Enhancing Competitive Advantage With Dynamic Management and Engineering

Carolina Machado
University of Minho, Portugal

J. Paulo Davim
University of Aveiro, Portugal

A volume in the Advances in
Logistics, Operations, and
Management Science (ALOMS) Book
Series

Published in the United States of America by
    IGI Global
    Business Science Reference (an imprint of IGI Global)
    701 E. Chocolate Avenue
    Hershey PA, USA 17033
    Tel: 717-533-8845
    Fax: 717-533-8661
    E-mail: cust@igi-global.com
    Web site: http://www.igi-global.com

Library of Congress Cataloging-in-Publication Data

Names: Machado, Carolina, 1965- editor. | Davim, J. Paulo, editor.
Title: Enhancing competitive advantage with dynamic management and
  engineering / Carolina Machado and J. Paulo Davim, editors.
Description: Hershey : Business Science Reference, [2018]
Identifiers: LCCN 2017040765| ISBN 9781522553601 (hardcover) | ISBN
  9781522553618 (ebook)
Subjects: LCSH: Organizational change. | Management--Technological
  innovations. | Decision making.
Classification: LCC HD58.8 .E5454 2018 | DDC 658.4/06--dc23 LC record available at https://
lccn.loc.gov/2017040765

This book is published in the IGI Global book series Advances in Logistics, Operations, and Management Science (ALOMS) (ISSN: 2327-350X; eISSN: 2327-3518)

British Cataloguing in Publication Data
A Cataloguing in Publication record for this book is available from the British Library.

All work contributed to this book is new, previously-unpublished material.
The views expressed in this book are those of the authors, but not necessarily of the publisher.

For electronic access to this publication, please contact: eresources@igi-global.com.

Advances in Logistics, Operations, and Management Science (ALOMS) Book Series

ISSN:2327-350X
EISSN:2327-3518

Editor-in-Chief: John Wang, Montclair State University, USA

MISSION

Operations research and management science continue to influence business processes, administration, and management information systems, particularly in covering the application methods for decision-making processes. New case studies and applications on management science, operations management, social sciences, and other behavioral sciences have been incorporated into business and organizations real-world objectives.

The **Advances in Logistics, Operations, and Management Science** (ALOMS) Book Series provides a collection of reference publications on the current trends, applications, theories, and practices in the management science field. Providing relevant and current research, this series and its individual publications would be useful for academics, researchers, scholars, and practitioners interested in improving decision making models and business functions.

COVERAGE

- Information management
- Operations management
- Production management
- Decision analysis and decision support
- Networks
- Finance
- Organizational behavior
- Political science
- Computing and information technologies
- Risk Management

IGI Global is currently accepting manuscripts for publication within this series. To submit a proposal for a volume in this series, please contact our Acquisition Editors at Acquisitions@igi-global.com or visit: http://www.igi-global.com/publish/.

The Advances in Logistics, Operations, and Management Science (ALOMS) Book Series (ISSN 2327-350X) is published by IGI Global, 701 E. Chocolate Avenue, Hershey, PA 17033-1240, USA, www.igi-global.com. This series is composed of titles available for purchase individually; each title is edited to be contextually exclusive from any other title within the series. For pricing and ordering information please visit http://www.igi-global.com/book-series/advances-logistics-operations-management-science/37170. Postmaster: Send all address changes to above address. ©© 2018 IGI Global. All rights, including translation in other languages reserved by the publisher. No part of this series may be reproduced or used in any form or by any means – graphics, electronic, or mechanical, including photocopying, recording, taping, or information and retrieval systems – without written permission from the publisher, except for non commercial, educational use, including classroom teaching purposes. The views expressed in this series are those of the authors, but not necessarily of IGI Global.

Titles in this Series

For a list of additional titles in this series, please visit:
https://www.igi-global.com/book-series/advances-logistics-operations-management-science/37170

Improving Business Performance Through Effective Managerial Training Initiatives
Luisa dall'Acqua (Scientific Lyceum TCO, Italy & Live Editions Inc., USA) and Dickson
Lukose (GCS Agile Pty. Ltd, Australia)
Business Science Reference • ©2018 • 316pp • H/C (ISBN: 9781522539063) • US $215.00

Lean Six Sigma for Optimal System Performance in Manufacturing and Service ...
Edem G. Tetteh (Rowan College at Burlington County, USA) and Hans Chapman (Cape
Fear Community College, USA)
Business Science Reference • ©2018 • 186pp • H/C (ISBN: 9781522540625) • US $165.00

Cubic Strategic Management in Contemporary Business
Mihai V. Putz (West University of Timişoara, Romania)
Business Science Reference • ©2018 • 215pp • H/C (ISBN: 9781522552581) • US $195.00

Contemporary Approaches and Strategies for Applied Logistics
Lincoln C. Wood (University of Otago, New Zealand)
Business Science Reference • ©2018 • 477pp • H/C (ISBN: 9781522552734) • US $215.00

Reputation Management Techniques in Public Relations
Ayse Erdemir (Istanbul Commerce University, Turkey)
Business Science Reference • ©2018 • 430pp • H/C (ISBN: 9781522536192) • US $225.00

Handbook of Research on Promoting Business Process Improvement Through Inventory ...
Nita H. Shah (Gujarat University, India) and Mandeep Mittal (Amity School of Engineering
and Technology, India)
Business Science Reference • ©2018 • 644pp • H/C (ISBN: 9781522532323) • US $345.00

Supply Chain Management Strategies and Risk Assessment in Retail Environments
Akhilesh Kumar (Indian Institute of Technology Kharagpur, India) and Swapnil Saurav
(JDA Software, India)
Business Science Reference • ©2018 • 351pp • H/C (ISBN: 9781522530565) • US $225.00

For an entire list of titles in this series, please visit:
https://www.igi-global.com/book-series/advances-logistics-operations-management-science/37170

701 East Chocolate Avenue, Hershey, PA 17033, USA
Tel: 717-533-8845 x100 • Fax: 717-533-8661
E-Mail: cust@igi-global.com • www.igi-global.com

Table of Contents

Detailed Table of Contents

This chapter primarily provides a thorough account of what the process perspective encompasses to address the attention that business processes perspective in today's postmodern organizations attracts. It exhibits how organizations designed around business processes are able to become more agile, competitive, dynamic, flexible, and adaptable to constantly shifting market realities. Accordingly, this chapter also covers the underlying logic behind business process orientation (BPO) as a comprehensive view of the process perspective. As BPO is thought to offer an integrated approach that encompasses structures of the organizations, their information technology systems and strategies, it is considered to possess qualities that will continuously create value for the global market.

Internationalization is a business strategy that normally aims at expanding the business of the firm outside its domestic market. It may also involve the creation of an integrated network of contacts and partners. The aim of this chapter involves a firm that distributes high-end wines and other alcoholic drinks to the domestic market and is seeking to expand its activities abroad. Taking into account the "nostalgia market," with many Portuguese living throughout Europe, this chapter seeks to analyze how a Portuguese firm seeks to embrace the internationalization strategy of serving these ex-pats, through local retailers, and afterwards the possibility of serving the market abroad using the contacts so far developed. As such, the firm seeks to serve both the ex-pats and the local market alike. The chapter analyzes the Spanish, French, and German market, and it is possible to conclude that France is the market with the higher likelihood of success, economically and culturally.

Chapter 3

Liliana Ávila, University of Aveiro, Portugal
Marlene Amorim, University of Aveiro, Portugal
Luis Miguel D. F. Ferreira, Universidade de Coimbra, Portugal

In recent years, hybrid organizations have been spreading in the competitive landscape, combining characteristics from both private and social sectors. To be successful, they need to do a great job managing limited resources. To this end, an effective operations strategy must be at the core of their priorities. Most of these organizations often rely on volunteer work to conduct their activities; therefore, mobilizing and engaging volunteers on a continuous basis is a key issue for many hybrid organizations. The present chapter aims to identify relevant workforce management practices in hybrid organizations. Building on the literature, the chapter offers a presentation of the main concepts underlying the setup of an operations strategy, highlighting the main particularities and challenges faced by hybrid organizations, and focusing on workforce management decisions. The chapter then identifies and discusses three workforce management practices employed by two hybrid organizations, whose operations are based on volunteer work.

Chapter 4

Alamuri Surya Narayana, Osmania University, India

Diversity and diversity management is a new organizational paradigm and a business imperative. We already have a vast and rich literature base on these two. Many and varied empirical findings are also available from earlier qualitative and quantitative research studies. An attempt is made in this chapter (1) to examine various theoretical concepts and constructs used in diversity and diversity management, (2) to come up with a synthesis of management research and current literature on diversity and diversity management, (3) to develop a theoretical framework, and (4) to suggest directions for future research as well. This chapter lists some of the challenges faced by firms, the major issues to be addressed, potential research directions, and themes in the Indian context before finally coming up with a conceptual model detailing the antecedents and consequences of diversity and diversity management.

Chapter 5
    Liliana Sofia Pinto, University of Aveiro, Portugal
    Maria Manuel Ribeiro, University of Aveiro, Portugal
    António Carrizo Moreira, University of Aveiro, Portugal

Internationalization involves an active behavior to compete in international markets. Several theories, as well as several entry modes, have been developed to explain why and how firms compete internationally. Nevertheless, the internationalization process is difficult to implement as it involves not only historical reasons, as well as traditional strategies that sometimes are usually not questioned by the firm. This chapter aims to depict a case study in which a firm is trying to deploy an opportunity-driven internationalization, shifting its traditional modus operandi. The firm is analyzed based on several theories, namely the Uppsala model, the network-based theory, the born globals and the born again globals, and it is possible to conclude that despite its more than 80 years of existence, neither of the four theories can be properly used to explain the firm's international behavior. Moreover, to embrace international challenges, the firm needs to reposition its traditional business behavior.

Chapter 6
    Pinar Yildiran, Marmara University, Turkey
    Huseyin Selcuk Kilic, Marmara University, Turkey
    Bahar Sennaroglu, Marmara University, Turkey

Today we are living in a constantly changing world and today's strong competition and changing market conditions enforce enterprises to adopt fundamental methods and new approaches to enhance their capabilities. Enterprises are goal-oriented, designed, and complex systems and they need to implement new strategies easily and control Key Performance Indicators to maintain their competitiveness. Enterprise engineering (EE) is a developing field and an enabler for informed decision making for addressing the required changes to be competitive and for tackling the complexity of enterprises' design issues on business, organization, information, and technology domains. Enterprise architecture (EA) is one of the basic elements of EE and it is about the structure of the whole of enterprise. There is an important and strong relationship between EE and EA. Although there are specific individual studies for EE and EA, this chapter aims to explore the fields of these two subjects in a collaborative system approach as a whole with existing literature review by assessing the core concepts and the methods used.

Purna Prabhakar Nandamuri, IFHE University, India
K. S. Venu Gopala Rao, IFHE University, India
Mukesh Kumar Mishra, IFHE University, India

Conventionally, businesses focus on their offerings for growth. But the increasingly unpredictable business environment is making them irrelevant in the market. So, businesses should resort to a system of dynamic management by innovating on the business models rather than a single aspect of the business. Business model innovation demands neither new technologies nor creation of new markets, but cares about delivering the existing products produced by existing technologies to the existing markets, through a unique model. Hence, defining, innovating, and evolving new business models have become the new basis of competition. A differentiated, hard-to-imitate, effective, and efficient business model is more likely to ensure higher profits and long-term survival. In this context, the present chapter attempts to furnish multiple global evidences and discuss the Indian perspective of business model innovation.

Shan Anjana Jayasinghe, University of Moratuwa, Sri Lanka
Galagedarage Dinesh Samarasinghe, University of Moratuwa, Sri Lanka
Theekshana Suraweea, Sri Lanka Institute of Information Technology, Sri Lanka

Due to inadequacy, there is a call for more research on the thought process of job seekers. This chapter argues that employers have to communicate their company's job-seeker value proposition to new graduates to create job-seeker perceived value in their minds. Job-seeker perceived value will lead to behavioral intention. Further, the chapter proposes that a company's job-seeker value proposition has a direct positive relationship with behavioral intention and the relationship is moderated positively by voluntariness and gender. The technology acceptance model and the unified theory of acceptance and use of technology (UTAUT) were used to develop arguments related to each relationship proposed in the conceptual framework. Marketing management literature was used to label both constructs: company's job-seeker value proposition and job-seeker perceived value; and the same is employed to complement the arguments borrowed from management information system. Theoretical contribution, practical contribution, limitations, and opportunities for future research are also discussed in the chapter.

Preface

Presently, we live a time in which there is a vast amount of uncertainty and ambiguity about the direction in which organizations are moving. While many advances have been made in understanding the complexity of manufacture/production engineering, the social and organizational context remains problematical. Interdisciplinary perspectives to further our knowledge and understanding of the development of manufacture/production engineering and related change processes and work practices are need. They will contribute to a better merge and interrelationship among organization, management and employee needs in order to increase efficiency, productivity and profitability.

Conscious of these needs, *Enhancing Competitive Advantage With Dynamic Management and Engineering* looks to provide relevant theoretical frameworks and the latest empirical research findings in the areas of management and engineering. Indeed, and taking present that in the business world there is a growing importance of sophisticated analysis for managers to support decision making, to use strategic information and innovative tools in order to guide thinking and behavior as well as to manage more strategically to adapt environments and achieve the organization's aims, this book looks to introduce new lines of research in management and engineering areas, at the same time that the models, theories and tools presented and discussed by the different chapter contributions allow management to take a more strategic role in todays' organizations.

This is why this book, with a specific emphasis in the dynamics in the Management and Engineering areas, will be critical and of great usefulness for all those - managers, engineers, researchers, human resource managers, academics, as well as professionals from different areas - that in their daily, academic and professional routines need to lead with management and engineering issues.

Organized in eight chapters; the book begins in Chapter 1 to present "Modern Approaches for Organizational Dynamism: Business Processes and Business Process Orientation". In Chapter 2, "Facing the Challenges of Nostalgia International Markets", is discussed. Chapter 3 covers "Workforce Management Practices in Volunteer-Based Operations for the Generation of Social and Economic Value", at the same time that Chapter 4 highlights the relevance of "Diversity Management Interventions for Enhancing Competitive Advantage: A Synthesis of Current Research and Literature". Chapter 5 discusses "Challenging the Theoretical Lenses of Internationalization: A Case Study Analysis", while a "Collaborative System Approach for Enterprise Engineering and Enterprise Architecture: A Literature Review" is explored in Chapter 6. A "Sustainable Competitive Advantage Through Business Model Innovation: The Indian Perspective" is addressed in Chapter 7, and finally, Chapter 8 gives a special focus "Thought Process of a New Graduate Which Leads to Behavioral Intention to Apply for a Job Vacancy: A Conceptual Model".

Although this is the order by which these chapters are presented, they don't need to be read by this order. Indeed, each one of them can be read independently as they offer a complete perspective about the particular topic they focus.

Giving a global, relevant and actual base of knowledge, critical to enhancing the competitive advantage with dynamic management and engineering, the professional and scientific interest of the content of this book is crucial for many Universities / Schools, all over the world, with courses in the Management and Engineering fields.

Carolina Machado
University of Minho, Portugal

J. Paulo Davim
University of Aveiro, Portugal

Acknowledgment

The editors acknowledge their gratitude to IGI Global for this opportunity and for their professional support. Finally, we also would like to thank to all chapter authors for their interest and availability to work on this project.

Chapter 1
Modern Approaches for Organizational Dynamism:
Business Processes and Business Process Orientation

Meral Dülger
Marmara University, Turkey

ABSTRACT

This chapter primarily provides a thorough account of what the process perspective encompasses to address the attention that business processes perspective in today's postmodern organizations attracts. It exhibits how organizations designed around business processes are able to become more agile, competitive, dynamic, flexible, and adaptable to constantly shifting market realities. Accordingly, this chapter also covers the underlying logic behind business process orientation (BPO) as a comprehensive view of the process perspective. As BPO is thought to offer an integrated approach that encompasses structures of the organizations, their information technology systems and strategies, it is considered to possess qualities that will continuously create value for the global market.

INTRODUCTION

The current marketplace that the organizations try to endure in has become very complex, instable, unforeseeable and fiercely competitive due to globalization, technological advances along with the proliferation of e-commerce activities. For instance, McCormack (2001) observes that organizations have to play against fierce

DOI: 10.4018/978-1-5225-5360-1.ch001

global competition, demanding customers with promptly shifting desires, decreasing response times, shorter product life cycles and employees with ever-changing requirements. He adds that all the comfortable corporate frictions such as geographical distance, price opacity, unquestioning brand allegiance that preserved organizational inefficiencies and status quo jobs are quickly disappearing (McCormack, 2001: 51).

To address these issues, the management literature prescribes organizations to become more agile, dynamic, flexible, adaptive and responsive if they are to survive and differentiate themselves from global competition. Apart from the managerial, financial and operational challenges, the fulfillment of this prescription has become a challenge within the widely accepted framework of hierarchic structures. The reason for this challenge lies behind Taylor's legacy of job specialization as an instrument to increase efficiency and productivity. As technological progress became widely available, the scale and scope of what humanity can create has reached tremendous levels. Thus, organizations lean towards even further specialization which unfortunately causes every task of each job to become more co-dependent on each other in order to be completed. Evidently, this keeps injecting complexity into the ways of conducting business within hierarchical structures.

Max Weber had laid the principles of functionalism, departmentalization and hierarchic organization which were widely adopted both by public and private organizations (Mulder, 2017). Those "reliable" bureaucratic structures are no longer adept in handling the constantly changing complexity, making sense of the information stemming from specialization and utilizing it efficiently and promptly. Gulick's (1937) classification of the functional management patterns, POSDCORB (Planning, Organizing, Staffing, Directing, Coordinating, Reporting, Budgeting), which serve the complex production/service provision processes of industries, has been moving constantly towards incorporating more and more execution of work. The sequentially dependent tasks and managerial levels of classical business administration, the chain-of-command approach coupled with the fixation of trying to gather every bit of information at the top levels of hierarchies hinder the indispensable maneuverability that is needed in order to survive under current circumstances.

Today, the requirements for fast production and marketing in ambiguous business environments require empowerment of lower levels of specialized staff, which compels organizations to become more horizontal. Consequently, as a response to increasing competition and more demanding customers, various authors have suggested companies to put less emphasis on hierarchical and functional structures, but instead focus and improve on entire chains of business operations, ranging often from client to client (Reijers, 2006:392). Thus, depending upon the complexity of the triggers from the internal and external business environment, business leaders may engage in doing things better through incremental improvements within the existing organizational structure and processes or introduce radical and transformational changes usually involving creation of new configurations with regard to systems, structure, process, technology, etc. (Sikdar & Payyazhi, 2014: 976). The business process perspective provides an organizationally transformational approach in addressing the aforementioned stakeholder expectations. Thus, it is thought that organizational designs based on processes could furnish a lasting solution. Accordingly, the main aim of this chapter is to introduce business processes and business process orientation (BPO) as possible approaches for making organizations less dependent on hierarchy in order to adapt to dynamic market requirements.

In its simplest sense, processes are the conceptual notation of what organizations do (Smart et al., 2009:12). In more technical terms, a process is a related group of tasks that together create a result of value to a customer (Hammer, 1996). However, the ability to implement the process perspective efficiently into organizational configurations requires business process orientation (BPO) which requires customer focus, cross-functional commitment and value chain concepts to be at the forefront of management thinking and acting (Spanyi, 2006). BPO connotes a state of mind where there are awareness and understanding of the "whole", how its main components relate to one another and how the big picture relates to creating value to attract and retain consumers. Processes, therefore, become central for organizational design pointing to a holistic view rather than thinking about the business functions one by one. Thus, here, it is maintained that BPO provides organizations the sophistication that they are soliciting in order to be able to relate to constantly changing customer and market requirements.

Therefore, this chapter primarily provides a thorough account of what the process perspective encompasses and exhibits how organizational designs based on business processes are able to become more agile, competitive, dynamic, flexible and adaptable relative to their competitors. Therefore, this chapter will also uncover the underlying logic behind BPO and its potential benefits for modern organizations as process-oriented thinking has become a sine qua non for organizations that seek competitive advantage in the marketplace.

This chapter is organized as follows: The following section provides an account of the evolution of the process perspective in the management literature. Next, a depiction of various definitions of processes is displayed supplemented with examples, explanations on various types of processes and objectives of processes. The succeeding section illuminates the scope of BPO as it depicts a state of mind and a vision of committing to staying flexible and adaptable in the face of constantly changing market dynamics. The ensuing section embarks upon the benefits of process-based organizational design and the chapter concludes with contributing remarks.

EVOLUTION OF THE PROCESS PERSPECTIVE
IN THE MANAGEMENT LITERATURE

Armistad et al. (1999:97) report that the initial attention to process can be seen in the original scientific management of Frederick Taylor and Henry Ford. Inspired by Henry Ford's success in reducing costs and increasing productivity in automotive assembly, Taylor's principles of scientific management were the prominent influencer of process perspective. Taylor argued for work simplification, time studies and systematic experimentation to identify the best way of performing a task, along with control systems that measured and rewarded output (Harmon, 2015). His primary aim was to elevate organizational productivity by applying the same engineering principles that solved technical problems in the workplace to human labor (Davenport and Short, 1990). The following two paragraphs explaining the evolution of process perspective are adapted from Harmon (2015: 37-54), Davenport and Short (1990) and Van der Aalst (2013:2):

Until 1950s, engineers worked to apply Taylor's ideas, analyzing processes, measuring and applying statistical checks. In the late 1970s, as more and more core processes began to be automated, the most popular quality control methodology was Total Quality Management (TQM). By the early 1980s, one realized that, eventually, nearly every process in every organization would either be automated, or performed by humans who relied on access to computers and information systems. This was when the strategic role of IT began to slowly unveil. Further, Porter (1985) discussed that competitive advantage grows out of the entire system of activities. From process perspective, this means that a value chain is actually a depiction of unique processes that give way to competitive advantage. The late-1980s began to be superseded by Six Sigma and Lean which became popular approaches for continuous process improvement. Six Sigma and Lean implement an organizational transformation that embraces process throughout the organization by emphasizing company-wide training efforts designed to make every employee responsible for process quality.

At the beginning of the 1990s, Business Process Reengineering (BPR) perspective was coined by Hammer's (1990), Davenport and Short's (1990), Davenport's (1993) and Hammer and Champy's (1993) writings. They insisted that companies must think in terms of comprehensive processes, similar to Porter's (1985) value chains. It was also around that time that organizations began to accept that IT was an integral part of every business process and a strategic asset. The way in which IT will change organizations is and will be is similar to the degree of what Taylorism did earlier. However, practitioners' reviews of BPR produced inconclusive results especially after Hammer's prescriptions turned out to be very challenging to apply. For instance, several companies tried to use existing technologies to pass information about their organizations and ended up with costly failures. However, one must keep in mind that these implementation attempts were taking place before the wide availability of the Internet.

Nevertheless, BPR prescriptions have largely been implemented. Whole industries are rapidly going out of business while customers now use online services allowing customers to swiftly move from information gathering, to pricing, to purchasing while many organizations have eliminated sales organizations and retail stores and interface with their customers online.

Over time, business processes have become more complex; relying heavily on information systems, and may span multiple organizations. The focus on the narrow technical perspective without giving enough emphasis on an integrated holistic approach is seen as one of the important reasons behind BPR failures (Al-Mashari et al., 2001, as cited in Sikdar & Payyazhi, 2014). The necessity for a holistic approach has paved the way for the development of Business Process Management (BPM) as a cross between management and computer science. Simply put, BPM formulates that the entire strategic planning, implementation and control of an organization need to be based on its most important – core – processes. BPM is "supporting business processes using methods, techniques and software to design, enact, control and analyze operational processes involving humans, organizations, applications, documents and other sources of information" (van der Aalst et al., 2003). In particular, BPM includes incremental change and radical change in business process, and emphasizes continuous improvement, customer satisfaction, and employee involvement (Ross, 1995). Choong (2013) observes that BPM is a holistic management philosophy whereas BPR is about radical process redesign.

Hung (2006:22) describes that the primary purpose of BPM is to improve business processes to ensure that the critical activities affecting customer satisfaction are executed in the most efficient and effective manner. Van der Aalst et al. (2003) note that BPM also includes tools and technologies, e.g. workflow management, balanced scorecard, expert systems and business rules, Computer Aided Software Engineering and process modelling tools. Hung (2006:24) classifies Continuous Improvement, Process Reengineering and Benchmarking as BPM initiatives and he identifies that BPM is comprised of:

- Process Alignment
  - How well an organization manages the fit between its processes and its institutional elements
- Customer Service
  - How well an organization can take preventative measures against lost customers
- Employees' Involvement

- ○ How well an organization involves people at all levels in the management of its processes
- Managers' Commitment
  - ○ The extent of commitment and support from top level of management

Furthermore, in their thorough account of the literature, Rosemann and von Brocke (2015:111-112) distinguish core elements for BPM signifying the fact that the process perspective requires an all-inclusive approach. These elements are:

- Strategic Alignment
  - ○ Processes have to be designed, executed, managed, and measured according to strategic priorities and specific strategic situations
- Governance
  - ○ Creating transparency and accountability and designing decision-making and reward mechanisms to guide process-related actions.
- Methods
  - ○ The set of tools and techniques that support and enable activities along the process lifecycle and within enterprise-wide BPM initiatives – such as Six Sigma
- Information Technology
  - ○ IT-based solutions such as process analysis and process modeling support that are of significance for BPM initiatives
- People
  - ○ The human capital who continually enhance and apply their process and process management skills and knowledge in order to improve business performance
- Culture
  - ○ Creating a facilitating environment that complements the various BPM initiatives

As a step further, Rohloff (2011:384) highlights the importance of the notion of *maturity* in BPM; it has been proposed to assess organizations' state in terms of implementing a specific program or the quality of a process. Paulk et al. (1993: 5) stress that improved maturity results "in an increase in the process capability of the organization". Rohloff (2011) reports that The Capability Maturity Model (CMM) was one of the first for maturity assessment followed by the Capability Maturity Model Integration (CMMI). DeBruin and Rosemann (2005) emphasize that Harmon (2004) developed a Business Process Management Maturity (BPMM) model. Wong et al. (2014) also list BPM Maturity Model (BPMMM) (Rosemann et al. 2006); the Business Process Orientation Maturity Model (BPOMM) (McCormack et al. 2009);

and the Business Process Maturity Model (BPMM Lee) (Lee et al. 2007). Trkman (2013: 49-50) provides a classification for the levels of maturity in organizations in relation to BPO:

- Ad Hoc
  - The processes are unstructured and ill-defined. Process measures are not in place and the jobs and organizational structures are based upon traditional functions, not processes.
- Defined
  - The basic processes are defined and documented in flow diagrams. Changes to these processes must now undergo a formal procedure. Representatives of functional areas have regular meetings to coordinate with each other
- Linked
  - The breakthrough level. Managers employ process management with strategic intent and results. Broad process jobs and structures are put in place outside the traditional functions and are centered on end-to-end processes.
- Integrated
  - Organizational structures and jobs are based on processes and traditional functions begin to be equal or sometimes subordinate to the process ones. Process measures and performance management systems are widely and frequently used in the organization.

In this rather brief account of the evolution of process perspective, it can be seen that the management literature has come a long way since Taylor. This section was written with the hopes to provide a framework for comprehending the attention that business processes in today's post-modern organizations attract. The next section will exhibit different definitions of processes along with examples as well as different types and purposes of processes.

THE DEFINITIONS AND SCOPE OF BUSINESS PROCESSES

Armistad et al. (1999) note that the word process has different associations across theology, sociology, anthropology, psychology and economics. Also, Hung (2006) informs that "process" as a term is found in other disciplines such as systems thinking (Checkland, 1981), cybernetics (Beer, 1966) and systems dynamics (Senge, 1990). Further, Monge (1990) highlights that organizational theorists have talked about processes within social and organizational contexts. Keen (1997) contends that most organizational processes are cross-functional and usually cut across traditional functional boundaries. Since processes cut across internal functional boundaries, they can serve as a means for breaking down hierarchical barriers (Rummler & Brache, 1990). Hence, as an increasingly popular approach from the 1980s and onwards, the management literature provides ample definitions for business processes. Table 1 below provides a substantial variety of these definitions in chronological order:

Table 1. Definitions for business processes

Author(s)	Definition
Pall (1987)	The logical organization of people, materials, energy, equipment, and procedures into work activities designed to produce a specified end result (work product)
Davenport and Short (1990)	A set of logically-related tasks performed to achieve a defined business outcome that have customers and cross organizational boundaries.
Hammer and Champy (1993); McCormack and Johnson (2001); Sethi and King (2003); Schutta (2006); Fields (2007)	Interconnected activities that transform particular inputs into customer focused outputs working across departments
Davenport (1993)	A structured and measured set of activities with specified business outcomes for a particular customer or market
Talwar (1993)	A sequence of pre-defined activities executed to achieve a pre-specified type or range of outcomes
Tenner and DeToro (1997); Harmon (2003)	A set of one or more linked procedures or activities that collectively realize a business objective by transforming a set of inputs into a specific set of outputs (goods or services) for another person (customer) by a combination of people, methods, and tools
Guha and Kettinger (1993); Strnadl (2006)	A complete, dynamically coordinated set of activities or logically related tasks that must be performed to deliver value to customers or to fulfill other strategic goals
Zairi (1997)	Has predictable and definable inputs; a linear, logical sequence or flow; a set of clearly definable tasks or activities; a predictable and desired outcome or result
Harrington (2006)	A series of interconnected activities that takes input, adds value to it, and produces output
Palmberg (2009)	A horizontal sequence of activities that transforms an input (need) to an output (result) to meet the needs of customers or stakeholders
Bergman (2010)	A network of activities that are repeated in time, the objective of which is to create value to external and internal customers
Anttila and Jussila (2013)	A set of interrelated or interacting activities which transforms inputs to outputs, and procedure is a specified way to carry out an activity or a process
Wong et al. (2014)	A complete, dynamically coordinated set of activities or logically related tasks that must be performed to deliver value to customers or to fulfill other strategic goals

Over time, these definitions have become more sophisticated and integrated with the advance of the business process perspective in the management literature while the activities of many devoted practitioners also contributed to these definitions. As a general theme; processes can be said to involve (Zairi, 1997):

- Predictable and definable inputs,
- A linear, logical sequence or flow,
- A set of clearly definable and interrelated activities,
- Predictable and desired outputs.

Accordingly, according to Palmberg (2009), overall, processes are:

- Horizontal or cross-functional,
- Performed by resources,
- Repeatable,
- Adding value for customers and stakeholders.

Also, Spanyi (2006: 110) sees processes as the "third dimension of management":

- The first dimension is the business itself which represents the domain of activities, or in other words, *where* the specific organizational operations are carried out to create value.
- The second dimension is the functions of the organization which define *what* is done to create the intended value.
- The third one is processes as they indicate *how* work is done as a critical component of management and as a means for achieving results for customers and stakeholders (Spanyi, 2006: 111).

Furthermore, Hammer (1996), notes that thinking in terms of business processes provides a novel diagnostic framework that facilitates breaking the functional mindset. Spanyi (2006: 53) lists the key elements of business process framework as:

- The critical enterprise level business processes that create value.
- The critical few measures that define performance.
- A plan for improving and managing enterprise level business processes.
- Accountability for results.
- A communication plan that inspires and moves people to action.

Such an approach would enhance customer focus by sidestepping the constraints of managing by vertical functions (McAdam, 1996). This ascertainment points to a holistic view of the whole organization rather than thinking about the business functions one by one.

Examples of Business Processes

As complicated as the various definitions of business processes might seem, examples of business processes might help solidify the concept in the minds of the readers. Davenport and Short (1990:4) note that common examples of processes include:

- Developing a new product
- Ordering goods from a supplier
- Creating a marketing plan
- Processing and paying an insurance claim
- Writing a proposal for a government contract

They also deconstruct the example of ordering goods from a supplier as it involves multiple organizations and functions as large-scale processes affecting the whole organization: The last user of the goods, the purchasing department, and the supplier organization are the participants. Thus, the user could be viewed as the customer of the process. Finally, the process outcome could be either the creation of the order, or perhaps more usefully, the actual receipt of the goods by the user.

Besides, they provide detailed process examples such as installing a windshield in an automobile factory, or completing a monthly departmental expense report. Further, training, development, manufacturing, budgeting, planning, sales, order fulfillment and service can be considered as other examples. Moreover, as goods and services are the results of processes (ISO, 2008/2009), products can also be provided as examples.

Finally, Coleman (1991), Binney (1992), Bemowski (1992), Davidson (1995), Boyer (1990), Zairi (1994) and Smith (1994) (cited in Zairi, 1997:67-68) provide real-life examples of effective management of strategic processes:

- When Rank Xerox Corp. made the commitment to adopt TQM in 1984, their first step was to articulate a simple and direct quality policy and to communicate it to all employees.
- Grundos have ensured that a quality policy containing strategy, goals, vision/mission and values is central to their efforts to win a sustainable competitive edge.

- At Procter and Gamble, through their CEO, strategic planning is management leadership's job.
- Mitel Telecom Ltd UK views the publishing of its quality policy as the first evidence of its commitment to quality improvement.
- Southern Pacific Airlines, in implementing continuous quality improvement, have emphasized that a strong and clear leadership statement of mission and strategy is essential underlining that quality is the strategy.
- Procter and Gamble, NEC Japan, Komatsu, Unilever Hewlett Packard, Rank Xerox, Florida Power and Light, in the process of ensuring success in developing, communicating and reviewing strategic plans at all levels, have heavily depended on a structured planning process termed quality policy deployment.
- At NEC Japan, the quality policy deployment process starts with the CEO first by setting the long-term policy in line with the aims and philosophy of the corporation.

Types of Business Processes

In order to grasp the concept further, business processes can be classified in several ways. Keen (1997) suggests that relevant processes are those that create value, processes that provide options and processes that sustain the value. Harrington (1997), on the other hand, considers the following classification in streamlining and designing processes:

- High-value adding activities
- Value adding activities
- Low-value adding activities

Finally, the following are the crucial business processes (Armistead et al., 1999; Earl, 1996; Harmon, 2003; Palmberg, 2009):

- *Core processes* describe the end-to-end work that starts from the customer and ends with the customer, and always using cross-functional activities (Hung, 2001).
  - Exert strategic significance to the organization's success, and have eminent bearings on customer satisfaction (DeToro & McCabe, 1997).
  - Involve production and delivery of products or services, contributing to value creation and directly related to external customers (Van Looy et al., 2011).

- ○ Gather around customer requirements and needs, are geared towards fulfilling them, and may very well involve cross-functional activities.
  - ○ May include activities such as new product development, marketing and sales, production and distribution.
- *Enabling processes* support the core processes by facilitating the smooth operation of work that is needed for the organization to function and perform.
  - ○ Characterized by internal customers, for instance, processes in information management or human resources (Van Looy et al., 2011).
  - ○ Managing payroll deductions or handling an office inventory can be considered as enabling processes.
- *Managerial processes* are, as the name implies, linked to the strategy and policy setting, serving the overall planning, and controlling all activities in the organization (Van Looy et al., 2011).

Objectives of Processes

This section is devoted to a brief account of the specific objectives for process redesign put forward by Davenport and Short (1990: 7-8):

- Cost Reduction
  - ○ Cost is an important redesign objective in combination with others, but insufficient in itself.
  - ○ Excessive attention to cost reduction results in tradeoffs that are usually unacceptable to process stakeholders.
  - ○ While optimizing on other objectives seems to bring costs into line, optimizing on cost does not bring about other objectives.
- Time Reduction
  - ○ Increasing numbers of companies are beginning to compete on the basis of time and processes are the ideal unit upon which to focus time reduction analysis.
  - ○ One common approach to cutting time from a product design process is to make the steps in the process begin simultaneously, rather than sequentially, using IT to coordinate design directions among the various functional participants.
- Output Quality
  - ○ All processes have outputs, such as in manufacturing a tangible product or adding data to a customer file.
  - ○ Output quality has frequently been the focus of process improvement in manufacturing and service industries.

- ◦ The specific measure of output quality may be uniformity, variability, or freedom from defects which needs to be defined by the customer of the process.
- Quality of Work Life (QWL)/Learning/Empowerment
  - ◦ A frequently neglected objective of process redesign is the work life quality of the individuals carrying it out.
  - ◦ IT can lead either to greater empowerment of individuals, or to greater control.
  - ◦ Moreover, Schein (1988, cited in Davenport and Short, 1990) has pointed out that organizations often do not provide a supportive context for individuals to introduce or innovate with IT.

Davenport and Short (1990) further stress that it is seldom possible to optimize all objectives simultaneously, and in most firms, the strongest pressures are to produce tangible benefits. For instance, they provide American Express and Hewlett Packard as examples. American Express set out to improve the cost, time, and quality of its process for making credit authorization decisions by embedding the knowledge of its best authorizers in an "Authorizer's Assistant" expert system. This successful redesign led to a $7 million annual reduction in costs due to credit losses, a 25% reduction in the average time for each authorization, and a 30% reduction in improper credit denials. Hewlett Packard, in applying IT to the redesign of several key manufacturing processes, also found that it could improve cost, time, and quality simultaneously (Davenport & Short, 1990:8).

This section provided a thorough account of the scope of process perspective as a useful tool and what it involves. The ensuing section will focus on business process orientation (BPO) as a necessary approach towards providing dynamism to today's organizations.

BUSINESS PROCESS ORIENTATION (BPO)

The globalized marketplace that the organizations try to endure in has become so complex and intricate that process oriented thinking has become a *sine qua non*. Hence, it is maintained that BPO provides organizations the sophistication that they seek in order to be able to become more dynamic, flexible, adaptive and responsive. As a solution, the BPO concept was coined by Davenport and Short (1990) and Hammer (1996) and was advanced by McCormack (2001). Hence, BPO seems to have the potential to diffuse a holistic view of businesses to the organizational members.

Seeing the literature, it becomes apparent that designing organizations around processes could overcome problems raised by the Taylorist view of structural specialization. Such a design would enable every employee in a particular organization – from the top management to the newly hired juniors – to become aware of how individual tasks combine to generate processes which in turn produce the outstanding goods and/or services that customers come back for. To McCormack (2001), "the BPO of an organization is the level at which an organization pays attention to its core processes such as end-to-end view across the borders of departments, organizations, countries, etc." BPO denotes an organization that, in all its thinking, emphasizes processes as opposed to hierarchies with a special emphasis on outcomes and customer satisfaction (McCormack & Johnson, 2001). Essentially, BPO connotes stance where there is awareness and understanding of the "whole". Managers and employees comprehend how their organization's main components relate to one another and how the big picture relates to creating value that attracts and retains consumers (Dülger, 2011). Processes therefore should become central for organizations and BPO should be made an integral part of any organization that seeks to get a full grasp of what is going on in the marketplace and craft its strategy accordingly.

McCormack and Johnson (2001) and Jaklic et al., (2012) note that BPO consists of several components:

- Process View
  - Extent to which an organization models, documents and understands a business process from the beginning to the end (McCormack & Johnson, 2001).
  - Involves a focus on processes across an organization that need to be defined and understood by the employees (Jaklic et al., 2012).
- Process Jobs
  - Focus on the extent to which employees' work is organized around the business processes that lead to final products or services (McCormack & Johnson, 2001).
  - Functional roles of the traditional hierarchical structure are replaced by process owners –leaders who are responsible for the operation and improvement of the core business (Tenner & DeToro, 1997).
  - Along with process owners, process teams become the main building element of an organization (Jaklic et al., 2012).
- Process Management and Measurement
  - Extent to which the efficiency and effectiveness (i.e. output quality, cycle time, process cost, and variability) of business processes are assessed (McCormack & Johnson, 2001).
  - Management and measurements systems that direct and assess these processes (Jaklic et al., 2012).
- Process Structures

- ○ Extent to which different elements, activities, and workflows are organized effectively (McCormack & Johnson, 2001).
  - ○ Structures that match these processes, with a flat hierarchy, cross-functional process teams and process ownership (McCormack, 2007).
- Process Culture
  - ○ It is embodied in all components, with values and beliefs such as a customer focus, empowerment and continuous improvement (McCormack & Johnson, 2001).

At this point it must also be highlighted that, considering the structure and culture components, BPO emerges as a much more comprehensive approach compared to BPM.

As for the probable positive probable outcomes of BPO, Zaheer et al. (2010:151) provide a thorough account of the literature. BPO helps to improve business processes by:

- Reducing cost.
- Improving process execution time.
- Eliminating bureaucratic activities such as excessive paperwork, signoffs and duplications.

Further, empirical evidence indicates the positive impact of business process orientation on organizational performance (McCormack & Johnson, 2001; Skrinjar et al., 2008). Having BPO results in enhancement of products/services, decrease in costs, and faster functions (Hinterhuber, 1995; Terziovski et al., 2003; Hammer, 2007; Hirzel, 2008; Kohlbacher, 2010; Psomas et al., 2011; Tiwari et al., 2008, as cited in Khosravi, 2016). Other empirical studies exhibited that BPO improves organizational dynamics, decreases interdepartmental conflicts, and promotes ''esprit de corps'' among employees and inspires greater connectedness within an organization, while improving business performance (McCormack & Johnson, 2001). Another study showed that BPO leads to better non-financial performance and indirectly to better financial performance (Skrinjar et al., 2008). Still, the empirical investigation of these ideas in real-life settings is lacking and will be a lucrative research area for academics.

As achieving BPO for organizations is a complex process done over a long period of time, companies can attain various degrees of BPO acceptance through adjustments of their business processes (Glavan et al., 2015) Thus, the levels of process orientation are often presented by a process maturity concept and models explained in the previous section. Hueffner (2004, as cited in Jaklic et al., 2012) states that increased process maturity is correlated with an increased probability of achieving effectiveness, efficiency and quality and can lead to a decreased gap between objectives and the current situation. Hence, for organizations to become process oriented, they need to gauge their level of achievement so as to be able to streamline this perspective with their inner workings and strategies.

As for the probable positive outcomes of BPO, Hammer (1996) contends that BPO expands the scope and breadth of jobs; requiring less administrative overhead, authorization, controls, reviews, audits and so forth. He also identifies the development of a customer focused process-oriented way of thinking, enabled by information technology (IT). BPO opens communication channels, fosters cooperation and information usage at the right time and right place (Kelly, 1995) whilst providing room for flexibility and innovation. It capitalizes on improving an organization's efficiency through high-level coordination of an organization's activities in a rationalized system of end-to-end processes (Benner & Tushman, 2002).

Moreover, Tang et al. (2013) emphasize that BPO fosters the shift from an input-focused, budget-driven managerial approach to an output-focused, market-driven approach. Accordingly, Glavan et al. (2015) note that BPO can slim down operational costs, promote customer relations by satisfying customer needs better and increasing employee satisfaction through harnessing the benefits of organizational knowledge. These positive effects of BPO seem to make it an approach that is fit to handle the challenges coming from the fiercely competitive and constantly changing market conditions.

Furthermore, BPO is an organizational and managerial outlook that empowers individuals while directing their focus on fulfilling customer expectations (Dülger, 2011). BPO offers a relief for individuals who are not at top management levels, and are stuck with a fragmented view of business outcomes due to their specialized, task-oriented jobs. BPO enables workers to become self-managed as they are responsible for both performing the work and assuring that it is well-done (Hammer, 1996) In other words, it is thought to permit employees to grow to be self-managed as they are accountable for both carrying out the work and ensuring it is well-done. As processes must become central to businesses (Hammer, 1996), Spanyi (2006) identifies that BPO includes:

- Customer focus.
- A view of processes as the building block.
- Jobs, management and measurement systems designed around these processes.
- Cross-functional commitment along with value chain concepts.

Finally, in order to systemize the concepts touched upon above, Kohlbacher (2010) suggests that the following dimensions can be utilized to identify a process oriented organization:

- Process design and documentation.
- Managerial support for process programs.
- Existence of process owners.
- Process performance measurement.
- A culture based on teamwork, readiness to change, customer orientation and a cooperative leadership style.
- Information technology as an enabler.
- Adaptation of organizational structure to process view.
- Presence of appropriate knowledge and incentive systems.
- Establishment of process oriented human resource systems.
- Existence of a formal instance coordinating and integrating all process projects.

Having gone over the scope and components of BPO, the following section will handle how organizations may utilize BPO with respect to organizational design.

BENEFITS OF PROCESS-BASED DESIGN

Traditionally, Taylorist view of specialization is the building block for job design and it is based on breaking a particular job into tasks. Task is a unit of work, a business activity normally performed by one person (Hammer, 1996). However, tasks create a fragmented view of the business activities/functions as organizational members may have a hard time conceiving how individual tasks combine into one whole that creates a value for the customers (Dülger, 2011). Furthermore, the market change is such a constant that, job designs, descriptions and requirements need to be altered more frequently than they can be crafted. Change is the main goal in process-based design because in today's market conditions, the ability to change is far more prized than the ability to create in the first place (Smith & Fingar, 2003). It is because the amount of uncertainty and unanticipated change that organizations experience is higher in this post-modern era and this calls for lateral coordination and usage of lateral organizational forms (Galbraith, 1994).

Further, hierarchies leave limited room for maneuver when faced with constantly changing features of the internal and external conditions. The process paradigm emphasizes viewing organizations based on the processes they perform rather than on the functional units, divisions, or departments they are divided into (Cooper et al., 1997; Trkman et al., 2007, as cited in Chen et al., 2009). In other words, the main difference between these organizational types is that the process-driven organization is geared towards meeting and satisfying customer needs while a functionally driven organization is one that is geared towards meeting its targets (Nadarajah et al., 2016: 1069).

On the other hand, the process approach broadens the focus of the organizations; the interaction across functions can create value in meeting customers' needs (Chen et al., 2009:215). According to Hammer (1996), thinking in terms of business processes provides a new analytic framework that aids crack the mold of thinking that is based only on functional units. This type of thinking will require employees and managers to think in terms of the system (i.e. the organization) they are operating within. Also, they will be obliged to think about how the components of the system are connected to one another and how those components might be affected when something internal or external forces the system to change and/or adapt (Dülger, 2011). Thus, it is proposed that only thinking around business processes can provide organizational flexibility against the rigidities of a hierarchic outlook. Therefore, importance of processes can be said to be their capacity to facilitate coordination across different functions.

However, it is important to emphasize that business processes are not replacements for business functions. In other words, possessing process oriented thinking in organizational design is a means for engendering the capacity of responsiveness, adaptability, prompt maneuver and flexibility rather than totally disregarding the functions and overall hierarchy. Thus, the process view never discounts the need for hierarchic structures; rather, it is a supplementary approach useful in diminishing the rigidities arising from such designs (Dülger, 2011).

Scholars also have argued that organizations should depart from any form of a vertical structure to a pure horizontal structure for improving the entire chain of business operations (Spector, 1999, as cited in Hung, 2006; Kohlbacher, 2009). Organizations that have successfully moved from a functionally driven organization to a process-driven organization tend to enjoy the benefits as outlined by Sever (2007, as cited in Nadarajah et al., 2014):

- Improved communications across the organization.
- Clearly defined inputs, outputs and work activities.
- Better understanding of end-to-end flow of activities until the product or service reaches the customers.

- Informed decisions made through tracking of process performance.
- Improved people management as the process culture focusses on raising the bar on performance.

Supporting this stance, Hammer (1996) highlights that processes are the essence of a company for its customers as they only see the products/services produced through the processes of that specific company. In the post-modern age, customers are kings since they have many options and they do not have to settle for anything that companies offer them. Thus, the major core process in a particular organization should be geared towards fulfilling the customers' needs and requirements as success lies in doing business the way customers want.

Hammer (1996: 32-52) notes that simple jobs and complex processes of the Industrial Age have given way to simple processes and complex jobs to address the constantly changing requirements of the market: Now, people do larger components of the work that needs to be done; rather than isolated fragments. Ultimately, larger jobs will inevitably require more sophisticated individuals or so called *professionals*. Such individuals do what it takes, reflect on their work; they become active learners. The nature of the work doesn't change; the individuals' ability and degree of sophistication do.

This stream of thought is related to Senge's (1990) systems thinking concept, where, just like thinking around process, understanding the relationships and interdependencies of variables in a given system which requires sophisticated specialists. Thus, the processes comprise many variables and the professionals are sophisticated enough to foresee the potential outcomes of their actions in terms of creating value for customers. Thus, such professionals and managers, have the responsibility for performing, supervising and controlling their work and ultimately, management becomes everyone's job (Hammer, 1996). As this becomes the case, process oriented structures leave enough room to cultivate people involvement.

Nevertheless, processes cannot always be carried out by mere individuals; thus, organizations employ teams in order to infuse direction, focus, efficiency and synergy within the organizational realm and produce value for their customers (Dülger, 2011). Even with the best efforts, an individual has a finite capacity to do everything that is needed for an entire process by himself/herself. Hence, the benefits of employing team mechanisms are repeatedly being stressed by academics within the scope of BPO.

Having covered the process perspective with respect to organizational design, the next subsection will deal with the applicability of these ideas in real-life situations and provide the alignment perspective as a support mechanism for structural change endeavors.

Process Alignment Perspective in BPO

Seeing the compelling evidence in the management literature, process perspective was widely adopted by organizations and they shifted their focus towards cross-functional teams and flattened organizational structures. Davenport and Short (1990) explain that organizations shifted their focus towards developing more flexible, team oriented, coordinated and communication-based work capabilities. Zairi (1997) reports that the pioneers in real-life application were companies such as Rank Xerox, IBM, ICL, Shell Chemicals UK, Smith Kline Beecham and British Telecom.

However, some of these structural transitions have been successful while others have not (Hung, 2006). One very important explanation for the failure of structural changes might lie with *process alignment* perspective. Process alignment can be interpreted as the organizational effort needed to make processes the platform for organizational structure, for strategic planning, and for information technology (Hammer, 1996). When an organization is appropriately aligned, organizational structure, IT and strategy correspond to organizational core processes and objectives, warranting competitive advantage (Hung, 2006). This perspective consists of the following aspects and their explanations are mainly adapted from Hung (2006: 25-27):

- Horizontal Structural Alignment
  - ◦ Mintzberg (1991) asserts that organizational alignment is the major underpinning for the organizational models; and this can facilitate analysis of the organizational context through his model of organizational configuration whilst also supporting an analysis of approaches to strategic planning.
  - ◦ Snow and Miles (1983) addressed an external-internal alignment model as an organizational theory to identify organization types: each with its own strategy and a particular configuration of technology, structure and process consistent with its strategy.
- Information Technology Alignment
  - ◦ IT facilitates the integration of business functions at all levels in an organization by making corporate-wide information more readily accessible (Scott-Morton, 1991, as cited in Hung, 2006).
  - ◦ IT systems support leadership, management control, and employee participation (Watkins, 1998, as cited in Hung, 2006).
  - ◦ Changes in IT systems accompany the transformation into a horizontal management style (Ostroff, 199, as cited in Hung, 2006).
  - ◦ IT alignment to support changes in core processes is therefore critical to implementation.

- ○ New IT systems alone do not produce sustainable performance, but must be carefully integrated into the way an organization operates its business processes (Gagnon & Dragon, 1998; Powell & Dent-Micallef, 1997, as cited in Hung, 2006).
  - ○ IT implementation is a component of organizational performance (Davenport, 1993; Hammer & Champy, 1993; Ostroff, 1999; Spector, 1999; Thompson & Strickland, 1999, as cited in Hung, 2006).
- Strategic Alignment
  - ○ Business success comes from better-quality processes as such processes facilitate the production of superior goods/services driven by organizational strategy.
  - ○ In strategic theory, the external-internal alignment model is widely employed (Andrews, 1980; Snow & Miles, 1983, as cited in Hung, 2006) that focuses on organizational strategies to fit with the various parts of work in an organization.
  - ○ Companies should first craft their strategies around their core processes and then develop functional strategies stemming from them.
  - ○ In order for a firm to compete successfully through its strategic objectives, alignment must exist between the firm's strategies, actions and performance measures (Keen, 1997; Pritchard & Armistead, 1999, as cited in Hung, 2006).
  - ○ In applying BPO principles, the program being followed must fit with the overall strategy of the company so as to provide a frame of reference.

This section stresses the importance of BPO and how it relates to organizational design. As attractive it may appear, for BPO principles to take hold in any organizational setting, these principles need to embedded into the organizations' architectures, IT systems and strategies. It seems that organizations that have reached such a maturity will reap the full advantages of agility and flexibility.

CONCLUSION

As mentioned in the beginning of the chapter, the challenging global markets drive organizations to seek novel ways to deal with the complex and unstable market conditions. Since Taylor's scientific management principles were developed under much foreseeable and stable market conditions, organizations' capabilities in agility, adaptation, flexibility and responsiveness for addressing today's markets seem rather limited. For example, hierarchies create a lot of over-head, repetition and waste just for the sake of running the business procedures. Approvals become problematic and time consuming as they need to travel higher up in the hierarchy or go to other departments. This leads to delays, conflict among employees and managers and eventually reflects on customers one way or another and in the expense of potential revenues. The way to combat such costs is by designing around processes that satisfy customers and able to generate new clients. Thus, it can be inferred that organizations can no longer rely on hierarchical models, complex processes and simple jobs to inflict and survive change.

Organizations are not to be visualized as a complex web of interpenetrating procedures, but as a set of simple processes, that are designed to operate with multi-skilled workforce towards the defined goal(s) for their customers' satisfaction, while being alert in identifying upcoming customer expectations. Achieving the mentioned capabilities would only be possible with the right organizational tools and designs. As a viable approach, BPO has the potential to provide the organizations and their members the opportunity to go beyond the familiar systems models and designs of the last century. BPO helps the shift from an input-focused, budget-driven managerial approach to an output-focused and customer-driven approach. Further, by empowering organizational members and ensuring their competency in communication and collaboration skills, BPO provides efficient and effective coordination throughout the organizational settings.

Therefore, within the framework of this study, it is believed that BPO will provide organizations the sophistication that they crave. Galbraith (1995) emphasizes that if structure is thought as the anatomy of the organization, processes are its physiology/ functioning. In other words, by placing business processes in the center, organizations can increase the capacity that will enable them to innovate, reenergize performance and deliver the value today's markets demand (Smith & Fingar, 2003). Nonetheless, it is important to emphasize that business processes are not replacements for business functions, but they are lateral support mechanisms for fast and productive coordination towards the goal.

Foremost, BPO has the potential to infuse a holistic view of the business activities by ensuring organizational members to understand the interconnections among the organizational components. In addressing day-to-day changes, the efforts of the top managers trying to possess the complete view of reality have begun to be inadequate. The constant flows of information and ever-changing market realities push them to update and/or alter their ways of perception almost any time. Besides, limited by their fragmented view due to hierarchical rigidities, specialization and functional orientation, many employees and managers – especially those who are not at the top management positions – face challenges in fully grasping the market realities and truly understanding their customers. Thus, BPO provides a modern management philosophy where they are able to acquire a holistic view of the various business activities and processes geared to a common goal and comprehend how these interact to create value for the customers while continuing to attract and retain them.

Customers, as they know a lot more than they did 50 years ago, have many specific requirements and demands and they have too many options on the market. Hence, it becomes quite challenging for organizations to rely on their customer base for being loyal. Since processes are defined as a group of tasks that generate value for the customer, the value that organizations have to strive to develop are worthy products and services that customers come back for repeatedly. Here, it is believed that if the organizations are able to put the customer at the heart of process and organizational design, value creation can be eventually created and then organizations can enjoy returning satisfied customers that will increase cash flow.

Further, as BPO enables the organizational members to work together and preferably in teams. By mitigating the hierarchical barriers, this engenders a cross-functional mindset where things can be approached from different angles so as to generate a well-rounded strategic, structural and technological alignment with the relevant organizational environment. BPO prescribes useful ways in which organizations can attract and retain customers while swiftly updating their product/service offerings. Thus, BPO should become an integral part of any organization that seeks to get a full grasp of what is going on in the marketplace and craft a strategy accordingly.

To summarize, being in tune with the current trends and realities is of utter importance. Today, success lies in doing business the way customers want. Applying post-modern design tools like BPO that are backed up with contemporary ways of thinking will presumably provide organizations the leap that they are looking for. Accordingly, those who are tenacious in the quest for becoming an integral part of the global community will find a quite unique approach in this chapter and may be able to address some of their pressing issues through business process-oriented thinking.

ACKNOWLEDGMENT

This chapter is built upon the literature review and interpretations of the author's Ph.D Dissertation *"Significance of Team-Based Organizations in Business Process Orientation and Effectiveness: An Application to Service Firms in Turkey" (2011)*.

This research received no specific grant from any funding agency in the public, commercial, or not-for-profit sectors.

REFERENCES

Anttila, J., & Jussila, K. (2013). An advanced insight into managing business processes in practice. *Total Quality Management & Business Excellence*, *24*(7-8), 918–932. doi:10.1080/14783363.2013.791105

Armistead, C., Pritchard, J. P., & Machin, S. (1999). Strategic business process management for organisational effectiveness. *Long Range Planning*, *32*(1), 96–106. doi:10.1016/S0024-6301(98)00130-7

Beer, S. (1966). Decision and control: The meaning of operational research and management cybernetics. *Knowledge and Process Management*, *4*, 31–36.

Benner, M. J., & Tushman, M. (2002). Process Management and Technological Innovation: A Longitudinal Study of the Photography and Paint Industries. *Administrative Science Quarterly*, *47*(4), 676–706. doi:10.2307/3094913

Bergman, K. (2010). *Quality from Customer Needs to Customer Satisfaction*. Lund: Studentlitteratur AB.

Checkland, P. B. (1981). *Systems Thinking Systems Practice*. Chichester, UK: Wiley.

Chen, H., Tian, Y., & Daugherty, P. J. (2009). Measuring process orientation. *International Journal of Logistics Management*, *20*(2), 213–227. doi:10.1108/09574090910981305

Choong, K. K. (2013). Are PMS Meeting the Measurement Needs of BPM? A Literature Review. *Business Process Management Journal*, *19*(3), 535–574. doi:10.1108/14637151311319941

Davenport, T. H. (1993). *Process Innovation: Reengineering Work through Information Technology*. Boston, MA: Harvard Business School.

Davenport, T. H., & Short, J. E. (1990). The New Industrial Engineering: Information Technology and Business Process Redesign. *Sloan Management Review*, *31*(4), 11–27.

De Bruin, T., & Rosemann, M. (2005). Towards a Business Process Management Maturity Model. *ECIS 2005 Proceedings of the Thirteenth European Conference on Information Systems*.

DeToro, I., & McCabe, T. (1997). How to Stay Flexible and Elude Fads. *Quality Progress*, *30*, 55–60.

Dülger, M. (2011). *Significance of Team-Based Organizations in Business Process Orientation and Effectiveness: An Application to Service Firms in Turkey*. İstanbul, Turkey: Boğaziçi University.

Earl, M. J. (1996). Business process reengineering: A phenomenon of organisation. In M. J. Earl (Ed.), *Information management. The organisational dimension* (pp. 53–76). New York: Oxford University Press.

Fields, J. (2007). *Conducting a Business Process Analysis*. The Dream Institute.

Galbraith, J. R. (1994). *Competing with Flexible Lateral Organizations*. Wesley Publication Company.

Galbraith, J. R. (1995). *Designing Organizations: An Executive Briefing on Strategy, Structure And Process*. Jossey-Bass Publishers.

Glavan, L. M., Vukšić, V. B., & Vlahović, N. (2015). Decision tree learning for detecting turning points in business process orientation: A case of Croatian companies. *Croatian Operational Research Review*, *6*(1), 207–224. doi:10.17535/crorr.2015.0017

Gulick, L. (1937). Notes on the theory of organization. In L. Gulick & L. Urwick (Eds.), *Papers on the science of administration* (pp. 1–45). New York: Institute of Public Administration, Columbia University.

Hammer, M. (1990). Reengineering Work: Don't Automate, Obliterate. *Harvard Business Review*, *68*(4), 104–113.

Hammer, M. (1996). *Beyond Reengineering: How the Process-Centered Organization is Changing Our Work and Our Lives*. HarperCollins Publishers.

Hammer, M., & Champy, J. (1993). *Reengineering the Corporation: A Manifesto for Business Revolution*. New York: Harper Business.

Harmon, P. (2003). *Business Process Change: A Manager's Guide to Improving, Redesigning, and Automating Processes*. San Francisco: Morgan Kaufmann Publishers.

Harmon, P. (2004). Evaluating an Organization's Business Process Maturity. *Business Process Trends*, *2*(3), 1–11.

Harmon, P. (2015). The scope and evolution of business process management. In *Handbook on business process management 1* (pp. 37–80). Springer Berlin Heidelberg. doi:10.1007/978-3-642-45100-3_3

Harrington, J. (2006). *Process Management Excellence – The Art of Excelling in Process Management*. Paton Press LLC.

Hung, R. Y. (2006). Business Process Management as Competitive Advantage: A Review and Empirical Study. *Total Quality Management*, *17*(1), 21–40. doi:10.1080/14783360500249836

ISO. (2008/2009). *ISO 9000 Quality Management Systems*. Geneva: Author.

Jaklic, J., Groznik, A., Huber, T., Svetina, M., Trkman, P., & Indihar Stemberger, M. (2012). A Link-up between Business Process Orientation and Efficiency Improvements in a Supply Chain: The Case Study from the Wholesale Business. *Transformations in Business & Economics*, *11*(2/26), 117-133.

Keen, P. G. W. (1997). *The Process Edge-Creating Value Where It Counts*. Boston, MA: Harvard Business School Press.

Kelly, K. (1995). *Out of Control: The New Biology of Machines, Social Systems and the Economic World*. Perseus Books.

Khosravi, A. (2016). Business process rearrangement and renaming: A new approach to process orientation and improvement. *Business Process Management Journal*, *22*(1), 116–139. doi:10.1108/BPMJ-02-2015-0012

Kohlbacher, M. (2009). The perceived effects of business process management. *Proceedings of Science and Technology for Humanity (TIC-STH), 2009 IEEE Toronto International Conference*, 399-402. 10.1109/TIC-STH.2009.5444467

Kohlbacher, M. (2010). The Effects of Process Orientation: A Literature Review. *Business Process Management Journal*, *16*(1), 135–152. doi:10.1108/14637151011017985

Lee, J., Lee, D., & Sungwon, K. (2007). *An overview of the business process maturity model (BPMM). International workshop on process aware information systems (PAIS 2007)*. Springer.

McAdam, R. (1996). An integrated business improvement methodology to refocus business improvement efforts. *Business Process Re-engineering & Management Journal*, *2*(1), 63–71. doi:10.1108/14637159610111482

McCormack, K. (2001, January). Business Process Orientation: Do You Have It? *Quality Progress*, 51–58.

McCormack, K. (2007). Introduction to the theory of business process orientation. In K. McCormack (Ed.), *Business Process Maturity. Theory and Application* (pp. 1–18). Booksurge Publishing.

McCormack, K., Willems, J., van den Bergh, J., Deschoolmeester, D., Willaert, P., Indihar Štemberger, M., ... Vlahovic, N. (2009). A Global Investigation of Key Turning Points in Business Process Maturity. *Business Process Management Journal*, *15*(5), 792–815. doi:10.1108/14637150910987946

McCormack, K. P., & Johnson, W. C. (2001). *Business Process Orientation – Gaining the E-Business Competitive Advantage*. St. Lucie Press. doi:10.1201/9781420025569

Mintzberg, H. (1991). The Effective Organization: Forces and Forms. *Sloan Management Review*, *54*(Winter), 54–69.

Monge, P. R. (1990). Theoretical and Analytical Issues in Studying Organizational Processes. *Organization Science*, *1*(4), 23–34. doi:10.1287/orsc.1.4.406

Mulder, P. (2017). *Bureaucratic Theory by Max Weber*. Retrieved November 9, 2017 from: https://www.toolshero.com/management/bureaucratic-theory-weber/

Nadarajah, D., & Latifah Syed Abdul Kadir, S. (2014). A Review of the Importance of Business Process Management in Achieving Sustainable Competitive Advantage. *The TQM Journal*, *26*(5), 522–531. doi:10.1108/TQM-01-2013-0008

Pall, G. A. (1987). *Quality Process Management*. Englewood Cliffs, NJ: Prentice-Hall.

Palmberg, K. (2009). Exploring Process Management: Are There Any Widespread Models and Definitions? *The TQM Journal*, *21*(2), 203–215. doi:10.1108/17542730910938182

Paulk, M. C., Curtis, B., Chrissis, M. B., & Weber, C. V. (1993). *The Capability Maturity Model for Software, Version 1.1 (No. CMU/SEI-93-TR-24)*. Software Engineering Institute. doi:10.21236/ADA263403

Porter, M. (1985). *Competitive Advantage: Creating and Sustaining Superior Performance*. New York: Free Press.

Reijers, H. A. (2006). Implementing BPM systems: The role of process orientation. *Business Process Management Journal*, *12*(4), 389–409. doi:10.1108/14637150610678041

Rohloff, M. (2011). Advances in business process management implementation based on a maturity assessment and best practice exchange. *Information Systems and e-Business Management*, *9*(3), 383–403. doi:10.100710257-010-0137-1

Rosemann, M., de Bruin, T., & Power, B. (2006). A Model to Measure Business Process Management Maturity and Improve Performance. In J. Jeston & J. Nelis (Eds.), *Business process management*. Oxford, UK: Butterworth-Heinemann.

Rosemann, M., & vom Brocke, J. (2015). The six core elements of business process management. In *Handbook on business process management 1* (pp. 105–122). Springer Berlin Heidelberg. doi:10.1007/978-3-642-45100-3_5

Ross, J. E. (1995). *Total Quality Management: Text, Cases and Readings*. St. Lucie Press.

Rummler, G., & Brache, A. (1990). *Improving Performance*. San Francisco, CA: Jossey-Bass.

Schutta, J. T. (2006). *Business Performance through Lean Six Sigma: Linking the Knowledge Worker, the Twelve Pillars, and Baldrige*. Milwaukee, WI: ASQ Quality Press.

Senge, P. (1990). *The fifth discipline: The Art and Practice of the Learning Organization*. New York: Doubleday Currency.

Sethi, V., & King, W. (2003). *Organizational Transformation through Business Process Reengineering*. Pearson Education.

Sikdar, A., & Payyazhi, J. (2014). A Process Model of Managing Organizational Change During Business Process Redesign. *Business Process Management Journal*, *20*(6), 971–998. doi:10.1108/BPMJ-02-2013-0020

Škrinjar, R., Bosilj-Vukšić, V., & Indihar-Štemberger, M. (2008). The Impact of Business Process Orientation on Financial and Non-Financial Performance. *Business Process Management Journal*, *14*(5), 738–754. doi:10.1108/14637150810903084

Smart, P. A., Maddern, H., & Maull, R. S. (2009). Understanding Business Process Management: Implications for Theory and Practice. *British Journal of Management*, *20*(4), 491–507. doi:10.1111/j.1467-8551.2008.00594.x

Smith, A., & Fingar, P. (2003). *Business Process Management: The Third Wave*. Meghan – Kiffer Press.

Snow, C. C., & Miles, R. E. (1983). The Role of Strategy in the Development of a General Theory of Organizations. *Advances in Strategic Management*, *2*, 231–259.

Spanyi, A. (2006). *More for Less: The Power Of Process Management*. Meghan – Kiffer Press.

Strnadl, C. F. (2006). Aligning Business and IT: The Process-Driven Architecture Model. *Information Systems Management*, *23*(4), 67–77. doi:10.1201/1078.10580 530/46352.23.4.20060901/95115.9

Talwar, R. (1993). Business Re-Engineering - A Strategy-Driven Approach. *Long Range Planning*, *26*(6), 22–40. doi:10.1016/0024-6301(93)90204-S

Tang, J., Pee, L. G., & Iijima, J. (2013). Investigating the Effects of Business Process Orientation on Organizational Innovation Performance. *Information & Management*, *50*(8), 650–660. doi:10.1016/j.im.2013.07.002

Tenner, A. R., & DeToro, I. J. (1997). *Process Redesign: The Implementation Guide for Managers*. Reading, MA: Addison-Wesley.

Trkman, P. (2013). Increasing Process Orientation with Business Process Management: Critical Practices. *International Journal of Information Management*, *33*(1), 48–60. doi:10.1016/j.ijinfomgt.2012.05.011

Van Der Aalst, W. M. (2013). Business Process Management: A Comprehensive Survey. *Software Engineering*, *2013*, 1–37. doi:10.1155/2013/507984

Van der Aalst, W. M. P., ter Hofstede, H. N., & Weske, M. (2003). Business Process Management: A Survey. *Proceedings of the International Conference of Business Process Management*. 10.1007/3-540-44895-0_1

Van Looy, A., De Backer, M., & Poels, G. (2011). Defining Business Process Maturity. A Journey towards Excellence. *Total Quality Management & Business Excellence*, *22*(11), 1119–1137. doi:10.1080/14783363.2011.624779

Wong, W. P., Ahmad, N. H., Nasurdin, A. M., & Mohamad, M. N. (2014). The Impact of External Environmental On Business Process Management and Organizational Performance. *Service Business*, *8*(4), 559–586. doi:10.100711628-013-0207-9

Zaheer, A., Rehman, K. U., & Khan, M. A. (2010). Development and Testing of a Business Process Orientation Model to Improve Employee and Organizational Performance. *African Journal of Business Management*, *4*(2), 149–161.

Zairi, M. (1997). Business Process Management: A Bounderyless Approach to Modern Competitiveness. *Business Process Management Journal*, *3*(1), 64–80. doi:10.1108/14637159710161585

KEY TERMS AND DEFINITIONS

Business Process Management: An approach where the main emphasis is on improving businesses processes improve business processes to ensure that the critical activities affecting customer satisfaction are executed in the most efficient and effective manner.

Business Process Orientation: An integrated managerial and strategic approach where the emphasis is on processes that create valuable outcomes and increase customer satisfaction.

Business Process Reengineering: The practice of rethinking and redesigning the way work is done by constantly assessing and improving business processes.

Business Processes: A set of specific activities that provide value to one organization's customers.

Organizational Design: Is a methodology which identifies dysfunctional aspects of work flow, procedures, processes, structures, and systems, and then realigns them to fit current business realities/goals.

Process Alignment: Has to do with how well an organization manages the fit between its processes and its external and internal organizational elements.

Process-Based Organization: An organizational configuration where processes are at the center of organizational design to address the changing contingencies.

Chapter 2
Facing the Challenges of Nostalgia International Markets

António Moreira
University of Aveiro, Portugal

Vitor Alves
University of Aveiro, Portugal

Tatiana Martins
University of Aveiro, Portugal

João Branco Pereira
University of Aveiro, Portugal

Sónia Conceição
University of Aveiro, Portugal

ABSTRACT

Internationalization is a business strategy that normally aims at expanding the business of the firm outside its domestic market. It may also involve the creation of an integrated network of contacts and partners. The aim of this chapter involves a firm that distributes high-end wines and other alcoholic drinks to the domestic market and is seeking to expand its activities abroad. Taking into account the "nostalgia market," with many Portuguese living throughout Europe, this chapter seeks to analyze how a Portuguese firm seeks to embrace the internationalization strategy of serving these ex-pats, through local retailers, and afterwards the possibility of serving the market abroad using the contacts so far developed. As such, the firm seeks to serve both the ex-pats and the local market alike. The chapter analyzes the Spanish, French, and German market, and it is possible to conclude that France is the market with the higher likelihood of success, economically and culturally.

DOI: 10.4018/978-1-5225-5360-1.ch002

INTRODUCTION

Business internationalization has been subject to extensive research. It can be understood as a strategy aiming at expanding and creating an integrated network of contacts and partners when firms seek to expand to new markets, despite the firms' risk embarking on international ventures (Dominguez, 2016). The firms' internationalization process has to be framed in accordance with the firms' competencies and competitive advantages, which normally are developed in the domestic market, and seen from a wide perspective taking into account a wider market and an extended competition (Moreira, 2004). Internationalization is important for firms to enhance competitive advantage as it involves a dynamic process (Stanisauskaite & Kock, 2016).

In recent years the Portuguese economy has embarked on an export-led strategy whose results surprised analysts. Faced with the downturn in the domestic market, many companies have deployed internationalization strategies to counterbalance the downfall of the domestic balance, where clearly the overseas markets were seen as a means of economic survival.

This chapter presents a case study of a reseller (B2B) firm – named OMEGA for confidentiality reasons – that distributes well known, high-end wines and other alcoholic drinks. It is an active player in the Centro region of Portugal that is considering expanding its business abroad. If the fierce competition felt in Portugal has sparked this risk-taking behavior, the number of Portuguese immigrants across Europe has opened a window of opportunity to explore the 'nostalgia market', which is a latent opportunity that has been traditionally neglected by many firms. Moreover, the agri-food sector has been one of the most dynamic ones among ex-pats, in particular, wine being one of the important products of Portuguese exports. As such, based on its competitive position in the domestic market, OMEGA seeks to exploit foreign markets and explore a calculated risk-taking behavior addressing an old social tradition based on socio-economic hardship during the 1960s, 1970s and 1980s, that has been growing as a result of the recent economic and financial crisis, that led to the emergence of this 'nostalgia market', made up of long-time migrant consumers of Portuguese products. OMEGA's internationalization strategy is to distribute its products, to resellers abroad to satisfy Portuguese ex-pats consumers.

The markets of Spain, Germany and France were analyzed in order to depict market potential and market risk. It was concluded that France is the market with the greatest potential for OMEGA.

The chapter is structured in eight sections. The first section addresses the literature on internationalization. The second section explores literature on motivations for internationalization. The third section addresses literature on modes of entry in international markets. The fourth section explores the importance of culture across countries. The fifth section addresses the research methodology used. The sixth section presents the case study of the firm under analysis, the analysis of the potential and risks of the three main Portuguese nostalgia markets in Europe: Spain, France, and Germany. It also discusses why France is the main market to start with the internationalization process. Finally, section seven presents the conclusions and section eighth presents future research direction.

INTERNATIONALIZATION

Internationalization normally refers to the process of increasing involvement of companies in business activities abroad (Grünig & Morschett, 2017). As such, it involves the company's operations in different markets or countries, both in terms of production factors, capital transfers, as well as in the development of projects in cooperation with foreign stakeholders or simply in marketing activities in other countries (Ribau et al., 2015).

With the globalization of the economic world, internationalization is an activity that has become increasingly important, with consequences for the growth and survival of firms, regardless of their size (Dicken, 2015; Moreira, 2009).

Over time, several theories have been put forward to explain how firms internationalize (Ribau et al., 2015), based not only on the globalization process, but also on how scholars have interpreted those theories and contexts. Ribau et al. (2015) summarize the ontological perspectives of the main strands of the literature on internationalization with the internationalization theories and the main constructs. Moreover, the literature on internationalization is vast, somewhat fragmented and dispersed. Over time, not only the globalization of business activity has evolved, but scholars' interpretations have also changed (Moreira, 2009; Ribau et al., 2015, 2017).

There are two well-known approaches in the firms' internationalization processes: (1) those that advocate an evolutionary, sequential, linear model with increasing international participation, known as the Uppsala Model (Johanson & Vahlne, 1977); and (2) those addressing a network-based view (Håkansson & Snehota, 2006). However, there are other theories that explain the internationalization processes based on innovation (Morgan & Katsikeas, 1997) or in rapid internationalization processes (Oviatt & McDougall, 1994).

The Uppsala model argues that firms follow a sequential path in their international operations, in which there are four stages that differ regarding the degree of involvement of the firm in the market (Johanson & Vahlne, 1977): no regular exports, exports through agents, sales through wholly owned subsidiary and international production subsidiaries. Both the degree of risk and commitment of resources increase as the internationalization process progresses.

This evolutionary process is based on a linear cumulative path in which the absence of international experience reduces the propensity of the firm to engage in unknown international markets. As such, the firm is committed to its domestic activities in the domestic market avoiding unnecessary business risks. This evolutionary process contends that only after the firm manages to internalize the knowledge and experience gained in dealing with international clients in foreign markets, the firm is willing to underpin its subsequent stages committing more resources and controlling its operations abroad (Johanson & Vahlne, 1977).

The progression of the firm's activities to far-flung international markets can be explained using the concept of psychic distance, which involves differences in culture, languages, education, industrial development, political systems, among other things (Ribau et al., 2015). As such, according to the Uppsala model, it is expected that firms begin their internationalization process to low psychic distant markets and once they gain experience in these markets they expand their activities to more psychic distant markets.

In a different vein, Johanson and Mattsson (2015) argue that the internationalization of a firm is the result of the development of (internal and external) network of relations with individuals and / or firms that have resources and experience / knowledge. This network approach is another way to analyze firms' internationalization paths, based on an interactive perspective among participants (suppliers, buyers, competitors or other institutions) involved in the business environment (Moreira & Alves, 2016). It is the complementarities of the participants that enable the creation of a network of relationships in which the company's internationalization takes place when the network is extended abroad. Håkansson and Snehota (2006) argue that relationships amongst players in foreign markets play an important role.

The internationalization of the firm means the establishment and development of positions in relation to other counterparts in foreign networks. As such, the internationalizing firm is initially engaged in a network which is primarily domestic and then further develops business relationships in networks in other countries (Ruzzier et al., 2006).

Johanson and Mattsson (2015) defend that the number and depth of relationships increase among clients, suppliers, distributors and competitors as firms internationalize. According to them, this occurs in three different ways: firstly, building relationships with companies in new countries (international expansion); secondly, increasing commitment in international networks (international penetration); finally, integrating their position in several networks in various countries (international integration).

Several factors influence the process of internationalization of small and medium-sized firms (SMEs) (Ribau et al., 2017): the type of products and activities; the international modes of entry and operation; the types of markets; internal competencies; the ability to manage cooperative relationships; financial constraints; and organizational structure. Moreover, as SMEs have very limited resources, establishing relationships with their clients can be a form of resource acquisition and international penetration (Moreira & Alves, 2016).

Johanson and Mattsson (2015) indicate that highly internationalized firms enjoy strong direct relationships with foreign network actors. Furthermore, when firms are positioned within a foreign internationalized network they manage to develop relationships that can lead to further linkages with other actors (Axelsson & Johanson, 1992; Johanson & Vahlne, 1992).

Clearly, the development of the internationalization process is influenced by several factors (Axelsson & Johanson, 1992; Johanson & Mattsson, 2015; Moreira & Alves, 2016): the firm and market level of internationalization; the partner level of internationalization; and the network level of internationalization. Thus, according to Johanson and Mattsson (2015), firms can be characterized as following four different types of behavior: the *Early Starter*; the *Late Starter*; the *Lonely International*; and the *International Among Others*.

The early starter firm has a low degree of internationalization, the same occurring with the network the firm belongs to (Johanson & Mattsson, 2015). This low degree of internationalization suggests that it possesses only weak channels with foreign networks. However, the relationship with the international network is considered important for the accumulation of knowledge.

Late starters are characterized by low levels of commitment and activity in international markets and low levels of international experience. However, it is generally argued that late starters enjoy a knowledge advantage *vis-à-vis* early starters, as they are more committed to international operations and acquire knowledge from an international wider network (Holm, Eriksson, & Johansson, 1996).

Lonely international firms possess a high degree of internationalization, which provides them with greater levels of experiential knowledge in international markets. As they may be present in various relationships, they tap into knowledge resources from several partners.

The international among others enjoys a high degree of internationalization (Johanson & Mattsson, 2015). Although they have established and developed positions and resources in foreign markets, like the lonely international, international among others also have a highly internationalized macro-position, which provides them with higher levels of experiential knowledge when compared with the lonely internationals.

MOTIVATIONS FOR INTERNATIONALIZATION

The prospect of internationalization should begin with the anticipation of the understanding and the reasons why companies intend to make greenfield investments, make foreign acquisitions, make international joint ventures, sign licensing agreements, or simply restrict themselves to export to a target market (Grünig & Morschett, 2017). Generically, the decision involves at least two main steps: first, spotting an opportunity abroad; and the selection among alternative ways to exploit this opportunity.

The most well-known classification of the main motivations for internationalization was proposed by Dunning (1993). In fact, motivations do not only support investment operations, but also modes of entry. This classification distinguishes the following four different types of motivations (Dunning, 1993):

1. *Resource seeking companies*, in which companies seek to access resources that are not available in their home market. For example, natural resources, raw materials, or even resources that have a higher cost in the domestic market, such as labor;
2. *Market seeking companies*, in which companies invest to capture consumers. In the more classic theories of international trade this motive can be framed in the attempt to avoid transportation costs, normally choosing to resort to foreign direct investment (FDI) as an alternative to exports;
3. *Efficiency seeking companies*, where companies resort to FDI if they can benefit from the differences between countries (regarding cost or availability of production factors), from economies of scale and scope, as well as from differences in consumer behavior and tastes;
4. *Strategic asset seeking companies*, in which companies undertake FDI in order to acquire new skills and resources, or dynamic capabilities, rather than simply exploiting the assets they already have. By undertaking FDI, the company is able to access specific knowledge specificities in host locations (countries, regions or even cities) and thus to set up subsidiaries there.

MODES OF ENTRY IN INTERNATIONAL MARKETS

Typologies of modes of entry in international markets are based on the degree of involvement in external markets, which in turn depend on the level of resources (investment) involved in external markets and on the degree of control over international operations (Grünig & Morschett, 2017; Moreira, 2004).

There are two different modes of market entry: exports, which involve production in the domestic market (direct export and indirect export), and a second type of exports that involve production abroad (production contract, licensing agreement, franchising agreement, technology transfer, service contracts, management contracts, strategic alliances, joint ventures and total ownership through direct foreign investment). These two modes of entry involve different costs and benefits (Katsikeas, Leonidou, & Samiee, 2009). There are clearly important differences in these two modes of entry, since exporting products to the destination market / country involves fewer resources and risks than the second mode of entry where there is the possibility of transferring the firm's resources (technology, capital and human labor) to a foreign country. Equally important is the fact that the products are sold directly to the end customer or shipped to be produced and sold in the destination market.

Grünig and Morschett (2017) propose the following modes of entry in international markets: exports (indirect and direct exports); contractual modes (licensing out; management contracts; international outsourcing); and foreign direct investment (joint-ventures; strategic alliances; subsidiaries partially or 100% controlled).

Exports are the most basic form firms use to address international expansion (Salomon & Shaver, 2005). Indirect exports occur when the company does not develop particular efforts in terms of international marketing, being dependent on third parties to sell in international markets (Moreira, 2004; Grünig & Morschett, 2017). Differently, direct exports mean that the company does not delegate any international marketing operation to third parties, using its own resources in the exploration of international markets. Clearly, indirect exports require less resource involvement and less risk than direct exports, since they do not involve gathering information and establishing the distribution, communication, and pricing policies / strategies in international markets. In turn, the knowledge generated from the international markets served is very limited, when compared to the necessary involvement of the company in international markets through direct exports.

Licensing agreements involve a deal signed between at least two parties where one company concedes the other company the right to use certain knowledge and / or to exploit industrial property rights (trademarks, patents, designs or designs) against a certain payment, usually through royalties (Grünig & Morschett, 2017). On the other hand, franchising is a specific form of licensing in which a franchisor licenses franchisees for them to market or produce a product / service in a particular territory or country, according to the business model created by the franchisor (Grünig & Morschett, 2017). Finally, international outsourcing involves an agreement between an international company or one that intends to internationalize (contractor), and a company in the country of destination (subcontracted), which manufactures the products or components thereof.

Joint ventures involve the participation of several companies in the capital of a business unit, in order to develop a productive and / or commercial activity, thus giving rise to the sharing of their assets, profits and business risk (Grünig & Morschett, 2017; Moreira, 2004). In turn, strategic alliances can be understood as a combination of two or more organizations to achieve common strategic objectives and encompass several situations of commercial relations between companies from different countries, often competing among them.

CULTURE

Defining culture is not an easy task. Even with the globalization process, in which it is expected that there is an increasing trend towards some behavioral homogenization among citizens from different countries in terms of food, clothing, leisure, among other things, one can contend that cultural differences across countries clearly exist, as the deepest manifestations of culture – values – are relatively stable over time (Hofstede, 1991).

Aware of the existence of distinct behavioral standards among countries, some researchers have been analyzing cross-cultural differences for the last decades (Hofstede, 1991; Trompenaars, 1993).

As culture is relatively stable over time, society tends to transmit to future generations the "solutions" (a set of basic common values) that have worked in the past that reflect the dominant values within their culture (Hofstede, 1991).

Hofstede's (1991) original work aimed at finding differences in values between individuals in their work context. He originally proposed four dimensions: uncertainty avoidance, individualism / collectivism, power distance and masculinity / femininity. Afterwards two dimensions were added: long-term / short-term orientation and indulgence versus restrain.

Uncertainty avoidance refers to a society's tolerance for uncertainty and ambiguity. In cultures ranking high in uncertainty avoidance individuals "want to have structure, to know precisely how they are supposed to behave and what is going to happen next. Predictability of events is highly valued" (Triandis, 2004, p. 92).

Individualism stands for a preference for a loosely-knit social framework in which individuals are expected to take care of themselves and their immediate families. In turn, collectivism, stands for a preference for a tightly-knit framework in society in which individuals can expect their relatives or members of a particular in-group to look after them in exchange for unquestioning loyalty.

Power distance stands for the degree to which the less powerful members of a society accept and expect that power is distributed unequally (Hofstede, 1991). It relates to the way each society manages the inequalities among their people. The higher the power distance, the more hierarchy the country is and the stiffer the control mechanisms used to control individuals.

In high power distance cultures, individuals are expected to be deferential and obedient to their hierarchical superiors (Shane, 1993) and do not believe in proposing initiatives (Hofstede, 1991). Power differences are translated into visible differences in status that contribute to the superior's authority that subordinates have to respect (Hofstede, 1991).

In feminine societies gender roles overlap while in masculine societies social gender roles are clearly distinct: men are supposed to be assertive, tough and focused in material success and women are supposed to be modest, tender and concerned with the quality of life (Hofstede, 2001).

In masculine societies the task is the absolute priority. As individuals are performance-oriented, more concerned with their careers, competitiveness is appreciated. In turn, in feminine societies making a career is less important. They are more concerned to reach welfare society (Hofstede, 1991).

Long-term orientation (LTO) involves certain characteristics: persistence, ordering relationships by status and observing this order, thrift and having a sense of shame. On the other hand, a short-term orientation (STO) is based on personal steadiness and stability, protecting your face, respect for tradition and reciprocating of greetings, favors and gifts.

Indulgence stands for a society that allows relatively free gratification of basic and natural human drives related to enjoying life and having fun. Restraint stands for a society that suppresses gratification of needs and regulates it by means of strict social norms.

Dantas, Moreira, and Valente (2015) used Hofstede's cultural values to analyze early-stage long-term orientation, necessity-driven entrepreneurship and opportunity-driven entrepreneurship among 44 countries using Global Entrepreneurship Monitor (GEM) Datasets from 2012 and 2013. They conclude that individualism and long-term orientation are of added value to explain early-stage long-term orientation. They also conclude that the higher the power distance among countries and the higher the uncertainty avoidance index the better they explain necessity-driven entrepreneurship. Finally, femininity and low uncertainty avoidance are of added value to explain opportunity-driven entrepreneurship. This is a clear indication that cultural values differ in explaining economic activity across countries

Following a different perspective, Dantas, Moreira, and Valente (2017) used Hofstede's cultural values and societal valued to analyze how necessity-driven and opportunity-driven entrepreneurship among 56 countries using GEM Datasets from 2016 and 2017. They conclude that individualism and long-term orientation are of added value to explain early-stage long-term orientation. They conclude cultural values marginally explain necessity-driven and opportunity-driven entrepreneurship.

METHODOLOGY

This empirical study investigates a contemporary phenomenon within its real-life context, where the limits between the phenomenon and the context are not clearly defined. The case study method, proposed by Yin (2004), is one of the most common research methods used in social sciences. In this chapter the use of the case study method is particularly appropriate as the aim is to understand, explore and describe certain unique events that are complex, and where researchers have no control over the real occurrences taking place (Yin, 2004).

The case study methodology is particularly indicated to respond to questions like "how?" and "why?" (Yin, 2004), clearly indicating the exploratory nature of the research being carried out. Moreover, this case study method is particularly useful, as a qualitative methodology, to explain complex and dynamic realities (Malhotra, 2017).

This chapter seeks to gather and analyze information about the company (history, mission, resources, evolution, etc.) known hereafter as OMEGA. To do so, accounting documents / reports were analyzed and an interview was held with the commercial director of the company. Moreover, the interviewee was willing to disclose information about the company, and subsequently clarify all doubts that emerged *en route*. Besides this, information available on the Internet about the firm was also used to shape the case study during the interviews.

CASE STUDY

This section contains a brief presentation of the company, its main business activity, the industry in which it operates, some relevant indicators and the markets it serves at present. The approaches are descriptive, with the help of tables and illustrations.

Presentation of the Company

OMEGA is a small, solid and dynamic family company, in operation for over three decades, having started up with only three employees. Its growth has been sustained on very well-defined principles and objectives and directed by a particular management recognized in the market as being a company of excellence in the drink-selling industry.

OMEGA's core business is the distribution of alcoholic drinks (wines, spirits, sparkling wines). The wines belong to different wine-producing regions in the country, namely Alentejo, Douro, Dão and Bairrada, particularly red, white and green wine, as well as port wine. Casal Garcia, Gazela, Esteva, Papa Figos and S. Domingos are examples of brands distributed by OMEGA. Most of its turnover (around 60%) is generated through the distribution channel, although Cash and Carry (sales to the final consumer) is also significant. In 2016, turnover amounted to 9 million euros, as presented in Table 1.

OMEGA's capital is currently 150,100 thousand euros and it has five partners. Shares are not distributed evenly among all partners, and it has 16 employees.

The company operates in the north and central regions of Portugal, its principal market being Aveiro, Portugal, where the firm is the industry leader. As for internationalization, although its strategy is not completely defined, it has some important contacts in the European market, where it intends to do business.

Analysis of the Company

This section analyses the company's internal and external context. Firstly, in the internal context, the firm's organizational, human and financial resources are analyzed, secondly, in the external context, competitors, market share and substitute products are analyzed, and finally, a SWOT analysis is elaborated.

The company has two main target markets: the Business to Business (B2B) market, which includes retailers and wholesalers (supermarkets, hotels, restaurants and cafés) and the Business to Consumer (B2C) market, since final consumers can purchase wine directly in the firm's Cash and Carry, situated in Águeda, Portugal.

OMEGA has storage facilities of 2,600 m^2 situated in the northern industrial estate in Águeda, which can hold a stock of up to 1.5 million products.

The company concentrates essentially on supplying the market in the Centro region, particularly the district of Aveiro, where OMEGA is the "industry leader".

The main competitor is situated in the city of Aveiro, Portugal. Although it is a strong company, "it has only mass-produced brands", OMEGA's product portfolio being "much more extensive" (according to our interviewee). The strategy to compete with this competitor consists of "negotiating lower prices with our supplier". It also has competitors nationally who "have around 50 salespeople and cover the

Table 1. Summary of OMEGA

	2012	2013	2014	2015	2016
Sales Volume	6,850,000€	7,350,000€	7,900,000€	8,650,000€	9,500,000€
Number of Employees	15	16	16	16	16
Number of Clients	1,200	1,200	1,200	1,200	1,200

autonomous regions of the Azores and Madeira", and although bigger than OMEGA, do not represent a "direct threat", according to the interviewee.

OMEGA presents a market share around 70%, in the district of Aveiro. Also in the medium-high restaurant sector OMEGA has a market share of 70%. To increase market share it would be necessary to increase the sales team available to bring in new clients, such as cafés and restaurants. The current strategy includes selling to retailers situated in Aveiro's adjoining regions such as Espinho, Vagos, Ovar and Esmoriz, who subsequently sell to local customers. Although this could be achievable, OMEGA is planning to expand internationally to exploit its brand portfolio abroad.

When confronted with competing / substitute products, the interviewee stated that

There are more wines in Portugal than in Spain, I don't know if I'm right, but I've heard that. In my opinion, it's very easy to create a brand in Portugal (register it, label it). The worst part is having the right distribution network, as there's no point in making wines if you don't have the right partner to sell them.

Considering OMEGA's product portfolio, what is important is not having products that clients need to buy directly from OMEGA, but to satisfy clients' needs with products intermediated by OMEGA. Obviously, all the brands commercialized by the firm can be acquired from any other shop or retailer, since OMEGA does not have its own brand. As far as could be gathered, OMEGA follows a differentiation strategy based on its wide product portfolio: it has around two thousand references, which means its supply base is more diversified than that of their direct competitors.

Strategy of the Company

OMEGA's mission is to "commercialize wine brands with a good price-quality relationship." The company's vision is "to be a market leader and sell the best brands". The brand's values are "trust and excellent service provision."

At present, OMEGA has not yet begun its internationalization process. However, the interviewee states that OMEGA "already sells indirectly to international markets through some of our other clients, and we think there is a market that could be a source of growth. Therefore, analyses are beginning so that in 2018, OMEGA can implement this internationalization strategy." As will be seen further on, the data analyzed from AICEP, the European market, and more specifically the ex-pat market (a market of Portuguese emigrants who look for familiar Portuguese products), seems to be the most viable for the type of product in question.

According to the firm's interviewee statements, indirect exports is the most viable route to initiate the internationalization process, i.e. through other companies who are already established in the foreign market and have a strong market presence abroad.

Clearly, this means resorting to the network-based approach, where international partners are firms whose main business is the sale of Portuguese products (including wine) and whose main target public is Portuguese emigrants.

The reasons leading OMEGA to consider entering international markets are "to make the company grow, and to some extent diminish the dependence on the domestic market" and take advantage of what is considered to be "a business opportunity", according to the interviewee.

When asked about what led to choosing indirect exports, as a way to access foreign markets, the interviewee indicates some benefits of exports, for example "increased sales, scale economies and less risk compared to the option of internationalization with investment abroad." But he is also aware of the problems arising from "legal matters, logistics and after-sales service." As a firm, OMEGA understands the importance of defining an internationalization strategy, but intends to minimize the risk of entry, taking advantage of the proximity to European countries and the Portuguese diaspora in Europe. In addition, the objective includes developing contacts in the destination market, so as to internalize knowledge about that market and establish networks to allow subsequent internationalization, minimizing the risk and maximizing the number of contacts.

In the context of exports, OMEGA aims to exploit the international market through indirect intermediaries, i.e. searching retailers and wholesalers to intermediate and decide the final product portfolio solution according to the intermediary's needs, at the same time satisfying the needs of the final customer.

Regarding possible changes to the marketing-mix for the external market, the products will be the same as those sold in Portugal, "of course, if a client asks for a brand and we don't have it, we'll try to get it, as long as it's good business for both of us, even here, this already happens." However, as the market will be fundamentally European countries, the selling price is going to be higher, as costs related to legal procedures, logistics and after-sales service will likely be higher. Concerning distribution and communication, this will be "the responsibility of the company we send the products to."

Table 2 displays OMEGA's main strengths, weaknesses, opportunities and threats.

Company Development

The company began its activity in 1984 in Águeda, at the time formed only of two people. With the growth of orders and consequent growth of stock and sales, OMEGA had to grow, and rented a store situated in Águeda. Due to constantly increasing sales, it had to take on someone else for company logistics, and in 1991, they created from scratch a new warehouse in Águeda, Portugal, which remains to this day the main company's warehouse.

Table 2. OMEGA's SWOT list

Strengths	Weaknesses
- Varied supply; - Own distribution; - Good price / quality relationship; - Well-known brands; - Leader in the Aveiro market;	- Lack of storage capacity; - Low national market share; - Not well known and weak positioning; - Weak marketing and non-existent digital marketing;
Opportunities	**Threats**
- External contacts; - Expand online sales and develop a strong presence on social networks; - High wine consumption abroad; - Presence in International Fairs such as ProWein; - Concentrating on the ex-pat market (Portuguese emigrants being the target public)	- Strong competition in the national and foreign market; - Competitors' strong presence online; - Dependence on suppliers; - Substitute products; - Strong competition in the destination market.

OMEGA has grown constantly over the years. Due to the growth in sales, OMEGA has 16 employees in 2017.

OMEGA was formed of two partners until 2008. In that year, one of the partner's quota was bought by the other party and four more partners joined the company, becoming a Public Liability Company (PLC). Since 2008, sales have grown by approximately 10% on average each year, from 5 million to 9 million euros turnover.

Market Opportunities

OMEGA operates in the Portuguese market, namely in the district of Aveiro. However, the company envisioned the Portuguese diaspora as an opportunity. The strategy, still in the early stages, is to provide Portuguese emigrants – the so-called "Nostalgia Market", at least to begin with – with the brands sold by OMEGA. Therefore, the reasons for internationalization include the sale and distribution of products to other intermediaries abroad, whose business is the sale of Portuguese wine brands, and where the target market is Portuguese emigrants.

As OMEGA sells several brands and covers the costs of distribution for the re-sale of products, it seeks to enter foreign markets where there is a certain geographical proximity. Furthermore, it intends to create synergies with commercial reselling companies abroad that are willing, strategically, to take on part of the distribution costs. Therefore, the firm wants the product distribution process to be from middle-man to middle-man, i.e., OMEGA receives the product from producers or suppliers, and sells to other intermediaries abroad. Figure 1 illustrates the distribution process OMEGA intends to exploit in international markets.

Figure 1. OMEGAS's intended distribution process for markets abroad

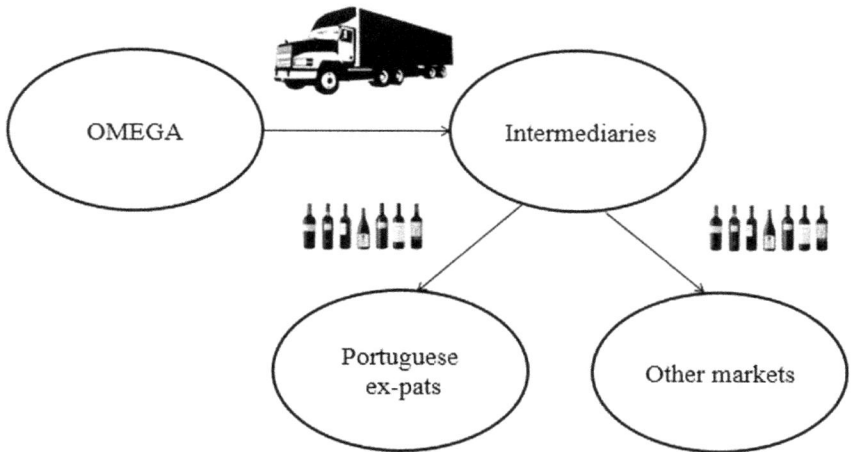

POTENTIAL MARKETS

OMEGA intends to gain, firstly, the ex-pat market, or in other words, Portuguese emigrants, and secondly, to maintain a great geographical proximity with the new markets to be exploited, since the company itself will bear the distribution costs. Therefore, criteria were adopted in selecting markets, reconciling the criterion of geographical proximity with that of the number of emigrants in the country. This suggests markets OMEGA seeks to select markets that are geographically closer to Portugal and have a greater number of Portuguese ex-pats.

Table 3 shows that the markets with the greatest number of emigrants are: Germany, Spain, France and the United Kingdom. However, considering the criterion of geographical proximity, France, in fourth position, has more potential than the United Kingdom. Therefore, bearing the criteria in mind, the potential markets for OMEGA are Germany, France and Spain, and these will be the subject of our study.

Table 4 presents information about the German, Spanish and French markets with the main macroeconomic indicators and the wine market.

German Market

According to studies carried out by the AICEP on external markets, Germany is a country with 81.9 million inhabitants, covering an area of 356,970 km², where the Euro is the currency unit. It has a GDP of more than three trillion dollars and GDP per capita of over 40 thousand dollars. The public debt is around 60% of GDP and the inflation rate is 1.6%. In 2016, it presented a negative balance of payments (AICEP, 2016a).

Commercial relations formed with Portugal are limited: 12% of Portuguese foreign exports are to Germany (AICEP, 2017a).

Regarding the wine market, Portugal has occupied the ninth position in wine exports to Germany in the period from 2008 to 2016, lying behind Greece (AICEP, 2017a). Although Portugal occupies a modest position regarding wine exports to Germany, OMEGA can take advantage of this as the country has a great diversity of wines and unique products that can enter the German market through exploiting the market offered by the Portuguese diaspora. However, the major obstacle may be German consumers' lack of knowledge, with the need to develop programs to promote wine brands in the German market immediately after entry. In addition, the opening up of the German market to Eastern European countries must be borne in mind, due to their geographical proximity (Novotná et al., 2017). Another important issue is the need to analyze the German wine market to understand its potential for exports, and to find out the potential intermediaries interested in establishing partnerships with OMEGA.

According to AICEP (2014), entry into the German market is difficult, as despite not having customs barriers and relatively little bureaucracy, all potential partner firms are rigorously analyzed according to strict criteria. Potential companies must understand what they could offer in terms of unique added value and appropriate to the needs of German consumers – beside the Portuguese diaspora – and have a good financial and business structure, to create business and long-term relations with German partners. The best way to enter the German market is through participation in the main trade fairs, where companies could find various business opportunities, as well as contacting German agents, to help OMEGA in the market entry process. The AICEP estimates a firm needs more than 100 thousand euros to form any commercial relationship with players in the German market (AICEP, 2014).

Spanish Market

Spain is the only country Portugal shares a border with. Spain has a resident population of 46.1 million inhabitants and a total area of 504,880 km^2. The currency is the euro and it is a monarchy. It has a GDP of over 1.2 trillion dollars and a GDP per capita around 30 thousand dollars, considerably less than Germany. The public debt is much higher than that of Germany, being almost 100% of GDP. In 2016, it has a negative rate of inflation, at -0.3% and a worse balance of payments than Germany (AICEP, 2017b).

Although the macroeconomic indicators are not favorable, in relation to Germany, Spain has more commercial relations with Portugal, the country being Spain's fifth biggest client. With a market share of 22.5%, regarding exports of Portuguese goods, Spain is the country that imports most from Portugal (AICEP, 2017).

Despite being a potential market, given its geographical proximity, the political and economic situation of Spain is one of crisis, affected by various internal nationalisms which influence the political and economic agendas. According to the study made by the AICEP, for companies to be able to enter the Spanish market they will need considerable production and financial capacity in order to respond to market needs and to adapt more easily to the emerging changes. Spain is a country where the processes of doing business are relatively simple for Portuguese firms, which is in OMEGA's favor. On the other hand, there is a major threat to foreign companies, as the Spanish consumer clearly prefers national and regional products, presenting a high degree of ethnocentricity.

As Spain is part of the European Union, there are no customs taxes, making international trade easier for OMEGA. Nevertheless, it has a special tax that is applied to exports such as spirits and other alcoholic drinks, tobacco and electric power (AICEP, 2017c).

In addition, Spain is divided into autonomous regions, each one having different cultures, policies and languages. Despite having to apply the main national policies, each autonomous region has control over its territory. Therefore, companies intending to enter this market must pay attention to the characteristics and language of each region, so as not to hinder the process of negotiating with Spanish firms. Negotiating processes are simplified, compared with the German market. However, in trade agreements in the wine sector, this market has a rigorous and hostile legislative framework (AICEP, 2017c). Another disadvantage is that Spain itself has good quality wines.

Table 3. Number of Portuguese immigrants per country in 2015

Countries	Portuguese Residents
Germany	347,162
Spain	346,875
United Kingdom	299,183
France	297,969

Source: Adapted from PorData (2017)

Table 4. Synthesis of Germany's, Spain's and France's macroeconomic indicators.

	Germany	Spain	France
Population (10^6 inhabitants)	81.2	46.1	66.9
Gross Domestic Product (trillion Dollars)	3	> 1.2	2.4
GPD per capita (10^3 USD \$)	40	30	38
Public Debt/GDP	60%	100%	97%
Inflation rate	1,6%	-0,3%	0,3%
Balance of payments	Negative	Negative	Positive
Share of Portugal's Exports	12%	22,5%	11,2%
Rank of Portuguese Imports	9th	1st	3rd
Strengths of the wine market	Variety of wines	Simplified processes	One of the main importers of Portuguese wine
Weaknesses of the wine market	Not well-known	Considerable production capacity	Little knowledge of Portuguese brands in the market
Threats to the wine market	Competition from the *New World*	Spaniards' preference for national products	Strong local competition
Opportunities in the wine market	Increased supply of modern-style wines	Close geographical proximity; similar language	Strengthening commercial relations with Portugal

French Market

France has 66.9 million inhabitants and a total area of 543,965 km^2. Its currency is the euro. In 2016, GDP was 2.4 trillion dollars and GDP per capita over 38 thousand dollars. In the same year, the public debt was around 97% of GDP and the inflation rate was 0.3%. Compared to the other two markets, France is the only country with a positive balance of payments in 2016. As for the commercial relations established with Portugal, France occupies the third position regarding exports of Portuguese goods, representing a share of 11.8% (AICEP, 2017d).

Due to the recent financial crisis of 2008, which led to economic crises of varying degrees of severity in several European countries, trade relations between France and Portugal diminished, leading the French to turn to emerging markets such as China where costs are lower. Nevertheless, in the current political and economic climate, commercial relations between the two countries have been re-established, due to the increased cost of the Chinese workforce and the costs of product distribution.

In the wine sector, France is one of Portugal's main clients, and holds various specialist wine fairs to stimulate relationships between companies and create international business opportunities. However, despite the good relations, Portuguese brands are little known to French consumers, as the typical French consumer is more demanding and sophisticated than the Portuguese consumer. As such, the demand for high added-value premium products is associated with greater purchasing power in the French market. Moreover, French brands are very well-known to French consumers, leading them to prefer national products and making it difficult for Portuguese companies to penetrate that market.

As a member of the European Union, France comes under the agreement of free movement of people, goods and capital, with no customs barriers. Similarly to Spain, France has a special tax applicable to spirits, other alcoholic drinks and tobacco. This market requires all imported goods to be labelled in French, as stated in the French legal framework (AICEP, 2016b).

France is one of the countries with the greatest number of Portuguese communities, which means a good opportunity for OMEGA to explore the ex-pat market. Many business-people in France have formed commercial relationships with foreign companies with strong links to immigrant communities resident in France, to be able to sell products from their native countries. Of all the markets analyzed, only France has concentrated on the ex-pat market with immigrants as the target public, and where food and drink are the most common products (AICEP, 2016b).

Given the proximity between France and Portugal historically and culturally, and the links formed both commercially and socially, this market has great potential for Portugal.

Cultural Values

Table 5 shows the differences across Portugal, Germany, France and Spain. It is clear that the differences between Portugal and Germany are more prevalent than the differences between Portugal and Spain and France, especially in terms of power distance (as Germany is clearly less hierarchical than Portugal, Spain and France), individualism (as Portugal is clearly a collectivist country), masculinity (as femininity characterizes Portugal), uncertainty avoidance (as Portugal is clearly the most conservative of the four), and Portugal is very short term oriented.

Table 5. Synthesis of Germany's, Spain's and France's macroeconomic indicators.

	Germany	Spain	France	Portugal	Δ Portugal vs Germany	Δ Portugal vs Spain	Δ Portugal vs France
Power Distance	35	57	68	63	28	6	5
Individualism	67	51	71	27	40	24	44
Masculinity	66	42	43	31	35	11	12
Uncertainty Avoidance	65	86	86	99	34	13	13
Long Term Orientation	83	48	63	28	55	20	35
Self-Indulgence	40	44	48	33	7	11	15
					199	85	124

Target Market Selection

According to Bradley (2004), target market selection must be tuned to specific market opportunities, and could be based on three main forms: opportunistic, systemic and mixed. The opportunistic form occurs when there is a stimulus that draws attention to an external market opportunity. The systemic form occurs when there is a comparative analysis of various markets, using pre-defined criteria that can be intrinsic or extrinsic to the company. The mixed form involves a mix of the two above-mentioned forms, evolving from an opportunistic approach to a systemic approach.

Initially, it can be argued that OMEGA used a systemic approach, as it is analyzing the Spanish, French and German markets to make up its mind, based on socio-economic, cultural and geographical reasons. However, it should be noted that OMEGA wishes to consolidate its position abroad not only targeting the Portuguese diaspora, but also taking advantage of intermediaries abroad according to the typical network-based view in order to gain more knowledge about the market and thereby serve adjacent local market segments. As such, OMEGA is seen to adopt a mixed form as it follows a systemic perspective and seeks to use intermediaries abroad to select the most suitable local market segments to position Portuguese wines. OMEGA establishes not only criteria for market selection, but also searches for potential local markets in order to make the final decision.

Therefore, and following a mixed selection approach, Table 6 presents the results of the market selection matrix, where a group of countries / markets with relevance for OMEGA was analyzed considering their attractiveness and risk. It should also be noted that this is a complex, subjective tool, requiring consideration of potential networks in the destination markets analyzed. These may be crucial for successful internationalization.

In this sense, the first task is to select the country / market that is likely to be interesting for OMEGA, from a socio-economic, geographical, and cultural point of view. Taking into consideration OMEGA's strategy, and considering the systemic selection process, France and Spain would be the first option, as Germany could be considered riskier due to cultural and linguistic differences. Following this, attractiveness indicators characterizing the markets are gathered, considering the industry and sector potential, as shown in Table 4.

The results of the taxonomic matrix are presented in Table 6, revealing that France is the most attractive market. France and Spain, with a low level of risk, are the most interesting markets in this respect. It is possible to conclude that the country combining a good level of attractiveness and risk is France.

From Opportunity Analysis to the French Market

As shown by the taxonomic matrix, concerning risk and attractiveness, the French market is the most suitable for OMEGA to expand its business, as contact with the Portuguese diaspora could enhance the likelihood of exploring local networks to approach other wine market segments.

Table 6. Synthesis of the market entry analysis

			France	Spain	
RISK	**Low**			Germany	
	Medium				
	High				
		High	High	Low	**Low**
			Medium		
			Attractiveness		

Therefore, OMEGA decided to start its internationalization process concentrating firstly on the French market, taking advantage of the opportunity to embrace exports as a form of learning, acquiring knowledge and establishing contacts and relationships. Moreover, the large and respected Portuguese community living in France is a permanent link between both countries and a reason for further exploration. Another factor was France's low risk, compared to Germany.

As a way to reduce any difficulties, OMEGA considers that building and maintaining partnerships is important. In this sense, OMEGA's goal is to consolidate its relationships with its French B2B clients / partners, to be able to create a solid position and gain market share, in order to sustain its future expansion in that market by establishing a branch.

CONCLUSION

Although internationalization is a phenomenon that has been intensively researched over the last few decades from a variety of viewpoints, it is a difficult issue for most SMEs, especially for those that are taking the initial steps towards internationalization.

OMEGA's case is interesting as it addresses how a small dynamic family company reselling alcoholic drinks in Portugal seeks to expand its competiveness abroad. As the company has a large market share in the Portuguese market segment it serves, OMEGA's market orientation is now focused on exploiting its competitive advantage exploiting opportunities in France.

Although several theories have been put forward to address internationalization, there is no single theory explaining the process of internationalization and strategies adopted by a firm. Based on this perspective, this chapter sought to explain OMEGA's internationalization process based on two theories: the Uppsala model and network-based theory.

The international network approach explains the internationalization process based on business networks (Johanson & Mattsson, 2015), in which the relationships a firm has with its customers, distributors, suppliers and competitors underpin the firm's internationalization. As referred to throughout, OMEGA seeks not only to serve the Portuguese diaspora in France, but also to become embedded in a relational network in order to initiate its entry to the French market. This approach clearly supports the view that the internationalization process occurs in an interactive environment established by a network of companies that includes local and external actors. They also argue that the interaction of these actors in networks can help firms acquire activities, resources and the information necessary to engage in internationalization processes.

Based on Johanson and Mattsson's (2015) typology, OMEGA cannot be defined as an Early Starter. However, OMEGA can clearly reach this status if it manages to internationalize through French distributors or close contacts within the French network.

One can argue that the firm's internationalization process might be developed in three steps: extension, penetration and integration. As such, based on OMEGA's intention, it is possible to claim that OMEGA's internationalization path involves construction of the network.

OMEGA is aware of its lack of experience and knowledge in foreign markets. It is clear that the Uppsala model can be seen as particularly applicable, since OMEGA prefers to internationalize to a country to which Portugal is psychologically close, to internalize knowledge gained through the relationship built with intermediaries to try to expand to other market segments. It can therefore be concluded that OMEGA should first exploit a familiar network before going on to explore unfamiliar markets where the risk is higher.

Although OMEGA is exploring a significant competitive advantage in the Portuguese market, it is important to note that in order to exploit its competitive advantage in France, it will first have to gain access to the French market, explore trust-commitment-based relationships with intermediaries, in order to have a solid market base in France to be able to serve the ex-pat market as well as to able to penetrate this unexplored market. Although the company has the resources and competencies to face the rivalry in Portugal, it is important to take into account that the competitive advantage will have to be adapted to be able to compete at the international level.

It is clear that OMEGA's market seeking behavior is an important tool form OMEGA to exploit its competitive advantage. Nevertheless, OMEGA is looking after Portuguese ex-pats to diminish market risk entry. Finally, exports are the main OEMGA's mode of entry. However, based on how OMEGA may develop over time, one cannot rule out the possibility for OMEGA to embark on an alliance with a French intermediary or even investing on a warehouse facility in France. However, this must be carefully analyzed taking into account a long-term perspective as a sudden success in France may change the minds of OMEGA's managers as serving Germany and / or Spain cannot be ruled out. However, this must be analyzed cautiously, as the firm needs to prove its market success abroad.

Clearly, although OMEGA has an interesting competitive advantage, it is important to understand that to succeed abroad it is mandatory to adapt the firm's competitive attitude acquiring new knowledge, internalizing it, and adapting the firm to new international realities.

FUTURE RESEARCH DIRECTIONS

Research on internationalization on service and commercial firms is quite specific when compared to industrial firms. As such, it would be interesting to analyze how trading firms embrace internationalization strategies, especially among SMEs, and overcome the liability of newness.

Although OMEGA sought to internationalize as it is facing stiff competition in its domestic market, it would be interesting to understand how the nostalgia international markets may underpin international opportunity-seeking behavior based on cultural familiarity.

REFERENCES

AICEP. (2014). *Guia Pratico de Acesso ao Mercado*. Retrieved May 16, 2017, from http://www.portugalglobal.pt/PT/Internacionalizar/Paginas/MercadosExternos. aspx?marketId=71

AICEP. (2016a). *Alemanha- Sintese Pais*. Retrieved May 16, 2017, from http://www. portugalglobal.pt/PT/Biblioteca/Paginas/Detalhe.aspx?documentId=1719618b-fdd4-48f7-b4e1-1d6c16ba4665

AICEP. (2016b). *França- Condições Legais de Acesso ao Mercado*. Retrieved May 16, 2017, from http://www.portugalglobal.pt/PT/Biblioteca/Paginas/Detalhe. aspx?documentId=1f14b44c-db40-4119-a532-8d70137aaa03

AICEP. (2017a). *Alemanha- Vinhos- Breve Apontamento*. Retrieved May 16, 2017, from http://www.portugalglobal.pt/PT/Biblioteca/Paginas/Detalhe. aspx?documentId=320cdc40-6702-4b85-b2b9-a486d0653590

AICEP. (2017b). *Sintese Pais- Espanha*. Retrieved May 16, 2017, from http://www. portugalglobal.pt/PT/Biblioteca/Paginas/Detalhe.aspx?documentId=a8457fad-912d-4e56-914f-c1b6164df82c

AICEP. (2017c). *Espanha- Condições Legais de Acesso ao Mercado*. Retrieved May 16, 2017, from http://www.portugalglobal.pt/PT/Biblioteca/Paginas/Detalhe. aspx?documentId=d13154c8-9337-419a-8c14-d8cec898353a

AICEP. (2017d). *Sintese Pais- França*. Retrieved May 16, 2017, from http:// www.portugalglobal.pt/PT/Internacionalizar/Paginas/MercadosExternos. aspx?marketId=03

Axelsson, B., & Johanson, J. (1992). Foreign market entry: The textbook vs the network view. In B. Axelsson & G. Easton (Eds.), *Industrial networks: A new view of reality* (pp. 218–234). London: Routledge.

Bradley, F. (2004). *International marketing strategy*. London: Prentice Hall.

Dantas, J. G., Moreira, A. C., & Valente, F. M. (2015). Entrepreneurship and national culture: How cultural differences among countries explain entrepreneurial activity. In L. C. Carvalho (Ed.), *Handbook of research on internationalization of entrepreneurial innovation in the global economy* (pp. 1–28). Hershey, PA: IGI Global. doi:10.4018/978-1-4666-8216-0.ch001

Dantas, J. G., Moreira, A. C., & Valente, F. M. (2017). National culture, societal values and type of economy. Are they relevant to explain entrepreneurial activity? In L. C. Carvalho (Ed.), *Handbook of research on entrepreneurial ecosystems and social dynamics in a globalized world*. Hershey, PA: IGI Global.

Dicken, P. (2015). *Global shift. Mapping the changing contours of the world economy*. New York, NY: Guilford Press.

Dominguez, N. (2016). Risk-seeking behaviours in SMEs' internationalization. In H. Etemad, S. Denicolai, B. Hagen, & A. Zucchella (Eds.), *The changing global economy and its impact on international entrepreneurship* (pp. 66–95). Cheltenham, UK: Edward Elgar.

Dunning, J. (1993). *Multinational enterprises and the global economy*. Reading, MA: Addison-Wesley.

Grünig, R., & Morschett, D. (2017). *Developing international strategies*. Berlin: Springer-Verlag. doi:10.1007/978-3-662-53123-5

Hadjikhani, A. (2015). A note on the criticisms against the internationalization process model. In M. Forsgren, U. Holm, & J. Johanson (Eds.), *Knowledge, Networks and Power* (pp. 64–87). London: Palgrave Macmillan. doi:10.1057/9781137508829_3

Håkansson, H., & Snehota, I. (2006). "No business is an island" 17 years later. *Strategic Management Journal, 22*(3), 271–274.

Hofstede, G. (1991). *Cultures and organizations: Software of the mind*. London: McGraw-Hill.

Hofstede, G. (2001). *Culture consequences. Comparing values, behaviors, institutions, and organizations across nations*. Thousand Oaks, CA: Sage Publications.

Holm, D. B., Eriksson, K., & Johanson, J. (1996). Creating value through mutual commitment to business network relationships. *Strategic Management Journal*, *20*(5), 467–486. doi:

Johanson, J., & Mattsson, L. G. (2015). Internationalisation in industrial systems — A network approach. In M. Forsgren, U. Holm, & J. Johanson (Eds.), *Knowledge, Networks and Power* (pp. 111–132). London: Palgrave Macmillan. doi:10.1057/9781137508829_5

Johanson, J., & Vahlne, J. E. (1977). The internationalization process of the firm – A model of knowledge development and increasing foreign market commitments. *Journal of International Business Studies*, *8*(1), 23–32. doi:10.1057/palgrave. jibs.8490676

Johanson, J., & Vahlne, J.-E. (1992). Management of foreign market entry. *Scandinavian International Business Review*, *1*(3), 9–27. doi:10.1016/0962-9262(92)90008-T

Katsikeas, C., Leonidou, L., & Samiee, S. (2009). Research into exporting: Theoretical, methodological, and empirical insights. In M. Kotabe & K. Helsen (Eds.), *The Sage handbook of international marketing* (pp. 165–182). Los Angeles, CA: Sage. doi:10.4135/9780857021007.n8

Leonidou, L., & Katsikeas, C. (1996). The export development process: An integrative review of empirical models. *Journal of International Business Studies*, *27*(3), 517–551. doi:10.1057/palgrave.jibs.8490846

Malhotra, N. K. (2017). *Marketing research: An applied approach*. Harlow: Pearson Education.

Moreira, A. (2004). Breve ensaio sobre a internacionalização. *Politécnica*, *15*, 23–33.

Moreira, A. C. (2009). The evolution of internationalisation: Towards a new theory? *Global Economics and Management Review*, *14*(1), 41–59.

Moreira, A. C., & Alves, C. (2016). Commitment-trust dynamics in the internationalization process: A case study of market entry in the Brazilian market. In Information Resources Management Association (Ed.), International business: Concepts, methodologies, tools, and applications, (vol. 3, pp. 1206-1229). Hershey, PA: IGI Global. Doi:10.4018/978-1-4666-9814-7.ch057

Morgan, J., & Katsikeas, C. (1997). Theories of international trade, foreign direct investment and firm internationalization: A critique. *Management Decision*, *35*(1), 68–77. doi:10.1108/00251749710160214

Novotná, L., Martins, I., & Moreira, A. C. (2017). Trade between the Czech Republic and Portugal: Analysis of the 2000-2015 period. In T. Dorożyński & A. Kuna-Marszałek (Eds.), *Outward foreign direct investment (FDI) in emerging market economies* (pp. 200–225). Hershey, PA: IGI Global. doi:10.4018/978-1-5225-2345-1.ch010

Oviatt, B. M., & McDougall, P. P. (1994). Toward a theory of international new ventures. *International Business Studies*, *25*(1), 45–64. doi:10.1057/palgrave.jibs.8490193

PorData. (2017). *Fluxos migratorios internacionais*. Retrieved April 28, 2017, from http://www.pordata.pt/Europa/Fluxos+migrat%C3%B3rios+internacionais-1622

Ribau, C. P., Moreira, A. C., & Raposo, M. (2015). Internationalisation of the firm theories: A schematic synthesis. *International Journal of Business and Globalisation*, *15*(4), 528–554. doi:10.1504/IJBG.2015.072535

Ribau, C. P., Moreira, A. C., & Raposo, M. (2017). SME internationalization research: Mapping the state of the art. *Canadian Journal of Administrative Sciences*. doi:10.1002/CJAS.1419

Ruzzier, M., Hisrich, R., & Antoncic, B. (2006). SME internationalization research: Past, present, and future. *Journal of Small Business and Enterprise Development*, *13*(4), 476–497. doi:10.1108/14626000610705705

Salomon, R., & Shaver, J. (2005). Export and domestic sales: Their interrelationship and determinants. *Strategic Management Journal*, *26*(9), 855–871. doi:10.1002mj.481

Shane, S. (1993). Cultural influences on national rates of innovation. *Journal of Business Venturing*, *8*(1), 59–73. doi:10.1016/0883-9026(93)90011-S

Stanisauskaite, V., & Kock, S. (2016). The dynamic development of international entrepreneurial networks. In H. Etemad, S. Denicolai, B. Hagen, & A. Zucchella (Eds.), *The changing global economy and its impact on international entrepreneurship* (pp. 119–135). Cheltenham, UK: Edward Elgar. doi:10.4337/9781783479849.00012

Triandis, H. (2004). The many dimensions of culture. *The Academy of Management Executive*, *18*(1), 88–93. doi:10.5465/AME.2004.12689599

Trompenaars, F. (1993). *Riding the waves of culture – Understanding cultural diversity in business*. London: Nicholas Brealey Publishing.

Yin, R. K. (2004). *Case study methods. Complementary methods for research in education*. Washington, DC: American Educational Research Association.

KEY TERMS AND DEFINITIONS

Case Study: It is a research method qualitative normally used in social sciences. It seeks to interpret a reality through a particular perspective. It is normally used to answer questions like "how" and "why." It is commonly used to address constructivist research processes.

Contextual Conditions: They normally characterize a country, a region, or a market, based on a set of political, social, economic, and cultural dimensions. These dimensions are useful to depict how those contextual conditions differ across countries, regions, or markets.

Culture: It is the collective programming of the mind that distinguishes the members of one group or category of people from others and causes them to display more or less the same behavior in similar situations.

Globalization: It is a worldwide movement toward economic, financial, trade, and communications integration. It is normally envisaged as a lack of trade barriers between nations, which are removed through free trade agreements throughout the world and between nation states. It implies the opening of local and nationalistic perspectives to a broader outlook of an interconnected and interdependent world with free transfer of capital, goods, and services across national frontiers, in which investment opportunities soar.

Internationalization: It is the process of increasing involvement of enterprises in international markets. It involves a strategy carried out by firms that decide to compete in foreign markets. It involves cross-border transactions of goods, services, or resources between two or more firms or organizations that belong to two different countries.

Internationalization Process: It involves the emphasis of a trajectory of a company in its transition from a national market to a particular foreign market. It normally involves several entry modes (exports, FDI, franchising, etc.) that exert a critical influence on the subsequent trajectory, as well as on cost related to the internationalization process. The two most important theories that explain the internationalization process are the Uppsala model and the network-based approach.

Network-Based Approach: It based on the industrial networks theory, which states that firms evolve on the basis of established relationships. It considers the companies' internationalization process through their integration into networks and relationships. Following this perspective, the internationalization process occurs in interactive environments where companies of a well-established network of companies have an opportunity to develop new relationships that give them access to broader markets in other countries.

Uppsala Model: It has been one of the most discussed dynamic theories in Nordic School and International Business Studies. It explains the process of internationalization of companies. It explains how organizations learn and the impact of learning on the companies' international expansion. This theory defends that the companies' internationalization process is carried out in stages, from non-regular exports to the establishment of companies abroad.

Chapter 3
Workforce Management Practices in Volunteer-Based Operations for the Generation of Social and Economic Value

Liliana Ávila
University of Aveiro, Portugal

Marlene Amorim
University of Aveiro, Portugal

Luis Miguel D. F. Ferreira
Universidade de Coimbra, Portugal

ABSTRACT

In recent years, hybrid organizations have been spreading in the competitive landscape, combining characteristics from both private and social sectors. To be successful, they need to do a great job managing limited resources. To this end, an effective operations strategy must be at the core of their priorities. Most of these organizations often rely on volunteer work to conduct their activities; therefore, mobilizing and engaging volunteers on a continuous basis is a key issue for many hybrid organizations. The present chapter aims to identify relevant workforce management practices in hybrid organizations. Building on the literature, the chapter offers a presentation of the main concepts underlying the setup of an operations strategy, highlighting the main particularities and challenges faced by hybrid organizations, and focusing on workforce management decisions. The chapter then identifies and discusses three workforce management practices employed by two hybrid organizations, whose operations are based on volunteer work.

DOI: 10.4018/978-1-5225-5360-1.ch003

INTRODUCTION

Operations strategy is a main topic within operations management field. According to an extensive literature review of survey research articles published between 1980 and 2000 in operations management conducted by Rungtusanatham, Choi, Hollingworth, Wu, & Forza (2003), operations strategy emerges as one of the most addressed topics. An operations strategy is made of a set of decisions regarding aspects such as the production process technology, the degree of vertical integration, as well as elements related to the facilities and plant location, planning and control systems, organizational structure, workforce management or quality management (Díaz Garrido, Martín-Peña, & García-Muiña, 2007; Espino-Rodriguez & Gil-Padilla, 2014). These decisions represent how the organization uses its resources and technologies to reach a sustainable competitive advantage in the sector (Lowson, 2002) and achieve the expected performance (Espino-Rodriguez & Gil-Padilla, 2014; Martín-Peña & Díaz-Garrido, 2008).

In the last years, there was a diversification of the existing organizational models and a spread of hybrid organizations in the competitive landscape (Walker, 2015). Hybrid organizations usually combine characteristics from both private and social sectors (Ebrahim, Battilana, & Mair, 2014; Pache & Santos, 2012), although there are some authors arguing they may also incorporate characteristics from the public sector or the civil society (e.g., Doherty, Haugh, & Lyon, 2014). Hybrid forms are attracting a growing interest from academics and practitioners (Doherty et al., 2014). Their emergence has been explained in a great extent by the economic crisis that has spread in the last years especially over some European countries, and that has resulted in substantial shortenings in the financial support provided by the State to non-for-profit organizations. Thus, the financial sustainability of such organizations is put at risk, forcing them to find alternative ways to fund their activities and keep pursuing their mission (Battilana & Lee, 2014; Smith et al., 2013). Social enterprises are also an example of hybrid organization, combining since their inception social and economic concerns in the same extent. Along the chapter will be used the term "hybrid organization" as it covers a wide range of organizations.

Hybrid organizations face many challenges. For instance, the separation between commercial and social activities may lead to a higher risk of mission drift (Ebrahim et al., 2014; Santos, Pache, & Birkholz, 2015) as well as to some ambidexterity in the field of operations management, depending on the level of integration of both types of activities. Examples of potential operational challenges include the need to deliver products or services to actors with different requirements and expectations about the organization (i.e., beneficiaries from social activities vs. customers for the commercial activities) as well as the need to effectively manage human resources with very heterogeneous capabilities and motivations (e.g., volunteers vs. employees; employees with commercial vs. social background).

In the last years, most of the studies addressing hybrid organizations have focused the definition and the characterization of their goals and activities, marked by the proliferation of arguments about their specificities (Doherty et al., 2014). However, to be successful, hybrid organizations need to do a great job managing limited resources (Roy & Karna, 2015), for which the definition of an effective operations strategy must be at the core of their priorities. The development of new managerial knowledge regarding the operations management of such organizations is of key importance for the field.

This chapter will focus the operations strategy of hybrid organizations from a workforce management perspective as they often rely on volunteer work to conduct their activities, including those aiming the generation of revenues. According to the cross-country report published by the SEFORIS project – in which were surveyed directors from more than 1000 social enterprises in 7 European countries, Russia and China – about 60% of the social enterprises surveyed have volunteers in their workforce. For instance, in Portugal, 80% of them have volunteers (SEFORÏS, 2016). Therefore, to mobilize and to engage these volunteers in a continuous manner for the generation of social value and economic value becomes a key issue for many hybrid organizations. Building on the literature and on the rationale derived from the practices of hybrid organizations acting in Portugal, where volunteers take part of the workforce of many organizations, this chapter aims to:

1. Present the main contributions for the literature on operations management, operations strategy, workforce management and hybrid organizations that can provide relevant insights for the understanding of workforce management practices in hybrid organizations;
2. Identify how volunteers are being involved in operations of hybrid organizations acting in the field aiming at the generation of social and economic value;
3. Understand which mechanisms have been adopted by such organizations to engage and to motivate volunteers in a continuous base;
4. Propose directions for future research on workforce management in hybrid organizations;

The chapter is organized as follows: after an introduction, a brief overview of the main concepts behind the setup of an operations strategy is offered, specially focusing on the aspects regarding workforce management decisions; then, the contextual circumstances, the particularities and the main challenges faced by hybrid organizations are presented; next, some of the practices and mechanisms concerning the management of a workforce mainly composed by volunteers are addressed, building on the analysis of the cases of two representative hybrid organizations acting in the field. Finally, conclusions are drawn and some directions for future research are suggested.

BACKGROUND

Operations Strategy, Operations Decisions, and Workforce Management

Operations Strategy and Decisions

Slack, Chambers and Johnston (2001) define operations strategy as "the pattern of strategic decisions and actions which set the role, objectives and activities of operations". A more elaborate definition is provided by Lowson (2001) who argues that "an operations strategy aims to perform key operational management activities better than rivals so as to provide support for the overall strategy of a firm as well as serving as a firm´s distinctive competence". Lowson's definition emphasizes two aspects that are often mentioned in the literature on operations strategy. First, the importance of operations for the overall strategy of a firm. Several authors have stressed in their work how it is fundamental the alignment between both - operations/manufacturing and business – strategies (Díaz Garrido et al., 2007; Khalili Shavarini, Salimian, Nazemi, & Alborzi, 2013; Raymond & Croteau, 2009; Thun, 2008). According to McDermott et al. (2003), the successful alignment between strategic objectives and operations decisions leads to a more effective and efficient use of resources, specially important when they are scarce. On the other hand, the lack of alignment would lead to wasted resources, missed opportunities and loss of competitiveness.

Second, the impact that the clear definition and implementation of an operations strategy can have in a firm's performance putting in evidence its competitive advantage over competition. Díaz Garrido, Martín-Peña, & García-Muiña (2007), Espino-Rodriguez & Gil-Padilla (2014) and Martín-Peña & Díaz-Garrido (2008) are among those who mentioned the role of operations strategy in performance. The key role of operations strategy in the pursuit of a competitive advantage was also noted by McDermott, Markman, and Balkin (2003) who argue that if entrepreneurs successfully identify opportunities but fail in their implementation at the operational level, their ability to sustain a competitive advantage will also fail. In the literature regarding typologies and taxonomies of operations strategies in manufacturing companies, cost, quality, flexibility and delivery are commonly pointed as the main competitive advantages pursued by such organizations (Martín-Peña & Díaz-Garrido, 2008b).

Service firms may pursue additional competitive advantages (e.g., service provision instead delivery considered for manufacturing firms, customer focus and know-how) due to their distinct characteristics (Ibrahim, 2010; Phusavat & Kanchana, 2008).

The formulation and implementation of an operations strategy has been essentially studied from two different approaches: process and content. On the one hand, process approaches deal with how to conduct the formulation and implementation of an operations strategy. For instance, Lowson (2003) and Thun (2008) refer resource-based and market-driven viewpoints whereas Slack et al. (2001) suggest the existence of four different perspectives: top-down perspective, market requirements perspective, bottom-up perspective and operations resources perspective. More recently, Rytter et al. (2007) proposed a conceptualization and model of operations strategy processes. On the other hand, content approaches deal with how operations can create competitive advantage through a set of operations decisions. These decisions are classified as structural and infrastructural. Structural decisions have strategic implications, require significant investment and have an impact in the long-term. They include choices such those regarding product and process technology, vertical integration, capacity, facilities and plant location.

Infrastructural decisions have a short-term impact, usually require lower investments and represent operational practices and decisions, for example, in terms of planning and control systems, organizational structure, quality management and workforce management (Díaz Garrido et al., 2007; Espino-Rodriguez & Gil-Padilla, 2014). Operational decisions pointed in the literature on the manufacturing field also apply to a great extent to service firms, although they present some specificities (Espino-Rodriguez & Gil-Padilla, 2014; Roth & Menor, 2003). For instance, in the context of services, structural decisions may also include those related to the touch points with clients as the relative allocation of service tasks to the front- and back-office or the number and types of distribution channels (Roth & Menor, 2003). Heineke (1995) argues that infrastructural decisions are even more critical in service organizations as structural decisions regarding location and capacity choices are determined by the customer and made through workforce decisions, respectively.

Structural and infrastructural decisions assume different degrees of importance depending on the competitive advantage the organization aims to pursue. For instance, if an organization wants to compete in the market by cost and delivery, it should pay special attention to location decisions. However, for organizations competing by flexibility are important the decisions regarding vertical integration, while supply chain management is more relevant for those aiming to provide high quality products and services (McDermott et al., 2003). According to Boyer and Pagell (2000), an organization pursuing several competitive advantages, probably is a world class organization and has access to the resources needed to successfully compete in more than one front, otherwise it does not have an operations strategy clearly defined.

The operations function tends to assume different roles over time as the organization evolves throughout different maturity levels. In 1984, Hayes and Wheelwright proposed a four-stage model to explain the development of the strategic impact of operations over time. The model was well accepted among other academics and has been referenced in several studies in manufacturing and services (Lillis & Sweeney, 2013; Slack et al., 2001). The authors suggest that the operations function evolves from an initial stage where it is internally focused - mainly reactive, working to correct the worst problems -, passing through intermediate stages to the ultimate stage, in which operations become the basis for ensuring a competitive advantage, enabling the organization to redefine industry expectations and to establish new standards (Slack et al., 2001; Wheelwright & Hayes, 1985).

Next, it will be presented in more detail the workforce management decisions and practices as the chapter focus on workforce management practices in volunteer-based operations.

Workforce Management Decisions and Practices

As mentioned previously, workforce management is often identified as one of the key decision areas at the infrastructural level that operations managers must consider when defining an operations strategy for their organization. Table I presents some of the authors and respective workforce management decisions that have been reported in the literature on operations strategy. Among them, for instance, are those related to the composition of the workforce, recruitment, training, reward systems and incentives.

Decisions regarding workforce management are operationalized through the implementation of a set of practices that should be in line with the organization's strategic objectives. Heineke (1995) argues that making workforce decisions in light of performance objectives increases the probability of achieving those objectives. This is supported by other studies which find workforce development practices to be directly related to a firm´s productivity (Díaz Garrido, Martín-Peña, & García-Muiña, 2007).

Kathuria and Davis (2001) and Kathuria and Partovi (1999) studied the workforce management practices that are most related to managerial performance when quality and flexibility are emphasized, respectively. In their studies, they considered relationship-oriented practices, leadership and delegation practices, and work-oriented practices. Both studies conclude that most of the relationship-oriented practices are effective in managing workforce when there is a high emphasis on quality or on flexibility. Using influence techniques to generate enthusiasm among employees,

Table 1. Workforce management decisions reported in the literature on operations strategy

References	Workforce Management Decisions
Wheelwright & Hayes (1985)	• Selection and training • Compensation • Security
Heineke (1995)	• Composition of the workforce • How the workforce will be scheduled and paid
Li, Benton, & Leong (2002)	• Staff composition • Staff increase and reduction • Staff overage and shortage management
Sumukadas & Sawhney (2004)	• Information sharing • Training • Improvement incentives • Non-monetary incentives • Team production incentives • Salary/skill based pay
Díaz Garrido et al. (2007)	• Job enrichment • Teamwork • Improving relations management workers • Decentralizing • Job enlargement • Worker training • Improving worker safety • Multi-functional project teams • Management training
Espino-Rodriguez & Gil-Padilla (2014)	• Improvement in labor relations between management and workers • Worker training • Management training • Expanding the variety of tasks to be performed by the workers

praising and recognizing effective performance, offering advice on how to advance career and acting friendly are some of the practices operations managers may adopt to manage the workforce more effectively. Regarding the remaining practices, both studies also highlight the importance of consulting subordinates before making important decisions (leadership practices), planning well and communicating task-relevant information (work-oriented practices).

Wheelwright and Hayes (1985) analyse how different workforce management approaches should be adopted as the organization moves along the different stages and operations are assuming different roles over time (considering the four-stage model they have proposed). According to these authors, in the first three stages, managers tend to adopt a command and control approach, focusing on the management of effort, coordinating information and directly supervising the workers. However, in stage 4, the command and control approach must be replaced by a management style that promotes teamwork and problem solving. The same authors also suggest that the strategic role of workforce policies increases over time. For instance, in the first stage, production is viewed as a low-tech operation that can be performed by low-skilled workers and managers. In that stage, there are little or no strategic issues involving workforce policies. In contrast, in the fourth (and last stage), organizations seek to acquire expertise in order to be able to anticipate the potential of new manufacturing practices and technologies.

The Emergence of Hybrid Organizations

In recent years, there was a spread of hybrid organizational forms in the competitive landscape. According to Doherty et al. (2014), hybrid organizational forms are structures and practices that allow the coexistence of values and artefacts from two or more sectors (e.g. private, public, non-profit). Hybrid organizations usually combine characteristics from both private and social sectors (Ebrahim, Battilana, & Mair, 2014; Pache & Santos, 2012), although there are some authors arguing they may also incorporate characteristics from the public sector or the civil society (e.g., Doherty, Haugh, & Lyon, 2014). Jäger and Schröer (2013) suggest that hybrid organizations are those who have a strong civil society identity as well as a strong market identity. They are different from socially responsible enterprises as the later incorporate the profit generation and its distribution among a group of shareholders as a core objective. They also differ from non-profit organizations who may run commercial activities as a way to get additional funds to pursue their social mission. Battilana et al. (2012) define the hybrid ideal as a fully integrated organization. Everything the enterprise does produces both social value and commercial revenue. Mission and profit aims are integrated in the same strategy. The authors of the present chapter agree with all these contributions, adopting the vision that a hybrid organization is an organization that has a social mission clearly defined and who should conduct commercial activities that allow it to generate a great part of their revenues in order to ensure its financial sustainability. Profits, if they exist, must be reinvested in efforts for scaling the social impact.

One of the main reasons pointed for the emergence of hybrid organizations is the economic crisis that has spread in the last year over some European countries, and that represented substantial shortenings in the financial support provided by the State to non-profit organizations, putting at risk their financial sustainability and pressing them to find alternative ways to fund their activities (Battilana & Lee, 2014; Smith et al., 2013). However, other arguments can be used to explain the emergence of organizations with social and economic concerns. On the one hand, traditional for-profit organizations are also dealing with increasingly informed and demanding customers, who search for more socially and environmentally friendly solutions. On the other hand, public services are not able to respond to all the citizens' needs, who become more attentive to the needs of the community and aware of the importance to exercise their citizenship and to be an active part in their resolution.

The emergence of these new organizational structures aiming to generate social and economic value brings many challenges due the combination of two sides (i.e. social and market) that were considered incompatible until then. This is especially true when the organization faces some transaction obstacles such as the inability of beneficiaries to pay, the difficulty to access or even the unwillingness to pay for the products or services the organization is offering (Santos et al., 2015). Despite the evidence that hybrid organizations generate great social impact, their hybridity make them fragile, exposed to the risk of internal tensions and mission drift (Ebrahim et al., 2014; Santos et al., 2015). In the last years, some authors have identified some organizational domains where there are tensions caused by the desire to pursue social and economic goals simultaneously. Wilson and Post (2011) suggest that these tensions are mostly at the operational than strategic level. This is supported by Doherty et al. (2014), who also argue that they have an operational impact on goals and acquisition of resources and suggest two operational mechanisms to manage such tensions: using the social mission as the main force for strategic direction and finding the optimum conditions to successfully align the creation of social value with the generation of revenues.

Recent work has identified some tensions arising from hybridity. Among the most referred are the tensions related to the legal structure chosen by the organization, the sources of financing and the management of human resources (Battilana & Lee, 2014; Cornforth, 2014; Doherty et al., 2014). Regarding the legal structure, hybrid organizations are confronted with the choice of registering as a for-profit organization, a nonprofit or choosing to adopt two different legal entities (a for-profit legal entity and a nonprofit form). For instance, having two legal entities can help them to get access to the benefits of both legal entities, namely in terms of sources of financing, searching for different sources of financing for social and income-generating activities or even opting by a mixed structure of funding (e.g. getting funds from public authorities in an early-stage and trying to attract venture capital later). Finally, regarding the management of human resources, once it is still hard to find people with a "hybrid" profile, they may opt by hiring people from the social sector, people from the private sector or hiring people from both sectors. Battilana, Sengul, Pache, and Model (2015) concluded that hybrid organizations who have a permanent staff with a social background are likely to prioritize systems and processes that help beneficiaries instead systems and processes that improve economic productivity. Most probably they will introduce more flexibility in production processes. Due to their ambidexterity, most of hybrid organizations are confronted with resource constraints and have no financial resources to pay high qualified staff to meet all their needs. This fact forces them to rely on some volunteer work to run their activities (Austin, Stevenson, & Wei-Skillern, 2006). Managing a workforce composed of employees and volunteers may also be a source of tension (Doherty et al., 2014).

Workforce management practices identified in the literature on operations management and strategy can be adapted to the domain of hybrid organizations. However, in this context, it should be kept in mind that the inclusion of volunteers in the workforce is a sensitive issue which requires special attention, especially when they are involved in activities which aim the generation of social and economic value. This way, issues regarding training, non-monetary incentives or task assignment become some of the key decision areas. An inadequate management of the workforce on volunteer-based operations may compromise the financial viability, the pursuit of the social mission and, therefore, the future of the organization.

In the following section, will be discussed some workforce management practices adopted by hybrid organizations whose operations rely on volunteer work. Based on some empirical evidence, the authors intend to answer the following research questions:

1. How are volunteers being involved in the operations of hybrid organizations aiming the generation of social and economic value?
2. Which mechanisms have been adopted by hybrid organizations to engage and to motivate volunteers in a continuous base?

The section begins with a brief introduction to the organizations studied, where are described the roles assumed by volunteers in the operations of each organizations. This is followed by the identification of three workforce management practices which are aligned with the workforce management decisions identified in the literature on operations management and strategy.

WORKFORCE MANAGEMENT PRACTICES IN HYBRID ORGANIZATIONS

As mentioned above, many hybrid organizations rely on volunteer work to conduct their activities, including those aiming the generation of revenues. The cross-country report published by the SEFORIS project – in which were surveyed directors from more than 1000 social enterprises in 7 European countries, Russia and China – about 60% of the organizations surveyed have volunteers in their workforce. In Portugal, 80% of them have volunteers. Mobilize and engage these volunteers in a continuous basis for the generation of social and economic value becomes a key issue for many of those hybrid organizations.

In order to contribute to the theory building, it was conducted an exploratory work that involved the collection of information on two hybrid organizations based in Portugal – Ajudaris and Vintage for a Cause – through the conduction of in-depth interviews with directors and volunteers. These organizations were selected because they are representative of organizations who followed different paths towards a hybrid model but both share the fact they have a workforce mainly composed of volunteers and they are pursuing ambidextrous goals. On the one hand, Ajudaris that was born with a more paternalistic approach and, then, evolved into a hybrid model when it launched the *Histórias da Ajudaris* project to ensure the financial sustainability of the organization. On the other hand, Vintage for a Cause that was created based on the principles of social entrepreneurship and proposes a solution that integrates social and economic concerns. The authors decided to focus on how workforce management practices are experienced by volunteers once the chapter aims at volunteer-based operations, in which paid employees represent a minority.

The main objective of this section is to understand how volunteers are being involved in the activities of these organizations and to explore some workforce managing practices they are employing in their operations, drawing some lessons which may help other organizations to effectively manage the presence of volunteers in their workforce.

Introducing Ajudaris and Vintage for a Cause

Ajudaris was established in 2008 by people who occasionally met to support local communities, especially elderly people and homelessness. Due the constant requests from the beneficiaries and the need to create more regular, organized and efficient responses, they decided to create Ajudaris. One year later, they have launched what becomes the most innovative and emblematic project of the organization – *Histórias da Ajudaris*. The project aims to promote reading, writing, art and solidarity. Stories written by children from schools across the country, helped by their teachers, are illustrated by professional artists and published every year. Revenues from bookselling are used to fund other programs developed by Ajudaris that support disadvantaged people (e.g. other children, youth and adults). Every year is defined a different theme. In the last years, children wrote their stories about grandparents, citizenship or the environment. The project is growing year by year, reaching more and more schools. Until 2014, Ajudaris has sold about 25000 books. In that year, were released for the first time two volumes. In 2016, were published five volumes with stories from 294 schools and illustrated by 518 artists. It is unquestionable the ability that Ajudaris has demonstrated to continuously engage students, teachers, artists and publishers in a volunteer basis.

Vintage for a Cause was founded in 2013 by three women who met a year before in a postgraduate program in Social Entrepreneurship and Innovation. It aims to promote the active aging, personal development, interpersonal relationship and social inclusion of women over 50 with no professional activity. Vintage for a Cause is a sewing club where old clothes donated are transformed by these women into new clothing with a vintage inspiration and unique design. For that, they are supported by professional fashion designers. After transformation, clothes are sold in the Vintage for a Cause's online shop and some stores in the city where it is based. The weekly ateliers (three hours) are a pretext to "transform lives through clothing transformation" (the organization's motto). The participation in the ateliers is free. The informal and creative context help these women developing new social relationships and acquiring new skills and new life goals. A year after running a pilot with 10 women, the ateliers were attended by 84 women aged between 52 and 88.

In both organizations, the paid workforce is composed by less than five people, which means that volunteers represent a great part of the workforce who performs the activities of the organization. In Ajudaris, children, teachers and artists are involved in writing and illustrating stories that will be compiled and published, whose revenues will be used to accomplish the social mission of the organization – the fight against persistent poverty and new forms of social exclusion among children and elderly. Ajudaris counts on these volunteers throughout the year in several activities promoted under the project, although there is no periodicity for such collaboration. Unlike the previous case, in Vintage for a Cause, most of volunteers are also the main beneficiaries of the organization (i.e., women over 50 with no professional activity). The contact with volunteers is established regularly, in the weekly ateliers. Vintage for a Cause also has fashion designers collaborating in a volunteer and regular basis, who support women in the transformation of clothes. In both cases, paid employees spend most of their time managing the activities carried out by volunteers.

Workforce Management Practices in Ajudaris and Vintage for a Cause

Both organizations presented rely on volunteer work to perform activities that generate social and economic value, which are crucial for the pursuing of their mission. In line with the workforce management decisions listed previously, it is possible to identify some practices adopted by Ajudaris and Vintage for a Cause which may be at the core of the successful conduction of their activities. Next, will be discussed three workforce management practices related to workforce management decision domains enumerated before: 1) Training; 2) Expansion of the variety of tasks; 3) Improvement of relations among volunteers and with other parties.

Training

One of the workforce management decision domains that has been emphasized in several works in the literature on operations management is training. Millette and Gagné (2008), who studied the impact of job characteristics on volunteers' engagement, suggest that offering volunteers the opportunity to learn new skills may contribute to their motivation. Ajudaris and Vintage for a Cause are encouraging continuous learning of their volunteers, although Vintage for a Cause is doing it in a more prominent way.

The ateliers of Vintage for a Cause can be attended by any woman over 50 without professional activity, even if she has no previous experience or knowledge in seam. There, they can learn several techniques as they transform different garments and there is an effort to continuously innovate and to create different types of accessories made from old clothes. For some of these women the acquisition of new skills was an opportunity to realise they still capable to have an active role in society. Some of the beneficiaries of Vintage for a Cause opened their own sewing workshops or returned to a professional activity after attending the ateliers.

As mentioned before, the project *Histórias da Ajudaris* aims to promote reading, writing, art and solidarity. Therefore, teachers can use it as a tool to develop reading and writing skills of their students. As volunteers of Ajudaris they may also benefit from training opportunities. Since 2014, Ajudaris organizes annually an international colloquium that intends to be a moment of learning and reflexion on topics such as reading, writing and citizenship. During those days, teachers can attend several workshops (e.g. creative writing). The participation of teachers in the annual colloquium is accredited by a training organization what is important for their career development.

Expansion of the Variety of Tasks

Another strategy to increase the motivation and the engagement of volunteers in the operations of the organization is to increase their self-commitment. For instance, the organization may provide them opportunities to perform new tasks or to allow the volunteers to represent the organization in activities opened to the public (Farmer & Fedor, 2001).

Regarding this aspect, Ajudaris has done an extensive work in the project's dissemination at the national level, involving children and their teachers as well as the artists who illustrate the books. During the year, several sessions are organized throughout the country to present the books to local communities. In these sessions, the little writers are invited for autograph sessions, what makes them and their teachers proud and motivated to continue writing stories year by year. In order to reward the solidarity of the artists who make the illustrations for the book, Ajudaris also organizes a roadshow with the book illustrations. The director of Ajudaris is present in the opening session in each place the roadshow goes. These are important opportunities to present the project to whom do not know it yet and get closer to people from the entire country who contribute in a volunteer way to the cause.

Vintage for a Cause faced some challenges to ensure its beneficiaries are committed with the organization. According to one of the founders, one year after the beginning of the ateliers, the team noticed a break in the attendance and punctuality of volunteers (i.e. the beneficiaries). They also realized that they were not communicating with the volunteers in an effective way. The volunteers did not seem to understand the purpose of Vintage for a Cause, all what its operationalization involves and how it is important their collaboration to ensure the continuity of the project. The founders decided to introduce some changes to transmit the message more clearly. They defined new rules and invested in the definition of roles to appeal to a greater involvement of volunteers. Thus, in each atelier were assigned roles to each participant. For instance, one person is responsible by taking photos to be published on the Facebook page, another person is responsible by welcoming the new volunteers or organizing the snack that happens at the end of each atelier. The volunteers have also started participating in public presentations of Vintage for a Cause (e.g. seminars, workshops, etc.), visiting the stores where the clothes they produce are sold and attending some fairs and street sales where they can directly contact with clients. Some volunteers were also invited to participate in training sessions directed to people from hybrid organizations with the management team and were involved in management tasks. Due to these improvement actions, the participation of volunteers in the ateliers became more regular and it is evident a greater commitment with the organization.

Improvement of Relations Among Volunteers and With Other Parties

The third workforce management practice identified in hybrid organizations is somewhat related with the previous one and regards the improvement of the interaction among volunteers and the interaction with partnering organizations. According to Millette and Gagné (2008), establishing contacts between volunteers and other involved parties can be used to increase task significance. All the activities in which volunteers are invited to represent the organization are already opportunities to strengthen ties with other parties. For instance, in Ajudaris, the interaction between volunteers and other involved parties is promoted through the organization of the roadshow as well as the colloquiums, which were described previously.

In Vintage for a Cause, there were created additional mechanisms to increase those interactions. To promote the social interaction between beneficiaries, at the end of each atelier, there is a moment reserved for a snack, when they may drink a tea, eat something and chat with each other before to go home. Sometimes, these snacks are also shared with fashion designers and other people who are invited to attend the ateliers. Occasionally, thematic workshops are organized to the public, usually available for a short period (e.g. two weeks). In these workshops, the participants can learn sewing and other techniques related to the transformation of clothes. They may happen at the same time of the ateliers, giving to the beneficiaries the opportunity to interact with the participants. When it happens, participants are also invited to join the team for the snack. In the past years, Vintage for a Cause has also organized three fashion shows with its creations. All these activities contribute to an improvement in labour relations between management and volunteers and represent nonmonetary incentives to volunteers for continuing collaborating with the organization.

FUTURE RESEARCH DIRECTIONS

As mentioned at the beginning of the chapter, hybrid organizational models are emerging mainly due to contextual pressures, which force traditional organizations to find new business models integrating social and economic concerns for the generation of social and economic value for the society. The chapter focused on the workforce management practices of such organizations from an operations management perspective, as most of them face resource constraints and, therefore, several have volunteer-based operations. This was a first attempt to address this topic, however many questions remain unanswered, claiming for future research efforts.

On the one hand, further studies are needed to measure the effects of the adoption of those practices in hybrid organizations and how they are experienced by paid employees compared to volunteers. Are the organizations adopting those practices in the workforce management retaining their volunteers longer? Is the adoption of those workforce management practices contributing to a better performance of the workforce? How are those practices experienced by employees? Is there some type of tension between paid employees and volunteers for instance regarding the access to training and the expansion of the variety of tasks? This can be done through the comparison between hybrid organizations and traditional non-profit and for-profit organizations or the study of a larger sample and the conduction of interviews with paid employees who are important stakeholders in workforce management issues.

On the other hand, there are opportunities to conduct research on other workforce management decisions that were not contemplated in this study. First, more research is needed to investigate the workforce composition (e.g. permanent staff with a social background, permanent staff with a commercial background and/or volunteers) of hybrid organizations and how it may influence other workforce management decisions, especially in volunteer-based operations. For instance, according to Battilana et al. (2015), who studied the productive tensions in work integration social enterprises, a permanent staff with a social background tends to be more permissive with workers than a staff with a commercial background, who tends to favor the economic productivity. It would be interesting to study if this applies to other kind of hybrid organizations integrating volunteers in their operations and how it influences volunteers' engagement. Second, there are research opportunities regarding selection and work assignment issues. Are hybrid organizations whose social and income-generating activities are performed separately recruiting more volunteers to their workforce than those adopting more integrated approaches in terms of operations? What kind of tasks are being assigned to them (tasks related to social or income-generating activities)? Furthermore, how do hybrid organizations choose between many volunteers dedicating a small amount of time and less volunteers dedicating a great amount of time to the organization? What are the criteria that guide this decision? Third, and finally, there is the opportunity to explore the incentives conceded to volunteers. What are the non-monetary incentives used by hybrid organizations to reward volunteers for their performance? In what extent do they differ from those used by traditional non-profit organizations?

Since workforce management practices in volunteer-based operations is a relatively unexplored field, answering all these questions requires, in a first instance, some exploratory work such as the one presented in this chapter in which was used qualitative data collected through interviews conducted with the directors and volunteers from both organizations. However, not belittling the importance of in-depth studies to support exploratory work, due to the great variety of hybrid organizational forms, the authors believe that future research will also evolve to quantitative data collection methods, which allow the study of larger samples and the generalization of results.

Revisiting the literature on human resources management may also help to understand the implications of workforce management decisions and practices in hybrid organizations.

CONCLUSION

In the forthcoming years, it is expected organizations from all sectors to incorporate social, economic and environmental concerns in their activities, evolving to hybrid models of organizing. This is already happening mainly in the non-profit and is attracting a growing interest among academics and practitioners from different sectors. Something that most hybrid organizations have in common is the fact they need to lead with resource constraints, namely in terms of human resources. A solution adopted by many of them to address this gap is to integrate volunteers in their workforce. However, managing a workforce composed of paid employees (with a social and/or a commercial background) can be a source of tension, especially in organizations aiming the generation of social and economic value in the same extent. A volunteer workforce must be managed differently than other employees because volunteers are not paid, therefore, other mechanisms must be used in order to keep them motivated and engaged.

This chapter aimed to identify some workforce management practices adopted by hybrid organizations acting in the field, using as background for the analysis the literature on operations management, operations strategy, workforce management and hybrid organizations. Three practices were identified - promoting continuous learning, fomenting self-commitment through role investment and establishing contacts between volunteers and with other parties-, and illustrated with the experiences of Ajudaris and Vintage for a Cause. The authors are aware of the limitations this approach presents in terms of the generalization of results, although they believe that the use of few cases allowed to describe more exhaustively each practice.

This was a good starting point to take the discussion to the next level. Studying the prevalent literature on operations management and strategy and transferring that knowledge, which was already extensively applied in manufacturing and service firms, to emergent research fields such as hybrid organizations represent a valuable contribute for the generation of new insights. It is urgent to draw theoretical contributions from what is being done in the field in order to inform practitioners and help them in the development of sustainable organizations focused on the generation of social and economic value.

ACKNOWLEDGMENT

This research was supported by the Fundação para a Ciência e a Tecnologia [grant number SFRH/BD/118584/2016].

REFERENCES

Austin, J., Stevenson, H., & Wei-Skillern, J. (2006). Social and Commercial Entrepreneurship: Same, Different, or Both? *Entrepreneurship Theory and Practice*, *30*(1), 1–22. doi:10.1111/j.1540-6520.2006.00107.x

Battilana, J., & Lee, M. (2014). Advancing Research on Hybrid Organizing – Insights from the Study of Social Enterprises. *The Academy of Management Annals*, *8*(1), 397–441. doi:10.1080/19416520.2014.893615

Battilana, J., Lee, M., Walker, J., & Dorsey, C. (2012). In Search of the Hybrid Ideal. *Stanford Social Innovation Review*, *10*, 51–55.

Battilana, J., Sengul, M., Pache, A. C., & Model, J. (2015). Harnessing productive tensions in hybrid organizations: The case of work integration social enterprises. *Academy of Management Journal*, *58*(6), 1658–1685. doi:10.5465/amj.2013.0903

Boyer, K. K., & Pagell, M. (2000). Measurement issues in empirical research: Improving measures of operations strategy and advanced manufacturing technology. *Journal of Operations Management*, *18*(1), 361–374. doi:10.1016/S0272-6963(99)00029-7

Brandsen, T., & Karré, P. M. (2011). Hybrid Organizations: No Cause for Concern? *International Journal of Public Administration*, *34*(13), 827–836. doi:10.1080/01900692.2011.605090

Cornforth, C. (2014). Understanding and combating mission drift in social enterprises. *Social Enterprise Journal*, *10*(1), 3–20. doi:10.1108/SEJ-09-2013-0036

Díaz Garrido, E., Martín-Peña, M. L., & García-Muiña, F. (2007). Structural and infrastructural practices as elements of content operations strategy. The effect on a firm's competitiveness. *International Journal of Production Research*, *45*(9), 2119–2140. doi:10.1080/00207540600735480

Doherty, B., Haugh, H., & Lyon, F. (2014). Social Enterprises as Hybrid Organizations: A Review and Research Agenda. *International Journal of Management Reviews*, *16*(4), 417–436. doi:10.1111/ijmr.12028

Ebrahim, A., Battilana, J., & Mair, J. (2014). The governance of social enterprises: Mission drift and accountability challenges in hybrid organizations. *Research in Organizational Behavior*, *34*, 81–100. doi:10.1016/j.riob.2014.09.001

Espino-Rodriguez, T. F., & Gil-Padilla, M. (2014). The structural and infrastructural decisions of operations management in the hotel sector and their impact on organizational performance. *Tourism and Hospitality Research*, *15*(1), 3–18. doi:10.1177/1467358414553866

Farmer, S. M., & Fedor, D. B. (2001). Changing the focus on volunteering: An investigation of volunteers' multiple contributions to a charitable organization. *Journal of Management*, *27*(2), 191–211. doi:10.1177/014920630102700204

Heineke, J. (1995). Strategic operations management decisions and professional performance in U.S. HMOs. *Journal of Operations Management*, *13*(4), 255–272. doi:10.1016/0272-6963(95)00035-6

Ibrahim, S. E. (2010). An alternative methodology for formulating an operations strategy: The case of BTC-Egypt. *Management Decision*, *48*(6), 868–893. doi:10.1108/00251741011053442

Jäger, U. P., & Schröer, A. (2013). Integrated Organizational Identity: A Definition of Hybrid Organizations and a Research Agenda. *Voluntas*, *25*(5), 1281–1306. doi:10.100711266-013-9386-1

Kathuria, R., & Davis, E. B. (2001). Quality and work force management practices: The managerial performance implication. *Production and Operations Management*, *10*(4), 460–477. doi:10.1111/j.1937-5956.2001.tb00087.x

Kathuria, R., & Partovi, F. Y. (1999). Work force management practices for manufacturing flexibility. *Journal of Operations Management*, *18*(1), 21–39. doi:10.1016/S0272-6963(99)00011-X

Khalili Shavarini, S., Salimian, H., Nazemi, J., & Alborzi, M. (2013). Operations strategy and business strategy alignment model (case of Iranian industries). *International Journal of Operations & Production Management*, *33*(9), 1108–1130. doi:10.1108/IJOPM-12-2011-0467

Li, L. X., Benton, W. C., & Leong, G. K. (2002). The impact of strategic operations management decisions on community hospital performance. *Journal of Operations Management*, *20*(1), 389–408. doi:10.1016/S0272-6963(02)00002-5

Lillis, B., & Sweeney, M. (2013). Managing the fit between the views of competitive strategy and the strategic role of service operations. *European Management Journal*, *31*(6), 564–590. doi:10.1016/j.emj.2012.10.001

Lowson, R. H. (2001). Retail Operational Strategies in Complex Supply Chains. *International Journal of Logistics Management*, *12*(1), 97–111. doi:10.1108/09574090110806253

Lowson, R. H. (2002). Operations strategy: Genealogy, classification and anatomy. *International Journal of Operations & Production Management*, *22*(10), 1112–1129. doi:10.1108/01443570210446333

Lowson, R. H. (2003). The nature of an operations strategy: Combining strategic decisions from the resource-based and market-driven viewpoints. *Management Decision*, *41*(6), 538–549. doi:10.1108/00251740310485181

Martín-Peña, M. L., & Díaz-Garrido, E. (2008a). Typologies and taxonomies of operations strategy: A literature review. *Management Research News*, *31*(3), 200–218. doi:10.1108/01409170810851294

Martín-Peña, M. L., & Díaz-Garrido, E. (2008b). Typologies and taxonomies of operations strategy: A literature review. *Management Research News*, *31*(3), 200–218. doi:10.1108/01409170810851294

McDermott, C. M., Markman, G. D., & Balkin, D. B. (2003). Operations strategy and new venture formation. *Management Research*, *1*(2), 195–205.

Millette, V., & Gagné, M. (2008). Designing volunteers' tasks to maximize motivation, satisfaction and performance: The impact of job characteristics on volunteer engagement. *Motivation and Emotion*, *32*(1), 11–22. doi:10.100711031-007-9079-4

Pache, A.-C., & Santos, F. (2012). Inside the Hybrid Organization: Selective Coupling as a Response to Competing Institutional Logics. *Academy of Management Journal*, *56*(4), 972–1001. doi:10.5465/amj.2011.0405

Phusavat, K., & Kanchana, R. (2008). Competitive priorities for service providers: Perspectives from Thailand. *Industrial Management & Data Systems*, *108*(1), 5–21. doi:10.1108/02635570810844052

Raymond, L., & Croteau, A.-M. (2009). Manufacturing Strategy and Business Strategy in Medium-Sized Enterprises: Performance Effects of Strategic Alignment. *IEEE Transactions on Engineering Management*, *56*(2), 192–202. doi:10.1109/TEM.2008.922646

Roth, A. V., & Menor, L. J. (2003). Insights into service operations management: A research agenda. *Production and Operations Management*, *12*(2), 145–164. doi:10.1111/j.1937-5956.2003.tb00498.x

Roy, K., & Karna, A. (2015). Doing social good on a sustainable basis: Competitive advantage of social businesses. *Management Decision*, *53*(6), 1355–1374. doi:10.1108/MD-09-2014-0561

Rungtusanatham, M. J., Choi, T. Y., Hollingworth, D. G., Wu, Z., & Forza, C. (2003). Survey research in operations management: Historical analyses. *Journal of Operations Management*, *21*(4), 475–488. doi:10.1016/S0272-6963(03)00020-2

Rytter, N. G., Boer, H., & Koch, C. (2007). Conceptualizing operations strategy processes. *International Journal of Operations & Production Management*, *27*(10), 1093–1114. doi:10.1108/01443570710820648

Santos, F. M., Pache, A.-C., & Birkholz, C. (2015). Making Hybrids Work: Aligning business models and organizational design for social enterprises. *California Management Review*, *57*(3), 36–58. doi:10.1525/cmr.2015.57.3.36

SEFORÏS. (2016). *SEFORÏS Cross-Country Report*. Retrieved from http://www.seforis.eu/cross-country-report

Slack, N., Chambers, S., & Johnston, R. (2001). *Operations managment* (3rd ed.). Harlow: Financial Times Prentice Hall.

Smith, W. K., Gonin, M., & Besharov, M. L. (2013). Managing Social-Business Tensions. *Business Ethics Quarterly*, *23*(3), 407–442. doi:10.5840/beq201323327

Sumukadas, N., & Sawhney, R. (2004). Workforce agility through employee involvement. *IIE Transactions*, *36*(10), 1011–1021. doi:10.1080/07408170490500997

Thun, J. H. (2008). Empirical analysis of manufacturing strategy implementation. *International Journal of Production Economics*, *113*(1), 370–382. doi:10.1016/j.ijpe.2007.09.005

Walker, J. (2015). Hybrid Organizations: Origins, Strategies, Impacts and Implications. *California Management Review*, *57*(3), 5–13. doi:10.1525/cmr.2015.57.3.5

Wheelwright, S. C., & Hayes, R. H. (1985). Competing through manufacturing. *Harvard Business Review*, *63*(1), 99–109.

Wilson, F., & Post, J. E. (2011). Business models for people, planet (& profits): Exploring the phenomena of social business, a market-based approach to social value creation. *Small Business Economics*, *40*(3), 715–737. doi:10.100711187-011-9401-0

KEY TERMS AND DEFINITIONS

Beneficiary: The main target group that a hybrid organization intends to serve (e.g., a disadvantaged group such as elderly, children and youth, victims of abuse, refugees, etc.).

Hybrid Organization: An organization that combines characteristics from different sectors.

Operations Strategy: A set of decisions made at the operational level in order to achieve a competitive advantage.

Social Enterprise: An organization that combines social and economic goals, performing social and commercial activities simultaneously.

Volunteer: A person who collaborates in activities with a social purpose without a financial compensation.

Workforce: The workers involved in the operations of an organization.

Workforce Management Decision: A decision at the operational level regarding aspects related to the management of the workforce such as its composition, recruitment, compensation, or training.

Chapter 4
Diversity Management Interventions for Enhancing Competitive Advantage:
A Synthesis of Current Research and Literature

Alamuri Surya Narayana
Osmania University, India

ABSTRACT

Diversity and diversity management is a new organizational paradigm and a business imperative. We already have a vast and rich literature base on these two. Many and varied empirical findings are also available from earlier qualitative and quantitative research studies. An attempt is made in this chapter (1) to examine various theoretical concepts and constructs used in diversity and diversity management, (2) to come up with a synthesis of management research and current literature on diversity and diversity management, (3) to develop a theoretical framework, and (4) to suggest directions for future research as well. This chapter lists some of the challenges faced by firms, the major issues to be addressed, potential research directions, and themes in the Indian context before finally coming up with a conceptual model detailing the antecedents and consequences of diversity and diversity management.

DOI: 10.4018/978-1-5225-5360-1.ch004

INTRODUCTION

In the face of the global meltdown, focus has shifted from expansion to consolidation. The organizations have concentrated on quality of hires instead of their number. This has revealed the shortage of talent in many regions. The hunt for talent has transcended the regional and national boundaries. The firms with a multi-racial, multi-ethnic, and multi-cultural work force have to tune themselves to the workforce diversity. They have to galvanize the diverse work force to a cohesive productive force to align with their organizational culture. Astounding progress of internet, coupled with fast communication system has brought the world close geographically. Despite geographical proximity, cultures prevalent in various parts of the world with divergence in individual orientation, tastes and preferences, attitudes and philosophies towards life and contrasting life styles have posed serious problems in integration of the varied and different national cultures with one organization culture.

Diversity of workforce means inclusion of people with different human qualities and from different cultural groups. Dimensions of diversity are both primary, such as age, gender, and race, and secondary, such as education, marital status, and income. Acceptance of diversity is becoming important because of socioeconomic changes and the changing workforce. Increasing diversity means that organizations must develop programs to deal with global as well as domestic diversity and with potential conflicts that arise. Two recent approaches to supporting and leveraging the power of diversity are *multicultural teams* and *employee network groups*. Many companies are now finding innovative ways to integrate diversity initiatives into their business. The list of HR initiatives that MNCs can use to manage workplace diversity is quite long and varied and their HR Managers need to understand the phenomenon of diversity and its causes and consequences before they effectively deal with the challenges through different organizational approaches and responses. They are required to create an environment that welcomes and values diverse employees in an effort to enhance the competitiveness of firms.

Effective management of a diverse workforce through appropriate interventions is critical for organizations that seek to obtain, improve, and maintain their competitive advantage. To celebrate diversity is to appreciate and value individual differences. This point became increasingly apparent and was also amply established through various research studies in the last two decades. It is not just a nice idea to focus on diversity and look for more and more ways to make an organization truly inclusive in its character. After all, it pays to make full use of the contributions of all employees. It is also good business sense as it definitely yields a competitive edge through greater overall organizational productivity. Diversity awareness training helps people become aware of their own cultural boundaries and prejudices besides learning to communicate with people from their cultural contexts.

It is no exaggeration to state that diversity has evolved from being *important* and the *correct thing* to do to being the *essential thing* to do as an imperative over the years. Progressive firms think of a company restructuring, an expansion, a merger, a corporate takeover, or any other similar episodic event in very highly businesslike manner. Diversity issues are no exception to this list and are expected to be addressed in the same manner before coming up with realistic action plans and solutions.

Building the business case for diversity in any given company will necessarily vary, but in general it can be stated in two compelling arguments: (i) For both large MNCs and small companies these days, the neighborhood in which they sell is the entire world, so it is essential that their workforces look and think like the world, in all of its ethnic, racial, and behavioral variety and (2) The demographics of almost every nation are changing so dramatically that over the coming decades it will be impossible for employers to fill their ranks with members of the traditional workforce. Diversity and diversity management is a new organizational paradigm. There is already a vast and rich literature base as well as empirical findings that are available from earlier qualitative and quantitative research studies.

In this context, an attempt is made in this Book Chapter (i) to examine various theoretical concepts and constructs used in diversity and diversity management (ii) to come up with a synthesis of management research and current literature on viz., diversity and diversity management, (iii) to develop a theoretical framework, and (iv) to suggest directions for future research as well.

DIVERSITY: CONCEPT AND MEANING

Diversity refers to differences among members of the group or organization on any characteristic. Diversity offers many benefits and organizations lose no opportunity to invest their resources in taking advantage of them. They do this strategically only to outperform their rivals who may fail to make such wise investments. Translating diversity into positive results requires its managers to focus on building and shaping an organizational culture. It also calls for suitable HR practices, the necessary supporting managerial competencies, and appropriate skills in group processes to derive benefits at the level of the organization, the work group, and the individual.

Today, we are in a position to make a persuasive business case for diversity. Moreover, available research evidence also suggests that there are few direct positive or negative effects of diversity on business performance in terms of productivity, quality of work life, and the bottom line. Some researchers even suggested that a more "nuanced" view of the business case for diversity may be more appropriate. Of late, in Human Resource Management (HRM) domain, diversity has assumed a top priority and a dominant theme for several reasons. They are as follows:

- Globalization of markets for most of the products and services.
- A perceptible shift from primarily manufacturing to a service economy.
- Increasing incidence of Mergers and Acquisitions that demand the synthesis of different corporate cultures.
- Formulation of newer business strategies requiring more teamwork.
- Ever evolving and changing labor market.

Diversity: Some Definitions

Kreitz defined diversity as "any significant difference that distinguishes one individual from another, covering a wide variety of factors that might be obvious to other individuals or hidden under the surface." One perspective argues that diversity results in better group functioning, group cohesion, and also in better team, group, and organizational performance. And then the other perspective argues that diversity results in conflict and collision.

As per Robbins, Judge and Vohra (2013), there are different bases of diversity such as age, sex, race, gender, ethnicity, religion, disability status, sexual orientation. While these demographic characteristics constitute *surface-level* diversity, others like personality, attitudes, and values represent *deep-level* diversity. Diversity is complex as it includes both (i) explicit and observable biographical characteristics and (ii) implicit factors that are within the individuals and not explicitly expressed. Diversity, therefore, is a wide, varied, and a manifold construct because there are different forms of diversity such as (i) Customer diversity, (ii) Supplier diversity, (iii) Diversity in the composition of the Board of Directors (BoD), and also (iv) Workforce diversity. It may be remembered here that diversity in organizations does not always bring about positive outcomes. Researchers have drawn on social categorization theory (Tajfel & Turner) and similarity-attraction paradigm (Byrne) to suggest the negative effect of diversity via such processes as conflict and reduced cohesiveness (as cited in Olsen & Martins, 2012). Hence, diversity has mixed consequences or repercussions in organizational functioning.

Diversity vs. Concepts of Inclusion and 'Field'

Another construct similar to diversity is *inclusion*. Shore *et al.,* (2011) argue that the construct of inclusion has remained nascent without consensus on the nature of this construct or its theoretical underpinnings. Building on Brewers' Optimal Distinctiveness Theory (ODT), they define inclusion as the degree to which an employee perceives that he or she is an esteemed member of the work group through experiencing treatment that satisfies his or her needs for belongingness and uniqueness. For the distinction between these two, Robertson (2006) suggests that they may not describe separate types of work environment but different approaches to Diversity Management (DM). As a corollary, though diversity and inclusion are used as two distinct concepts, benefits from the two might however be similar.

Diversity and DM draw support from Bourdieu's concept of "field" where fields are "contested terrains" in which actors compete for appropriation of different forms of capital (Tatli & Ozbilgin, 2012). Further, according to them, relating this line of argument of Bourdieuan concept of capitals into the study of workforce diversity is based on the premise that limitations of the dominant *etic* approaches in the current diversity research can be overcome by using the emic approach suggested by Bourdieu. Hence, they propose *emic (ex post)* approach to researching diversity at work than focusing only on pre-established (ex-ante) or *etic approach* to workforce diversity. *Emic* perspective identifies emergent and situational categories of diversity, as embedded in specific time and place. However, there are few research studies which have tried to operationalize diversity using the *emic* approach (Tatli, 2011).

This suggests that situational antecedents to diversity relatively need more exploration than other antecedents. While suggesting different approaches to diversity, Podsiadlowski *et al.,* (2013) contend that diversity strategy, diversity orientation, and diversity perspective are often used synonymously. Moreover, strategic response to diversity can be episodic, freestanding, or systemic (Dass & Parker, 1999) or can range from "not doing anything" to having a full blown diversity strategy that integrates various interventions into an organization-wide general framework (Bhawuk, Podsiadlowski, Graf & Triandis, as cited in Podsiadkiwski, et al., 2013).

DIFFERENT APPROACHES TO DIVERSITY MANAGEMENT IN THEORY AND RESEARCH

As there are different concepts of diversity, so are there different concepts of Diversity Management (DM). DM has been a subject of popular discourse for management practitioners ever since it was started first in 1980s. DM has remained prime agenda in the twenty first century as today's organizations are required to deal with diverse workforce more than ever before. Effective DM allows organizations to get access to the widest possible pool of skills, abilities, and ideas. DM has been defined as "enabling every member of the workforce to perform his or her potential" (R.R. Thomas, as cited in Olsen & Martins, 2012).

Cox defines DM as the sum of organizational practices for managing people to maximize potential advantages and as policies for recruiting and retaining talent from different backgrounds (Cox & Blake, as cited in Podsiadlowski et al., 2013).

Olsen and Martins (2012) defined Diversity Management broadly as "the utilization of Human Resource (HR) Management practices to (1) increase or maintain the variation in human capital on some given dimension(s), and/or (2) ensure that variation in human capital on some given dimension(s) does not hinder the achievement of organizational objectives, and/or (3) ensure that variation in human capital on some given dimension(s) facilitates the achievement of organizational objectives." In this definition, though the focus is on demographic characteristics, they are taken as a proxy for other deeper level diversity.

White (as cited in Ollapally & Bhatnagar, 2009) uses a metaphor and defines DM as "creating a level playing field"—an environment where each individual has the same opportunity to score.

Cox and Beale (as cited in Curtis & Dreachslin, 2008) conceptualized DM as a three-stage developmental process: awareness, understanding, and action. They argue that action or behaviors are required to translate awareness to reality ranging from diversity training, education, mentoring, and Organizational Development (OD) activities. DM interventions have been found to affect outcomes at the individual, group, and the organizational level.

Bassett-Jones (2005) defined Diversity Management as "the systematic and planned commitment on the part of organizations to recruit and retain employees with diverse backgrounds and abilities."

Current Corporate Approaches to Diversity

In order to effectively manage workplace diversity, a HR Manager of an MNC needs to change from an ethnocentric view ("our way is the best way") to a culturally relative perspective ("let's take the best of a variety of ways"). This paradigm shift in philosophy has to be very much ingrained in the managerial framework of the HR Manager in his/her managerial and operative functions performed towards the organization's diverse human resources. The role of the HR manager must parallel the needs of the changing situations in businesses. Successful organizations are becoming more adaptable, resilient, quick to change direction, and customer-centric. Currently, MNCs face a three-fold challenge while dealing with workplace diversity.

1. Enable the heterogeneous workforce to work together harmoniously toward their common goals
2. Maximize the contributions of each member of what is in fact a large team. And,
3. Ensure fair treatment for all, irrespective of their background.

Today's MNCs are searching for inclusive practices that go well beyond affirmative action to confront the obstacles that prevent women and minorities from advancing to senior management positions. In addition, to prepare for and respond to an increasingly diverse business climate, managers in most companies are expanding the organization's emphasis on diversity beyond race and gender to consider such factors as ethnicity, age, physical ability, religion, and sexual orientation. Once managers create and define a vision for a diverse workplace, they can analyze and assess the current culture and systems within the organization. Actions to develop an inclusive workplace that values and respects all people include three major steps: (a) building a corporate culture that values diversity; (b) changing structures, policies, and systems to support diversity; and (c) providing diversity awareness training.

The underlying culture of an organization should change or else, all the other efforts to support diversity will fail. Companies are addressing this issue by using surveys, interviews, and focus groups to identify how the cultural values affect other groups. Others can set up structured networks of people of color, women, and other minority groups to explore the issues they face in the workplace and to recommend changes to senior management. Organizations' policies designed to fit the stereotypical male employee should be changed. For example, a good way to revitalize the recruiting process is for the company to examine employee demographics, the composition of the employee pool in the area, and the composition of the customer base before working toward reflecting the same in the latter.

One of the most successful structures to accomplish elimination of glass ceiling is the mentoring relationship, wherein a mentor, a highly ranking, senior organizational member is committed to providing upward mobility and support to a *protégé's* professional career. Many organizations are struggling with generational diversity, striving to meet the needs of employees at different ages and life cycles. Changing organizational structures and policies is important because it demonstrates a concrete commitment to supporting diversity. If managers talk about the value of diverse workforce but do nothing to ensure that ensure diverse employees have opportunities and support in the workplace, employees are not likely to trust that the company truly values diversity.

Diversity Management as a Pragmatic Business Strategy

Over the past two decades DM has become a major competitive factor for many companies and even something they are proud of. Yet others remain to be convinced. They want the business justification for diversity to be sound and demonstrable. To do that, it's necessary to address at least five major issues. They are: how does diversity (i) help an organization expand into global markets, (ii) help build brand equity, (iii) support the organization's human asset/resource strategies, (iv) build corporate image among our consumers, and (iv) enhance operational efficiency? In an equitable work environment, no member or group of members of an organization should have an undue advantage or unfair disadvantage.

The essence of diversity management is establishment of a heterogeneous employee force and making it to perform to its maximum potential. Any business strategy would become pragmatic only when it meets the needs of the diverse consumer/ customer groups by focusing on maximizing the creativity, commitment, and productivity of the employee force. Diversity Management is a pragmatic business strategy that focuses on maximizing the productivity, creativity, and commitment of the workforce while meeting the needs of diverse consumer groups. However, overall challenge is to create a work setting where in everyone would be performing to his full potential in the long-run. It is a situation where all employees would be competing for incentives, rewards, and promotions only on the basis of merit alone. An examination of the factors that have contributed significantly for the effective management and successful performance of companies at once reveals that such organizations do the following much better than the rest. They are as follows:

- They purposefully focus on attracting and brining in the best possible talent.
- They are not interested in just meeting the numerical goals.
- They believe in establishment of mentoring programs among employees of same and different races as well.
- They ensure that management is held accountable for meeting all diversity-related goals.
- They conceptualize, design, and develop career plans for employees as part of their performance reviews.
- They consciously make it a point to promote women and minorities to important and significant decision-making positions in the organizations instead of confining or relegating them to mere staff jobs.
- They even go to the extent of making the composition of the Board of Directors also highly diverse.

These are all the compelling reasons for making the workforce diverse and managing it. They all represent sound business principles and have the potential to contribute to the shareholder value and make it more and ever increasing.

Diversity and Linking HR Practices to Business Practices

An organization's capacity to learn as to how to manage diversity effectively gets stunted and limited should it fail to link HR practices to business performance. Any company's claims for diversity as a strategic imperative would remain hollow and shallow if it doesn't justify the same through suitable supporting financial investments. There are many factors that affect the relationship between diversity and measurable business outcomes. This is precisely the reason for the difficulty in identifying and establishing a simple and direct cause-effect relationship between these two. Diversity can always be made as an input and a resource for learning, change, and organizational renewal. However, managers attempting it are bound to face challenges and experience difficulties in their efforts in this direction. To surmount these impediments, HR managers need to promote cultures of mutual learning and cooperation among the members of the employee force with the help of enabling management practices. Maximizing the overall returns to shareholders i.e., increases in stock prices as well as in dividends continues to remain the basic objective of profit-making businesses. Company earnings have a direct bearing on this objective. In this context, management has to determine the degree to which diversity interventions, like any other management programs, do impact the bottom line.

In reality, organizations, however, have a tendency to measure the success of such programs not by looking at the bottom line but by watching other indicators. Diversity awareness and implementation initiatives like affirmative action programs definitely entail costs but with *no* or *little* financial benefits to the company that commensurate with the expenditure making the critics to strongly oppose them. For this reason, they can be justified only on moral or philosophical grounds.

A SYNTHESIS OF MANAGEMENT RESEARCH AND CURRENT LITERATURE ON DIVERSITY AND DIVERSITY MANAGEMENT

From the time the concept was popularized, the process of conceptualizing and coming up with a generic model monopolized the interest of scholars for a very long time. Diversity as a concept, by and large, has a strong theoretical root in various related concepts giving different perspectives about it. Diversity and Diversity Management concepts were found to have evolved and expanded overtime. Lorbiecki and Jack (2000) identified four major overlapping turns in ideas of DM labeled as demographic, political, economic, and critical. And each turn represents a shift in the way thinking gets changed about DM. Historical evolution of DM can be traced through the report "Workforce 2000" prepared by Johnson and Packer in 1987. They indicated that by 2000 North American workforce would comprise of African-Americans, Hispanics, Native Americans, women, and other minority groups. Triggered by this news, organizations and academicians started taking note of the changing demographic situation to consider the effect of demographic in the workplace.

Konrad (2003) reviewed six articles on workforce diversity and suggested that diversity in the workforce is an extension of Heider's Balance Theory. He even argued that balancing among conflicting parties cannot be attained until the individuals sharing important identity group memberships achieve supportive relationships among themselves.

Resource-based Theory is concerned with performance heterogeneity among organizations based on variety of resources: physical capital, financial capital, human capital, and corporate capital. It is also suggested (Richard, 2000; Richard, Barnett, Dwyer, & Chadwick, 2004) that diversity can be valuable, rare, and inimitable resource that enhances a firm's competitiveness (as cited in Yang & Konrad, 2011). They provided empirical evidence that racial diversity and cultural diversity are positively related with financial performance. It was found that firm with more diversity management practices witnessed less turnover and more innovation. Resource-based Theory is concerned with firms' competitive advantage. So, dynamic DM programs and policies can be a competitive asset for a firm which is difficult to copy and hence ensure sustained competitiveness. Organizations are likely to adopt workforce diversity management practices for social legitimacy and to gain resources needed for survival as per Institutional Theory perspective which is concerned with firms' homogeneity. The theory, in itself, comprises of regulative forces, normative forces, and cognitive forces promoting or ensuring homogeneity and act as antecedents for diversity and Diversity Management.

Person-Organization Fit Theory is yet another theoretical perspective for diversity. It is concerned with the congruence between individuals' values, beliefs and personal characteristics on one side and those of the organization on the other side. Generally, women and minorities would perceive organizations to be very attractive employers if they provide opportunities and a work environment that is free from discrimination. This feeling is in consonance with the literature available on Person-Organization Fit Theory.

Olsen and Martins (2012) theorized diversity from value perspective. Some organizations treat DM as an instrumental value as it is responsible for achieving favorable business outcomes. It becomes a terminal value for organizations that view diverse workforce itself as an objective and an end result. The value-in-diversity perspective argues that diverse workforce is generally beneficial for business. The benefits include but are not limited to corporate profits and earnings. The dynamics of labor and consumer markets were altering because of demographic changes and this became a crucial argument in favor of diversity programs.

Inclusive philosophy was seen as an attractive alternative to affirmative action initiating the political turn. Affirmative action former was designed as a temporary measure to redress past discrimination and was eventually got replaced by DM. The political interest turned 'economic' through various articles that were published warned organizations that the performance and image of the organization would be in jeopardy if they did not pay immediate attention to manage diversity.

The domain of DM turned critical when problems were encountered in its implementation. For instance, Gilbert, Stead, and Ivancevich (1999) argued that negative perception combined with poor implementation at the organizational level has resulted in more ineffective and unjust society and not due to the goal of affirmative action to ensure equal opportunities for all. They also proposed a Model for effective Diversity Management. They contend that the CEO's initiation of diversity movement and its continuation as a prerequisite for effective DM. They believed that it would finally lead to and result in transformation of HR functions (mentoring, recruitment, friendly policies, diversity councils and more), individual level outcome (integration, organizational attachment, and psychological dissonance), and positive attitudes towards diversity (acceptance, appreciation of differences, and multiculturalism).

This would benefit the organization in terms of better decision making, representation of qualified minorities, retention of qualified minorities, business with diverse and multinational customer base, and product line development. It is contended that the above stated benefits would be instrumental in achieving positive organizational outcomes (profit, market share, stock price), and public recognition.

Today, diversity has been conceptualized with different terminologies providing a modified and an expanded view. The expansion was guided more by the need of the time rather than any other thing. The rhetoric of diversity has been shifted from affirmative action to DM. Of late, the focus of DM has been shifted towards inclusion. The aspects of inclusion demand organization to reduce problems associated with demographic diversity and create environment such that individuals from all background are fairly treated, valued, and included in decision-making (Nishii, 2013).

It is the essence of decision making that makes the concept of inclusion totally different in the context of DM. Prior to that, DM was concerned only with treating each employee fairly and equitably by choice rather than compulsion. Inclusion, as a new concept or as an expansion of DM concept, focused on all aspects associated with DM with additional decision-making feature.

Bassett-Jones (2005) in their conceptual analysis included range of factors associated with diversity. This might include a range of differences in ethnicity, nationality, gender, functions, ability, language, religion, lifestyle, tenure, culture, or intellectual capacities.

In its primitive form diversity in the organization was concerned with demographic aspects but globalization and organizational complexities have enhanced the domain of diversity from mere demographic to cultural diversity.

Prasad and Mills (1997) argued that the notion that traditional monoculture organizations cannot function effectively in the context of today's and tomorrow's workforce and has embedded the same within the philosophy of managing diversity.

They broadly conceptualized diversity as a corporate asset that contributes indirectly towards the performance of the organization. The authors viewed that the concept of diversity signifies different things to different groups and individuals within organizations and society. For some, diversity means demographic representation and for others, it may involve overcoming cultural prejudice and instilling new values about difference in the organization.

Kersten (2000) argued that racial equality through DM differs from previous approaches to discrimination in four aspects. First one advocates for systematic transformation of organization by changing the culture in such a way that it becomes an open, welcome, and supportive environment for all people. Second approach is concerned with the presentation of diversity which advocates it as positive and voluntary effort on the part of organization rather than negative and external mandated. As per the third aspect, difference is justified with economic rather than legal arguments. Lastly, diversity is defined in the form of inclusive definition in which any and all differences are considered as part of the diversity project.

Majority of the conceptual work concerning diversity was more towards labeling diversity as necessity rather than choice by generating positive outcomes. Many scholars viewed diversity and its management in the workplace as valuable assets for sustained competitive advantage. Contrary to these conceptualizations, Lorbiecki and Jack (2000) argued that DM initiatives have increased rather than decreased inequalities. They emphasized the need to get involved in more critical and reflexive debate before theorizing diversity in a philosophically and socio-politically different manner.

There isn't one single best way for DM in the workplace. The approach of the organization towards diversity depends on the degree of pressure for diversity, the type of diversity in question, and managerial attitudes. In the larger context, the practice of diversity is more guided by legal compliance rather than choice. So, people from disadvantaged groups act as diversity champions. DM is similar to marketing for many organizations. Organizations with global presence tend to promote and preserve diversity within their organizations by appealing towards larger stakeholders including customers.

The general understanding that can be derived from the conceptual review will be that planned and systematic diversity management can yield positive outcomes for the organization. One should not be involved in affirmative action in the name of diversity. Such actions would discourage qualified and capable pool of candidates from entering the organization. DM can also be an indicator of economic condition for organization and to a large extent for the nation. Diversity movement emerged from developed economies and the effort helped them achieve the greater global market share.

India, as a nation is still struggling with the affirmative action perspective of diversity, providing quota for diverse population, and ensuring their representation. In doing so, representation from political to organizational level is more guided by constitutional requirement and such representation was found to be less meaningful.

RESEARCH STUDIES ON GENDER, AGE, AND RACE AS THE BASES OF DIVERSITY

Gender

Among other forms of diversity at the surface level, *gender* has been associated with positive outcomes. If we look into the vast and varied literature that is available on diversity, compared to other bases of diversity, gender as a basis looms large and figures out to be more prominent than others. Gender as a base for diversity has garnered worldwide attention as the number of females joining the workforce has increased significantly in the current era compared to the earlier times. Most researches have examined as to how the inclusion of female workforce in the BOD has resulted in increased financial performance (Campbell & Vera, 2007). However, not all the studies suggest consistent findings with gender and firms' performance. Dwyer, Richard, and Chadwick (2003) posit that the effect of gender diversity at the management level is moderated by a firm's strategic orientation and organizational culture in which it resides. Hence, they suggest that a supportive environment needs to be put in place to reap the benefits of gender diversity.

In similar lines, Smith, Smith, and Verner (2006) found that proportion of women in top management jobs had positive effect on firm's performance while keeping firm's other characteristics constant. Of course, the positive effects, however, depend on the qualification of female top managers. Francoeur, Labelle, and Desgagne (2008) found that firms operating in complex environments generated exceptionally positive and unusually significant returns when they have higher proportion of women officers in the employee force. Though women in positions of directors made no difference but women working in management and governance system generated enough value to keep up with stock market returns.

All the research studies provide consistent findings with regard to effect of gender and performance though these effects cannot be measured in isolation. Hence, possible role of moderating variables must be taken into account.

Cumming, Leung, and Rui (2015) studied the impact of gender diversity and securities fraud and found that the former can reduce the likelihood and severity of fraud.

Effect of gender diversity was compared across full samples in male-dominated and female dominated industries and found that the presence of women was more effective in reducing frequency and severity of fraud in male dominated industries.

Research on gender has explored whether gender has made progress with regard to management and leadership over a period of time (Broadbridge & Simpson, 2011; Embry, Padgett, & Caldwell, 2008). Braodbridge and Simpson (2011) in their purely conceptual paper discuss how gender over the period of 25 years to the current stage has now reduced to gender denial and gender concealment. This has led to both disadvantage and privilege. Embry, Padgett, and Caldwell (2008) found that men using *gender inconsistent* (feminine) style were evaluated more positively than men using a *gender consistent* style. In addition, a perceived female leader who used a gender-inconsistent (masculine) style was evaluated more positively than a perceived male leader who used a masculine style, but only by female participants.

Another study by Powell, Butterfield, and Parent (2002), suggested that though there has been a significant increase in the proportion of women managers, there was no significant change in the perception of women managers and leaders. A good manager is considered as predominantly masculine. Atwater, Brett, Waldman, DiMare, and Hayden (2004) found that some sub-roles were found to be more masculine while others were found to be more feminine.

Allocating resources, networking, problem-solving delegation, and strategic decision making would be perceived as more masculine, while supporting and consulting others were perceived as more feminine. Additionally, male respondents saw most sub-roles as masculine than female respondents.

Nishii (2013) found that within inclusive climates, interpersonal bias is reduced in a way that gender diversity is associated with lower levels of conflicts. All these research studies on gender and management, or gender and leadership suggest that these are largely influenced by stereotypes or perceptions.

The purpose of postmodernism is to make us aware about the connections among meaning, power and language, and that constructivist view of gender theorizing in contemporary psychology reveals gender as a continuum of psychological differences (Hare-Mustin & Marecek, 1988). Constructivist view challenge an idea of single meaning of reality and concern themselves with the way meaning is represented. Gender has its theoretical root in many other theories. Sex role theory explains gender pattern by appealing to the social expectations that define proper behavior for women and men. This theory has been criticized on the ground of intellectual weakness as it does not consider the issue of power, violence, or material inequality, misses the complexities within masculinity and femininity and that it offers very limited opportunities for change.

Categorical theory treats women and men as pre-formed categories. This approach though it addresses the issue of power, does not consider gender complexities. Feminist

Theory has often been critical of naturalistic explanations of sex and sexuality that assume that the meaning of women's social existence can be derived from some fact of their physiology and distinguished sex from gender, feminist theorists have disputed causal explanations that assume that sex dictates or necessitates certain social meanings for women's experience (Butler, 1988). Masculinity refers to male bodies but is not determined by male biology and thus it is perfectly logical to term masculine women.

Masculinity studies view gender as unstable and fluid whereas feminist perspective views gender as a social practice that involves creation, negotiation and maintenance of difference in specific social and institutional context that created ground for conceptualization of gender identities (Broad Bridge & Simpson, 201). Most of the quantitative research approaches to gender and performance have used correlations, descriptive statistics, and regressions to study the impact of gender diversity on organizational level outcomes (Dwyer, Richard, and Chadwick, 2003; Smith, Smith, and Verner, 2006; Francoeur, Labelle, & Desgagne, 2008).

Cumming, Leung, and Rui (2015) employed robust measures to study the impact of gender diversity and security fraud. They used control firm approach to create group of control firms (non-fraud firm). They came up with empirical models to test their hypotheses while controlling firms' characteristics like age and governance factors. They took 742 control firms out of a sample of 1484. Logistic regression was employed with two stage estimates of determinants of fraud. The findings were subjected to robustness by bootstrap technique. They also addressed the endogeneity between likelihood of fraud and number of female directors on board.

Age

Apart from gender, age is also one of the demographic measures of diversity. Kunze, Boehm, and Bruch (2011) examined the effect of age diversity and age discrimination climate on performance. They found that age diversity seems to be related to the emergence of an age discrimination climate in the organizations, which negatively impacts the overall performance. Sluiter (2006) argued that in high-demand jobs which can be physical, mental, or psychological in their origin are more likely to overtax the capacities of older workers than those of younger workers. This calls for a shift from 'no diversity thinking' to 'diversity thinking' in the context of deciding about the work ability of ageing workers in high-demand jobs.

Contrary to that Walker (2005) proposed that promoting age diversity and providing an environment in which each individual is able to achieve his or her potential without being disadvantaged by their age should be the policy and that employees should not be discriminated by their age. Limited work on age has contradictory findings which place sufficient doubt over age as probable researchable construct that would be of interest to researcher.

Riach (2009) put forward and interesting argument in regard to considering old workforce as diverse and found that there is difficultly in translating age diversity as an abstract managerial concept into policies and practices. Moreover, particularly age and gender has been taken as control variables in majority of the studies that has diminished its actual relevance as a potential variable of interest. More studies taking age and gender as influential variables in the studies would increase its relevance and expand its domain. The conceptual work on the area of diversity needs to be backed by sufficient empirical studies, mostly quantitative, in order to validate the conceptualization under this theme.

Race

Herring (2009) has identified racial diversity to be associated with increased sales revenue, more customers, greater market share, and greater relative profit. Avery, Mckay, Wilson, and Tonidandel (2007) studied whether racial discrimination is associated with absenteeism. They found that underprivileged group within a given race tends to be more absent than the privileged one. And it was more significant on two occasions: first, when the supervisor is racially similar and second, when diversity has no value in the organization. Paug, Dietz, Brief, and Wiley (2008) found that when few racial minorities live in the community within an organization's periphery, workforce diversity has an impact on employees' diversity climate perceptions. Whenever the share of minorities increased, the workforce diversity loses its significance. Richard (2000) studied the interface between racial diversity and business strategy and found that it is important in determining firm performance measured in three different ways viz., productivity, return on equity, and market performance. Like age and gender, the association of racial diversity has been studied with more of the hard measures of performance than others.

Diversity as the Source of Competitive Advantage: The Empirical Evidence

Bassett-Jones (2005) argued about the two facets of diversity in the workplace. Diversity can be a source of competitive advantage as it promotes creativity and innovation in the workplace. It can also be a cause of misunderstanding, suspicion, and conflict in the workplace that can result in absenteeism, turnover, poor quality, low morale, and loss of competitiveness. A need for diversity arises because of discrimination. If an employee is perceived to be discriminated because of his/ her demographic or any other difference in identity, the overall performance of the organization deteriorates. As was found out by one research study, employees who grew up in a favorable culture tend to have a less degree of perceived discrimination and thereby leaving a positive impact on employee outcomes. Further, the effect of perceived discrimination on organizational commitment, job satisfaction, and work tension was moderated by superior culture, salary, and work experience.

In their research study, Ng and Burke (2005) found out diversity management to be important when accepting offers of employment by women and ethnic minorities. In the same study, new immigrants rated organizations with DM initiatives as more attractive as their potential employers.

Nishii and Ozbilgin (2007) identified several outcomes of effective global workforce DM practices. They are: effective global knowledge creation, sharing and dissemination of information, lower level of backlash, more commitment, greater satisfaction, and perceived fairness, improved organizational performance and innovation, and employee engagement.

Nishii (2013) found that relationship and task conflict were significantly lower in gender-diverse groups with high scores on *climate for inclusion* than in diverse groups with lower scores on *climate for inclusion*. Similarly, they also observed that any negative association between relationship conflict and satisfaction disappears when climate for inclusion is high. Herring (2009) identified that gender diversity is associated with increased sales revenue, more customers, and greater relative profits.

Curtis and Dreachslin (2008) discussed that the measurable effectiveness of organizational performance through diversity interventions has not been researched adequately. Moreover, the limited work on this issue lacks rigor as there was a total domination of quasi-experimental designs, qualitative methods, and self-reported data. There is a need to investigate the relationship of DM interventions with various performance indicators in more objective ways rather than through the ongoing subjective ones.

It was evident from literatures that men are most likely to use task-oriented and autocratic style of leadership than women, and women are more likely to use interpersonal and democratic leadership styles than men. Based on this premise, Embry, Padgett, and Caldwell (2008) conducted one study and found out that males using a feminist style of leadership were evaluated positively than males using masculinity style. On the contrary, a female leader using a masculine style was evaluated more positively by female participants when compared to a male leader using a masculine style.

Powell, Butterfield, and Parent (2002) carried out a study and its results indicated that a good manager is one who predominantly possesses masculinity characteristics giving support to the stereotype associated with gender. But some other pieces of evidence suggested that women bring a different set of personal characteristics in the managerial roles than men. This would help in changing the stereotype based on bookkeeping and also the conversion models of stereotype change. In today's competitive era of business, the role of managers has shifted towards good communication, coaching, and people skills from the erstwhile competitiveness, aggression, and task orientation. The former is more associated with feminist characteristics. Now, the demand for managers with such characteristics is growing and is becoming instrumental in shifting stereotypical paradigm.

Managerial roles, allocating resources, problem solving, delegating, strategic decision-making, disciplining, and punishing were perceived as more masculine in nature. On the contrary, supporting, mentoring, recognizing and rewarding, communicating, and planning were seen as more feminine in character indicating that management is not entirely a bundle of masculine roles. Francoeur, Labelle, and Sinclair-Desgagne (2008) carried out a research study concerning corporate governance and top management. They found out that organizations with relatively more female officers generate positive and significant much more than normal returns in the complex environments while those with high proportion of females in management and governance systems generate good value to keep up with normal stock market returns.

Cumming, Leung, and Rui (2015) revealed that gender diversity has influence on the effective operation and fraud minimization in the organization. Similarly, women in top positions broaden the talent pool and pave the way for more talented Board. Providing for a diversity of views encourages constructive discussion. Gender diversity also gives rise to more conflict and less trust among Board members, and hence increases scrutiny and less fraud from organizational perspective.

The research work concerning gender and diversity in general is more towards a qualitative inquiry. The limited quantitative work under this domain was more concerned towards objective measures of performance. Subjective measurement of diversity was found to be insufficient as it is still one of the emerging concepts in behavioral sciences domain. Hard measures of performance have been found to be tested with diversity whereas more of the soft measures like the effect of diversity on satisfaction, commitment, engagement, and so forth have not been adequately considered for research work. Further, not much of moderating or mediating tests concerning DM have been performed. This trend provides sufficient doubt over the reliability of diversity as a concept in the organizational setting. Limited empirical work on DM lead us to believe that diversity is more guided by political agenda and interest rather than academic and/or organizational interest.

METHODOLOGICAL APPROACH

Both quantitative and qualitative research has been conducted in the domain of diversity and DM. Yang and Konrad (2011) reviewed relevant extant literatures on antecedents and outcomes of diversity management practices. They developed a research model by applying institutional and resource-based theories. Olsen and Martins (2012) conducted proposition based qualitative inquiry for formulating conceptual framework. Bassett-Jones (2005) came up with a conceptual and discursive paper. Prasad and Mills (1997) research studies were reviewed for a Book Chapter. Kelly and Dobbin (1998) performed exploratory study on the concepts of evolution and dissolution. Gilbert, Stead, and Ivancevich (1999) carried out qualitative narrative study where a model for effective diversity management was proposed.

Likewise, the study conducted by Lorbiecki and Jack (2000) was based on a narrative inquiry. Miller and Rowney (1999) study was exploratory in nature where the extent of adoption and implementation of DM initiatives in organizations was examined. Kersten (2000) performed a critical examination of DM by using Habermas model of dialogue. Nishii and Ozbilgin (2007) study was a paper review with a purpose of formulation of conceptual framework for Global Diversity Management. Also, the study of Dass and Parker (1999) was concerned with conceptual review and framework design. Hare-Mustin and Marecek (1988) performed qualitative inquiry on the study of post-modernism approach in gender. The study of Sluiter (2006) and Walker (2005) was a study in the form of conceptual paper. Riach (2009) carried out a conceptual inquiry with in-depth interview as a research tool. Curtis and Dreachslin (2008) carried out integrative literature review.

Curtis and Dreachslin (2008) adopted a unique methodology in this context. They took an integrative approach by means of going through 26 relevant portions from the available literature on diversity intervention programs by means of training, education, mentoring, and organizational development activities. They find that most of those interventions were carried out using experimental, quasi-experimental, case study, descriptive, and developmental methods. Majority of the intervention programs employed quasi-experimental research designs. Pre- and post-test surveys were also carried out among participants who attended diversity course.

Self-reported measures were carried out to assess the change in attitudes of the participants that attended the diversity course. Similar kinds of study designs were adopted for education, mentoring, and OD interventions. Most research on gender and leadership as well as gender and management have taken more of a qualitative approach for studying the progress of the latter over a period of time (Broadbridge & Simpson, 2011).

Embry, Padgett, and Caldwell (2008) have used surveys among undergraduate business students and it is alleged that their sample is not an appropriate one as they do not mention whether the students are working or full time students. If the students are not working, their perception of the leader will be far from reality and may not give the accurate result. The major problem with the methodology is the simulated situation where the leaders and subordinates were fictional characters, which might have led to biased findings and stereotypes. Also, there was no clue over the composition of perceived leaders in terms of male and female. Hence, this study was subjected to a number of methodological lapses and the sample size was also small.

Similar problems in methodology were found in another research study on gender and stereotypes where the sample consisted of undergraduate and part time students (Powell, Butterfield, & Parent, 2002) there by missing the context. Relying on student samples can be taken as drawback for this study as well. Methodology was not rigorous as they carried out mean analysis and basic descriptive one. It lacked robust measures of data analysis. Atwater, Brett, Waldman, Di Mare, and Hayden (2004) used Yukl taxonomy of 14 managerial roles. It used non-parametric binomial tests. Though the results were tested by means of means score, z-tests, and chi-square values, in terms of methodology, they could have employed other rigorous methods than simple descriptive and comparison checks by means of chi-square. Despite the fact that samples drawn were students and 75% of them had supervisory experiences, there is no proper justification for the choice of sample.

Sanchez and Brock (1996) study was cross-sectional in nature with quantitative hierarchal regression analysis and questionnaire as a tool to gather data. The study of Ng and Burke (2005) was hypothesis testing mean significance study. Kunze, Boehm, Bruch (2011) study was cross organizational quantitative study by using SEM as a technique for data analysis.

Herring (2009) study was based on determining racial diversity through racial index of diversity and then performing regression analysis on the data. Avery, Mckay, Wilson, and Tonidandel (2007) dealt with questionnaire survey with hierarchical multiple regression analysis as a technique to analyze data. Richard (2000) carried out logistic regression analysis for the data acquired from secondary sources. Francoeur, Labelle, and Sinclair-Desgagne (2008) performed a model-based multivariate analysis where comparison of average monthly returns, average return on equity, and average monthly abnormal returns between high and low representation of women was carried out.

Powell, Butterfield, and Parent (2002) performed quantitative inquiry using chi-square test to determine the difference in samples for different time periods. Cumming, Leung, and Rui (2015) conducted a model-based logistic regression analysis with 'fraud' as a dependent variable and 15 other independent variables. Samples were divided into control group and treatment group for comparison purposes. Atwater, Brett, Waldman, DiMare, and Hayden (2004) used non-parametric binomial test and chi-square test to see the difference in the perceptions of male and female employees about the manager roles. Nishii (2013) performed confirmatory factor analysis on the data and ran SEM program. Paug, Dietz, Brief, and Wiley (2008) performed simple regression analysis.

The research work by Embry, Padgett, and Caldwell (2008) was a quantitative inquiry with business students as respondents among whom 81% were having prior work experiences. The responses from 19% with no work experience couldn't be validated as they were not exposed to the leadership style in organizational settings.

The methodological approach on diversity and diversity management was more inclined towards qualitative inquiry. Various conceptual models on diversity management have been formulated and many of the studies on this domain were guided towards enriching conceptual understanding. Only limited quantitative inquiry to test and validate the proposed conceptual framework was initiated. In the quantitative front, the studies were more focused towards measuring hard performance measures. In majority of the quantitative studies, data were collected from secondary sources and one can witness the use of logistic regression for the data concerning this domain. In many studies, financial models for measuring the effect of one variable on other were presented. This showed that diversity management has been more an area of interest within finance domain rather than that of behavioral science. In order to incorporate diversity within behavior science there is a serious need to conduct more quantitative studies to be able to establish the effect of diversity management on behavioral science variables.

Potential Directions and Research Issues in Indian Context

The issue of diversity is more prominent in Indian society. Diversity is so much into Indian society in the form of gender, ethnicity, religion, and language that the slogan *"unity within diversity"* is being promoted to ensure societal and cultural harmony. Diversity in Indian context is much more a political agenda than an organizational agenda. In this regard, diversity is much more driven by affirmitive action rather than meaningful inclusion. Diversity has been found to be encouraged and promoted especially in the development sectors. Research to explore and identify whether (i) diversity in the development sector is because of the mandatory requirement and is limited to affirmitive inquiry or (ii) is it really following the norms of inclusion in the workforce, can be carried out. The perception of employees from marginalized domains (female, dalits, and religious minorities) can add valuable insights in the diversity movement as it has been practiced by developmental sectors. The probable research issue is: What are the reasons that force the firms to claim that their organization is forcefully or willingly practicing diversity management within the organization?

It is evident from the review of literature that very limited work on examining the impact of demographic variables (age, gender, tenure, and ethnicity) on outcome variables (job satisfaction and organizational commitment) has been performed in the Indian context. In this regard, quantitative inquiry to examine the above mentioned relationship can be carried out. The findings from this study will enrich the domain of diversity management and enable organization to formulate diversity strategies on retirement schemes or continuing benefits concerning age and tenure, and formulate selection policies in regard to gender and ethnicity. The research can be carried out for banks and financial institutions because banking sector till date has not been forced to recruit employees on the ground of diversity management. Hence, this sector can carry out diversity management practices as per their requirement based on the findings of this study. The probable research issue is: *Do age, gender, tenure, and ethnicity affect job satisfaction and organizational commitment in Indian Banks and Financial Institutions?*

As there has been not much published work in the area of gender and diversity management in the Indian organizational context, this is a potential research area requiring in depth investigation. The issue of *inclusion* has garnered significant attention starting from government organizations to development agencies. The fact that NGOs have been recruiting employees from marginalized communities and minorities including women suggests that diversity will be more of a rule than exception in the days to come. In this regard, it would be meaningful to explore the perceptions of workforce diversity and inclusion among the employees from the development sector.

A pertinent research question to be raised for seeking a meaningful answer is to come up with a universally acceptable definition for the concept of diversity such that it includes the concept of *inclusion* as well. It is no denying the fact that the number of females joining the workforce especially in the post-economic reforms era in corporate houses continues to witness an upward swing. In this backdrop, it would be meaningful to study if the participation of women in the workforce leads to increased corporate financial performance in general and sectors like banking and insurance in particular that have more women representation compared to other formal sectors.

Diversity, of late, has become a major competitive factor for many companies. However, others are yet to be convinced about it and they want the business justification for diversity and expect it to be sound and demonstrable. To do that, it's necessary to address five *major issues.* They are:

- How does diversity help an organization expand into global markets?

- How can diversity help build brand equity?
- How does diversity support the organization's human asset/resource strategies?
- How does diversity build corporate image among its consumers?
- How does diversity enhance operational efficiency?

In the context of diversity management, some of the *challenges* the firms face are:

- What is the objective of building and managing a diverse workforce?
- Can firms make a persuasive business case for diversity with compelling arguments in their respective contexts?
- What could be the possible direct positive or negative effects of diversity on business performance in terms of productivity, quality of work life, bottom line, etc.?
- How can managers take a more "nuanced" view of the business case for diversity?
- Is there additional information beyond the five issues that we need to feel is necessary to make the business case for diversity?
- What steps can one take as a manager to become more effective in a work environment that is more diverse than ever?
- Does diversity management conflict with maximizing shareholder's value?
- How can a company come up with a list of suggested actions that managers can take to deal with and manage effectively the multiple and varied changes taking place in the internal organizational environment now and in the future?
- What are the implications of diversity management when it is seen from more closely?

FINDINGS FROM EARLIER RESEARCH STUDIES AND EMPIRICAL EVIDENCE

There is good amount of qualitative and quantitative research on the theme of diversity and Diversity Management. The qualitative research is concerned with defining or operationalizing the construct of diversity, diversity strategy, diversity discourse, and DM practices. Review of available literature shows that single category diversity dominates the multi-category diversity. Also, there is no meta-analysis carried out by considering all aspects of diversity. Meta-analysis on demographic diversity and team performance suggested that specific demographic variables (functional background, organizational tenure, etc.) had small positive relationship with team performance as well as team creativity and innovation (Bell et al., 2011). Literature considering the antecedents and consequences of diversity is also minimal. The focus of most of the studies on diversity has been only at the surface level. Also, vast literature on diversity and DM has focused on the positive outcomes than compared to the negative outcomes. Moreover, research studies have considered diversity as an antecedent in most cases. There is sparse literature on diversity as a moderating variable. In one study, diversity strategy was found to moderate the relationship between racial diversity and organizational performance (Cunningham, 2009).

Diversity Management: Some Practical Examples From Corporate World

Many MNCs are now finding innovative ways to integrate diversity initiatives into their business. These initiatives teach current employees to value differences, direct corporate recruiting efforts, influence supplier decisions, and provide development training for women and minorities. Some managers value diversity and enforce the value in day-to-day decision making. Now organizations recognize that everyone is not the same and that the differences people bring to the workplace are valuable. Rather than expecting all employees to adopt similar attitudes and values, managers are learning that these differences enable their companies to compete globally and to tap into rich sources of new talent. Although diversity in India has been a reality for some time now, genuine efforts to accept and manage diverse people begin in right earnest. Managers must take a proactive approach so that differences are valued and capitalized upon. Diversity will turn into an opportunity and enhance the organization's market presence and market share by prudent and pragmatic management practices.

A number of World famous MNCs like Coca-cola, Xerox, AT&T, Proctor & Gamble, and 3M strongly believe in the positive aspects of diversity and attuned their managers to utilize the diversity to the utmost advantage of their organizations. Experience of these businesses suggests that diverse workforce broadens customer base and helps managing customer service more efficiently and effectively. In fact to be successful, MNCs must continue to look forward to the future, not the past. The CEOs, senior line and HR management, and diversity leaders play a key role in that process. If MNCs are to address the complex issues of child and eldercare, the emerging issues of multiculturalism, tolerance of religious practices, and full inclusion of people with disabilities in the workplace, then diversity professionals must lead from the front. They alone must lead as MNCs cannot get there by themselves. In this context, MNCs have developed many HR practices in order to improve the efficacy of the approach they adopt while managing diversity.

CONCLUSION

More Recent Approaches to Diversity Management

- Constitution of employee-initiated and employee-funded *caucus groups* based on the various dimensions of diversity to sponsor activities such as training workshops, conferences, and mentoring programs for their members.
- Designing and keeping in place a *Management Resources Planning*, a company-wide formal succession planning process for identifying, developing, and tracking the flow of women and other disadvantaged groups through the company. This is done to ensure their upward mobility while making the business unit leaders responsible for the process.
- Adopting a *balanced workforce strategy* wherein we set numerical targets, based on employee market demographics that specify the percentages of these diverse groups to be hired and promoted into each major job category. Incentive pay and promotions of managers are to be explicitly tied to their achievement of balanced workforce goals.
- Provision for *work and family programs* to include financial grants, alternative work schedules including job sharing, flextime, and compressed workweeks, and a variety of family friendly benefits.
- Tracking and *monitoring Workforce demographics* at all levels and within all units of the company
- Conducting *Annual Employee Surveys* to include questions that assess satisfaction with all aspects of work life, and analyzing the results to assess whether satisfaction differs by gender or ethnicity.
- Organizing *community outreach and development* and stimulating interest in science and technology among all members of the future workforce and to combat early gender and ethnic occupational stereotyping.

The list of HR initiatives that MNCs are currently using to manage workplace diversity is quite long and varied. Managers need to target specific efforts and set priorities for implementing them. An organization's choice of specific efforts will reflect the nature of diversity that is important for the organization, the goals set, the actions of other organizations in the industry, and so on. The rise in consumerism has led to a management style quite divorced from the traditional paternalistic organization. Even the psychological contract between the employer and employee has changed over the years.

On the other hand, there have been perceptible shifts in the individual perceptions of what the main springs of human actions are and what motivates them at workplace as well as in their personal lives. Both the management and the individual employees need to play a positive role in managing diversity. Any attempt to resist the change that comes with it is only self-defeating and fool hardy. Perceptions have an important role to play in diversity management and the role of Personnel practitioners becomes imperative. Various tools such as brainstorming etc. can be used effectively here. Challenging the deep-rooted stereotypes is the crux of the matter in managing diversity. Collaborative and cooperative workplace behavior, training, communication and other such related practices need to be modulated to achieve management of diversity. The imperativeness to review, measure, and reinforce and the steps taken by the organization in this direction on a continuous basis and their importance need not be overemphasized here.

REFERENCES

Ableson, R. (2000, September 10). Can Respect Be Mandated? May be Not Here. *The New York Times*.

Adamson, J. (2000, Winter). How Denny's Went from Icon of Racism to Diversity Award Winner. *Journal of Organizational Excellence*, 55-68.

Atwater, L. E., Brett, J. F., Waldman, D., DiMare, L., & Hayden, M. V. (2004). Men's and Women's Perceptions of the Gender Typing of Management Sub-roles. *Sex Roles*, *50*(3/4), 191–200. doi:10.1023/B:SERS.0000015551.78544.35

Belkin, L. (2003, October 26). The Opt-Out Revolution. *New York Times Magazine*, 43-47, 58+.

Bell, S. T., Villado, A. J., Lukasik, M. A., Belau, L., & Briggs, A. L. (2011). Getting Specific about Demographic Variable and Team Performance Relationships: A Meta-Analysis. *Journal of Management*, *37*(3), 709–743. doi:10.1177/0149206310365001

Black, J., & Mendenhall, M. (1990). Cross-Cultural Training Effectiveness: A Review and a Theoretical Framework for Future Research. *Academy of Management Review*, *15*, 113–136.

Broadbridge, A., & Simpson, R. (2011). 25 Years On: Reflecting on the Past and Looking to the Future in Gender and Management Research. *British Journal of Management*, *22*(3), 470–483. doi:10.1111/j.1467-8551.2011.00758.x

Campbell, K., & Vera, A. M. (2007). Gender Diversity in the Boardroom and Firm Financial Performance. *Journal of Business Ethics*. doi:10.100710551-007-9630-y

Childs, J. T. (2005). *Workplace Diversity: A global HR topic that has arrived in 'The Future of Human Resource Management* (M. Losey, S. Meisinger, & D. Ulrich, Eds.). Society for Human Resource Management.

Cox, T. H. Jr, & Blake, S. (1991). Managing Cultural Diversity: Implications for Organizational Competitiveness. *The Academy of Management Executive*, *5*(3), 45–56. doi:10.5465/AME.1991.4274465

Cumming, D., Leung, T. Y., & Rui, O. (2015). Gender Diversity and Securities Fraud. *Academy of Management Journal*, *58*(5), 1572–1593. doi:10.5465/amj.2013.0750

Cunningham, G. B. (2009). The Moderating Effect of Diversity Strategy on the Relationship between Racial Diversity and Organizational Performance. *Journal of Applied Social Psychology*, *39*(6), 1445–1460. doi:10.1111/j.1559-1816.2009.00490.x

Curtis, E. F., & Dreachslin, J. L. (2008). Diversity Management Interventions and Organizational Performance: A Synthesis of Current Literature. *Human Resource Development Review*, *7*(1), 107–136. doi:10.1177/1534484307311700

Dwyer, S., Richard, O. C., & Chadwick, K. (2003). Gender diversity in management and firm's performance: The influence of growth orientation and organizational culture. *Journal of Business Research*, *56*(12), 1009–1019. doi:10.1016/S0148-2963(01)00329-0

Embry, A., Padgett, M. Y., & Caldwell, C. B. (2008). Can Leaders Step Outside of the Gender Box? An Examination of Leadership and Gender Role Stereotypes. *Journal of Leadership & Organizational Studies*, *15*(1), 30–45. doi:10.1177/1548051808318412

Forsythe, J. (March 28, 2004). Winning with Diversity. *New York Times Magazine*, 65-72.

Francoeur, C., Labelle, R., & Desgagne, B. S. (2007). Gender Diversity in Corporate Governance and Top Management. *Journal of Business Ethics*, *81*(1), 83–95. doi:10.100710551-007-9482-5

Harris, R. (2001, May). The Illusion of Inclusion. *CFO,* 42-50.

Impact of Diversity Initiatives on the Bottom Line. A SHRM Survey of the Fortune 1000. (June 3, 2001). *Fortune*. Retrieved from http://www.fortune.com/sections

Lennie Copeland, L. (1988, June). Valuing Diversity, Part I: Making the Most of Cultural Differences at the Workplace. *Personnel*, 52–60.

Milliken, F. J., & Martins, L. I. (1996). Searching for Common Threads: Understanding the Multiple Effects of Diversity in Organizational Groups. *Academy of Management Review*, *21*(2), 402–433.

Nishii, L. H. (2013). The Benefits of Climate for Inclusion for Gender-Diverse Groups. *Academy of Management Journal*, *56*(6), 1754–1774. doi:10.5465/amj.2009.0823

Ollapally, A., & Bhatnagar, J. (2009). The Holistic Approach to Diversity Management: HR Implications. *Indian Journal of Industrial Relations*, *44*(3), 454–472.

Olsen, J. E., & Martins, L. L. (2012). Understanding organizational diversity management programs: A theoretical framework and directions for future research. *Journal of Organizational Behavior*, *33*(8), 1168–1187. doi:10.1002/job.1792

Podsiadlowski, A., Groschke, D., Kogler, M., Springer, C., & Zee, K. (2013). Managing a culturally diverse workforce: Diversity perspectives in organizations. *International Journal of Intercultural Relations*, *37*(2), 159–175. doi:10.1016/j. ijintrel.2012.09.001

Powell, G. N., Butterfield, D. A., & Parent, J. D. (2002). Gender and Managerial Stereotypes: Have the Times Changed? *Journal of Management*, *28*(2), 177–193. doi:10.1177/014920630202800203

Ragins, B. (1989). Barriers to Mentoring: The Female Manager's Dilemma. *Human Relations*, *42*(1), 1–22. doi:10.1177/001872678904200101Ragins, B. R., Townsend, B., & Mattis, M. (1998). Gender Gap in the Executive Suite. *The Academy of Management Executive*, *12*(1), 28–42.

Rice, F. (1994, August 8). How to Make Diversity Pay. *Fortune*, 78-86.

Roberson, Q. M. (2006). Disentangling the Meanings of Diversity and Inclusion in Organizations. *Group & Organization Management*, *31*(2), 212–236. doi:10.1177/1059601104273064

Shore, L. M., Randel, A. E., Chung, B. G., Dean, M. A., Ehrhart, K. H., & Singh, G. (2011). Inclusion and Diversity in Work Groups: A Review and Model for Future Research. *Journal of Management*, *37*(4), 1262–1289. doi:10.1177/0149206310385943

Smith, N., Smith, V., & Verner, M. (2006). Do women in top management affect firm performance? A panel study of 2500 Danish firms. *International Journal of Productivity and Performance Management*, *55*(7), 569–593. doi:10.1108/17410400610702160

Sujansky, J. (2004, February). Lead a Multi-Generational Workforce. *The Business Journal of Tri-Cities*, 21-23.

Survey results reported in "Diversity Initiatives Shown to Be Critical to Job Seekers". (2003, September 14). *The New York Times Magazine,* 100.

Tatli, A. (2011). A Multi-layered Exploration of the Diversity Management Field: Diversity Discourses, Practices and Practitioners in the UK. *British Journal of Management*, *22*(2), 238–253. doi:10.1111/j.1467-8551.2010.00730.x

Tatli, A., & Ozbilgin, M. F. (2012). An Emic Approach to Intersectional Study of Diversity at Work: A Bourdieuan Framing. *International Journal of Management Reviews*, *14*(2), 180–200. doi:10.1111/j.1468-2370.2011.00326.x

Towers Perrin and Hudson Institute. (1990). *Workforce 2000: Competing in a Seller' Market*. Valhalla, NY: Towers Perrin.

Wellington, S., Brumit Kropf, M., & Gerkovich, P. R. (2003, June). What's Holding Women Back? *Harvard Business Review*, 18–19.

APPENDIX

Figure 1. A Conceptual model of diversity and diversity management in terms of its antecedents and consequences

A Conceptual Model of **Diversity and Diversity Management** in terms of its Antecedents and Consequences

Moderating Variables

Diversity strategy
Firms Strategic Orientation
Organizational Culture

Antecedents   **Consequences**

Surface-Level Diversity
Age, Gender, Sex, Sexual
Orientation, Race,

Deep Level Diversity

Personality, attitude,
values

**Diversity Management
Interventions**

- Training,
- Education,
- Mentoring, and
- OD interventions

Outcomes
Individual level (attitude
towards multicultural change
initiative, increased
awareness)

Group level (group cohesion,
team performance, improved
creativity and decision
making, team conflict)

Organizational level
(Firm's performance, firms

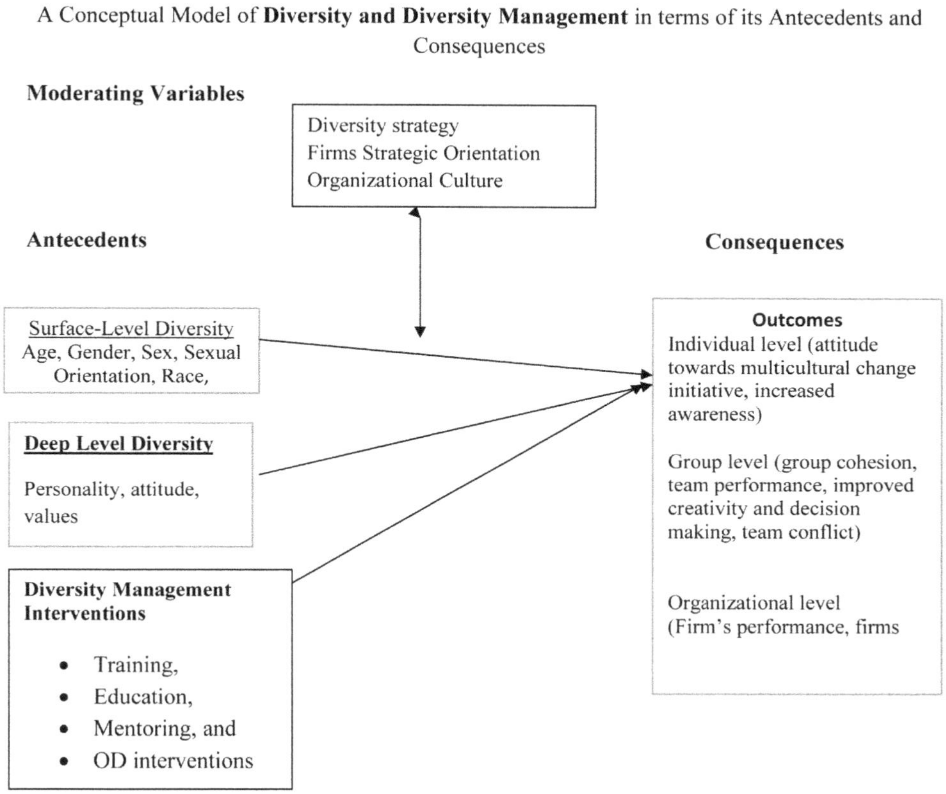

Chapter 5
Challenging the Theoretical Lenses of Internationalization:
A Case Study Analysis

Liliana Sofia Pinto
University of Aveiro, Portugal

Maria Manuel Ribeiro
University of Aveiro, Portugal

António Carrizo Moreira
University of Aveiro, Portugal

ABSTRACT

Internationalization involves an active behavior to compete in international markets. Several theories, as well as several entry modes, have been developed to explain why and how firms compete internationally. Nevertheless, the internationalization process is difficult to implement as it involves not only historical reasons, as well as traditional strategies that sometimes are usually not questioned by the firm. This chapter aims to depict a case study in which a firm is trying to deploy an opportunity-driven internationalization, shifting its traditional modus operandi. The firm is analyzed based on several theories, namely the Uppsala model, the network-based theory, the born globals and the born again globals, and it is possible to conclude that despite its more than 80 years of existence, neither of the four theories can be properly used to explain the firm's international behavior. Moreover, to embrace international challenges, the firm needs to reposition its traditional business behavior.

DOI: 10.4018/978-1-5225-5360-1.ch005

INTRODUCTION

Internationalization is very important for firms across the world. It is important for a wide range of firms, including small and medium-sized firms (SMEs) as internationalization is a dynamic process that is the result of the exploitation of competitive advantages (Stanisauskaite & Kock, 2016).

The globalization of markets and production, underpinned by a pervasive technological change, has made the business world a common "battle ground" for all companies whether large, medium or small. On the other hand, international competition is ever present even for firms competing in their "local" markets (Ribau, Moreira, & Raposo, 2015). As such, internationalization is ever present in basically all contemporary business activities. However, if some companies choose not to export, therefore not competing in international markets, others fail to compete abroad as a result of their lack of competitive advantages (Stanisauskaite & Kock, 2016).

Internationalization is a strategy aiming at expanding and creating an integrated network of contacts and partners when firms seek to expand to new markets, despite the firms' risk embarking on international ventures (Dominguez, 2016). Although the less risky mode of entry in international markets, exporting can be very difficult as it is a dynamic and complex process separating buyers and sellers in international markets. As such, companies need to be aware of the international business context. However, non-exporting companies seek challenging objectives, such as export-led sales growth, growth output and increased profits from foreign markets. For that they need to be tuned to increase their competitive advantage.

According to Welch and Luostarinen (1988), internationalization refers to the process of increasing involvement in international activities and is related to how the firm explores international markets. Many studies analyze the internationalization process based on two main strands: the Uppsala model, that advocates an evolutionary, sequential and linear model with growing international involvement (Ribau et al., 2015); and the network-based view of the firm (Håkansson & Snehota, 2006), based on a relational-based perspective among market players.

However, those theories of internationalization do not fully disclose the internationalization of a firm, especially from an entrepreneurial perspective based on a combination of innovative and risky behaviors at cross border level (McDougall & Oviatt, 2000). As such, *born global* and *born again global* firms are typologies that have been put forward to explain why firms internationalize rapidly or suddenly, based on entrepreneurial behaviors empowered by powerful, open minded entrepreneurs/ managers, guided by the generation of new and innovative ideas, with riskier decisions and able to detect unique opportunities at an international level. This leads to the creation of a much more motivating, attractive and ambitious environment inside the company (Bell, McNaughton, & Young, 2001).

In the business context, the process of internationalization might be considered an entrepreneurial act as firms move away from its comfort zone (home market) adapting their strategy to the new market conditions. The search for competitive advantages has traditionally pushed firms to embrace opportunities in foreign markets. However, traditional theories explaining the internationalization process depict certain specificities, but sometimes fail to capture the dynamic changes certain firms go through. As such, not only certain theories fail to explain how firms internationalize, but also certain firms do not fit within what theories postulate.

Based on a case study that analyzes a 70-year old Portuguese firm that went through difficult times and decided to turnaround their internal operations and business model and is striving to internationalize their activities so that growth and profitability will not fade away, the objective of this chapter is to examine and debate the internationalization process from a historical perspective and debate the intricacies of the following main internationalization theories: the Uppsala perspective; the network-based view of the firm; the *born global* and *born again global* theories. The aim is to confront these four theories in order to address the particularities of the firm within the four theoretical grounds.

The case study depicts the way the firm is analyzing new market entry opportunities abroad, based on the firm's strategy to deploy their new services to international markets, which is a very significant advance for this company. However, when one analyzes the competitive behavior of the firm one realizes that, in order to embrace the new strategy, the firm left behind its passive position in international markets deploying an active, risk-taking behavior, analyzing opportunities and weighting risks in a much more entrepreneurial way. Accordingly, the aim of this chapter is to examine the firm from a business historical perspective and the internationalization process involving an opportunity-driven perspective. In order to achieve the above-mentioned goals several theories about internationalization are presented and discussed throughout this chapter.

The document is structured in three main parts. The first part addresses the importance of internationalization, following an entrepreneurial, opportunity-seeking perspective. For that, a literature review addresses internationalization theories from four different perspectives: Uppsala model, the network-based approach, the born globals and the born again globals. The second part presents the case study of a small and medium-sized firm – that despite its long successful behavior in the Portuguese market it has been quite passive on international grounds –, the selection and assessment market entry process and how the firm is trying to overcome the "stuck-in-the-middle" positioning it has been facing over time and to rely in the provision of high-end services to position the firm as a reliable international partner. Finally, the third part of the chapter discusses and concludes the main benefits of the entrepreneurial process *vis-à-vis* with more traditional internationalization perspectives and presents some future research direction.

INTERNALIZATION THEORIES

Uppsala Model

The Uppsala model is essentially based on two articles by Johanson and Wiedersheim-Paul (1975) and Johanson and Vahlne (1977). Afterwards they were reviewed by Johanson and Vahlne (1990, 2009) and Vahlne and Nordström (1993). Moreover, since the first article published, the literature on the internationalization process has been growing (Ribau et al., 2015, Ribau et al., 2017). The Uppsala model deals with the acquisition of knowledge, namely with learning, i.e., how organizations learn and how their learning affects their progressive investment behavior in international markets. This model is based on four fundamental concepts, namely market knowledge, market commitment, commitment decisions and current activities (Forsgren, 2002).

This model is based on three basic assumptions (Forsgren, 2002). First, the companies' lack of knowledge regarding external markets is a serious obstacle for companies to embrace international activities; however, this knowledge can be acquired. Second, the decision and the implementation of investments abroad are made incrementally, as a result of the uncertainties of international markets. Finally, the third concerns knowledge that is highly dependent on individuals and therefore difficult to transfer to other contexts and individuals. Moreover, to explain the company internationalization, the concept of psychic distance was put forward to explain how companies would enter first close, cultural familiar markets, and afterwards new, distant and culturally different markets, as occurs for example between Czech and German firms (Novotná, Martins, & Moreira, 2017).

According to what is exposed above, the Uppsala model argues that a company's knowledge and market commitment determine the company's path throughout the stages of internationalization (Geldres-Weiss et al., 2016). As far as knowledge is concerned, companies enter external markets after acquiring the necessary knowledge to generate new opportunities and reduce uncertainty. Moreover, the market commitment can be related to the amount of resources that a company allocates to that market (Geldres-Weiss et al., 2016).

According to Ribau et al. (2015), in the Uppsala stage model, the company gradually increases its international participation, through information and experience. In summary, the model basically includes the following steps:

1. Non-regular exports;
2. Exports through independent representatives (agents or distributors);
3. The establishment of a sales branch abroad;
4. The establishment of production / manufacturing units abroad.

Geldres-Weiss et al. (2016) and Johanson and Vahlne (2009) state that the Uppsala model emphasizes the possibility of acquiring and internalizing knowledge dynamically through interactions with foreign partners. This is an adaptation to the initial model, as Johanson and Vahlne (2009) argued that when the model was presented there was a rather rudimentary understanding of the complexities that could explain internationalization difficulties. In addition, further research on international marketing and procurement has given a different perspective on the international inter-organizational network faced by companies. Therefore, Johanson and Vahlne (2009) present two conclusions: the first is that markets are networks of relationships in which companies are linked together in several complex patterns; the second is that relationships contribute to learning and to build trust and commitment.

Complementing the above-mentioned vision, some researchers argue that this model is static as it does not explain or predict the dynamic patterns of the companies' internationalization process. In addition, this and other static models do not explain how and when internationalization processes begin, as they only focus on what drives companies' activities in an internationalization process already underway (Ribau et al., 2015). As a result, stage models have a limited explanatory power to explain the behavior of certain firms, hence the emergence of new theory such as the Born Globals (Ribau et al., 2015).

According to Forsgren (2002), the Uppsala model is about how organizations learn and the impact of learning on organizational behavior. However, there may be different paths and "shortcuts" to gaining knowledge, such as acquiring other companies or hiring employees with the necessary international knowledge, which complements the concept of organizational learning (Forsgren, 2002).

Summarizing, the Uppsala model is one of the most important and studied theories explaining internationalization. This theory defends that the companies' internationalization process is carried out in stages, from non-regular exporter to the establishment of companies abroad. However, not all companies internationalize following strictly these steps. As a result, this theory was subject to criticisms as was complemented by the networked-based approach.

Networked-Based Model

Personal contacts and social interactions play a very important role in the development of international markets (Welch & Luostarinen, 1988), since it is important to establish international networks that include buyers and sellers from abroad. These networks are at the basis of effective communication (Welch & Luostarinen, 1988).

Networks are usually defined as sets of inter-organizational exchange relationships (Franco, Mainardes, & Martins, 2011; Popp et al., 2014). The inter-organizational connection is the core of the business network approach, since it is through the company's commitment that they gradually expand the connections to the networks (Franco et al., 2011; Popp et al., 2014).

According to Ribau et al. (2015), the network-based approach is considered an expansion of the Uppsala model and describes industrial markets as business networks, based on the resource dependence theory. They also point out that the basic assumption of the network-based approach defends that actors (companies) depend on resources controlled by other companies, since access to resources and the construction of relationships represent the process of resource consumption. In short, since the company's basic objective is to survive, internationalization is a way to increase the likelihood of short- and long-term survival (Ribau et al., 2015).

It is important to refer that the creation of networks can be a very demanding, time-consuming process, as there are sometimes large differences between the seller and the buyer, which indicates that it is important to invest in a knowledge-based relationship to overcome the lack of knowledge on both sides. This enables the overcoming of the barriers that exist at both cultural and physical distance levels (Welch & Luostarinen, 1988). As such, it is not unexpected to witness that buyers prefer local suppliers because they end up being more "familiar", which make them feel more secure. However, overcoming the liability of newness is part of the first phases companies must go through, in order for the gap between sellers and buyers diminish over time. As such the growth of the company is expected to grow with a more diversified experience, with more contacts abroad and with greater cultural exposure, which ultimately deepen inter-organizational relationships, strengthening commitment (Welch & Luostarinen, 1988).

In addition to promote growth, these inter-organizational networks also end up being extended to international partners (Moreira, 2007; Moreira, & Alves, 2016; Moreira, & Silva, 2015). These market "fluctuations" are driven by innovation-based international activities (Törnroos, 2002). The ARA (Actors-Resources-Activities) model is used to explain how actors behave, and what resources are deployed to embrace different activities (Törnroos, 2002), forming an inter-organizational network in which it is profitable and safe for all companies to cooperate and use their diverse skills, capabilities, and knowledge. When actors create, develop, combine or exchange resources they perform their activities in international markets (Håkansson & Snehota, 2006), they expand the Uppsala model to address how companies resort to the network theory of internationalization.

The company's position in a network turns out to be a key factor in maintaining and developing the company's objectives, both in terms of the company's degree of internationalization and in terms of the level of internationalization of the market (Axelsson & Johanson, 1992; Carvalheira & Moreira, 2016; Törnroos, 2002).

Johanson and Mattsson (1988) put forward the following typology to address how companies are influenced by the level of internationalization of both the market and the company: the *Early Starter*, the *Late Starter*, the *Lonely International* and the *International among Others*.

Early starters have few, or even insignificant, network relationships with foreign companies. As they have very limited knowledge of international business, these companies use local agents or even other companies that have international business experience so they can learn and start their operations abroad gradually.

Lonely internationals depict companies in already highly internationalized markets, although with a low level of internationalization. These companies have experience and know how to operate in international markets. These companies need to adjust their differences to the international markets, learn as they enter other networks and, in order to able to expand their networks and operations. It should be noted that these lonely internationals are better known for being "promoters" of the international expansion of their counterparts in the network, as they tend to be quite independent of the other agents of the network.

Late starters are companies that have or are looking for international networks to be able to start their activities at an international level. Relationships in international markets may turn out to be important to facilitate entering international markets. Investments in developing important capabilities to conquer the domestic market can be seen as assets that can be used when late starters move abroad.

International among others are highly internationalized companies in international contexts. In these cases, the extension of their networks or the entry into international networks only means a gradual change in their international position. These companies have the capability to use their own networks to be able to join other networks if they feel it is necessary.

In business to business markets, companies are involved in the production, distribution, and use of goods and services (Johanson & Mattsson, 1987). There is a division of labor across the network, which means that firms become dependent on one another, so their activities have to be well coordinated. This coordination is not carried out through a central plan or organizational hierarchy. It occurs, rather, through an inter-organizational interaction among companies of the network (Geiger, Dost, Schönhoff, & Kleinaltenkamp, 2015; Kleinaltenkamp, Rudolph, & Claßen,

2012). It should be noted that there is a need for adjustments between interdependent firms as to the quantity and quality of the goods and services exchanged and also the timing of such exchanges (Geiger et al., 2015; Johanson & Mattsson, 1987; Kleinaltenkamp et al., 2012).

Networks provide opportunities for smaller companies to internationalize (Carvalheira & Moreira, 2016; Dana, 2001). Large companies encourage skilled workers to leave their jobs, in order to set up their own businesses, aiming at signing business contracts from their former employers (Dana, 2001). These emerging small businesses are gaining platforms for growth and internationalization through those business relationships with large companies (Dana, 2001). However, these new ventures remain free to create the relationships they find most convenient, even though large companies give them advice on how to get started. When smaller companies connect with larger scale companies, they are able to get their products / services to international markets faster, and at lower costs, because smaller companies feel they can count on larger companies to facilitate their internationalization activities (Dana, 2001; Moreira, 2007; Moreira & Silva, 2015).

The capability to embrace new opportunities abroad is not limited to large companies (Dana, 2001, Moreira, 2007, Carvalheira & Moreira, 2016). According to Dana (2001), the recent expansion of markets has not been associated with an expanded role for large companies. The role of small companies is quite varied in international markets (Ribau et al., 2017). Clearly, there is a major change in international business activities: traditionally, large companies opted for setting up branch offices abroad as the preferred means of internationalization, because of the company's desire to remain independent and to maximize control of its own activities. However, the recent evolution of networking activities suggests that companies are looking for balanced, symbiotic interdependent relationships based on dynamic complementarities between firms (Dana, 2001; Franco et al., 2011).

Summarizing, the network-based approach is based on the industrial networks theory, which states that firms evolve on the basis of established relationships (Ribau et al., 2015). As such, companies stablish long-term relationships that go well beyond the transaction-based perspective (Carvalheira & Moreira, 2016; Ribau et al., 2015). Clearly, the company's home network and its relationships can be a starting point for the company's internationalization. When entering new international markets, companies have the opportunity to develop new relationships that give them access to broader markets in other countries (Ribau et al., 2015). Therefore, internationalization is understood as a process led by inter-organizational relationships that co-ordinate the evolution of the company's network in international markets (Ribau et al., 2015). Moreover, the availability of market information from network partners can be a potential source of competitive advantage for the company's internationalization through the sharing of information, support and assistance (Carvalheira & Moreira, 2016; Moreira & Silva, 2015; Ribau et al., 2015).

Born Globals

The contemporary world of international business is characterized by globalization, which is related to the dissipation of different obstacles of international business activities (Dicken, 2015). This notion of globalization has been popularized as the lack of barriers to trade among nations, through free trade agreements throughout the world and among nation states (Törnroos, 2002), giving rise to investment opportunities rapidly materialized (Dicken, 2015).

According to Törnroos (2002), both temporal and spatial processes can be reduced and compressed in the "here and now" perspective. An example of this is the global financial market, as the acceleration of the speed of information, together with the development of Information and Communication Technologies (ICT) and the possibility of information exchange in real time, makes everything faster and reaches more people and places in the world (Törnroos, 2002). These changes in the economic context gave rise to a set of strategies that allowed both large multinationals and small companies to be present in international markets (Ribau et al., 2015, 2017; Covielo, 2015).

Globalization has given rise not only to a global geographic market reach, but also to a global competition for global trade and investment (Zander, McDougall-Covin, & Rose, 2015).

Globalization has given rise to new competitive positions, where born globals (BG) and International New Ventures (INV) stand out as examples of internationalization, based on rapid internationalization processes where innovation plays a fundamental role in the early stages of the firm's internationalization process (Ribau et al., 2015). The number of companies that conduct international business since its inception are growing significantly throughout the world (Weerawardena et al., 2007; Covielo, 2015).

BGs are companies that expand to international markets, taking advantage of both new global contextual conditions and new needs, based on rapid internationalization approaches (Ribau et al., 2015). It is the rapid internationalization processes that allow questioning the classical behavioral theories, given the emergence of new typologies such as INV, *High Technology Start-Ups*, *Infant Multinationals*, *BG* and *Born Again Globals* (Ribau et al., 2015). These new phenomena, which marked the beginning of the 21st century, have been studied by researchers looking for new theories to describe the internationalization of companies (with special attention to SMEs), trying to circumscribe the ineffectiveness of the traditional theories of internationalization. However, the research that has been developed so far does not seem to be enough to anchor a new consensual theory about the definition of new internationalization phenomena (Ribau et al., 2015). Despite the scarce financial and human resources that characterize most SMEs, born globals have been heavily involved in international business very early on. In short, BGs are business organizations that, from the outset, seek competitive advantages from the use of resources and the sale of products in several countries (Weerawardena et al., 2007; Covielo, 2015).

Born globals have as main characteristics: a global vision from the beginning of their business activity; their managers have international experience prior to the internationalization of the company (making them aware of international opportunities); access to international networks; strong technological base with strong capabilities (Ribau et al., 2015). However, as the technology of the BGs becomes obsolete, they need to exploit its advantages, causing BGs to rapidly develop international activities (Ribau et al., 2015).

Born globals can be considered as very recent companies, as a result of the consequences of the opening up of international markets. On the other hand, the use of emerging technologies and small-scale production systems has brought profound changes to the traditional way of competing. The fact that new production systems support the manufacture of complex, non-standard parts and components relatively easily enables smaller firms to be catapulted to an international competitive base previously only achieved by large multinationals (Knight & Cavusgil, 1996).

Born globals are young, entrepreneurial companies with a strong culture of innovation and a strong tendency to internationalize, eventually achieving a sustainable performance in foreign markets (Knight & Cavusgil, 2004). In fact, as mentioned earlier, BGs may be characterized by a shortage of both financial and human resources, and may also lack equipment and other physical resources. However, they are rich in their assets of key intangible skills based on knowledge of foreign markets, since the very beginning of their international evolution. It should be noted that BGs have a great ability to acquire knowledge, which is a key success factor for achieving superior international performance among entrepreneurial companies, based on their R&D capabilities and on knowledge of international markets they are able to internalize (Knight & Cavusgil, 2004). The capacity to consistently acquire the capabilities the company needs to compete in a variety of markets and to support international expansion is what gives BGs a competitive edge (Knight & Cavusgil, 2004).

According to Weerawardena et al. (2007), the combination of the dynamic capabilities perspective of competitive strategy with the theory of organizational learning is important. The process of having the capacity to build a new global company is present among entrepreneurs / owners / managers who have a global mindset, previous international experience and a learning orientation (Weerawardena et al., 2007). Clearly, they build and nurture the "distinctive capabilities of market-focused learning, internally focused learning and networking capabilities which enable the small, innovative, international new venture to develop leading-edge knowledge intensive products" (Weerawardena et al., 2007, 298). As a consequence, it is the development of superior marketing capabilities that facilitates these combined capabilities to produce rapid internationalization and, possibly, superior performance when entering international markets (Weerawardena et al., 2007).

Born globals are examples of successful international SMEs. In short, these firms challenge conventional theories of internationalization and the belief that strategic choices of small firms are limited because of the scarcity of their resources, rapidly entering international markets (Weerawardena et al., 2007).

In conclusion, the debate about BGs is still in its infancy and research on this topic is still ongoing (Cesinger, Danko, & Bouncken, 2012). There is little research on the factors that give rise to rapid internationalization (Weerawardena et al., 2007). So this is a key area for possible future research.

Born Again Globals

Although BGs and international new ventures have been extensively used to explain international activities, the traditional process model of internationalization is considered as one of the most influential theories explaining firms' internationalization (Coviello and McAuley, 1999; Ribau et al., 2017). They clearly differ from each other as in the Uppsala model internationalization is perceived as an incremental process, while born globals, based on the entrepreneurship theory, are considered rapid internationalizers (Oviatt & McDougall, 1994; Bell, McNaughton, & Young, 2001).

Knowledge is considered a competitive weapon in those two types of models of internationalization. In the Uppsala model knowledge about international markets enables the company to penetrate psychic and geographically distant markets. In turn, knowledge of international markets enables to explore the dynamics of an increasingly global market environment (Bell et al., 2001), which allows INVs and BGs to internationalize rapidly. This thought led to the study of another type of companies, the *born again globals*, which are established in their internal markets that apparently do not have a strong motivation to internationalize (Bell et al., 2001).

The literature on born again globals, that are different from BGs, presents the emergence of a new phenomenon, which is still little explored, because born again globals adopt a different trajectory: instead of gradually penetrating the markets with very close psychic distance to their home market, represented by low risk (Schueffel et al., 2014), they embrace this new international venture in a more spontaneous, albeit late, way. Bell et al. (2001) have classified born again globals as the combination of process theory and INV theory, since they present characteristics of both theories.

Born again globals are business organizations that do not seek to obtain a significant competitive advantage using their resources to compete essentially in the domestic market, as opposed to BGs that seek rapid internationalization right after their inception (Schueffel et al., 2014). It is only after a strategic change that born again globals seek to gain a competitive advantage of the use of their resources and product sales in various countries (Schueffel et al., 2014).

The internationalization of born again globals are often triggered by certain "critical incidents", and domestic, foreign, or network partners may exert some influence on the company that ultimately has to adjust its internationalization activities significantly (Schueffel et al., 2014). The most common critical incident in these cases is related to the change of ownership or management and / or administration of the company, thus triggering the internationalization process, which may not be linear, incremental or unidirectional (Schueffel et al., 2014).

Although born again globals have focused on domestic markets in their early years, it does not mean that they cannot begin the path of rapid and dedicated internationalization. Born again globals can be equally well-structured, proactive and flexible in their modes of entry into international markets (Schueffel et al., 2014). An interesting example of this phenomenon refers to the born again globals that are able to decrypt international opportunities, however, they are prevented from exploiting them because of lack of resources (Bell et al., 2001).

In conclusion, born again globals are characterized as being very focused on the domestic market and suddenly being able to radically change their strategic focus in order to increase their sales volume. They differ from both traditional companies and BGs, since they omit some internationalization stages and present a different trajectory from BGs.

CASE STUDY

The aim of this section is to present the case study of ALFA, which by confidentiality reasons cannot be disclosed, explaining ALFA's history, as well as ALFA's international business history.

ALFA was founded in 1935. During its more than 80 years ALFA has gone through several phases. Initially, its business area was the wood sawing band. Later on, in 1939/1945, ALFA embraced a new business area – special steels – starting a partnership with Uddeholm and becoming its exclusive representative in Portugal.

In 1950s, ALFA began the provision of heat treatments services complementing the previous activity. In 1954 ALFA was renamed and opened company branches in Porto, Lisbon, Águeda, Marinha Grande, Portugal and Luanda, Angola. Some of these branches do not currently exist for reasons which will be explained later in this chapter. In 1958, the first perforated shelf bracket was produced in Portugal, under license from Dexion (another ALFA's partnership).

With its increasing development, in 1962, ALFA decided to create a new industrial unit in Ovar, Portugal, where the activities of cold-rolled steel and cold-drawn steel would be developed. In the 1970s, ALFA began to invest in its production capacity and built a new warehouse linked to the manufacturing of special steel.

At the end of the 1980s ALFA renewed the heat treatment unit and started using the vacuum heat treatment technology. In 1997, ALFA started with machining services, namely the assembly machines and straightening presses. In 2002, ALFA obtained the ISO 9001: 2000.

More recently, the company started the provision of oxy cutting service and the product range was expanded with the commercialization of stainless steels, with the development of brass-based products and with the development of machining services – controlled material-removal process and drilling of water. Finally, ALFA started a brand new unit producing anti-wear steels and high elastic limit steels.

In 2014, another machining service is integrated in this company: the milling custom machined parts. In 2017, ALFA's headquarters is relocated in Ovar and there are now branches in Braga, Lisbon, Marinha Grande, Águeda and Porto. However, the branches are considered just logistical platforms. In addition to that, the company currently has 223 employees and the company's turnover is now around 75 million euros.

Clearly, ALFA has been developing throughout its 80 years. ALL its business areas have been addressing and integrating innovation in order to keep abreast of technological knowledge. ALFA can be considered a market leader in Portugal with partners from all over the world. As the company's largest partner is Uddholm, as previously mentioned, ALFA has been a unique reference in Portugal for more than 50 years. Its partnership with the Swedish company drives important competitive advantage based on knowledge acquisition that otherwise would have been difficult to generate internally.

As can be seen in Figure 1, ALFA offers a variety of services. Furthermore, ALFA commercializes products such as:

- Special steels and alloys;
- Rapid steels, steels for molds, steels for cold or hot working tools, aluminum alloys, technical plastics, among others;
- Cutting tools: Milling and turning tools, drilling and boring tools, threading tools, saws, fastening systems.

Figure 1. Services provided by ALFA

ALFA's Internationalization

This subsection analyzes ALFA's internationalization.

Almost all the products that ALFA manufactures end up in international markets. However, direct exports reach only 2%, to nearby Galicia, Spain. Although indirect exports are important, ALFA is aware that to increase added value to final clients, it is important to transform steel internally and to exploit competitive advantage with their resources.

In the past, ALFA apart from its exports to Spain, has exported to Brazil as a response to a Portuguese major client with an affiliate in Brazil. However, as the client has headquarters in Portugal, the relationship was directly carried out afterwards with the headquarters in Portugal and not with the affiliate in Brazil. As a result, ALFA resorts to indirect exports to Brazil, as well as to several other markets.

One of the reasons pointed out by ALFA for having such a residual (2%) percentage of exports, two answers were given: firstly, that steel, as a heavy material, is cheap to transport abroad, which may be quite expensive as a commodity; secondly, ALFA has signed contracts with several international partners, like Uddholm for example, representing them in the Portuguese market. Moreover, those deals give ALFA a competitive edge in the Portuguese market, however, hinder ALFA's strategy to internationalize exporting steel to other markets. As such, ALFA decided to embrace an added-value service-based strategy to serve international markets in order to circumvent the possibility to export raw steel.

As previously mentioned, ALFA had already had a branch in Luanda, Angola, at an earlier stage of its internationalization path. However, before setting up the branch, ALFA has already exported products to Angola. ALFA choose this market because it was a Portuguese colony and because they were dedicated to the commercialization of machetes, which currently represent only 10% of the total sales volume in Angola (which previously represented 100% of the business). As a result of the economic turmoil in Portugal and Angola, this branch is no longer active.

ALFA's strategy is changing. The company is changing its business model as aims to provide added-value services transforming steel and supplying directly to international clients/markets (Spain, England, Italy, Germany and France), where it seeks to enter in international value chains to take the most of international contacts. This is expected to change the international competitive landscape and is expected to provide a more international market orientation. In order to implement this change, ALFA is seeking to expand its facilities, to be able to increase competitiveness and profitability. As such, the company is seeking to abandon an indirect internationalization strategy and to embrace in an active one.

In order to expand its international market penetration, ALFA has started to negotiate and hire representatives, mimicking the strategy it has deployed in Galicia, Spain. This market penetration strategy is currently going through a market test phase. The feasibility and outcome of this process is still under research.

Three main factors led ALFA to seek the international markets:

- Firstly, the success of spot exports to Brazil, which clearly demonstrated that ALFA has a competitive edge, albeit unexploited in international markets;
- Secondly, the fact that they are heavily investing in the development of the company infrastructure and in brand new technology (equipment and machinery). As the investment needs to generate above average returns, ALFA considered that the exploitation of international markets could be potentially interesting, instead of relaying in indirect exports;
- Thirdly, the fact that ALFA needs to grow in order not to stagnate and be able to take on very strong competition. Clearly, the Portuguese market is not large enough for ALFA to grow. As such, internationalization is an important issue as the firm is willing to compete (directly) on international grounds.

It is clear that ALFA has already international experience, albeit a very passive one. However, ALFA's strategy has traditionally aimed at the domestic market, jeopardizing its market position in far-flung markets. This is perhaps a result of a very conservative strategy, as well as a result of the contract signed with Uddeholm and Dexion, among others. However, ALFA realized that can explore international markets without jeopardizing their contract as long as it is able to add value to steel. Based on its domestic experience, ALFA realized that it is possible to capitalize its competences in international markets and not be so dependent on a domestic saturated market.

DISCUSSION

The search for competitive advantage drives the strategy among all companies. In the quest for a new competitive behavior, ALFA has been changing its strategy, abandoning a passive behavior and taking on active, risk taking posture to embrace new business opportunities. However, when analyzing the firm through theoretical lens, there is hardly any fit between internationalization theories and ALFA's strategic behavior, as can be observed in Table 1.

ALFA has traditionally been involved in the commercialization of commodities, which normally shrinks profit margins as they are subject to international market fluctuations. As it normally commercializes raw material, its price is determined by the fluctuations of the supply and demand of international markets. In addition, ALFA has been traditionally dependent on its biggest partner (supplier of steel): Uddholm.

After exploring the Portuguese market, and overcoming all the intricacies of entering foreign markets, namely to Brazil and Angola, one can argue that ALFA began its internationalization process following the Uppsala model, i.e. based on progressive steps, which eventually ended up not succeeding as originally predicted. As knowledge is an important part of the Uppsala stage-based model, one can argue that ALFA has failed in taking advantage of the necessary knowledge to proceed with its internationalization process to other distant markets, taking advantage of its domestic competitive position.

It is clear that ALFA is not a BG at all. Nevertheless, it would have been almost impossible, based on the year it was set up. However, its 2% of sales in international markets gives a clear picture how passive the firm has behaved on international business grounds.

Based on its passive international behavior, ALFA realized it had to start gaining international market share and decided to analyze the relevance of its international contacts and the relationships with international actors through indirect internationalization process. This recalls immediately to the network-based theory. As previously stated, networks play an important role in explaining why and how companies internationalize their operations / activities, and their position in the network is a key factor, both internally and externally, for companies to become interdependent in sharing resources and in overcoming the vulnerabilities they may face.

It is important for a company to be embedded in an international network, in order to exchange and internalize knowledge, maintain stable relationships and perspective the market as a business relationship network. Belonging to these networks gives companies the possibility of increasingly acquiring contacts and being able to embrace active internationalization strategies. However, in this case study, ALFA showed a clear inability to embrace this active outward internationalization process. One possible explanation for this is the fact that ALFA, after signing its partnership with Uddholm was very focused in conquering the domestic market that ignored their possibilities of gaining market share abroad. Moreover, the first strategy deployed by ALFA was to sell raw steel in the domestic market. As such, mimicking this strategy in international markets was doomed as steel is difficult and costly to transport. As such Uddholm ends up exporting the steel and it has a bigger role in the international contact network. Clearly, this is changing nowadays.

One can argue that the network-based approach is perfectly suitable to explain ALFA's position with regards to internationalization. However, it is difficult to explain why it is not as successful as it could have been. The born again global behavior is a possible outcome, yet to be proved by ALFA.

One can argue that ALFA might behave as an early starter or as a late starter. ALFA behaves as an early starter in the sense that the company does not have, as already mentioned, a lot of knowledge about international business, and therefore uses local agents or even other companies that have export experiences, so that ALFA can learn and thus start their international operations more gradually. As a late starter, ALFA uses its networks to be able to start its activities at an international level. These international actors and activities can be very important so that ALFA's entry in international markets can be, in a certain way, smoother.

Finally, if the company really wants to succeed it is important to focus on its competitive advantage to embrace internationalization with a different approach: not behaving as a traditional small and medium-sized firm. For that a new strategic mindset is important. As such, it is not strange that the firm is trying to abandon its commodity transaction-based strategy to embrace a technology-based one, in which the added value provided to the customer makes a difference. For that the company needs to understand that its strategic position in international markets depends not only on their internal capabilities, but also on their willingness to embrace it.

Given this, it is difficult to categorize ALFA, as neither the Uppsala model nor the network-based approach can be easily used to explain ALFA's international behavior. Moreover, neither we can use the born global nor the born again global concepts. Let us see, ALFA did not internationalize gradually, nor installed production facilities

Table 1. Summary table depicting ALFA position

	Main Ideas of Theories	Theoretical Framework of the Company in the Different Theories Analyzed
Uppsala Model	It is based on two articles: Wiedersheim-Paul (1975) and Johanson and Vahlne (1977); This theory deals with the acquisition of knowledge, regarding international markets; Four fundamental concepts: market knowledge; the market commitment; decisions; and current activities; Company's knowledge and market commitment determine the path of the company through the stages of internationalization; Stages of the internationalization process: non-regular exports; independent representatives (agents or distributors); creation of a sales subsidiary abroad; establishment of foreign production / manufacturing units; Static model.	ALFA does not fit the Uppsala model, once it did not manage to internationalize following a progressive, stage-based perspective. ALFA took advantage of the knowledge acquired to achieve a competitive position in the domestic market and in indirectly internationalized (through indirect exports).
Network Theory	Sets of connected exchange relationships; Expansion of the Uppsala Model; Main rationale: companies depend on resources controlled by other companies, since access to resources and the construction of relationships represent the process of resource consumption; Networking is a time-consuming process; Typology of companies in this internationalization model: *early starter*, *lonely international*, *late starter* and *international among others*; In business to business markets, companies are involved in the production, distribution and use of goods and services. There is a network division and an interaction between the companies inserted in the network; Networks provide opportunities for smaller companies to internationalize; Internationalization is a process governed by relationships and the evolution of a company's network.	Based on its international indirect exports, ALFA can be considered a *late starter*. However, based on ALFA's poor reach of international penetration it is an early starter as it has many relationships with its partners. However, ALFA is seeking to change its strategy competing through adding value while avoiding the mere trade of commodities.
Born Globals	Companies that, from the outset, seek competitive advantages from the use of resources and the sale of products in several countries; Technology-based companies; Innovation plays a key role; Global networks; The debate on BGs is still growing and research on this topic is still ongoing. There is little research on the factors leading to rapid internationalization. So this is a key area for possible future research.	ALFA is certainly not a BG, because it has not internationalized early on. However, only in the 1980s the international economic/business context started to experience an open, global environment.
Born Again Globals	Companies that are very focused on the domestic market, but with the objective of increasing their sales volume. They internationalize suddenly; They differ from traditional companies as well as from BGs;	If taking advantage of international opportunities, ALFA could be a born again global, exploiting their competencies and capabilities in foreign markets.

abroad, having concentrated its production in its headquarters in Ovar, Portugal. Therefore, the company did not follow an internationalization process consistent with any traditional model, explained previously. In addition, the company exports only 2% of its production. This situation is depicted in Table 1.

Accordingly, if ALFA is willing to succeed in the strategic change it is deploying, ALFA needs to be aware to establish agreements and secure relationships with other companies. Moreover, ALFA needs to position itself as a technology service provider. The relationship with other companies is extremely important so that ALFA can acquire certain knowledge, giving ALFA more confidence and motivation to evolve in international markets. Finally, the major challenge ALFA has to overcome is to stop behaving as a traditional company focused on the domestic market. If opportunities are meant to be taken, risk taking behavior is important to success.

CONCLUSION

Studies on internationalization and globalization have been fruitful in studying companies and theories. They have also addressed the main forms and strategies that have been used by successful companies in international markets. However, there are companies that despite their long experience in the market still have difficulties in embracing competitive strategies in far-flung markets. Clearly, almost all studies support internationalization, with few studies analyzing less-successful companies in their internationalization process.

A first conclusion that can be drawn from ALFA's case is that exporting may not be easy, since it implies the adequacy of resources to the environment, which apparently ALFA has never achieved.

The ALFA's case study portrays the difficulty of exporting, based on the type of product, and the lack of an adequate strategy on the part of the company. As such, this case portrays an important lesson: companies need to clearly define their strategies to cope with the intricacies of the market. As such, the first challenge ALFA needs to overcome is the abandonment of its commodity transaction-based strategy to embrace an opportunity-based one, in which ALFA can provide added value to their customers, whether in the domestic market or in international markets. Another challenge for the company is to understand that what matters are both the firm's internal capabilities and the willingness to embrace change.

Taking into account the objectives set out in the introduction, this chapter presented the main theories related to the internationalization process, such as the Uppsala model, the network-based model, the born globals and the born again globals. Moreover, one has seen that the case analyzed does not fit into any of these theories or typologies, which depicts the particular character of this company, which may reflect its traditional strategic posture. It is important to make clear that it is important for the company to define a clear strategy to exploit its competitive advantage in wider markets.

It is important to refer that although certain theories try to explain how firms evolve over time in their internationalization process, certain firms do not fit within what theories postulate. As such, it is important to be aware that change, as an important driver of competitive advantage, needs to be addressed to understand the theoretical stances that support the theoretical rationales of internationalization.

FUTURE RESEARCH DIRECTIONS

Although research on internationalization is quite reach, it would be interesting to analyze pre-internationalization behavior to depict the possible causes that hinder the internationalization process among many small and medium-sized firms.

It was clear that ALFA wanted to reposition its business activities as it was following a very passive strategic behavior, and only recently ALFA started seeking to approach the market from a technology-based, opportunity-seeking behavior. This opens up new opportunities for research as it would be of added value to analyze how managers' behavior might generate proactive internationalization behavior, which might explain why some firms suddenly embrace born again global behaviors.

REFERENCES

Andersen, O. (1993). On the internationalization process of firms: A critical analysis. *Journal of International Business Studies*, *24*(2), 209–231. doi:10.1057/palgrave. jibs.8490230

Axelsson, B., & Johanson, J. (1992). Foreign market entry: The textbook vs. the network view. In B. Axelsson & G. Easton (Eds.), *Industrial networks: A new view of reality* (pp. 218–234). London: Routledge.

Bell, J., McNaughton, R., & Young, S. (2001). 'Born-again global' firms. An extension to the 'born global' phenomenon. *Journal of International Management*, *7*(3), 173–189. doi:10.1016/S1075-4253(01)00043-6

Carvalheira, A., & Moreira, A. C. (2016). Searching for opportunities and trust in internationalization markets. Entrepreneurial perspective of a traditional industry SME. In L. C. Carvalho (Ed.), *Handbook of research on entrepreneurial success and its impact on regional development* (pp. 675–701). Hershey, PA: IGI Global. doi:10.4018/978-1-4666-9567-2.ch028

Cesinger, B., Danko, A., & Bouncken, R. (2012). Born globals: (almost) 20 years of research and still not 'grown up'? *International Journal of Entrepreneurship and Small Business*, *15*(2), 171–190. doi:10.1504/IJESB.2012.045203

Coviello, N. (2015). Re-thinking research on born globals. *Journal of International Business Studies*, *46*(1), 17–26. doi:10.1057/jibs.2014.59

Dana, L. P. (2001). Networks, internationalization & policy. *Small Business Economics*, *16*(2), 57–62. doi:10.1023/A:1011199116576

Dicken, P. (2015). *Global shift. Mapping the changing contours of the world economy*. New York, NY: Guilford Press.

Dominguez, N. (2016). Risk-seeking behaviours in SMEs' internationalization. In H. Etemad, S. Denicolai, B. Hagen, & A. Zucchella (Eds.), *The changing global economy and its impact on international entrepreneurship* (pp. 66–95). Cheltenham, UK: Edward Elgar.

Forsgren, M. (2002). The concept of learning in the Uppsala internationalization process model: A critical review. *International Business Review*, *11*(3), 257–277. doi:10.1016/S0969-5931(01)00060-9

Franco, M., Mainardes, E., & Martins, O. (2011). A review of inter-organizational networks: Evidence from studies published in 2005-2008. *Cuadernos Americanos*, *24*(43), 133–155.

Geiger, I., Dost, F., Schönhoff, A., & Kleinaltenkamp, M. (2015). Which types of multi-stage marketing increase direct customers' willingness-to-pay? Evidence from a scenario-based experiment in a B2B setting. *Industrial Marketing Management*, *47*, 175–189. doi:10.1016/j.indmarman.2015.02.042

Geldres-Weiss, V., Uribe-Bórquez, C., Coudounaris, D., & Monreal-Pérez, J. (2016). Innovation and experiential knowledge in firm exports: Applying the initial U-model. *Journal of Business Research*, *69*(11), 5076–5081. doi:10.1016/j.jbusres.2016.04.083

Håkansson, H., & Snehota, I. (2006). "No business is an island" 17 years later. *Strategic Management Journal*, *22*(3), 271–274.

Johanson, J., & Mattsson, L. G. (1987). Interorganizational relations in industrial systems: A network approach compared with the transaction-cost approach. *International Studies of Management & Organization*, *17*(1), 34–48. doi:10.1080/00208825.1987.11656444

Johanson, J., & Mattsson, L.-G. (1988). Internationalisation in industrial system: A network approach. In N. Hood & J.-E. Vahlne (Eds.), *Strategies in global competition*. London: Croom Helm.

Johanson, J., & Vahlne, J.-E. (1977). The internationalization process of the firm – a model of knowledge development and increasing foreign market commitments. *Journal of International Business Studies*, *8*(1), 23–32. doi:10.1057/palgrave.jibs.8490676

Johanson, J., & Vahlne, J.-E. (1990). The mechanism of internationalization. *International Marketing Review*, *7*(4), 11–24. doi:10.1108/02651339010137414

Johanson, J., & Vahlne, J. E. (2009). The Uppsala internationalization process model revisited: From liability of foreignness to liability of outsidership. *Journal of International Business Studies*, *40*(9), 1411–1431. doi:10.1057/jibs.2009.24

Johanson, J., & Wiedersheim-Paul, F. (1975). The internationalization of the firm: Four Swedish cases. *Journal of Management Studies*, *12*(3), 305–322. doi:10.1111/j.1467-6486.1975.tb00514.x

Kleinaltenkamp, M., Rudolph, M., & Claßen, M. (2012). Multi-stage marketing. In M. Glynn & A. Woodside (Eds.), *Business-to-business marketing management: Strategies, cases, and solutions, advances in business marketing and purchasing* (Vol. 18, pp. 141–174). Bingley, UK: Emerald Group Publishing Ltd.

Knight, G. A., & Cavusgil, S. T. (1996). The born global firm: A challenge to traditional internationalization theory. *Advances in International Marketing*, *8*, 11–26.

Knight, G. A., & Cavusgil, S. T. (2004). Innovation, organizational capabilities, and the born-global firm. *Journal of International Business Studies*, *35*(2), 124–141. doi:10.1057/palgrave.jibs.8400071

McDougall, P. P., & Oviatt, B. M. (2000). International entrepreneurship: The intersection of two research paths. *Academy of Management Journal, 43*(5), 902–906. doi:10.2307/1556418

Moreira, A. C. (2007). La internacionalización de Pymes industriales a través de multinacionales. Presentación de algunos casos de los sectores automotor y electrónico. *Cuadernos de Administración, 20*(34), 89–114.

Moreira, A. C., & Alves, C. (2016). Commitment-trust dynamics in the internationalization process: A case study of market entry in the Brazilian market. In Information Resources Management Association (Ed.), International business: Concepts, methodologies, tools, and applications, (vol. 3, pp. 1206-1229). Hershey, PA: IGI Global. Doi:10.4018/978-1-4666-9814-7.ch057

Moreira, A. C., & Silva, P. M. (2015). New product development and the challenges of internationalization. In L. C. Carvalho (Ed.), *Handbook of research on internationalization of entrepreneurial innovation in the global economy* (pp. 65–87). Hershey, PA: IGI Global; doi:10.4018/978-1-4666-8216-0.ch004

Novotná, L., Martins, I., & Moreira, A. C. (2017). Trade between the Czech Republic and Portugal: Analysis of the 2000-2015 Period. In T. Dorożyński & A. Kuna-Marszałek (Eds.), *Outward foreign direct investment (FDI) in emerging market economies* (pp. 200–225). Hershey, PA: IGI Global; doi:10.4018/978-1-5225-2345-1.ch010

Oviatt, B. M., & McDougall, P. P. (1994). Toward a theory of international new ventures. *International Business Studies, 25*(1), 45–64. doi:10.1057/palgrave.jibs.8490193

Popp, J., Milward, H., MacKean, G., Casebeer, A., & Lindstrom, R. (2014). *Interorganizational networks. A Review of the literature to inform practice.* Washington, DC: IBM Center for The Business of Government.

Ribau, C. P., Moreira, A. C., & Raposo, M. (2015). Internationalisation of the firm theories: A shematic synthesis. *International Journal of Business and Globalisation, 15*(4), 528–554. doi:10.1504/IJBG.2015.072535

Ribau, C. P., Moreira, A. C., & Raposo, M. (2017). SME internationalization research: Mapping the state of the art. *Canadian Journal of Administrative Sciences*. doi:10.1002/CJAS.1419

Ruzzier, M., Hisrich, R., & Antoncic, B. (2006). SME internationalization research: Past, present, and future. *Journal of Small Business and Enterprise Development*, *13*(4), 476–497. doi:10.1108/14626000610705705

Schueffel, P., Baldegger, R., & Amann, W. (2014). Behavioral patterns in born-again global firms: Towards a conceptual framework of the internationalization activities of mature SMEs. *Multinational Business Review*, *22*(4), 418–441. doi:10.1108/MBR-06-2014-0029

Stanisauskaite, V., & Kock, S. (2016). The dynamic development of international entrepreneurial networks. In H. Etemad, S. Denicolai, B. Hagen, & A. Zucchella (Eds.), *The changing global economy and its impact on international entrepreneurship* (pp. 119–135). Cheltenham, UK: Edward Elgar. doi:10.4337/9781783479849.00012

Törnroos, J. Å. (2002). Internationalisation of the firm–a theoretical review with implications for business network research. In *18th IMP Conference*, Dijon, France.

Trudgen, R., & Freeman, S. (2014). Measuring the Performance of Born-Global Firms Throughout Their Development Process: The Roles of Initial Market Selection and Internationalisation Speed. *Management International Review*, *54*(4), 551–579. doi:10.100711575-014-0210-y

Vahlne, J. E., Ivarsson, I., & Johanson, J. (2011). The tortuous road to globalization for Volvo's heavy truck business: Extending the scope of the Uppsala model. *International Business Review*, *20*(1), 1–14. doi:10.1016/j.ibusrev.2010.05.003

Weerawardena, J., Mort, G. S., Liesch, P. W., & Knight, G. (2007). Conceptualizing accelerated internationalization in the born global firm: A dynamic capabilities perspective. *Journal of World Business*, *42*(3), 294–306. doi:10.1016/j.jwb.2007.04.004

Welch, L. S., & Luostarinen, R. (1988). Internationalization: Evolution of a concept. *Journal of General Management*, *14*(2), 83–98. doi:10.1177/030630708801400203

Zander, I., McDougall-Covin, P., & Rose, E. (2015). Born globals and international business: Evolution of a field of research. *Journal of International Business Studies*, *46*(1), 27–35. doi:10.1057/jibs.2014.60

KEY TERMS AND DEFINITIONS

Born Again Globals: They are characterized as being focused on the domestic market and suddenly being able to radically change their strategic focus in order to increase their sales volumes in international markets.

Born Global: It is a type of company that from its inception seeks to derive a competitive advantage to compete in many countries. It normally pursues a vision of becoming global and globalizes rapidly without any preceding long term domestic or internationalization period or experience. Usually born globals are small, technology-oriented companies that operate in several international markets.

Case Study: It is a qualitative methodology, normally used in social sciences, that seeks to interpret a reality through a particular perspective. It is normally used to answer questions like "how" and "why." It is commonly used to addresses constructivist research processes.

Globalization: It is a worldwide movement toward economic, financial, trade, and communications integration. It is normally envisaged as a lack of trade barriers between nations, which are removed through free trade agreements throughout the world and between nation states. It implies the opening of local and nationalistic perspectives to a broader outlook of an interconnected and interdependent world with free transfer of capital, goods, and services across national frontiers, in which investment opportunities soar.

Internationalization: It is the process of increasing involvement of enterprises in international markets. It involves a strategy carried out by firms that decide to compete in foreign markets. It involves cross-border transactions of goods, services, or resources between two or more firms or organizations that belong to two different countries.

Internationalization Process: It involves the emphasis of a trajectory of a company in its transition from a national market to a particular foreign market. It normally involves several entry modes (exports, FDI, franchising, etc.) that exert a critical influence on the subsequent trajectory, as well as on cost related to the internationalization process. The two most important theories that explain the internationalization process are the Uppsala model and the network-based approach.

Network-Based Approach: It based on the industrial networks theory, which states that firms evolve on the basis of established relationships. It considers the companies' internationalization process through their integration into networks and relationships. Following this perspective, the internationalization process occurs in interactive environments where companies of a well-established network of companies have an opportunity to develop new relationships that give them access to broader markets in other countries.

Uppsala Model: It has been one of the most discussed dynamic theories in Nordic School and International Business Studies. It explains the process of internationalization of companies. It explains how organizations learn and the impact of learning on the companies' international expansion. This theory defends that the companies' internationalization process is carried out in stages, from non-regular exports to the establishment of companies abroad.

Chapter 6
Collaborative System Approach for Enterprise Engineering and Enterprise Architecture:
A Literature Review

Pinar Yildiran
Marmara University, Turkey

Huseyin Selcuk Kilic
Marmara University, Turkey

Bahar Sennaroglu
Marmara University, Turkey

ABSTRACT

Today we are living in a constantly changing world and today's strong competition and changing market conditions enforce enterprises to adopt fundamental methods and new approaches to enhance their capabilities. Enterprises are goal-oriented, designed, and complex systems and they need to implement new strategies easily and control Key Performance Indicators to maintain their competitiveness. Enterprise engineering (EE) is a developing field and an enabler for informed decision making for addressing the required changes to be competitive and for tackling the complexity of enterprises' design issues on business, organization, information, and technology domains. Enterprise architecture (EA) is one of the basic elements of EE and it is about the structure of the whole of enterprise. There is an important and strong relationship between EE and EA. Although there are specific individual studies for EE and EA, this chapter aims to explore the fields of these two subjects in a collaborative system approach as a whole with existing literature review by assessing the core concepts and the methods used.

DOI: 10.4018/978-1-5225-5360-1.ch006

INTRODUCTION

Today, the fast pace of rapidly changing world is the prominent motivation for Enterprises. Dynamics of Enterprise need to be adaptive and evolving in every aspect like social, technical and economic etc. Under frequently changing conditions, the creation, design and development of Enterprises are required to address management and decision-making issues effectively and systematically. At this point, Enterprise Engineering, as an interdisciplinary and emerging field, provides insights both from Information Systems and Organizational Sciences (Molnar & Korhonen, 2014). Collaborative perspective of Enterprise Engineering and Information Sciences is clearly highlighted by Albani and Dietz (2010). In this study, with comprehensive literature review, it is pointed out that Enterprise Engineering closely cooperates with Information Science and Enterprise Architecture.

Enterprise has its products and services through its core components: processes, people, information and technology. The relationship among Enterprise's core components is the primary motivation of Enterprise Architecture in design and change perspective. Enterprises are complex and dynamic systems (Kosanke et al., 1999) and change of their core components and elements is rather continuous in its nature. One of the effective way of evaluation of changes is making comparison of scenarios and solutions. For current and future strategy of Enterprises, the business people need high level abstractions of Enterprise core components as defined in Enterprise Architecture Models such as business architecture, information architecture, software architecture and technical architecture (Tang et al., 2004).

In literature, an extensive body of literature has been generated around Enterprise Architecture and its related concepts, however the purpose of this chapter is to highlight the collaboration between Enterprise Engineering and Enterprise Architecture. This chapter has aims to present a general entry for Enterprise Engineering and Enterprise Architecture domains with a collaborative system approach. A literature review is proposed to highlight the related prominent concepts and to provide important definitions for these domains consequently.

Starting with the general definition of Enterprise Engineering, it is as follows: "define, structure, design and implement enterprise operations as communication networks of business processes, which comprise all their related business knowledge, operational information, resources and organization relations" (Kosanke et al., 1999).

Evaluation of changes requires comparison of alternative scenarios and different situations, from this point, the design and improvement of processes benefit from modeling and simulation activities of Enterprise Engineering. Enterprise Engineering is dealing with enterprise operations to increase the efficiency, effectiveness and competitiveness in a dynamically changing environment. Major task of Enterprise

Engineering is structuring and maintaining the enterprise knowledge base efficiently for decision support.

In Enterprise organizations strategic, tactical, and operational decisions are common activities that occur every day. These decisions, which have a huge impact on profitability and sustainability, provide four essential branches of the enterprise: Design, Business, Engineering, and Production (Rabelo et al., 2007). Enterprise Perspectives of Enterprise Architecture are process, information, application and technology (Albani & Dietz, 2010) and Enterprise design domains are business, organization, information and technology (Dietz & Hoogervorst, 2012). Starting from these definitions, the key enabling factors of Enterprise are Information Technology and Enterprise Architecture that is initially developed in and have a vast scope in the Information Technology (IT) domain for the benefits of enterprise integration and decision support. Enterprise Architecture is a way of fast and efficient analysis of information through simulation and prediction of Enterprise behavior under specific conditions and constraints.

The body of knowledge for Enterprise Engineering contains such titles like enterprise engineering, business engineering, and enterprise architecture (BKCASE Editorial Board, 2017). An enterprise typically goes beyond its organizational boundaries with the scope of supply chain such as Virtual Enterprises (VEs) or Collaborative Networked Organizations (CNOs).

A comprehensive literature review of scientific journals, books, standards, technical reports, white papers, thesis and conference proceedings etc. were performed in scientific databases. To provide preliminary data, 98 research papers published between years 1996–2016 were examined. Regarding the existing literature review studies on Enterprise Engineering and Enterprise Architecture, this study provides the systematic analysis and comparison with respect to various characteristics or elements. This study can be regarded as important with its comprehensive assessment of the body of knowledge with an up-to-date information pertaining to Enterprise Engineering and Enterprise Architecture. A systematic review of the literature is followed to identify and validate the following research questions in the context of Enterprise:

- Practical implementations of Enterprise Engineering and Enterprise Architecture
- Key concepts of Enterprise Engineering and Enterprise Architecture
- Quantitative and qualitative approaches for Enterprise Engineering and Enterprise Architecture
- Enterprise Engineering domain coverage

This Chapter is organized as follows. In Section 2, Background Research is introduced in order to provide evaluation and assessment of Enterprise Engineering and Enterprise Architecture for research and practice, and the alignment of the related constructs is presented. Next in Section 3, the literature review method and research procedure are explained. In Section 4, the main steps of the literature review and the results of it are demonstrated with proper representation methods. Finally, the limitations of this study and suggested future researches are expressed consequently.

BACKGROUND RESEARCH

A literature search provides invaluable insight into research subjects and makes the researchers benefit from use of previous works in the interested area. This section presents a brief summary of the major concepts with an overview of the Enterprise Engineering and Enterprise Architecture definitions in the literature. The Background research delineates a kind of sequential relationship between these prominent concepts and highlights the boundaries and span of them in the research field.

System, Complex System and System Approach

System Thinking is seeing the connected wholes in a complete view and understanding the situation or circumstances by discovering the relations between its elements (Checkland, 1999). General System Theory (GST) defines system as interactive elements such as software, hardware, firmware, information, people, techniques, services, facilities, and other support elements to realize a target objective (INCOSE, 2012). A System is a complex network with combined and interactive elements related with enterprise's goals and strategies (Bertalanffy, 1968). In Systems Engineering, engineered system has product system, service system, enterprise system and system of systems (BKCASE Editorial Board, 2017). Complex system has hierarchy in its structure and it is assembled with its sub-systems or they are near-decomposability that is a way of tackling the complexity (Simon, 1962).

Systems approach is a problem-solving view and specifically needed for the description of a system with all the information pertinent to design, architecture, development of it. A "systems approach" to the study of enterprises provides understanding them with increasing levels of details. Thus well documented and detailed common views ensure the organizations having all benefits from systems that Enterprise operates in. Additionally, this approach as enterprise architecture framework guarantees that all related parties and stakeholders have a common layout for Enterprise's delivery systems.

Enterprise, Enterprise as a System

An enterprise is a collection of business processes to deliver products and services to realize the targeted enterprise results (Presley et al., 1993).

By making analogy with the complex system definition, the enterprise has hierarchical organized complexity that comes from interactions between people and with other organizations. These interactions are summarized as information exchange, transformation of inputs to outputs, giving reactions and changing themselves according to circumstances that they operate in. So as Dietz pointed out that "an enterprise is as *a complex, open, heterogeneous and adaptive socio-technical system"*(Dietz et al., 2009).

As Real-life organizations, Enterprises are complex systems with integrated processes, information, organizations, and technology infrastructure as components of the system. Enterprises' structural complexity comes from the great number of interconnections of its parts. Interaction of these components are difficult to anticipate for any individual or group with limited cognitive capacity. Enterprise systems are specific to themselves and they are constantly changing and evolving. Complexity brings difficulty to understand and to predict the behavior of the systems after a change or evolution occurs. It is practically impossible to accurately predict how any changes to Enterprise may impact its behavior without required tools for the analysis of the behavior and its drivers. Several dimensions of enterprises should be revised according to changing and evolving conditions that Enterprises operate in.

Enterprise Engineering

Enterprise Engineering explains the principles and practices for design, analysis, implementation and operation of an enterprise (Liles et al., 1996) and addresses "how to design and improve all elements associated with the total enterprise through the use of engineering and analysis methods and tools to more effectively achieve its goals and objectives" (SEE,1995). ISO definition of Enterprise Engineering is "the discipline applied in carrying out any efforts to establish, modify, or reorganize any enterprise" (ISO 15704:2000). Enterprises must be operated as a unified and integrated with their business processes. Enterprises can only be well managed with clearly defined and controlled business processes (Bernus et al. 2003). Business process models explain the functionalities and operational activities of Enterprises with their process plans, products, orders, resources, responsibilities, authorizations and the relationships among the internal and external environments (Kosanke et al., 1999). These models lead to support the decision-making activities in the enterprise for the evaluation of business processes alternatives due to constant change in its the environment and in its business strategies (Martin, 1995). Enterprise Engineering is analyzing, reshaping, designing and optimizing business entities for producing product and services in line with Enterprise's mission and goals (Chen & Vernadat, 2004). The Enterprise Engineering develops new theories, models, methods for the design, analysis, implementation, and enterprise governance by applying management and organization techniques, by using information systems methods and tools (Dietz, 2011). Enterprise Engineering follows scientific principles to design, implement new methodologies and to forecast Enterprise's behaviors under specific operating conditions such as different functionalities, economics and safety (Greefhorst & Proper, 2011).

Enterprise Engineering implements approaches and strategies for the transformation from 'as is' state of enterprise to a 'to be' state. Theoretical and methodological approaches to Enterprise Engineering are needed for mastering complexity for managing Enterprise changes and re-engineering. Enterprise engineers investigate alternative models, evaluate the impact of change and determines the design of enterprises.

Enterprise Engineering Methodologies and Tools

Enterprise Engineering Methodologies explain the enterprise integration process and enterprise modelling. Some examples of Enterprise Engineering tools are as follows: ARIS Toolset (ARIS), FirstSTEP (CIMOSA), METIS, Process wise, etc. Some of Enterprise Engineering Methodologies are the Purdue Guide for Master Planning, GIM (Grai Integrated Methodology), Globemen1 Reference Model and Virtual Enterprises (VEs).

DEMO and Design science research (DSR) are main research methodology in enterprise engineering.

Enterprise Architecture and Architecture Frameworks

Companies face many competitive challenges and threats. Adaptation to changing requirements of Enterprise under these conditions mandates effective foundation for execution with organizational structures, processes, supporting information systems and technologies. For analyzing and designing enterprises business process management is another popular approach. The main focus of Enterprise Architecture is the relationship between processes, people, information, technology in Enterprises (Rocha et al., 2014). The Enterprise Architecture provides the identification of the enterprise including its strategy, mission, vision and organization. Enterprise architecture describes the fundamental structure of an enterprise and reduces the complexity of the enterprise (Halpin et al., 2009). The Enterprise Architecture is a knowledge base and support for decisions from the high-level concepts to physical level such as enterprise premises and networks. Enterprise Architecture activities are understanding the enterprise artefacts and joint conceptualization, building a shared understanding with 'as-is' and 'to-be' approach, organizational contexts, possible impacts of the changes, identifying and communication with stakeholders (Op't Land et al., 2008). Developing architecture addresses trade-offs, conflicts, risk assessment and mitigation, assesses alternatives and decisions. Enterprises Architecture adopts models to mitigate the challenges of changes and build maps for future directions of the company (Armour et al., 1999). It defines technical entities such as functionality, data, physical infrastructure, interfaces and applications, and organizational entities such as goals, business processes, organizational units, and workflow under circumstances of reference models, standards, and methodologies (The Open Group, 2002).

There is a variety of definitions of Enterprise Architecture, ISO/IEC/IEEE 42010 standard defines an Enterprise Architecture as "fundamental concepts or properties of an Enterprise in its environment embodied in its elements, relationships, and in the principles of its design and evolution". ANSI/IEEE STD 1471-2000 defines architecture as "the fundamental organization of a system, embodied in its components, their relationships to each other and the environment, and the principles governing its design and evolution". The IEEE recommendation explains an architecture as the system's fundamental organization and its components, their relationships, the environment and the principles for design and evolution (IEEE, 1999).

The vision of an enterprise is moving to Digital era which brings globalization - Borderless Enterprise, Networked Community Capabilities - Extended Enterprise, collaboration and flexibility – Virtual Enterprise. To enable and to build more collaborative works among firms and with their partners and suppliers, Enterprise Architecture frameworks are interconnection or integration points for various information systems' design and operation in terms of collaboration concept. Indeed, Enterprise Architecture is a decision support tool in order to manage the business and IT solutions, relations and alignments strategically. However Enterprise Architecture is not limited to IT, it deals with strategy, organization, processes, and products in addition to information systems of the organizations. Enterprise Architecture focuses business and technical architectures with organizational and technical aspects in which the IT systems operate the models of high-level abstractions of enterprise entities. Enterprise Architecture has information, business, application, infrastructure, technology and service oriented architecture domains.

The Enterprise Reference Architecture is the main concept and the essence of the construction and operation used in enterprise engineering.

Architecture Frameworks are standards and tools for the description of architectures for providing a system-level description of the enterprise. It has two parts as an ontology for describing the elements and relationships and reference architecture for creating generic enterprise architectures. The complexity of the enterprise depends on the size of the enterprise and there is no one-size-fits-all approach for building the proper architecture for it. Enterprise complexity with modeling and simulation with the architecture frameworks provides graphical artifacts, domain-specific views for the analysis and design to capture the effects of changes and comparison of alternatives. For the needs of decision-makers Enterprise architecture is a way of to control this complexity. Architecture Frameworks define the outputs of architecting and use views to depict the perspectives of overall architecture. Architectural views reduce complexity and provide focus to the needs of the stakeholders in the enterprise and assist to understand the whole enterprise (Gorman, 2004).

The framework of an architecture includes standardized view templates, viewpoints, meta-models, model templates which enable the development system architecture views. A metamodel is a pattern, a language representation for the architectural models' instantiation for creating main concept in Enterprise Architecture.

Enterprise architecting was born in the late 1980s and first enterprise architecture framework was stated in an article in IBM Systems Journal by John Zachman in 1987. Enterprise Architecture Frameworks have been constructed by two communities: (1) the Enterprise Integration (EI) movement of the Industrial Engineering community, for manufacturing systems for information, control and material flows, supply chain across the enterprise and (2) the Information Systems (IS) community for development of software systems in enterprise information systems (Romero & Vernadat, 2016). The frameworks from 1st community are the Computer-Integrated Manufacturing Open System Architecture (CIMOSA), Purdue Enterprise Reference Architecture (PERA), GERAM, which stands for Generalized Enterprise Reference Architecture and Methodology, GRAI-GIM method. The generalization of these and similar frameworks was formalized as ISO 15704:2000 as a set of concepts for manufacturing or service enterprises. The frameworks developed by 2nd community on IS development are the Open Group Architecture Framework (TOGAF), ARIS, the Federal Enterprise Architecture (FEA) framework, the Department of Defense Architecture Framework, ArchiMate. In 1995 and the first version of TOGAF was published. The Open Group Architecture Framework (TOGAF) is a popular framework that connects Data Architecture, Business Architecture, Application Architecture, and Technology. TOGAF has three components: The enterprise continuum; the architecture development method (ADM); the resource base. Other international standards have also been constructed for additional important subjects considering architecture descriptions within the software engineering viewpoint, e.g. ISO 42010: 2011.

Enterprise Architecture Planning is the plan for implementing the Enterprise Architecture that addresses the business processes plan and develops the IS plan. IS planning and Enterprise Architecture planning are different concepts in terms of goal and scope. Enterprise Architecture has a broader scope that identifies integration of business view on top of Information Systems planning with technology driven approach. Enterprise Architecture planning puts the required information to conduct the business in the future and it works with Enterprise Architecture as-is documentation and Enterprise Architecture analysis processes with different sub-architectures as Enterprise Architecture Planning (Winter et al., 2010).

Enterprise Model and Enterprise Modelling

Enterprise modelling concept is a key concept for enterprise engineering and information systems. An enterprise model is a computational representation of the organizational elements of Enterprise such as processes, information, people, business activities including constraints of a business, government or other enterprise in its circumstances (Bernus et al., 2003). Enterprise environment is so complex and very detailed in its nature that this complexity can be modeled with different views to show the enterprise elements interactions and abstractions of enterprise system entities. The enterprise elements such as processes, information, organizations, and enabling infrastructure are linked properly and integrated into Enterprise models which give insights to business people and decision makers to indicate their requirements, to understand the relevant solutions. Organized Enterprise operations and enterprise knowledge by suitable representations are visible to users with enterprise models. Enterprise modeling constructs models of enterprise systems to predict the impact of change within an organization. The power of a model is the ability of simplification of the real world (Wood, 1994). Enterprise modelling helps to analyze and control business operations and consequently to build improvements for the usage of resources (Vernadat, 1996). Solutions of difficult enterprise problems take into consideration both aspects and need to be developed in a systematic way. Different modelling methods may have similar approaches, the differences between them come from mostly the object types and the symbols for representations that have descriptive and definitional approach to design, analysis, control and evaluation purposes.

Several methodologies have been developed to practice enterprise design and engineering for example Business Engineering (Österle & Winter, 2003), Design and Engineering Methodology for Organizations (DEMO) (Dietz, 2006), Business Process (Re) engineering (Davenport & Short, 1990; Hammer & Champy, 1993), PICTURE (Becker et al., 2007) or ARIS (Scheer & Schneider, 2005), E3-Value (Gordijn & Akkermans, 2003), UML (UML ISO IEC 2005), IDEF (IDEF, 1993).

Enterprise Integration

Interoperability provides flexibility and synergy in enterprise's organizations with common terminology and representation models (Ciociou et al., 2001). Enterprise integration enables communication and enriches enterprise information between Enterprise's core elements. Enterprise Integration heavily depends on Enterprise Architecture for reaching the right enterprise information and having clear rules for architecting the integration while keeping the requirements addressed properly and effectively with alignment of future strategic directions.

Enterprise Information Systems

Enterprises require Enterprise Information Systems which are made of software, computers, people, data and processes. Enterprise Information System addresses the operations of the enterprise's organization with software systems. Such operations are like business management, planning, manufacturing, sales, marketing, logistics, accounting, human resources, finance, warehouse management, service management, and project management etc. Depending on the size of the enterprise, Enterprise Information System contains lots of complex software systems including system interface integrations among themselves and/or with other enterprises' organizations.

With developments in computer systems, today Enterprise Information Systems are mandatory systems nearly for all enterprises to support their business processes, information flows and data. With the review of the evaluation of Enterprise Information Systems after 60's besides reporting systems, production related systems were in charge, after 70s, the new definition as Management Information Systems (MISs) appeared. Material Resource Planning (MRP) and MRP II and Enterprise Resource Planning (ERP) are major concepts from 80s and 90s. In the 2000s, with ERP II the 'extended enterprise' concept was introduced for better organizational collaboration for nearly all business functions (Moller, 2004).

Another recent concept the ERP/III, a new definition was added as 'borderless enterprise' for enhancing the collaboration even further beyond from the enterprise business functions to across the enterprises' supply chains, customers and the marketplace (Hurbean et al., 2014).

The newest concept Industry 4.0 puts the technological advances with Information and Communication Technologies (ICT) as a solution pathway for Enterprise Information Systems for the integration needs of enterprises in manufacturing, supply chain and service operations.

Enterprise Interoperability

Enterprise interoperability is a major stepping stone for seamless enterprise operation for providing communication between information systems, devices and applications. The ability of information exchange requires common understanding for related functionalities and services between those elements to be connected (Vernadat, 1996). Interoperability for Enterprises' ICT systems, technical and organizational standards provide elaboration mostly in global scale by commissions, interest groups, institutions, associations, engineering consortiums etc.

Networked Enterprises

Spanning organizational structure of the Enterprises are "networked enterprises meaning joint activities and providing support for business people interaction via Computer Supported Cooperative Work (CSCW) (Grudin, 1994), with the coordination of business processes based on Workflow Management Systems (WfMS) (Chen et al., 2001).

Collaborative Networked Organizations operations heavily depend on collaboration and require interconnected and synchronized flows for supporting different types of digital transactions. For such organizations, extensive and advanced functionalities via information systems and computer networks, help business people to collaborate among themselves, to execute the business services, to share business knowledge and information at all levels and to interconnect business processes between organizations (Rabelo et al., 2008).

Extended Enterprise

For some strategic reasons, sometimes Enterprises' close cooperation and collaboration with some of their partners, suppliers require temporary relations for a certain time. With the concept of Extended Enterprise network by Browne et al. (1999), Virtual Enterprises occurred for the implementation of product lifecycles (Globeman21, 1999).

In competitive environment, Extended Enterprise is a way of handling the difficulty of highly distributed structures in order to form a cooperation and collaboration solution with partners, suppliers or customers in a harmonized way. This solution requires changing of standard way of working, adapting new business processes and practices alignment between parties and working together under agreed goals with different legal and organizational structures. With this approach collaboration between extended enterprises may discontinue after a certain time (Costanzo et al., 2009).

Virtual Enterprise

The competitive conditions put forward the need for gaining rapid information for Enterprises as a major challenge. For enhancing the capabilities and the potentials of the Enterprises Virtual Enterprise may be an option to complement Enterprises' competencies temporarily or for a long period. Customer focus Partnering or R&D capability sharing provide quick response for competitive market conditions. Classic example of virtual enterprises can be seen in movie industry (Goranson, 1999). This kind of Co-operation between enterprises also derives solutions for cost reduction, gaining flexibility or enhancing the existing enterprise capabilities to a new level (Bernus et al., 2003). The Virtual Enterprise Methodology (VEM) works with the Virtual Enterprise Reference Architecture (VERA) to define methods and to guide the enterprises for building Virtual Enterprise systematically.

Enterprise Engineering gives rise to Enterprises via all these co-operation and collaboration opportunities to provide short path for Enterprises' organizational developments and capability advancements (Costanzo et al. 2009).

METHODOLOGY AND RESEARCH PROCEDURES

Before conducting literature review, different approaches for literature reviews were investigated in terms of building structure. Our research methodology for conducting this literature review is systematically constructed. The systematic literature review requires all procedures documented for auditing purpose of other researchers (Moustaghfir, 2008). Systematic review ensures comprehensive coverage of the highly influential works in research space. However, use of the systematic approach may lead to omit the relevant publications due to looking for terminology other than the search criteria. Therefore, an exploratory approach was consulted in parallel to include highly relevant studies that would otherwise have been lacking for the exploratory review does not follow a strictly systematic approach. A systematic procedure was followed within the literature review as shown in Figure 1.

This chapter, with chronological and categorical approach, is supposed to provide up-to-date information on Enterprise Engineering and Enterprise Architecture themed articles published in time interval between 1996 and 2017 concerning the variety aspects of Enterprise Engineering and Enterprise Architecture.

To identify the relevant literature, online databases like Springer, Elsevier, Mendeley, Research Gate etc. were used to search for the terms Enterprise Engineering and Enterprise Architecture in academic journals, conference proceedings, standards and books/book chapters. The search yielded to finding out related concepts and identifying the relevance of subjects to focus area for having good coverage.

Consequently, only the influential works with Enterprise Engineering and Enterprise Architecture were chosen for further analysis and also to define boundaries of focus subject area. As a part of the analysis, the key themes of each publication were identified to develop a better understanding of the primary areas of interest in Enterprise Engineering and Enterprise Architecture research. These publications are listed in Appendix (Table 7) with a high-level analysis according to classification coding frame defined below. However, the analysis is performed for only some of the selected headings in the classification coding frame.

During data collection, compilation, analysis and interpretation the following classification was performed as explained below:

- Publication Year, the year that study was published officially in the literature
- Publication Title, name of the study as appeared in literature
- Authors, the performers of the study
- Published in, the medium, university or company that published the related study
- Primary Theme, main area of the study related with our research subjects
- Type, study type as Journal Article, Conference Proceedings, White Paper – Report, Book Chapter, Standard – Specification, PhD or MSc Thesis
- Research Questions, Study Aims & Objectives
- Research Methodology, the research methodology expressed in the study by authors specifically
- Types of Research Methods According to the Purpose of the Study
  ◦ Fundamental Research (Pure or Basic Research), acquiring or enhancing or improving the knowledge with theoretical and experimental approach
  ◦ Applied Research (Action Research), practical problem solving with analysis and scientific approach by using the findings of fundamental or basic research
- Types of Research Methods According to Nature of the Study
  ◦ Descriptive, describes, explains and predicts the situations, identifies concepts and facts, no cause and effect relationship presents, observational methods, case-study methods, survey methods are applied
  ◦ Analytical, evaluation using available facts and information, Theory, Model, Experimental - Controlled Environment/Simulation are applied
  ◦ Conceptual,
  ◦ Exploratory,
  ◦ Experimental,
- Evaluation Method Category
  ◦ Comparison, Observational, Case/Field Study, Survey (*Descriptive*)
  ◦ Theory – Model, Methods, Facts (*Analytic*)

- ◦ Idea, Concepts (*Conceptual*)
- ◦ Hypothesis (*Exploratory*)
- ◦ Experiments, Controlled Environment, Simulation (*Experimental*)
- ◦ No Evaluation
- Design Artifact, main focus of the study in terms of Design Science Research
  - ◦ Construct
  - ◦ Model, relationships among constructs
  - ◦ Method, algorithm or steps for the representation of constructs
  - ◦ Instantiation, real world application of the construct
- Common Abbreviations, abbreviations mostly related with the focus of the study
- Research Q1, *Practical implementations of Enterprise Engineering and Enterprise Architecture,* whether the real life application presented in the study or not
- Research Q2, *Quantitative or qualitative approaches for Enterprise Engineering and Enterprise Architecture,* Research Methods Type in the study

MAIN STEPS OF THE LITERATURE REVIEW METHODOLOGY

In this study, the applied "Literature Review Methodology" that can be seen in Figure 1 has 3 major stages as "Planning", "Conducting" and "Reporting". In planning phase related preparation activities before conducting literature review were performed, then all paper works, context review and selection processes were accomplished. As last step, proper demonstration of the conclusions of the literature review was presented as reporting.

Planning

Our initial research efforts have the general aim of understanding and clarifying what an organization's functional perspective should be. The aim of the planning stage is to identify the related peripherals of literature review. To determine which articles are of further interest, it is necessary to decide which papers are eligible according to literature review framework.

In the planning phase of the proposed literature review methodology, identification of the research questions was the first step. The presented literature review framework focuses on the following questions:

Figure 1. Literature review methodology

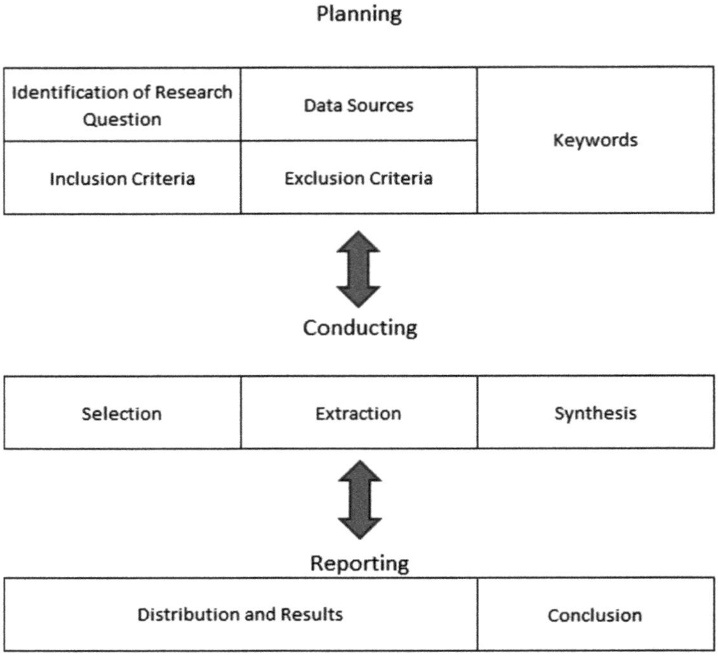

Planning

Identification of Research Question	Data Sources	Keywords
Inclusion Criteria	Exclusion Criteria	

Conducting

Selection	Extraction	Synthesis

Reporting

Distribution and Results	Conclusion

- Practical implementations of Enterprise Engineering and Enterprise Architecture
- Quantitative and qualitative approaches for Enterprise Engineering and Enterprise Architecture
- Key concepts of Enterprise Engineering and Enterprise Architecture

The following digital data sources included in our research:

- Elsevier
- Emerald
- IEEE
- Google Scholar
- ProQuest
- Science Direct
- Mendeley
- Springer Link
- Wiley

The keywords search strings were determined accordingly, and the following terms, Enterprise, Enterprise Engineering, Enterprise Architecture, Enterprise Model, Enterprise Reference Architecture, Reference Architecture Framework, Business Process Management, Architecture Framework, Enterprise Integration and Enterprise Interoperability were selected for literature search.

Inclusion criteria have the following approaches

- Studies that include target keywords
- Studies in search timeline
- Studies evaluating our main subject area Enterprise Engineering and Enterprise Architecture (Primary Theme)
- Studies that include not only Information Communication Technology perspective

Exclusion criteria have following approaches

- Studies that did not explicitly discuss target keywords
- Studies out of search timeline

Conducting the Literature Review

The main structure of the literature review is based on the classification of 98 proposed studies. Initially, 150 papers were reviewed according to the determined research inclusion and exclusion criteria and compliance of Primary Theme as Enterprise Engineering and Enterprise subjects. The outputs were checked, non-related scientific papers are eliminated, and 98 scientific papers are selected for this literature review. The majority of reviewed studies vary in different extents and for our literature review assessment foundation we focused on the analysis of our primary theme subjects and all related reference areas for our primary theme subjects identified and addressed based on the surveyed articles as presented in this section. This study provides an analysis on our primary theme subjects in order to facilitate broader view, clarification of related terminology and contribution to making Enterprise Engineering more actionable for researchers.

Based on the articles found in the literature, a frequency analysis of various subjects of Enterprise Engineering and Enterprise Architecture has been conducted as explained in detail in the Reporting section.

First analysis expresses the type of the reference. Eight different types are "Book", "Book Chapter" "*Conference Proceedings*", "*Journal Article*", "*Master Thesis*", "*PhD Thesis*", "Standard" and "*White Paper - Report*" as shown in Table 1.

Table 1. Classification of the reviewed papers with respect to "publication type"

Publication Type	# of Publication
Book	2
Book Chapter	8
Conference Proceeding	43
Journal Article	27
Msc Thesis	1
Phd Thesis	3
Standard	1
White Paper - Report	13
Grand Total	98

Second analysis is based on timeline, the publication year classification, publication year distribution and timespan distribution.

Third analysis is an evaluation according to Types of Research Methods according to Purpose of the Study, Nature of the Study and Evaluation Method category.

Fourth analysis is evaluation of Common Abbreviations and Key Concepts of Enterprise Engineering and Enterprise Architecture in our literature review with word cloud visual representation

Fifth analysis is based on Publications' Primary Theme by Research Methodology.

Sixth analysis is according to Design Science Research design artifact by Evaluation Method.

Last analysis includes frequency distribution of Common Terms and Common Abbreviations in publications.

One of the challenges that is faced in conducting this literature review is the identification and differentiation of the research methodology, and nature of the research as analytic, descriptive, conceptual, experimental etc. It is difficult to get a precise interpretation about the methodology used in studies as researchers do not always present the methodology they use in a coherent way in their publications. So Research Methodology and Design Science Research Methodology are selected as the reference frame for main classification of the studies in the literature review. Another difficulty is to address common abbreviations and key terms in a variety of studies. Some of the researches do not include the related terminology, abbreviations detailed enough to comprehend the subject area well, so word cloud were used to visualize most common areas covered in the studies subjected in the presented literature review.

In an attempt to assist with understanding and comparison, graphs, data tables for each of the analyses described above are presented in Reporting section.

The Article Coding Frame and Full details of the studies reviewed and evaluated during in the literature review are presented in Appendix (Table 6 and Table 7) in the hope that they may provide useful summaries and references for future studies.

Reporting

For providing better evaluation and understanding for the literature, two approaches have been proposed. First approach is clear identification of the coverage of the literature review. Second is presenting the results of analysis of the literature review.

For the literature review, various publication types have been selected in order to get a broader coverage. Among the publications mostly Conference Proceedings and Journal Articles were taken as references due to high relevance of literature review focus, beside that other type of publications contributed to complete the understanding the primary theme of the study as seen in Figure 2.

Another important factor for literature review studies is the number of studies published in the previous years. The related data is provided in Figure 3.

As seen in Table 2, Purpose Type of Research was detailed according to Nature of the Study and Evaluation Method categories. This analysis provides which existing works applied what type of research in order to understand practical and or theoretical approach. In the literature review, Applied Research (Action Research) as practical problem-solving approach is common with 65% of 98 studies. Among the Applied Research Studies, Analytic nature of research with Theory – Model evaluation method is the most frequent method as observed. This means that lots of theoretical models are proposed but less real-life case studies or observations appeared.

In Figure 4, Word Cloud is presented in order to highlight the frequently encountered subject areas that the primary theme Enterprise Engineering and Enterprise Architecture have been studied and how these topics were approached by researchers. Enterprise Architecture Frameworks like GERAM, GRAI, and TAFIM etc. and Enterprise Architecture Models like DEMO, ARIS, and UML etc. have frequent usage in studies. Also ICT and System can be seen as prominent concepts within the primary themes.

In Table 3, analysis is based on Publications' Primary Theme by Research Methodology, Enterprise Engineering is leading theme in our literature review within special coverage of Enterprise Architecture. It may lead to identify a gap such as the making connection strong between Enterprise Engineering and Enterprise Architecture. Also another potential study area is to present more real life applications or case studies for Enterprise Engineering in line with Enterprise Architectural approach. Another conclusion derived out from this analysis is that most of the publications don't have clearly stated research methodology or no methodology

Figure 2. Publication type distribution

Figure 3. Number of publications by publication year

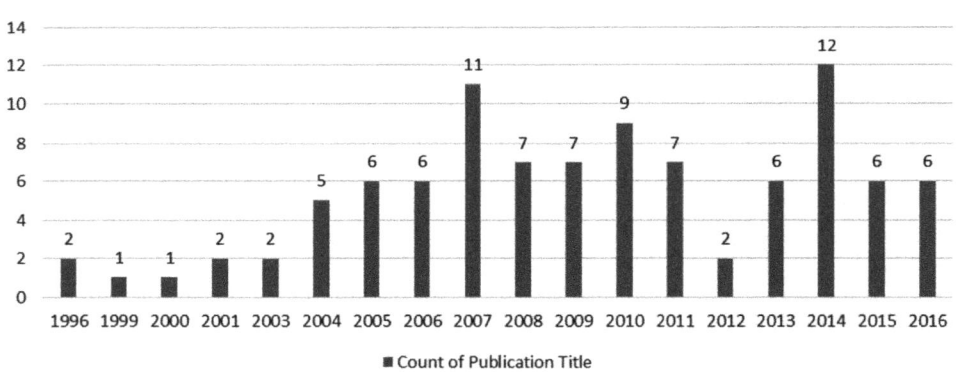

has been put forwarded. Most common research methodology observed during this study is Design Science Research with 8% of 98 studies.

In Table 4, the analysis is based on the view of design artifact of Design Science Research by Evaluation Method. Again theoretical approach is observed most frequently and Construct and concepts are widely seen ways of evaluation method for researchers in this literature review.

Table 5 provides an overview of which primary themes of reviewed publications are relevant in this literature review.

Table 2. Number of publications by research type, nature of research and evaluation method

Purpose Type of Research	Nature of Research	Category of Evaluation Method	Total
Applied Research	Analytic	Methods	1
		Model	2
		Theory-Model	19
		Theory-Model; Method	2
	Analytic; Descriptive	Case Study; Method	2
		Case Study; Theory-Model	1
		Model; Case Study	1
		Survey; Theory-Model	1
		Theory-Model; Case Study	1
	Conceptual	Concepts	3
	Conceptual; Exploratory	Hypothesis; Concepts	1
	Descriptive	Case Study	3
		Case Study; Interviews	1
		Interview	2
		Observation	5
		Observation; Case Study	2
		Survey	5
		Theory-Model	1
	Descriptive; Analytic	Case Study; Method	2
		Case Study; Theory-Model	4
	Descriptive; Conceptual	Concepts; Field Study	2
	Descriptive;Experimental	Simulation; Case Study	1
	Descriptive; Exploratory	Observation; Survey;Case Study; Hypothesis	1
		Survey;Theory-Model	1
	Total		**64**
Fundamental Research	Analytic	Theory-Model	2
	Analytic;Conceptual	Concepts; Method	1
		Theory-Model; Concepts	2
	Conceptual	Concepts	24
		No Evaluation	1
	Conceptual; Descriptive	Comparison;Concepts	1
	Descriptive	Comparison	2
	Descriptive; Exploratory	Hypothesis;Case Study	1
	Total		**34**

Figure 4. Word cloud

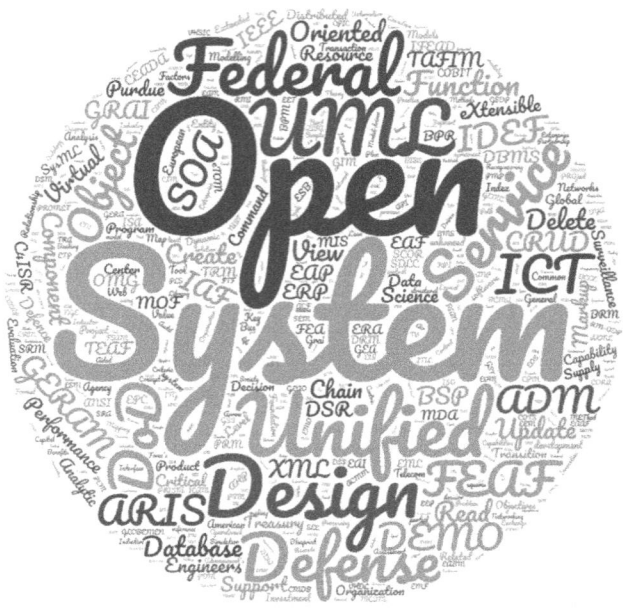

In Figure 5, the analysis demonstrates the results of Research Question 1 as a frequency distribution of Common Terms and Common Abbreviations in publications. This analysis brings two points. One is the common terms related with the presented primary theme and second is which subthemes come with Enterprise concept under Enterprise Engineering and Enterprise Architecture. All subthemes may be interpreted as potential subject areas of main topics that have been studied in this literature review. Also in Figure 6, common abbreviations appeared in studied publications give another perception for related terms.

Last analysis includes the results of Research Questions 1, and 2. For the classification of the reviewed publications Practical implementations of Enterprise Engineering and Enterprise Architecture is about 35% of the 98 publications. Also for the classification of Quantitative and qualitative approaches for Enterprise Engineering and Enterprise Architecture is about 95%. This may be interpreted that descriptive studies as real life applications are scarce when it is compared to theoretical and/or conceptual studies in this literature review. Moreover as a supportive point to this qualitative approach, it is concluded that less practical implementations, experiences are observed during the literature review.

Table 3. Publication primary theme by research methodology

Publication Primary Theme by Research Methodology	# of Publication
Business Modelling	**1**
Design Science Research	1
Business Transformation	**1**
NA	1
Enterprise Architecture	**62**
Canonical Action Research	1
Design Science Research	8
Exploratory Empirical Analysis	1
Functional Reference Model	1
NA	46
Simulation Model	1
Systematic and Exploratory Review	2
Web-based Survey; Analytic Hierarchy Process; Pair-wise Comparison	1
Design Science Research; CEADA; Exploratory Survey	1
Enterprise Architecture Framework	**2**
NA	2
Enterprise Engineering	**20**
Design Science Research	1
Meta-Methodology	3
Multiscale Analysis	1
NA	13
ProCEM - Process-Centric Enterprise Modeling & Management	1
Survey	1
Enterprise Governance	**2**
NA	2
Enterprise Information Systems	**1**
NA	1
Enterprise Modelling	**6**
Case Study; Interview	2
Design Science Research	2
NA	2
Enterprise Simulation	**1**
Discrete Event Simulation (DES), System-Dynamics (SD) Simulation	1
Information Systems	**1**
NA	1
Process Modelling	**1**
Fuzzy Mapping; Triangular-norm-based Combination Rule	1
Grand Total	**98**

Table 4. Design artifact by evaluation method

Designed Artifact by Evaluation Method	Evaluation Methods	# of Publication
Construct	Comparison; Concepts	1
	Concepts	27
	Interview	2
	No Evaluation	1
	Theory-Model; Concepts	1
Construct; Model; Method; Instantiation	Model; Case Study	1
Construct; Model	Hypothesis; Concepts	1
	Theory-Model	1
	Theory-Model; Concepts	1
Instantiation	Case Study; Theory-Model	1
	Observation	3
	Survey	3
	Survey; Theory-Model	1
Method	Case Study	1
	Case Study; Method	4
	Methods	1
	Observation	2
	Survey	2
	Theory-Model	2
	Observation; Case Study	2
	Concepts; Field Study	2
Model	Case Study	2
	Case Study; Theory-Model	4
	Comparison	2
	Simulation; Case Study	1
	Survey; Theory-Model	1
	Theory-Model	18
	Theory-Model; Case Study	1
	Case Study; Interviews	1
	Model	2
Model; Instantiation	Hypothesis; Case Study	1
	Observation; Survey; Case Study; Hypothesis	1
Model; Method	Theory-Model	1
	Theory-Model; Method	2
Construct; Method	Concepts; Method	1
Grand Total		98

Table 5 Primary Theme of Publications

Primary Theme of Publications	Book	Book Chapter	Conference Proceeding	Journal Article	Msc Thesis	Phd Thesis	Standard	White Paper Report	Grand Total
Business Modelling						1			1
Business Transformation								1	1
Enterprise Architecture	3	7	22	15		2	1	12	62
Enterprise Architecture Framework			2						2
Enterprise Engineering		3	10	5				2	20
Enterprise Governance					2				2
Enterprise Information Systems				1					1
Enterprise Modelling			4	2					6
Enterprise Simulation				1					1
Information Systems				1					1
Process Modelling			1						1
Grand Total	**3**	**10**	**39**	**25**	**2**	**3**	**1**	**15**	**98**

Figure 5. Frequency distribution of common terms in publications > 4 counts

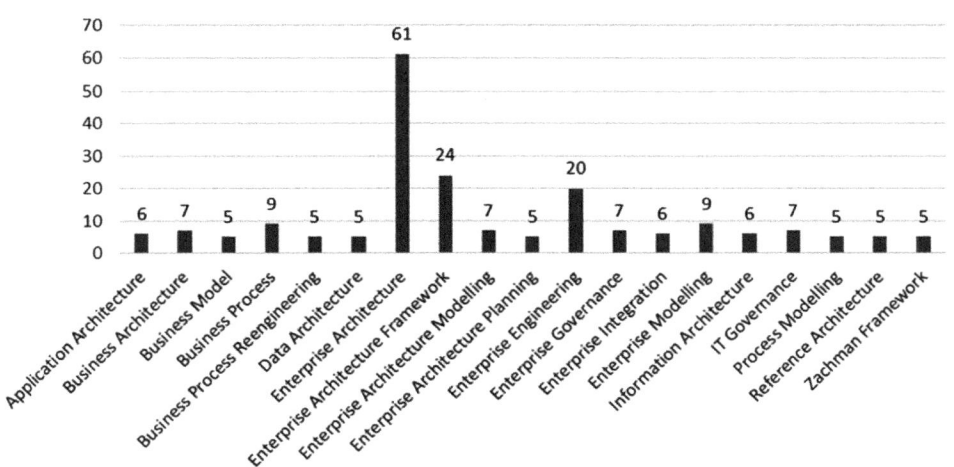

Figure 6. Frequency distribution of common abbreviations

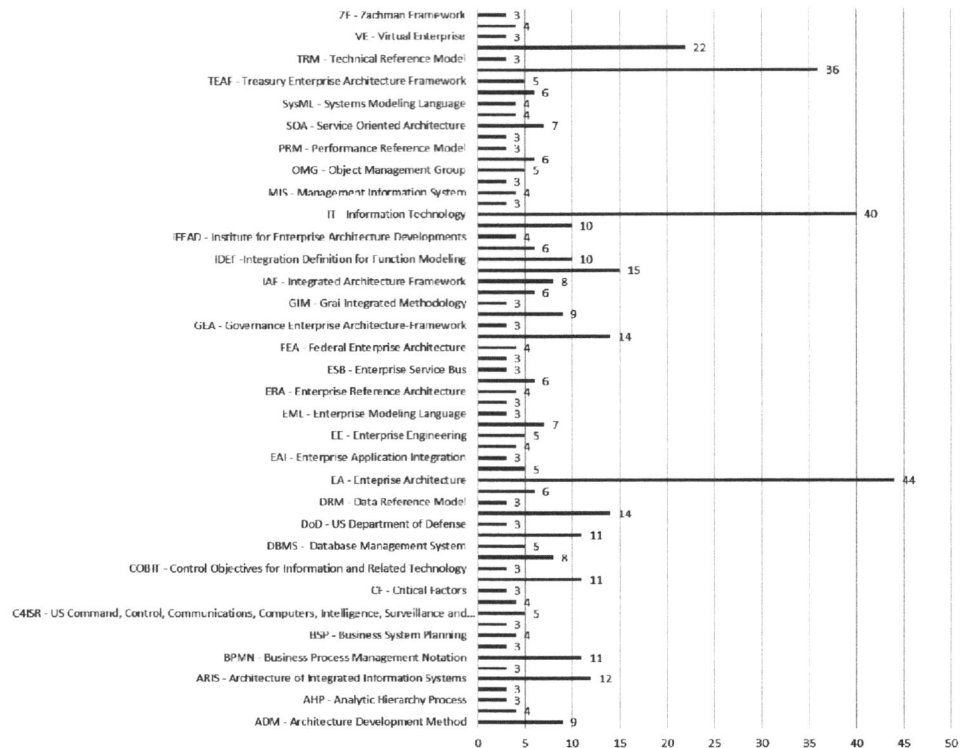

CONCLUSION

Limitations and Future Research

The aim of this study is to develop a systematic review of literature in order to provide a critical assessment of work to date. This study is conducted by collecting information about existing publications and the extracted information about the publications is grouped for communicating major findings and insights. The study is performed according to a detailed research framework on assessed related publications under consideration of the research questions. The 98 various publications are reviewed and classified based on proposed "Article Coding Frame" as explained in Appendix (Table 6), in which a number of different criteria are selected to identify appropriate studies for inclusion and exclusion and classify them from current literature review. The categorization results are demonstrated as graphics and data tables for summarizing the literature review. Identified and extracted information from systematic literature review regarding the primary themes of this study summarizes an overview of each publication and provides a comprehensive understanding of what is known about the topics.

Presently, Enterprise Engineering has a unifying role for Information Systems Development. Far more than 20 years, Enterprise Architecture has business process reengineering focus to take a deeper view of the Enterprise structure and conceptual design of Enterprise. Mostly, Enterprise Architecture is positioned as decision-aid mechanism for Information Technology and Enterprise Architecture is frequently used for IT Architecture of whole Enterprise Architecture. After reviewing 98 studies, it may be emphasized that the majority of the studies on Enterprise Engineering and Enterprise Architecture are on IT perspective. It may be concluded that Information, Communication and Technology (ICT) is the most popular area and it is in the recent research areas of the literature. Although IT is one of the significant supportive lines of the Enterprise, it is only the small part of Enterprise. In the core of the enterprise what it does, and in the context of Enterprise Architecture which is the integration point of the whole enterprise, there is no special treatment and emphasis for IT.

In this literature review, regarding the research question 1 as "Practical implementations of Enterprise Engineering and Enterprise Architecture" it is observed that most of the publications have conceptual and/or theoretical approach and empirical evidence to theoretical explanations is so limited. Very few studies provide real life case studies and experiences. Enterprise Engineering and Enterprise Architecture practices must support strategic direction of Enterprise and also everyday business concerns and problems.

During the past decade, there have been many Enterprise Architecture Frameworks, standards, modeling languages and tools developed to support building or transforming the enterprise. The systematic literature review shows that despite of defined many frameworks currently available, there is no commonly accepted scientific and theoretical foundation agreed upon among researchers and practitioners. Within the various type of 72 frameworks it is very difficult to compare and evaluate the recommendations and practical implementations proposed by these frameworks. Nevertheless, there is no generally accepted architectural representation view or content that exists in Enterprise Architecture. According to the classification in this study, it is observed that researchers mostly focus on TOGAF as a most popular architecture reference framework. It can be seen that only few Enterprise Architecture Reference models are known as in wide usage.

Enterprise Architecture and Enterprise Engineering consist of lots of concepts and relationships among them. In this classification of the literature review, it is seen that there is no comprehensive review and assessment of the research in Enterprise Engineering and Enterprise Architecture as a whole. The most notable point about Enterprise Engineering and Enterprise Architecture is the design decisions of Enterprise. Formal and systematic approaches for making decisions must be based on relevant and up-to-date information. One of the shortfalls seen during this literature review appears to be the scarcity of decision support in practice in Enterprise, especially in IT organization.

While practical solutions, implementations and measuring or testing the benefits or effects of methods are fundamental for enhancing the existing theoretical and conceptual models, most of the publications are based on qualitative approaches, so few studies include quantitative method as observed in this study. Quantitative analysis of Enterprise Engineering and Enterprise Architecture is largely missing in design and decision-making literatures. Many research publications focus on theoretical contributions related to Enterprise Engineering and Enterprise Architecture. Some use case studies exemplifying the contributions, but very few publications use hypotheses and statistical tools/approaches related to Enterprise Engineering and Enterprise Architecture. Thus, this leads to difficulty of finding any proof of applicability. It may be concluded that the actual employment of Enterprise Engineering and Enterprise Architecture among companies is limited or there is no considerable attention to subjects due to explaining their roles empirically in achieving organizational benefits from abstraction or theoretical foundation to move to practice of Enterprise Architecture and Enterprise Engineering. It is vital for organizations to successfully address Enterprise structure. Despite its importance, little consideration has been given to Enterprise Engineering.

Another observation is that most of the publications do not describe the methodology clearly and purposefully. Furthermore, it seems that with very few exceptions, no systematic methods have been used. Indicating in general, very limited publications are identified that devote considerable attention to methodology.

Key conclusions are explained from the findings of the literature review presented above. Regarding the existing literature, it can be concluded that there requires a literature review study about Enterprise Engineering and Enterprise Architecture. Hence, in this chapter, it is aimed to reveal the research questions coverage to address Research Questions 1, 2, and 3. As a result of this systematic literature review, it is identified that conceptual and model-driven studies are much more common than descriptive studies, this is a barrier for understanding the applicability of Enterprise Engineering and Enterprise Architecture in real life widely. It is believed that this literature review details the concepts and classifies the publications that can be used to provide a foundation for future studies and to raise practitioners' and researchers' awareness of extant research. Building and maintaining Enterprise Architecture based on a selected Architecture Reference Framework associated with the implementation of Enterprise Engineering activities, is vital to the success of organizations for embracing inevitable fast paced changes of today.

As in all literature reviews the current review has a number of limitations. The Enterprise Engineering and Enterprise Architecture subjects in this study are reviewed based on theoretical foundation, but all theoretical aspects are not covered as a continuous search throughout year by year evaluation. During this literature review, the most relevant databases are taken into consideration, and the most suitable and related terms are selected, however as with all literature reviews, this study is limited with key terms and databases used. Moreover, this literature review has an interpretative analysis, the findings are based on the authors' subjective interpretations.

For future studies, the Small Medium size Enterprise should embrace the outcomes of Enterprise Engineering and Enterprise Architecture. Moreover, new methodologies and relevant case studies will enhance the applicability of Enterprise Architecture models in real life organizations. Thus, practice-oriented research methodologies can be an opportunity for future direction.

REFERENCES

Aier, S., & Gleichauf, B. (2010). Application of Enterprise Models for Engineering Enterprise Transformation. *Enterprise Modelling and Information Systems Architectures*, *1*(5), 58–75.

Aier, S., Gleichauf, B. (2010). Applying design research artifacts for building design research artifacts: A process model for enterprise architecture planning. *Global Perspectives on Design Science Research*, 333-348.

Aier, S., Riege, C., & Winter, R. (2008). Classification of Enterprise Architecture Scenarios – An Exploratory Analysis. *Enterprise Modelling and Information Systems Architectures*, *3*(1), 14–23.

Aier, S., & Gleichauf, B. (2015). Application of enterprise models for engineering enterprise transformation. *Enterprise Modelling and Information Systems Architectures*, *5*(1), 58–75.

Albani, A., & Dietz, J. (2010). Advances in Enterprise Engineering IV. In *6th International Workshop, CIAO 2010*. Springer.

Albani, A., Raber, D., & Winter, R. (2016). A Conceptual Framework for Understanding the Essence of Enterprise Engineering Methodologies. *Enterprise Modelling and Information Systems Architectures*, *11*(1), 1–26.

Alter, S. (2014, July). Potentially valuable overlaps between work system theory, DEMO, and enterprise engineering. In *Business Informatics (CBI), 2014 IEEE 16th Conference on* (Vol. 2, pp. 25-32). IEEE.

ANSI/IEEE Std 1471-2000, IEEE Recommended Practice for Architectural Description of Software- Intensive Systems

Antunes, G., Barateiro, J., Caetano, A., & Borbinha, J. L. (2015, May). Analysis of Federated Enterprise Architecture Models. ECIS.

Arbab, F., Boer, F., Bonsangue, M., Lankhorst, M., Proper, E., & Torre, L. (2007). Integrating Architectural Models. *Enterprise Modelling and Information Systems Architectures*, 2(May), 40–57.

Armour, F. J., Kaisler, S., & Liu, S. (1999). Building an Enterprise Architecture Step by Step‖. *IT Professional*, 4(1), 31–39. doi:10.1109/6294.781623

Barroero, T., Motta, G., & Pignatelli, G. (2010). Business Capabilities Centric Enterprise Architecture. *Enterprise Architecture, Integration and Interoperability IFIP TC 5 International Conference, EAI2N 2010*, 32–43. 10.1007/978-3-642-15509-3_4

Becker, J., Pfeiffer, D., & Räckers, M. (2007). Domain Specific Process Modelling in Public Administrations – The PICTURE-Approach. In *Electronic Goverment: 6th International Conference, EGOV 2007, Proceedings*. Springer.

Bernus, P., Nemes, L., & Schmidt, G. (2003). *Handbook on Enterprise Architecture*. Springer. doi:10.1007/978-3-540-24744-9

Bernus, P., Noran, O., & Riedlinger, J. (2003). Using the Globemen Reference Model for Virtual Enterprise Design in after Sales Service. *VTT Symposium (Valtion Teknillinen Tutkimuskeskus)*, 71–90.

Bernus, P., Noran, O., & Molina, A. (2015). Enterprise architecture: Twenty years of the GERAM framework. *Annual Reviews in Control*, 39, 83–93. doi:10.1016/j.arcontrol.2015.03.008

von Bertalanffy, L. (1968). *General System Theory: Foundations, Development, Applications* (rev. ed.). New York: Braziller.

BKCASE Editorial Board. (2017). *Guide to the Systems Engineering Body of Knowledge*. Author.

Braun, C., & Winter, R. (2007). Integration of IT Service Management into Enterprise Architecture. *Applied Computing 2007, 1-2*, 1215–19.

Browne, J., Harhen, J., & Shivnan, J. (1996). *Production Management Systems – An Integrated Perspective* (2nd ed.). Boston: Addison-Wesley.

Buckl, S., Ernst, A. M., Lankes, J., Matthes, F., Schweda, C. M., & Wittenburg, A. (2007). Generating visualizations of enterprise architectures using model transformations. Enterprise Modelling and Information Systems Architectures-An International Journal, 2(2).

Martinez, C., Cane, S., Abdul-Rauf, S., Smith, K., & Lee, K. (2008). *Application of network visualization to identify gaps in complex information system architectures*. The Mitre Corporation.

Checkland, P. (1999). *Systems thinking, systems practice*. New York: Wiley.

Chen, Q., & Hsu, M. (2001). Interenterprise collaborative business process management. *Proceedings of the 17th IEEE International Conference on Data Engineering*, 253–260. 10.1109/ICDE.2001.914836

Chen, D., & Vernadat, F. (2004). Standards on Enterprise Integration and Engineering–State of the Art. *International Journal of Computer Integrated Manufacturing*, *17*(3), 235–253. doi:10.1080/09511920310001607087

Ciocoiu, M., Gruninger, M., & Nau, D. (2001). Ontologies for integrating en- gineering applications. *Journal of Computing and Information Science in Engineering*, *1*(1), 45–60. doi:10.1115/1.1344878

Cochran, D. S., Sereno, R., & Aldrich, W. (2014). *Enterprise Engineering of Lean Accounting and Value Stream Structure through Collective System Design*. Academic Press.

Costanzo, F., Kanda, Y., Kimura, T., Kühnle, H., Lisanti, B., Singh Srai, J., . . . Williams, P. M. (2009) Enterprise Organization and Operation. Applications in Mechanical Engineering. doi:10.1007/978-3-540-30738-9_15

Davenport, T. H., & Short, J. E. (1990). The New Industrial Engineering – Information Technology and Business Process Redesign. *Sloan Management Review*, *31*(4), 11–27.

Deschamps, F., de Lima, E. P., Santos, E. A. P., & Van Aken, E. (2013, January). Development of Enterprise Engineering Guidelines for Enterprise Diagnosis and Design. In *IIE Annual Conference. Proceedings* (p. 807). Institute of Industrial and Systems Engineers (IISE).

de Vries, M., Gerber, A., & van der Merwe, A. (2015, June). The enterprise engineering domain. In *Enterprise Engineering Working Conference* (pp. 47-63). Springer.

de Vries, M., Gerber, A., & van der Merwe, A. (2014, April). The Nature of the Enterprise Engineering Discipline. In EEWC (pp. 1-15). doi:10.1007/978-3-319-06505-2_1

Debbabi, M., Hassaïne, F., Jarraya, Y., Soeanu, A., & Alawneh, L. (2010). Architecture Frameworks, Model-Driven Architecture, and Simulation. In Verification and Validation in Systems Engineering (pp. 15-35). Springer Berlin Heidelberg.

Dietz, J. L., Hoogervorst, J. A., Albani, A., Aveiro, D., Babkin, E., Barjis, J., & Mulder, H. (2013). The discipline of enterprise engineering. *International Journal of Organisational Design and Engineering*, *3*(1), 86–114. doi:10.1504/IJODE.2013.053669

Dietz, J. L. G. (2006). *Enterprise Ontology – theory and methodology*. Heidelberg, Germany: Springer. doi:10.1007/3-540-33149-2

Dietz, J. L. G. (2011). *Enterprise Engineering Manifesto*. Retrieved from www.ciaonetwork.org. www.ciaonetwork.org

Dietz, J. L. G., & Hoogervorst, J. A. P. (2012). The principles of enterprise engineering. *Second Enterprise Engineering Working Conference, EEWC 2012*, 15–30.

Fischer, R., Aier, S., & Winter, R. (2007). A Federated Approach to Enterprise Architecture Model Maintenance. *Enterprise Modelling and Information Systems Architectures*, *2*, 14. doi:10.1145/253260.253294

Dietz, J. L. G., & Hoogervorst, J. A. P. (2011). A Critical Investigation of TOGAF - Based on the Enterprise Engineering Theory and Practice. *Enterprise Engineering Working Conference 2011*, 76–90.

Executive Office of the President of the United States. (2007). *Federal Enterprise Architecture (FEA) Consolidated Reference Model: Version 2.3*. Author.

Fattah, A. (2009). *IBM Enterprise Reference Architecture*. Academic Press.

Franke, U., Ekstedt, M., Lagerström, R., Saat, J., Winter, R. (2010). Trends in Enterprise Architecture practice–A survey. *Trends in Enterprise Architecture Research*, 16-29.

Feltus, C., Petit, M., & Vernadat, F. (2009). Refining the Notion of Responsibility in Enterprise Engineering to Support Corporate Governance of IT. *IFAC Proceedings Volumes, 13*(1), 924–29. 10.3182/20090603-3-RU-2001.0126

Fischer, R., Aier, S., & Winter, R. (2007). A Federated Approach to Enterprise Architecture Model Maintenance. *Enterprise Modelling and Information Systems Architectures*, *2*(2), 14.

Foorthuis, R., & Brinkkemper, S. (2008). Best Practices for Business and Systems Analysis in Projects Conforming to Enterprise Architecture. *International Journal of Enterprise Modelling and Information Systems Architectures*, *3*(August), 36–47.

Frank, U., & Strecker, S. (2007). Open Reference Models: Community-Driven Collaboration to Promote Development and Dissemination of Reference Models. *Enterprise Modelling and Information Systems Architectures*, *2*(2), 32–41.

Franke, U., Ekstedt, M., Lagerström, R., Saat, J., & Winter, R. (2010). Trends in Enterprise Architecture practice–A survey. *Trends in Enterprise Architecture Research*, 16-29.

Gaaloul, K., & Molnar, W. (2014, November). Research Methodologies in Enterprise Engineering: Insights from a Workshop. In *Advanced Information Systems for Enterprises (IWAISE), 2014 International Workshop on* (pp. 58-64). IEEE.

Gammelgård, M. (2007). Business Value Assessment of It Investments. KTH, Royal Institute of Technology.

Giachetti, R. E. (2010). *Design of Enterprise Systems*. Boca Raton, FL: CRC Press.

Glazner, C. G. (2009). *Understanding Enterprise Behavior Using Hybrid Simulation of Enterprise Architecture*. Massachusetts Institute of Technology.

Globemen21. (1999). *Global Engineering and Manufacturing in Enterprise Networks*. Globemen.

Goranson, H. T. (1999). *The Agile Virtual Enterprise—Cases, Metrics, Tools*. Quorum Books.

Gordijn, J., & Akkermans, J. M. (2003). Does e-Business Modeling Really Help? In *36th Hawaii International Conference On System Sciences*. Hawaii, HI: IEEE.

Gorman, M. (2004). Enterprise's Architecture. Enterprise Architectures, 1–10.

Greefhorst, D., & Proper, E. (2011). The Role of Enterprise Architecture. Architecture Principles. doi:10.1007/978-3-642-20279-7_2

Gorman, M. (2004). Enterprise's Architecture. *Enterprise Architectures*, 1–10.

Graves, T. (2008). *Tetradian enterprise-architecture series Real Enterprise-Architecture: Beyond IT to the Whole Enterprise*. Academic Press.

Greefhorst, D., & Proper, E. (2011). The Role of Enterprise Architecture. *Architecture Principles*.

Gregor, S. (2006). The nature of theory in information systems. *Management Information Systems Quarterly*, *30*(3), 611–642. doi:10.2307/25148742

Grudin, J. (1994). Computer-supported cooperative work: History and focus. *Computer*, *27*(5), 19–26. doi:10.1109/2.291294

Hall, C., & Harmon, P. (2005). *BPTrends.com The Enterprise Architecture, Process Modeling, and Simulation Tools Report*. Academic Press.

Hammer, M., & Champy, J. (1993). *Reengineering the Corporation – A Manifesto for Business Revolution*. New York: HarperCollins Publishers.

Van Der Beek, W.T.H., Trienekens, J., & Grefen, P. (2012). The Application of Enterprise Reference Architecture in the Financial Industry. *Lecture Notes in Business Information Processing, 131*, 93–110.

Henriques, M., Tribolet, J., & Hoogervorst, J. (2010). *Enterprise Governance and DEMO* (Doctoral dissertation). Department of Computer Science and Engineering, Technical University of Lisboa, Instituto Superior Técnico, Lisboa.

Hoogervorst, J. A. (2009). *Enterprise governance and enterprise engineering*. Springer Science & Business Media. doi:10.1007/978-3-540-92671-9

Hurbean, L., & Doina, F. (2014). *ERP III the promise of a new generation*. 13th International Conference on Informatics in Economy, Education, Research & Business Technologies, ASE, Bucharest, Romania.

IBM. (2006). *IBM Industry Models for Financial Services The Information FrameWork (IFW)*. Overview.

IDEF. (1993). *Federal Information Processing Standards Publication 183: Integration Definition For Function Modeling (IDEF0)*. IDEF.

IEEE. (1999). *Draft for Standard, IEEE P1471/D5.1 Draft Recommended Practice for Architectural Description, October 1999*. IEEE.

INCOSE. (2012). Systems Engineering Handbook: A Guide for System Life Cycle Processes and Activities, version 3.2.2. San Diego, CA: International Council on Systems Engineering (INCOSE), INCOSE-TP-2003-002-03.2.2.

ISO 15704:2000 Industrial automation systems — Requirements for enterprise-reference architectures and methodologies

ISO/IEC, ISO/IEC/IEEE 42010 Systems and Software Engineering—Architecture Description, 2011

Iyamu, T., Mphahlele, L., & Hamunyela, S. (2014). The Connective Scheme between the Enterprise Architecture and Organisational Structure. In *New Perspectives in Information Systems and Technologies* (Vol. 2, pp. 9–21). Cham: Springer. doi:10.1007/978-3-319-05948-8_2

Jonkers, H., Groenewegen, L., Bonsangue, M., van Buuren, R., Quartel, D. A., Lankhorst, M. M., & Aldea, A. (2017). A language for enterprise modelling. In *Enterprise Architecture at Work* (pp. 73–121). Springer Berlin Heidelberg. doi:10.1007/978-3-662-53933-0_5

Jorgensen, H. D., Lillehagen, F., & Karlsen, D. (2005). Collaborative Modelling and Metamodelling with the Enterprise Knowledge Architecture. *Enterprise Modelling and Information Systems Architectures*, *1*, 36–45.

Karlsen, A. (2011). Enterprise Modeling Practice in ICT-Enabled Process Change. *IFIP Working Conference on The Practice of Enterprise Modeling 2011*, 208–22. 10.1007/978-3-642-24849-8_16

Kosanke, K., Vernadat, F., & Zelm, M. (1999). CIMOSA: Enterprise Engineering and Integration. *Computers in Industry*, *40*(2), 83–87. doi:10.1016/S0166-3615(99)00016-0

Kotusev, S. (2016a). *British Computer Society Enterprise Architecture Frameworks: The Fad of the Century*. Academic Press.

Kotusev, S. (2016b). The History of Enterprise Architecture: An Evidence-Based Review. *Journal of Enterprise Architecture*, *12*(1), 29–37.

Kuras, M.l., & White, B.E. (2005). *Engineering Enterprises Using Complex-System Engineering*. INCOSE Foundation.

Leelawat, N., Suppasri, A., Kure, S., Carine, J. Y., Mateo, C. M. R., & Imamura, F. (2015). Disaster Warning System in the Philippines Through Enterprise Engineering Perspective: A Study on the 2013 Super Typhoon Haiyan. *Journal of Disaster Research*, *10*(6), 1041–1050. doi:10.20965/jdr.2015.p1041

Liles, D. H., Johnson, M. E., & Meade, L. (1996). The enterprise engineering discipline. *Proceedings of the Fifth Industrial Engineering Research Conference*, 479–484.

Liles, D.H., Huff, B.L., & Rogers, K.J. (2001). A Manufacturing Reference Model For The Enterprise Engineer. *The Journal of Engineering Valuation and Cost Analysis*.

Liles, D. H., & Presley, A. R. (1996). Enterprise Modeling Within An Enterprise Engineering Framework. *The 1996 Winter Simulation Conference*.

Lindström, Å., Johnson, P., Johansson, E., Ekstedt, M., & Simonsson, M. (2006). A survey on CIO concerns-do enterprise architecture frameworks support them? *Information Systems Frontiers*, *8*(2), 81–90.

Liu, Y., & Iijima, J. (2015, June). A Case Study of Business Process Simulation in the Context of Enterprise Engineering. In *Enterprise Engineering Working Conference* (pp. 96-110). Springer.

Ma, S., & Wang, R. (2013). A Study on Meta-synthesis Mode of the Systems Engineering of Governance of Large Enterprise Group. In *Proceedings of the Sixth International Conference on Management Science and Engineering Management* (pp. 761–771). Springer London; doi:10.1007/978-3-319-19297-0_7.

Madarasz, L., Timko, M., & Racek, M. (2005). Enterprise Modeling and Its Applications in Company Management Systems. *Proceedings of 5th International Symposium of Hungarian Researchers on Computational Intelligence*, 1–82.

Marashi, E., & Davis, J.P. (2005). A Systems Approach to Resolving Complex Issues in a Design Process. *Complexity in Design and Engineering*, 160–69.

Marques, A. F., Borges, J. G., Sousa, P., & Pinho, A. M. (2011). An Enterprise Architecture Approach to Forest Management Support Systems Design: An Application to Pulpwood Supply Management in Portugal. *European Journal of Forest Research*, *130*(6), 935–948. doi:10.100710342-011-0482-8

Martin, J. (1995). *The Great Transition. Using the Seven Principles of Enterprise Engineering to Align People, Technology and Strategy*. American Management Association.

Mitre Corporation. (2014). Retrieved from http://www2.mitre.org/public/eabok/pdf/Using-EAs-14-1210.pdf

Moller, C. (2004). ERP II: next-generation extended enterprise resource planning. In J. Damsgaard, J. Hørlück, P. Kræmmergaard, & J. Rose (Eds.), Organizing for Networked Information Technologies: Readings in Process Integration and Transformation, Aalborg Universitetsforlag (pp. 108–118). Aalborg: Academic Press.

Molnar, W. A., & Korhonen, J. J. (2014). Research paradigms and topics in Enterprise Engineering analysis of recent conferences and workshops. *Proc - Int Conf Res Challenges Inf Sci*. 10.1109/RCIS.2014.6861071

Molnar, W. A., & Proper, H. A. (2013, June). Engineering an enterprise: Practical issues of two case studies from the luxembourgish beverage and tobacco industry. In *Working Conference on Practice-Driven Research on Enterprise Transformation* (pp. 76-91). Springer. 10.1007/978-3-642-38774-6_6

Moustaghfir, K. (2008). The dynamics of knowledge assets and their link with firm performance. *Measuring Business Excellence*, *12*(2), 10–24. doi:10.1108/13683040810881162

Nakakawa, A., van Bommel, P., & Erik Proper, H. A. (2010). On Supporting Collaborative Problem Solving in Enterprise Architecture Creation. *Working Conference on Practice-Driven Research on Enterprise Transformation PRET 2010*, 156–81. 10.1007/978-3-642-16770-6_7

Nakakawa, A., van Bommel, P., & Proper, E. (2010, June). Towards a Theory on Collaborative Decision Making in Enterprise Architecture. In DESRIST (pp. 538-541). doi:10.1007/978-3-642-13335-0_40

Nightingale, D. J., & Rhodes, D. H. (2004). Enterprise Systems Architecting : Emerging Art and Science within Engineering Systems. *Proceedings of the ESD External Symposium*, 1–13.

Noran, O. (2007). Discovering and Modelling Enterprise Engineering Project Processes. Handbook of Enterprise Systems Architecture in Practice. doi:10.4018/978-1-59904-189-6.ch003

Noran, O. (2009). A Decision Support System for Enterprise Engineering. *Information Systems Development: Challenges in Practice, Theory, and Education*, 93–104.

Ogush, M., Coleman, D., & Beringer, D. (2000). *Hewlett Packard A Template for Documenting Software and Firmware Architectures*. Academic Press.

Op 't Land, M., Proper, H. A., Waage, M., Cloo, J., & Steghuis, C. (2008). *Enterprise architecture—creating value by informed governance*. Berlin: Springer.

Ortner, E. (2008). From Software Engineering to Enterprise Engineering–Introduction to a Language-Critical. *Innovative Techniques in Instruction Technology*, 135–143.

Osterwalder, A. (2004). The Business Model Ontology A Proposition. In *A Design Science Approach*. UNIVERSITE DE LAUSANNE.

Österle, H., & Winter, R. (2003). Business Engineering. In Business Engineering – Auf dem Weg zum Unternehmen des Informationszeitalters (Vol. 2). Springer.

Presley, A. R., Huff, B. L., & Liles, D. H. (1993). A Comprehensive Enterprise Model for Small Manufacturers. In *Proceedings of the 2nd Industrial Engineering Research Conference* (pp. 430-434). Institute of Industrial Engineers, Atlanta, Georgia

Rabelo, L., Helal, M., Jones, A., & Min, H. S. (2007). *Enterprise simulation: a hybrid system approach. Int J Comput Integr Manuf.* doi:10.1080/09511920400030138

Rais, A. A. (2016). Interface-Based Software Integration. *Journal of Systems Integration*, (3).

Rocha, Á., Correia, A. M., Tan, F. B., & Stroetmann Editors, K. A. (2014). *Advances in Intelligent Systems and Computing 276 New Perspectives in Information Systems and Technologies* (Vol. 2). Springer.

Romero, D., & Vernadat, F. (2016). Enterprise information systems state of the art: Past, present and future trends. *Computers in Industry*, *79*, 3–13. doi:10.1016/j.compind.2016.03.001

Ross, J.W., Weill, P., & Robertson, D.C. (2006). Enterprise Architecture as Strategy. *Enterprise Architecture as Strategy*, 1–10.

Sakas, D., & Kutsikos, K. (2014). An adaptable decision making model for sustainable enterprise interoperability. *Procedia: Social and Behavioral Sciences*, *148*, 611–618. doi:10.1016/j.sbspro.2014.07.087

SAP. (2007). *Sap Eaf Overview Guide*. SAP.

Scandura, T. A., & Williams, E. A. (2000). Research methodology in management: Current practices, trends, and implications for future research. *Academy of Management Journal*, *43*(6), 1248–1264. doi:10.2307/1556348

Scheer, A. W., & Schneider, K. (2005). ARIS – Architecture of Integrated Information Systems. In P. Bernus, K. Mertins, & G. Schmidt (Eds.), *Hand-book on Architectures of Information Systems* (Vol. 2, pp. 605–623). Berlin: Springer.

Schekkerman, J. (2003). *Extended Enterprise Architecture Maturity Model*. Institute for Enterprise Architecture Developments.

Schekkerman, J. (2006). Creating or Choosing an Enterprise Architecture Framework. In *How to Survive in the Jungle of Enterprise Architecture Frameworks: Creating or Choosing an Enterprise Architecture Framework*. Academic Press.

SEE. (1995). *Society For Enterprise Engineering Conference Announcement, 1995*. SEE.

Sembiring, J., & Siregar, M. I. H. (2013). A Decision Model for IT Risk Management on Disaster Recovery Center in an Enterprise Architecture Model. *Procedia Technology*, *11*, 1142–1146. doi:10.1016/j.protcy.2013.12.306

Simon, H. A. (1962). The architecture of complexity. *Proceedings of the American Philosophical Society*, *106*(6), 467–482.

Singh, A., Mudholkar, P., & Balani, L.L. (2015). *Contemporary Enterprise Architecture Frameworks (A Comparative Study of TOGAF and Zachmans â€TM EA Frameworks)*. Academic Press.

Sousa, P., Lima, J., Sampaio, A., & Pereira, C. (2009). An Approach for Creating and Managing Enterprise Blueprints: A Case for IT Blueprints. *Advances in Enterprise Engineering III, 5th International Workshop, CIAO! 2009, and 5th International Workshop, EOMAS 2009*, 70–84. 10.1007/978-3-642-01915-9_6

Sultanow, E., Brockmann, C., Schroeder, K., & Cox, S. (2016). *A multidimensional Classification of 55 Enterprise Architecture Frameworks*. Academic Press.

Svee, E. O., & Zdravkovic, J. (2015, June). Extending enterprise architectures to capture consumer values: the case of TOGAF. In *International Conference on Advanced Information Systems Engineering* (pp. 221-232). Springer. 10.1007/978-3-319-19243-7_22

Tamm, T., Seddon, P. B., Shanks, G., & Reynolds, P. (2011). How Does Enterprises Architecture Add Value to Organisations? *Communications of the Association for Information Systems*, *28*(1), 141–168.

Tang, A., Han, J., & Chen, P. (2004). A Comparative Analysis of Architecture Frameworks Technical Report: CeCSES Centre Report. Software Engineering Conference, 2004. 11th Asia-Pacific, 640–647.

The IT Governance Institute. (2007). *0 The IT Governance Institute TOGAF TM and COBIT Mapping of TOGAF 8.1 with COBIT 4.0*. Author.

Timmers, P. (1998). *Business Models for Electronic Markets. Journal on Electronic Markets*, *8*(2), 3–8.

Treasury Board of Canada. (2004). *Business Transformation Enablement Program Strategic Design & Planning Methodology*. Author.

Tribolet, J., Sousa, P., & Caetano, A. (2014). The role of enterprise governance and cartography in enterprise engineering. Enterprise Modelling and Information Systems Architectures-An International Journal, 9(1).

UML ISO IEC - UML Specification, Version 1.4.2, formal/05-04-01 (2005)

Urbaczewski, L., & Mrdalj, S. (2006). A comparison of enterprise architecture frameworks. *Issues in Information Systems*, *7*(2).

U.S. Government. (2009). *Improving Agency Performance Using Information and Information Technology*. Author.

Velitchkov, I. (2008). Integration of IT Strategy and Enterprise Architecture Models. *International Conference on Computer Systems and Technologies*, 1–6. 10.1145/1500879.1500955

Vernadat, F. B. (1996). *Enterprise Modeling and Integration: Principles and Applications*. London: Chapman & Hall.

Vernadat, F. (2014). Enterprise Modeling in the context of Enterprise Engineering: State of the art and outlook. *International Journal of Production Management and Engineering*, *2*(2), 57–73. doi:10.4995/ijpme.2014.2326

Vesterager, J., Tølle, M., & Bernus, P. (2003). VERA: Virtual Enterprise Reference Architecture. *VTT Symposium (Valtion Teknillinen Tutkimuskeskus)*, 39–51.

Wan, H., Luo, A., & Luo, X. (2014, May). How Enterprise Architecture Formative Critical Success Facets Might Affect Enterprise Architecture Success: A Literature Analysis. In ICISO (pp. 197-209). doi:10.1007/978-3-642-55355-4_20

Whitman, L., & Huff, B. (2001). On the Use of Enterprise Models. *International Journal of Flexible Manufacturing Systems*, *13*(2), 195–208. doi:10.1023/A:1011187602935

Winter, R., Zhao, J. L., & Aier, S. (2010). Global Perspectives on Design Science Research. *5th International Conference, Desrist 2010*. 10.1007/978-3-642-13335-0

Wood, J. T. (1994). *Organismic Modeling of Organizations: A Dynamic Enterprise Model*. Arlington, VA: The University of Texas at Arlington.

Wolff, F. (2008). An Evaluation Framework for Enterprise Architecture Modelling. *Enterprise Modelling and Information Systems Architectures*, *3*(1), 48–60.

Zia, M. J., Azam, F., & Allauddin, M. (2011). A survey of enterprise architecture analysis using multi criteria decision making models (MCDM). *Intelligent Computing and Information Science*, 631-637.

APPENDIX

Table 6. Article coding frame

Publication Year
Publication Title
Authors
Published in
Primary Theme
Type *Journal Article /* *Conference Proceeding /* *White Paper - Report /* *Book Chapter /* *Standard - Specification /* *PhD Thesis*
Research Questions Study Aims & Objectives
Research Methodology
Purpose Type of Research Applied Research - Action Research (Generalization, basics, forecasting..) Fundamental(Pure) Research (solving problem)
Nature of Research Descriptive Analytic Conceptual Exploratory Experimental
Category of Evaluation Method Comparison; *Observation - Case/Field Study, Survey (Descriptive)* *Theory-Model, Methods, Facts (Analytic)* *Idea, concepts (Conceptual)* *Hypothesis (Exploratory)* *Experimental - Controlled Environment/Simulation (Experimental)* *No Evaluation*
Designed Artifact *Construct / Model /* *Method / Instantiation*
Common Abbreviations
Research Q1 - Practical implementations of Enterprise Engineering and Enterprise Architecture
Research Q2 - Quantitative and qualitative approaches for Enterprise Engineering and Enterprise Architecture

Table 7. Analysis of primary studies with respect to selected criteria

Publication Year	Publication Title	Authors	Published in	Type *Journal Article / Conference Proceeding / White Paper - Report / Book Chapter / Standard - Specification / PhD Thesis*	Research Questions Study Aims & Objectives	Research Methodology	Research Q1 - Practical implementations of Enterprise Engineering and Enterprise Architecture	Research Q2 - Quantitative and qualitative approaches for Enterprise Engineering and Enterprise Architecture
1996	Enterprise Modeling Within An Enterprise Engineering Framework	Liles, Donald H. Presley, Adrien R.	The 1996 Winter Simulation Conference	Conference Proceeding	describes a multi-view reference architecture for modeling an enterprise. presents a modeling scheme under development which supports the architecture and acts as a tool for Enterprise Engineering provide a valuable tool for the modeling of enterprises	NA	NA	Qualitative
1996	The Enterprise Engineering Discipline	Liles, D. H. Johnson, M. E. Meade, L. Underdown, D. R.	Society for Enterprise Engineering Conference	Conference Proceeding	discusses the emerging discipline of Enterprise Engineering	NA	NA	Qualitative
1999	CIMOSA: Enterprise Engineering and Integration	Kosanke, K. Vernadat, F. Zelm, M.	Computers in Industry	Journal Article	discusses enterprise engineering as an enterprise life-cycle oriented discipline for identification, design, and implementation of enterprises and their continuous evolution identification of current problems in the field	NA	NA	Qualitative
2000	A Template for Documenting Software and Firmware Architectures	Ogush, Ma Coleman, Derek Beringer, Dorothea	HP	White Paper - Report	defines a template for producing architectural documentation specifies a common structure for document and illustrates its use with examples tackles the problem of how an architecture should be documented	NA	Yes	Qualitative

continued on following page

Table 7. Continued

continued on following page

Publication Year	Publication Title	Authors	Published in	Type Journal Article / Conference Proceeding / White Paper - Report / Book Chapter / Standard - Specification / PhD Thesis	Research Questions Study Aims & Objectives	Research Methodology	Research Q1 - Practical implementations of Enterprise Engineering and Enterprise Architecture	Research Q2 - Quantitative and qualitative approaches for Enterprise Engineering and Enterprise Architecture
2001	A Manufacturing Reference Model For The Enterprise Engineer	Liles, D. H. Huff, B. L. Rogers, K. J.	The Journal of Engineering Valuation and Cost Analysis: Special Issue on Enterprise Engineering	Journal Article	presents a manufacturing reference model for enterprise engineering provides an overview of models, a description of their use, a survey of other enterprise reference models, and a description of the manufacturing enterprise reference model	NA	NA	Qualitative
2001	On the Use of Enterprise Models	Whitman, Larry Huff, Brian	International Journal of Flexible Manufacturing Systems	Journal Article	field study designed to determine how enterprise models are used survey was conducted to focus attention on current limitations in enterprise models and modeling practices in general	Survey	Yes	Qualitative
2003	Using the globemen reference model for virtual enterprise design in after sales service	Bernus, Peter Noran, Ovidiu Riedlinger, Joachim	VTT Symposium	Conference Proceeding	a step-by-step methodology for designing virtual enterprises for after sales service a step-by-step procedure for VE creation The management and service delivery processes are designed through customising the Globemen Reference Model	NA	Yes	Qualitative
2003	VERA: Virtual Enterprise Reference Architecture	Vesterager, Johan Tolle, Martin Bernus, Peter	VTT Symposium (Valtion Teknillinen Tutkimuskeskus)	Conference Proceeding	describes Globemen's main contents and presents examples of its use and potentials	NA	NA	Qualitative

179

Table 7. Continued

Publication Year	Publication Title	Authors	Published in	Type *Journal Article / Conference Proceeding / White Paper - Report / Book Chapter / Standard - Specification / PhD Thesis*	Research Questions Study Aims & Objectives	Research Methodology	Research Q1 - Practical implementations of Enterprise Engineering and Enterprise Architecture	Research Q2 - Quantitative and qualitative approaches for Enterprise Engineering and Enterprise Architecture
2004	A Comparative Analysis of Architecture Frameworks	Tang, A. Han, J. Chen, P.	Software Engineering Conference, 2004. 11th Asia-Pacific	Conference Proceeding	provides a model of understanding through analyzing the goals, inputs and outcomes of six Architecture Frameworks propose a method to delineate architecture activities from detailed design activities to analyze AF in terms of their goals, inputs and outcomes	NA	NA	Qualitative
2004	Business Transformation Enablement Program Strategic Design & Planning Methodology	Treasury Board of Canada	Government Publication	White Paper - Report	developing an integrated toolkit for planning, designing and implementing business transformation using business design best practices and models suited to public sector organizations overall process methodology for business transformation	NA	NA	Qualitative
2004	Enterprise Systems Architecting: Emerging Art and Science within Engineering Systems	Nightingale, Deborah Rhodes, Donna H	Proceedings of the ESD External Symposium	Conference Proceeding	propose enterprise system architecting as an emerging art and science	NA	NA	Qualitative

continued on following page

Table 7. Continued

Publication Year	Publication Title	Authors	Published in	Type Journal Article / Conference Proceeding / White Paper - Report / Book Chapter / Standard - Specification / PhD Thesis	Research Questions Study Aims & Objectives	Research Methodology	Research Q1 - Practical implementations of Enterprise Engineering and Enterprise Architecture	Research Q2 - Quantitative and qualitative approaches for Enterprise Engineering and Enterprise Architecture
2004	Enterprise's Architecture	Gorman, Michael	Enterprise Architectures	Book Chapter	describes the contents of the enterprise's architecture and describes at a high level how the enterprise's architecture is created describes the work products, how they are interrelated, and how these work products fit with the work products of the other architectures is about the various classes of architectures that exist within the enterprise	NA	NA	Qualitative
2004	The Business Model Ontology A Proposition In A Design Science Approach	Osterwalder, Alexander	Universite De Lausanne	Phd Thesis	How can business models be described and represented in order to build the foundation for subsequent concepts and tools, possibly computer based? propose a rigorous conceptual model of business models to tackle the concept of business models with an ontological approach in order to provide the basis for new management tools generic business model ontology	Design Science Research	NA	Qualitative
2005	A systems Approach to Resolving Complex Issues in a Design Process	Marashi, Emad Davis, John P	Complexity in Design and Engineering	Conference Proceeding	propose a systemic methodology based on discourse and negotiation among participants to help in the resolution of complex issues in engineering design	Fuzzy Mapping; Triangular-norm-based Combination Rule	Yes	Quantitative

continued on following page

Table 7. Continued

Publication Year	Publication Title	Authors	Published in	Type: Journal Article / Conference Proceeding / White Paper - Report / Book Chapter / Standard - Specification / PhD Thesis	Research Questions Study Aims & Objectives	Research Methodology	Research Q1 - Practical implementations of Enterprise Engineering and Enterprise Architecture	Research Q2 - Quantitative and qualitative approaches for Enterprise Engineering and Enterprise Architecture
2005	Collaborative Modelling and Metamodelling with the Enterprise Knowledge Architecture	Jorgensen, Howard D Lillehagen, Frank Karlsen, Dag	Enterprise Modelling and Information Systems Architectures	Journal Article	presents the Modelling Platform for Collaborative Enterprises (MPCE) introduce the metamodelling framework of the MPCE, known as the Enterprise Knowledge Architecture (EKA) interoperability challenges associated with heterogeneous modelling architectures	NA	NA	Qualitative
2005	Engineering enterprises using complex-system engineering	Kuras, MI White, B.E.	INCOSE International Symposium	Conference Proceeding	summarizes a complex-system engineering (cSE) regimen for the deliberate and accelerated management of the natural processes that shape the development of complex-systems and proposes an approach for applying this regimen to enterprises introduces a fundamental process of cSE, multiscale analysis	Multiscale Analysis	NA	Qualitative
2005	Enterprise Modeling and its Applications in Company Management Systems	Madarasz, Ladaislav Timko, Maros Racek, Michal	Proceedings of 5th International Symposium of Hungarian Researchers on Computational Intelligence	Conference Proceeding	presented main reasons that lead to a state that enterprise models were not maintained in actual (living) state	NA	NA	Qualitative

continued on following page

Table 7. Continued

Publication Year	Publication Title	Authors	Published in	Type Journal Article / Conference Proceeding / White Paper - Report / Book Chapter / Standard - Specification / PhD Thesis	Research Questions Study Aims & Objectives	Research Methodology	Research Q1 - Practical implementations of Enterprise Engineering and Enterprise Architecture	Research Q2 - Quantitative and qualitative approaches for Enterprise Engineering and Enterprise Architecture
2005	Enterprise simulation: a hybrid system approach	Rabelo, Luis Helal, Magdy Jones, Albert Min, Hyeung-Sik	International Journal of Computer Integrated Manufacturing	Journal Article	focus on the impact of production decisions, evaluated using discrete-event- simulation models, on enterprise-level performance measures integrating discrete-event simulation models with system dynamics models in a hybrid approach to the simulation of the entire enterprise system focus on the interactions between the production and business branches approach through an example of a semiconductor enterprise	Discrete event simulation (DES); system-dynamics (SD) simulation	Yes	Quantitative
2005	The enterprise architecture, process modeling, and simulation tools report	Hall, Curtis Harmon, P.	BPTrends.com	White Paper - Report	to provide our members with an overview of the various types of business process software products available today focuses on tools that companies use to analyze and modify business processes the capabilities of modeling tools in several ways	NA	Yes	Qualitative

continued on following page

Table 7. Continued

Publication Year	Publication Title	Authors	Published in	Type Journal Article / Conference Proceeding / White Paper - Report / Book Chapter / Standard - Specification / PhD Thesis	Research Questions Study Aims & Objectives	Research Methodology	Research Q1 - Practical implementations of Enterprise Engineering and Enterprise Architecture	Research Q2 - Quantitative and qualitative approaches for Enterprise Engineering and Enterprise Architecture
2006	A Comparison Of Enterprise Architecture Frameworks	Urbaczewski, Lise Mrdalj, Stevan	Issues in Information Systems	Journal Article	provides a comparison of several frameworks that can then be used for guidance in the selection of an EAF that meets the needed criteria views and abstractions comparisons guidelines in selecting an EAF and determining a best-fit of a framework	NA	NA	Qualitative
2006	A survey on CIO concerns- do enterprise architecture frameworks support them	Lindström, Asa Johnson, Pontus Johansson, Erik Ekstedt, Mathias Simonsson, Mårten C Johansson, E	Information Systems Frontiers	Journal Article	presents the results of a survey in which Swedish CIOs have prioritized their most important concerns a brief review over how well two existing Enterprise Ar- chitecture frameworks address the surveyed concerns of the CIO foci of two frameworks, the Department of Defense Architecture Framework and the Zachman Frame- work for Enterprise Architecture, are therefore compared to the results of the survey	web-based survey; Analytic Hierarchy Process; Pair-wise comparison	Yes	Qualitative
2006	Creating or Choosing an Enterprise Architecture Framework	Schekkerman, Jaap	How to Survive in the Jungle of Enterprise Architecture Frameworks: Creating or Choosing an Enterprise Architecture Framework	Book Chapter	general information about some of the Enterprise Architecture Frameworks	NA	NA	Qualitative

continued on following page

Table 7. Continued

Publication Year	Publication Title	Authors	Published in	Type Journal Article / Conference Proceeding / White Paper - Report / Book Chapter - Standard - Specification / PhD Thesis	Research Questions Study Aims & Objectives	Research Methodology	Research Q1 - Practical implementations of Enterprise Engineering and Enterprise Architecture	Research Q2 - Quantitative and qualitative approaches for Enterprise Engineering and Enterprise Architecture
2006	Enterprise Architecture: Driving Business Benefits from IT	Jeanne W. Ross	Center for Information Systems Research	White Paper - Report	four stages of architecture maturity as Enterprises learn to enhance the strategic capabilities of IT	NA	Yes	Qualitative
2006	IBM Industry Models for Financial Services	IBM	IBM	White Paper - Report	IFW business models that assist a bank in implementing a flexible, reusable, extensible and easily customizable architecture	NA	NA	Qualitative
2006	The Nature Of Theory In Information Systems	Gregor, Shirley	MIS Quarterly	Journal Article	examine the structural nature of theory in Information Systems addresses issues of causality, explanation, prediction, and generalization that underlie an understanding of theory presented a number of ideas about theory in IS and proposed a taxonomy for classifying the theories we develop	NA	NA	Qualitative

continued on following page

Table 7. Continued

Publication Year	Publication Title	Authors	Published in	Type *Journal Article / Conference Proceeding / White Paper - Report / Book Chapter - Standard - Specification / PhD Thesis*	Research Questions Study Aims & Objectives	Research Methodology	Research Q1 - Practical implementations of Enterprise Engineering and Enterprise Architecture	Research Q2 - Quantitative and qualitative approaches for Enterprise Engineering and Enterprise Architecture
2007	A Federated Approach to Enterprise Architecture Model Maintenance	Fischer, Ronny Aier, Stephan Winter, Robert	Enterprise Modelling and Information Systems Architecture	Journal Article	discusses the shortcomings of existing approaches to enterprise architecture model maintenance, proposes a federated approach, and reports on its implementation at a large financial service provider How should an EA maintenance concept be designed to ensure the sustainable and effi- cient usage of EA as an instrument for stra- tegic change and alignment?	NA	Yes	Qualitative
2007	Business Value Assessment of It Investments	Gammelgård, M.	KTH, Royal Institute of Technology	Phd Thesis	IT investment evaluation method is presented that indicatively assesses the differences in contribution to business value from IT-investment alternatives	Functional Reference Model	Yes	Qualitative

continued on following page

Table 7. Continued

Publication Year	Publication Title	Authors	Published in	Type Journal Article / Conference Proceeding / White Paper - Report / Book Chapter / Standard - Specification / PhD Thesis	Research Questions Study Aims & Objectives	Research Methodology	Research Q1 - Practical implementations of Enterprise Engineering and Enterprise Architecture	Research Q2 - Quantitative and qualitative approaches for Enterprise Engineering and Enterprise Architecture
2007	Discovering And Modelling Enterprise Engineering Project Processes	Ovidiu Noran	Handbook of Enterprise Systems Architecture in Practice	Book Chapter	proposes a way to assist the inference of processes and to facilitate the selection and use of AF elements needed to accomplish EE projects the description of the meta-methodology principle and of the assessment reference used a case study presents a sample application of the meta-methodology for a real EE project. proposes a basic method to guide the creation of a set of activity type descriptions expressing what needs to be done in a particular EE project, based on domain knowledge – i.e., based on project stakeholder / champion knowledge about the participating entities and their relations	Meta-Methodology	Yes	Qualitative
2007	Enterprise Architecture as Strategy	Ross, J. W., Weill, P. Robertson, D. C.	Harvard Business School	Book Chapter	handbook for building foundation; how to define operation model; how to desig and implement enterprise architecture; how to adopt IT engagement model	NA	NA	Qualitative

continued on following page

187

Table 7. Continued

Publication Year	Publication Title	Authors	Published in	Type Journal Article / Conference Proceeding / White Paper - Report / Book Chapter / Standard - Specification / PhD Thesis	Research Questions Study Aims & Objectives	Research Methodology	Research Q1 - Practical implementations of Enterprise Engineering and Enterprise Architecture	Research Q2 - Quantitative and qualitative approaches for Enterprise Engineering and Enterprise Architecture
2007	Federal Enterprise Architecture (FEA) Consolidated Reference Model: Version 2.3	Executive Office of the President of the United States	www.reginfo.gov	Standard	a common language and framework to describe and analyze IT investments, enhance collaboration and ultimately transform the Federal government consists of a set of interrelated "reference models" designed to facilitate cross-agency analysis and the identification of duplicative investments, gaps and opportunities for collaboration within and across agencies	NA	NA	Qualitative
2007	Generating visualizations of enterprise architectures using model transformations	S., Buckl A.M., Ernst I., Lankes C.M., Schweda A., Wittenburg	Enterprise Modelling and Information Systems Architecture	Journal Article	points to the fundamental principles of software cartography, an approach for EA modeling, including a method for the automatic creation of visualizations based on EA models. brief overview of a prototypic implementation of this approach illustrates the practical applicability for visual modeling and documenting EA a visualization model containing elements representing graphical concepts.	NA	NA	Qualitative

continued on following page

Table 7. Continued

Publication Year	Publication Title	Authors	Published in	Type Journal Article / Conference Proceeding / White Paper - Report / Book Chapter - Standard - Specification / PhD Thesis	Research Questions Study Aims & Objectives	Research Methodology	Research Q1 - Practical implementations of Enterprise Engineering and Enterprise Architecture	Research Q2 - Quantitative and qualitative approaches for Enterprise Engineering and Enterprise Architecture
2007	Integrating Architectural Models	Arbab, Farhad Boer, Frank de Bonsangue, Marcello Lankhorst, Marc Proper, Erik Torre, Leendert van der	Enterprise Modelling and Information Systems Architectures	Journal Article	how the distinctions can be used for model integration within the architectural approach illustrate how symbolic models can be integrated using an architectural language. how integrated models can be updated using the distinction between symbolic models and their visualization, and how semantic models can be integrated using a new kind of enterprise analysis called semantic analysis	NA	Yes	Qualitative
2007	Integration of IT Service Management into Enterprise Architecture	Braun, Christian Winter, Robert	SAC '07 Proceedings of the 2007 ACM symposium on Applied computing	Conference Proceeding	proposes an enterprise architecture extension that achieves such an integration the integration of Service Oriented Architecture is discussed as a further extension	Design Science Research	NA	Qualitative

continued on following page

Table 7. Continued

Publication Year	Publication Title	Authors	Published in	Type Journal Article / Conference Proceeding / White Paper - Report / Book Chapter / Standard - Specification / PhD Thesis	Research Questions Study Aims & Objectives	Research Methodology	Research Q1 - Practical implementations of Enterprise Engineering and Enterprise Architecture	Research Q2 - Quantitative and qualitative approaches for Enterprise Engineering and Enterprise Architecture
2007	Open Reference Models: Community-driven Collaboration to Promote Development and Dissemination of Reference Models	Frank, Ulrich Strecker, Stefan	Enterprise Modelling and Information Systems Architecture	Conference Proceeding	notion of open reference models based on analogies to free and open source software development how "openness" of reference models affects their development and use, and outline strategic options for a first open reference modelling initiative suggest that community-driven collaborative modelling projects resolve the current paradox of reference model research and practice investigates whether FOSS development serves as a suitable orientation for over-coming the reference model paradox	NA	NA	Qualitative
2007	Sap Eaf Overview Guide	SAP	SAP	White Paper - Report	Overview of SAP EAF	NA	NA	Qualitative

continued on following page

Table 7. Continued

Publication Year	Publication Title	Authors	Published in	Type *Journal Article / Conference Proceeding / White Paper - Report / Book Chapter - Standard - Specification / PhD Thesis*	Research Questions Study Aims & Objectives	Research Methodology	Research Q1 - Practical implementations of Enterprise Engineering and Enterprise Architecture	Research Q2 - Quantitative and qualitative approaches for Enterprise Engineering and Enterprise Architecture
2007	TOGAF and COBIT Mapping of TOGAF 8.1 with COBIT 4.0	The IT Governance Institute	www.opengroup.com	White Paper - Report	provides a detailed mapping of TOGAF 8.1 with COBIT 4.0 and also contains the classification of the standards discussed in this publication	NA	NA	Qualitative
2008	An Evaluation Framework for Enterprise Architecture Modelling	Wolff, Frank	Enterprise Modelling and Information Systems Architectures	Journal Article	The process of judging the economic impact and interdependencies with the concept of evaluation chains. a dedicated reference evaluation chain based on an extensive compilation of existing knowledge on economic relationships in enterprise architecture modelling is proposed.	NA	NA	Qualitative

continued on following page

Table 7. Continued

Publication Year	Publication Title	Authors	Published in	Type Journal Article / Conference Proceeding / White Paper - Report / Book Chapter - Standard - Specification / PhD Thesis	Research Questions Study Aims & Objectives	Research Methodology	Research Q1 - Practical implementations of Enterprise Engineering and Enterprise Architecture	Research Q2 - Quantitative and qualitative approaches for Enterprise Engineering and Enterprise Architecture
2008	Application of Network Visualization to Identify Gaps in Complexs Information System Architectures	Cane, Carlos E. Martinez. Cane, Sheila a. Abdul-Rauf, Salwa Smith, Kevin Lee, Kristin	MITRE Corporation	White Paper - Report	follows earlier work aimed at ensuring a connection between the information sharing needs of a large number of participants comprising a distributed command, control, and coordination network and the underlying communications capabilities that they possess; and on the relational model and database built as part of a subsequent effort to analyze the complex relationships involved. examines the applicability of network visualization techniques linked directly to the underlying relational data elements to analyze and portray information in a more intuitive way, including identification, comprehension, and presentation of participant interdependent relationships and capability gaps	NA	NA	Qualitative

continued on following page

continued on following page

Table 7. Continued

Publication Year	Publication Title	Authors	Published in	Type Journal Article / Conference Proceeding / White Paper - Report / Book Chapter / Standard - Specification / PhD Thesis	Research Questions Study Aims & Objectives	Research Methodology	Research Q1 - Practical implementations of Enterprise Engineering and Enterprise Architecture	Research Q2 - Quantitative and qualitative approaches for Enterprise Engineering and Enterprise Architecture
2008	Best Practices for Business and Systems Analysis in Projects Conforming to Enterprise Architecture	Foorthuis, Ralph Brinkkemper, Sjaak	International Journal of Enterprise Modelling and Information Systems Architectures	Journal Article	Canonical Action Research approach is applied to participate in two business process redesign projects Focus Group interviews to elicit knowledge about carrying out projects conforming to architecture present seven observations and ten best practices What best practices can be identified for eliciting business and IT requirements in local projects that have to comply with Enterprise Architecture? how enterprises can deal practically with project conformance to EA, mainly from a business and systems analysis perspective	Canonical Action Research	Yes	Qualitative
2008	Classification of Enterprise Architecture Scenarios – An Exploratory Analysis	Aier, Stephan Riege, Christian Winter, Robert	International Journal of Enterprise Modelling and Information Systems Architectures	Journal Article	a basic classification of EA scenarios	exploratory empirical analysis	Yes	Quantitative

continued on following page

Table 7. Continued

Publication Year	Publication Title	Authors	Published in	Type Journal Article / Conference Proceeding / White Paper - Report / Book Chapter - Standard - Specification / PhD Thesis	Research Questions Study Aims & Objectives	Research Methodology	Research Q1 - Practical implementations of Enterprise Engineering and Enterprise Architecture	Research Q2 - Quantitative and qualitative approaches for Enterprise Engineering and Enterprise Architecture
2008	From Software Engineering to Enterprise Engineering– Introduction to a Language-Critical Approach	Ortner, Erich	Innovative Techniques in Instruction Technology, E-learning, E-assessment, and Education	Conference Proceeding	how the philosophy of science has developed throughout the twentieth century seems to imply that a) the primarily American analytic philosophy of science paired with b) the methodical constructivism of predominantly German origin (Erlangen and Constance) could form this common basis. In this paper, both philosophies will form the foundation substantiating practical development in the field of service-oriented architecture.	ProCEM - Process-Centric Enterprise Modeling & Management	NA	Qualitative
2008	Integration of IT Strategy and Enterprise Architecture Models	Velitchkov, Ivaylo	International Conference on Computer Systems and Technologies	Conference Proceeding	provides the rationale and concept for integration of models and modeling objects of Enterprise Architecture and IT Strategies	NA	NA	Qualitative

Table 7. Continued

Publication Year	Publication Title	Authors	Published in	Type *Journal Article / Conference Proceeding / White Paper - Report / Book Chapter / Standard - Specification / PhD Thesis*	Research Questions Study Aims & Objectives	Research Methodology	Research Q1 - Practical implementations of Enterprise Engineering and Enterprise Architecture	Research Q2 - Quantitative and qualitative approaches for Enterprise Engineering and Enterprise Architecture
2008	Real enterprise-architecture: beyond IT to the whole enterprise	Graves, Tom	Tetradian Books	Book	This book is about the practice of enterprise-architecture, particularly at the level of the whole enterprise.	NA	NA	Qualitative
2009	A Decision Support System for Enterprise Engineering	Noran, O.	Information Systems Development: Challenges in Practice, Theory, and Education	Book Chapter	to support decision-making in Enterprise Engineering projects approach based on the analysis of the interactions between	meta-methodology	NA	Qualitative

continued on following page

Table 7. Continued

continued on following page

Publication Year	Publication Title	Authors	Published in	Type Journal Article / Conference Proceeding / White Paper - Report / Book Chapter / Standard - Specification / PhD Thesis	Research Questions Study Aims & Objectives	Research Methodology	Research Q1 - Practical implementations of Enterprise Engineering and Enterprise Architecture	Research Q2 - Quantitative and qualitative approaches for Enterprise Engineering and Enterprise Architecture
					approach to handle blueprints of the Enterprise Architecture, based on several years and projects in large organizations, both in the financial and telecommunication industry overview of the underlying model, the applied methodology and the blueprints that we found to be a valuable instrument amongst elements of different communities: Project Management, IT Governance and IT Architecture			
2009	An Approach for Creating and Managing Enterprise Blueprints: A Case for IT Blueprints	Sousa, Pedro Lima, José Sampaio, André Pereira, Carla	Advances in Enterprise Engineering III, 5th International Workshop, CIAO! 2009, and 5th International Workshop, EOMAS 2009,	Conference Proceeding	Are the IT artifacts referred in IT project planning the ones that appear in IT architectural blueprints? Are project plans up-to-date enough so they can be a trustful source of information? Can we provide to each IT project a blueprint no more complex than it should be? Can changes in such blueprints be automatically propagated back to enterprise-wide and more complex blueprints? To what level of detail/ semantic should one define artifacts and concepts? How can one decide which architectural blueprints to use and what artifacts should each blueprint represent?	NA	NA	Qualitative

Table 7. Continued

Publication Year	Publication Title	Authors	Published in	Type Journal Article / Conference Proceeding / White Paper - Report / Book Chapter / Standard - Specification / PhD Thesis	Research Questions Study Aims & Objectives	Research Methodology	Research Q1 - Practical implementations of Enterprise Engineering and Enterprise Architecture	Research Q2 - Quantitative and qualitative approaches for Enterprise Engineering and Enterprise Architecture
2009	Enterprise Reference Architecture	Fattah, Ahmed	IBM	White Paper - Report	the gap/disconnect between EA and project- level architecture. Huge challenges face many in realising the promised benefits of EA on regular basis. ERA can help demonstrating the value of EA to the business.	NA	Yes	Qualitative
2009	Improving Agency Performance Using Information and Information Technology	U.S. Government	http://www.whitehouse.gov/sites/default/files/omb/assets/fea_docs/OMB_EA_Assessment_Framework_v3_1_June_2009.pdf	White Paper - Report	the use of key performance indicators (KPIs) to measure the effectiveness of EA relative to the three EA capabilities areas of Completion, Use, and Results a template-based model aimed at improving reporting and assessment via an automated process and delivery mechanism.	NA	NA	Qualitative
2009	Refining the Notion of Responsibility in Enterprise Engineering to Support Corporate Governance of IT	Feltus, Christophe Petit, Michaël Vernadat, François	13th IFAC, Information Control Problems in Manufacturing 2009	Conference Proceeding	Generic responsibility mode built on the concepts of accountability, capability and commitment and combines that model with CIMOSA Enhanced CIMOSA model	NA	Yes	Qualitative

continued on following page

Table 7. Continued

Publication Year	Publication Title	Authors	Published in	Type *Journal Article / Conference Proceeding / White Paper - Report / Book Chapter / Standard - Specification / PhD Thesis*	Research Questions Study Aims & Objectives	Research Methodology	Research Q1 - Practical implementations of Enterprise Engineering and Enterprise Architecture	Research Q2 - Quantitative and qualitative approaches for Enterprise Engineering and Enterprise Architecture
2009	The Enterprise Architecture	Op'tland, Martin Proper, Erik Waage, Maarten Cloo, Jeroen Steghuis, Claudia	Springer	Book		NA	Yes	Qualitative
2009	Understanding enterprise behavior using hybrid simulation of enterprise architecture	Glazner, Christopher G	Massachusetts Institute Of Technology	Phd Thesis	seeks to extend the practice of enterprise architecting by developing an approach for creating simulation models of enterprise architectures that can be used for analyzing the architectural factors affecting enterprise behavior and performance. matches the content of each of the "views" of an enterprise architecture framework with a suitable simulation methodology such as discrete event modeling, agent based modeling, or system dynamics, and then integrates these individual simulations into a single hybrid simulation model. how a process and methodology for creating hybrid simulation models of enterprise behavior using the enterprise's architecture can be created and applied in practice.	Simulation Model	Yes	Qualitative

continued on following page

Table 7. Continued

Publication Year	Publication Title	Authors	Published in	Type Journal Article / Conference Proceeding / White Paper - Report / Book Chapter - Standard - Specification / PhD Thesis	Research Questions Study Aims & Objectives	Research Methodology	Research Q1 - Practical implementations of Enterprise Engineering and Enterprise Architecture	Research Q2 - Quantitative and qualitative approaches for Enterprise Engineering and Enterprise Architecture
2010	An Introduction to Enterprise Engineering	Albani, Antonia Dietz, Jan	6th International Workshop, CIAO 2010	Conference Proceeding	transition from the era of information systems engineering to the era of enterprise engineering	NA	NA	Qualitative
2010	Application of Enterprise Models for Engineering Enterprise Transformation	Aier, Stephan Gleichauf, Bettina	Enterprise Modelling And Information Systems Architectures	Journal Article	propose a method to systematically derive an enterprise transformation model based on existing models representing enterprise structures at different points in time research artefact (the method) is finally demonstrated in a case study	Design Science Research	Yes	Qualitative
2010	Applying Design Research Artifacts for Building Design Research Artifacts: A Process Model for Enterprise Architecture Planning	Aier, Stephan Gleichauf, Bettina	5th International Conference, Desrist 2010	Conference Proceeding	builds a process model for EA planning as a design research artifact Which activities should be performed for EA planning and how can these activities be structured in an EA planning process?	Design Science Research	Yes	Qualitative
2010	Architecture Frameworks, Model-Driven Architecture, and Simulation	Debbabi, Mourad Hassaine, Fawzi Jarraya, Yosr Soeanu, Andrei Alawneh, Luay	Verification and Validation in Systems Engineering	Book Chapter	concept of architecture frameworks as well as the most relevant initiatives in this field	NA	NA	Qualitative

continued on following page

199

Table 7. Continued

Publication Year	Publication Title	Authors	Published in	Type Journal Article / Conference Proceeding / White Paper - Report / Book Chapter / Standard - Specification / PhD Thesis	Research Questions Study Aims & Objectives	Research Methodology	Research Q1 - Practical implementations of Enterprise Engineering and Enterprise Architecture	Research Q2 - Quantitative and qualitative approaches for Enterprise Engineering and Enterprise Architecture
2010	Business Capabilities Centric Enterprise Architecture	Barroero, Thiago Motta, Giannmario Pignatelli, Giovanni	Enterprise Architecture, Integration and Interoperability IFIP TC 5 International Conference, EAI2N 2010	Conference Proceeding	to link changes of business to data, application and technology architectures Business Component approach into the TOGAF framework	NA	Yes	Qualitative
2010	Enterprise Governance and DEMO	Henriques, Miguel Tribolet, José Hoogervorst, Jan	Instituto Superior Tecnico	Msc Thesis	to exploit how this organizational competence labeled enterprise governance (EG) can deal with this issue by using the enterprise ontological models produced using DEMO.	NA	NA	Qualitative
2010	On Supporting Collaborative Problem Solving in Enterprise Architecture Creation	Nakakawa, Agnes van Bommel, Patrick Proper, H A Erik	Working Conference on Practice-Driven Research on Enterprise Transformation PRET 2010	Conference Proceeding	to demonstrate how GSSs can also be used to support collaborative prob- lem solving in enterprise architecture creation a method designed to support collaborative problem solving during architecture creation evaluated using an experiment and two real life cases.	Design Science Research	Yes	Qualitative

continued on following page

Table 7. Continued

Publication Year	Publication Title	Authors	Published in	Type Journal Article / Conference Proceeding / White Paper - Report / Book Chapter / Standard - Specification / PhD Thesis	Research Questions Study Aims & Objectives	Research Methodology	Research Q1 - Practical implementations of Enterprise Engineering and Enterprise Architecture	Research Q2 - Quantitative and qualitative approaches for Enterprise Engineering and Enterprise Architecture
2010	Towards a Theory on Collaborative Decision Making in Enterprise Architecture	Nakakawa, Agnes vanBommel, Patrick Proper, Erik	5th International Conference, Desrist 2010	Conference Proceeding	presents an evolving theory that is currently being used to guide the development of a method for supporting collaborative decision making during enterprise architecture creation	Design Science Research; CEADA; Exploratory Survey	Yes	Qualitative
2010	Trends in enterprise architecture practice–a survey	Franke, U Ekstedt, M Lagerström, R Saat, Jan Winter, Robert	Trends in Enterprise Architecture Research 5th International Workshop, TEAR 2010	Conference Proceeding	investigates the actual application of EA, by giving a broad overview of the usage of enterprise architecture in Swedish, German, Austrian and Swiss companies a survey originally focusing on the relation between IT/ business alignment (ITBA) and EA For how many years have companies been using EA models, tools, processes and roles? How is ITBA in relation to EA perceived at companies? investigation quality attributes of EA, related to IT-systems, business and IT governance	NA	NA	Quantitative

continued on following page

201

continued on following page

Table 7. Continued

Publication Year	Publication Title	Authors	Published in	Type Journal Article / Conference Proceeding / White Paper - Report / Book Chapter / Standard - Specification / PhD Thesis	Research Questions Study Aims & Objectives	Research Methodology	Research Q1 - Practical implementations of Enterprise Engineering and Enterprise Architecture	Research Q2 - Quantitative and qualitative approaches for Enterprise Engineering and Enterprise Architecture
2011	A Critical Investigation of TOGAF – Based on the Enterprise Engineering Theory and Practice	Dietz, Jan L G Hoogervorst, Jan A P	Enterprise Engineering Working Conference 2011	Conference Proceeding	report on an investigation of TOGAF (version 9) regarding the extent to which it satisfies the indispensable requirement of unity and integration	NA	NA	Qualitative
2011	A Survey of Enterprise Architecture Analysis Using Multi Criteria Decision Making Models (MCDM)	Zia, Mehmooda Jabeen Azam, Farooque Allauddin, Maria M.J., Zia F., Azam M., Allauddin	International Conference, ICICIS 2011	Conference Proceeding	survey two multi-criteria decision making models (AHP, ANP) to determine that to what extent they have been used in making powerful decisions in complex enterprise architecture analysis find out the comparative strengths of these models	NA	NA	Qualitative
2011	An enterprise architecture approach to forest management support systems design: an application to pulpwood supply management in Portugal	Marques, A F Borges, J G Sousa, @bullet P Pinho, @bullet A M	European Journal of Forest Research	Journal Article	an approach to pulp- wood supply system architecture	NA	Yes	Qualitative
2011	Enterprise Engineering Manifesto	Dietz, Jan L G	www.ciaonetwork.org	White Paper - Report	focal topics and objectives of the emerging discipline of enterprise engi- neering, as it is currently theorized and developed within the CIAO! Network	NA	NA	Qualitative

Table 7. Continued

Publication Year	Publication Title	Authors	Published in	Type Journal Article / Conference Proceeding / White Paper - Report / Book Chapter / Standard - Specification / PhD Thesis	Research Questions Study Aims & Objectives	Research Methodology	Research Q1 - Practical implementations of Enterprise Engineering and Enterprise Architecture	Research Q2 - Quantitative and qualitative approaches for Enterprise Engineering and Enterprise Architecture
2011	Enterprise Modeling Practice in ICT-Enabled Process Change	Karlsen, Anniken	IFIP Working Conference on The Practice of Enterprise Modeling	Conference Proceeding	findings from a study where the use of enterprise modeling has been empirically investigated in eight combined process change and information technology initiatives Artifacts, guidelines and tools used in enterprise modeling practice (1) How is the modeling process organized? (2) How is participation and involvement in the modeling process? (3) Which tools, languages and guidelines are used for modeling? (4) Which artifacts are produced in each type of modeling initiative? (5) What might influence the selected way of organizing the modeling process as for example workshops with oral participation or workshops with active par- ticipation? (6) Are there any barriers to modeling to be identified	Case Study; Interview	Yes	Qualitative
2011	How does enterprises architecture add value to organisations?	Tamm, Toomas Seddon, Peter B. Shanks, Graeme Reynolds, Peter	Communications of the association for information systems	Journal Article	How does EA lead to organisational benefits? consolidates the fragmented knowledge on EA benefits and presents the EA Benefits Model (EABM)	Systemac and Exploratory Review	NA	Qualitative

continued on following page

Table 7. Continued

Publication Year	Publication Title	Authors	Published in	Type Journal Article / Conference Proceeding / White Paper - Report / Book Chapter / Standard - Specification / PhD Thesis	Research Questions Study Aims & Objectives	Research Methodology	Research Q1 - Practical implementations of Enterprise Engineering and Enterprise Architecture	Research Q2 - Quantitative and qualitative approaches for Enterprise Engineering and Enterprise Architecture
2011	The Role of Enterprise Architecture	Greefhorst, D. Proper, Erik	Architecture Principles	Book Chapter	the role of enterprise architecture, and more specifically, the role of architecture principles	NA	NA	Qualitative
2012	The Application of Enterprise Reference Architecture in the Financial Industry	Wijke ten Harmsen van der Beek1, Jos Trienekens2, and Paul Grefen2	7th Workshop, Trends in Enterprise Architecture Research and Practice TEAR 2012, and 5th Working Conference, PRET 2012	Conference Proceeding	a working definition for the concept of Enterprise Reference Architecture (ERA) a conceptual model wherein ERA is positioned What is an ERA? What are the requirements to an ERA? Are ERA's already available and how are they used? Can an ERA enhance the quality of the enterprise architecture products in the sense that expectations of stakeholders are fulfilled? Can an ERA speed up the enterprise architecting design process and deliv- ery of enterprise architecture results? Can an ERA provide improved support to the business in decision making regarding the business/IT alignment and during the EA design, realization and maintenance?	Design Science Research	NA	Qualitative

continued on following page

Table 7. Continued

Publication Year	Publication Title	Authors	Published in	Type Journal Article / Conference Proceeding / White Paper - Report / Book Chapter / Standard - Specification / PhD Thesis	Research Questions Study Aims & Objectives	Research Methodology	Research Q1 - Practical implementations of Enterprise Engineering and Enterprise Architecture	Research Q2 - Quantitative and qualitative approaches for Enterprise Engineering and Enterprise Architecture
2012	The Principles of Enterprise Engineering	Dietz, Jan L G Hoogervorst, Jan A P	Second Enterprise Engineering Working Conference, EEWC 2012	Conference Proceeding	generic objectives of enterprise engineering, formulated seven principles for dealing effectively with enterprise changes	NA	NA	Qualitative
2013	A Language for Enterprise Modelling	Lankhorst, Marc	Enterprise Architecture at Work	Book Chapter	explains what the added value of a separate enterprise modelling language is in addition to existing, more detailed design languages for business processes or software	NA	NA	Qualitative

continued on following page

206

Table 7. Continued

Publication Year	Publication Title	Authors	Published in	Type *Journal Article / Conference Proceeding / White Paper - Report / Book Chapter / Standard - Specification / PhD Thesis*	Research Questions Study Aims & Objectives	Research Methodology	Research Q1 - Practical implementations of Enterprise Engineering and Enterprise Architecture	Research Q2 - Quantitative and qualitative approaches for Enterprise Engineering and Enterprise Architecture
2013	The Discipline of Enterprise Engineering	Dietz, Jan L G Hoogervorst, Jan A P Albani, Antonia Aveiro, David Babkin, Eduard Barjis, Joseph Caetano, Artur Huysmans, Philip Iijima, Junichi Van Kervel, Steven J H Mulder, Hans Op 't Land, Martin Proper, Henderik A Sanz, Jorge Terlouw, Linda Tribolet, José Verelst, Jan Winter, Robert Jan A.P. Hoogervorst	International Journal of Organisational Design and Engineering	Journal Article	evaluate a century of enterprise development, and conclude that a paradigm shift is needed for dealing adequately with the challenges that modern enterprises face. Three generic goals are identified:	NA	NA	Qualitative
2013	A Decision Model for IT Risk Management on Disaster Recovery Center in an Enterprise Architecture Model	Sembiring, Jaka Ikhsandana, Mohammad Siregar, H	he 4th International Conference on Electrical Engineering and Informatics (ICEEI 2013)	Conference Proceeding	to show the possibility of designing a decision suppport in case of risk	NA	Yes	Quantitative

continued on following page

Table 7. Continued

Publication Year	Publication Title	Authors	Published in	Type Journal Article / Conference Proceeding / White Paper - Report / Book Chapter / Standard - Specification / PhD Thesis	Research Questions Study Aims & Objectives	Research Methodology	Research Q1 - Practical implementations of Enterprise Engineering and Enterprise Architecture	Research Q2 - Quantitative and qualitative approaches for Enterprise Engineering and Enterprise Architecture
2013	Engineering an Enterprise: Practical Issues of Two Case Studies from the Luxembourgish Beverage and Tobacco Industry	Molnar, Wolfgang A Proper, Henderik A	Practice-Driven Research on Enterprise Transformation, Pret 2013	Conference Proceeding	practical issues in engineering enterprises that do not embrace classical enterprise architecture frameworks	NA	Yes	Qualitative
2013	A Study on Meta-synthesis Mode of the Systems Engineering of Governance of Large Enterprise Group	Ma, Sheng Wang, Rui	Proceedings of the Sixth International Conference on Management	Conference Proceeding	defines the concept and connotations of large enterprise group, then describes and analyzes the main content and the framework model of the governance of large enterprise groups.	NA	NA	Qualitative
2013	Development of Enterprise Engineering Guidelines for Enterprise Diagnosis and Design	Deschamps, Fernando Pinheiro De Lima, Edson Gouvea Da Costa, Sergio Eduardo Santos, Eduardo Alves Portela Van Aken, Eileen	Industrial and Systems Engineering Research Conference	Conference Proceeding	proposing a set of guidelines to be used for diagnosing and (re)designing organizations	NA	NA	Qualitative

continued on following page

Table 7. Continued

Publication Year	Publication Title	Authors	Published in	Type: Journal Article / Conference Proceeding / White Paper - Report / Book Chapter / Standard - Specification / PhD Thesis	Research Questions Study Aims & Objectives	Research Methodology	Research Q1 - Practical implementations of Enterprise Engineering and Enterprise Architecture	Research Q2 - Quantitative and qualitative approaches for Enterprise Engineering and Enterprise Architecture
2014	An Adaptable Decision Making Model for Sustainable Enterprise Interoperability	Sakas, Damianos Kutsikos, Konstadinos	Procedia - Social and Behavioral Sciences	Journal Article	to introduce new ways for managing: a) information flow (re-)configurations; b) equilibrium state transitions in evolving collaboration networks the development of an adaptability model that helps entities in a collaboration network manage inter-enterprise information flows, in the presence of dynamic re-configurations of the network.	NA	NA	Qualitative
2014	Enterprise Modeling in the context of Enterprise Engineering: State of the art and outlook	Vernadat, François	International Journal of Production Management and Engineering	Journal Article	recalls definitions and fundamental principles of enterprise modelling, which goes far beyond process modeling new features of enterprise modeling languages including risk, value, competency modeling and service orientation	NA	Yes	Qualitative

continued on following page

Table 7. Continued

Publication Year	Publication Title	Authors	Published in	Type *Journal Article / Conference Proceeding / White Paper - Report / Book Chapter / Standard - Specification / PhD Thesis*	Research Questions Study Aims & Objectives	Research Methodology	Research Q1 - Practical implementations of Enterprise Engineering and Enterprise Architecture	Research Q2 - Quantitative and qualitative approaches for Enterprise Engineering and Enterprise Architecture
2014	Potentially Valuable Overlaps between Work System Theory, DEMO, and Enterprise Engineering	Alter, Steven	Proceedings - 16th IEEE Conference on Business Informatics, CBI 2014	Conference Proceeding	1) establishing links between WST/WSM and enterprise engineering in general and 2) comparing aspects of WST/WSM and DEMO and demonstrating similarities, thereby implying the possibility of converting DEMO models into work system models that can be developed further using other methods and tools designed around WST	NA	Yes	Qualitative
2014	How Enterprise Architecture Formative Critical Success Facets Might Affect Enterprise Architecture Success: A Literature Analysis	Wan, Haining Luo, Aimin Luo, Xueshan	Service Science and Knowledge Innovation: 15th IFIP WG 8.1 International Conference on Informatics and Semiotics in Organizations	Conference Proceeding	how EA formative critical success facets/factors would affect the achievement of EA success	Abductive reasoning; Prescriptive literature analysis	NA	Qualitative
2014	Research Paradigms and Topics in Enterprise Engineering	Molnar, Wolfgang A. Korhonen, Janne J.	Proceedings - International Conference on Research Challenges in Information Science	Journal Article	a debate on the need for alternative research paradigms and for research on social aspects in the field of EE.	NA	NA	Qualitative

continued on following page

Table 7. Continued

Publication Year	Publication Title	Authors	Published in	Type Journal Article / Conference Proceeding / White Paper - Report / Book Chapter / Standard - Specification / PhD Thesis	Research Questions Study Aims & Objectives	Research Methodology	Research Q1 - Practical implementations of Enterprise Engineering and Enterprise Architecture	Research Q2 - Quantitative and qualitative approaches for Enterprise Engineering and Enterprise Architecture
2014	Research Methodologies in Enterprise Engineering: Insights from a Workshop	Gaaloul, Khaled Molnar, Wolfgang	Proceedings - 2014 International Workshop on Advanced Information Systems for Enterprises, IWAISE 2014	Conference Proceeding	present insights from a workshop about research methodologies in EE	NA	NA	Qualitative
2014	The Connective Scheme between the Enterprise Architecture and Organisational Structure	Iyamu, Tiko Mphahlele, Leshoto Hamunyela, Suama	The 2014 World Conference on Information Systems and Technologies (WorldCIST'14)	Conference Proceeding	The impact of agents on the deployment of EA in organizations, using the lens of structuration theory in the analysis of the data.	NA	Yes	Qualitative
2014	Enterprise Engineering of Lean Accounting and Value Stream Structure through Collective System Design	Cochran, David S Aldrich, Wendell Sereno, Rich	2014 IIE Engineering Lean and Six Sigma Conference	Conference Proceeding	to provide a systems engineering perspective about the future of Enterprise Engineering that includes the design of the value stream(s) and performance measurement, including lean accounting structure	Collective System Design (CSD)	Yes	Qualitative
2014	Enterprise Architectures A Just-in-Time Approach for Decision-Making	MITRE Corporation	http://www2.mitre.org/public/eabook/pdf/Using-EAs-14-1210.pdf	White Paper - Report	a summary of the range of potential uses of enterprise architectures (EAs), some of the challenges facing the users of EAs, and practical approaches for developing them incrementally over time to provide "just in time" utility to decision makers	NA	NA	Qualitative

continued on following page

Table 7. Continued

Publication Year	Publication Title	Authors	Published in	Type Journal Article / Conference Proceeding / White Paper - Report / Book Chapter - Standard - Specification / PhD Thesis	Research Questions Study Aims & Objectives	Research Methodology	Research Q1 - Practical implementations of Enterprise Engineering and Enterprise Architecture	Research Q2 - Quantitative and qualitative approaches for Enterprise Engineering and Enterprise Architecture
2014	The Role of Enterprise Governance and Cartography in Enterprise Engineering	Tribolet, José Sousa, Pedro Caetano, Artur	Enterprise Modelling and Information Systems Architecture	Journal Article	defines a set of enterprise cartography principles and provides an account of its role in understanding the dynamics of an organisation	NA	NA	Qualitative
2014	The Nature of the Enterprise Engineering Discipline	de Vries, Marne Gerber, Aurona van der Merwe, Alta	4th Enterprise Engineering Working Conference	Conference Proceeding	argue that a research agenda for EE should start with the first class of questions, concerning the domain of the discipline and suggest that an existing model, the Enterprise Evolution Contextualisation Model (EECM), could be used to define the domain of the EE discipline	NA	NA	Qualitative

continued on following page

Table 7. Continued

Publication Year	Publication Title	Authors	Published in	Type Journal Article / Conference Proceeding / White Paper - Report / Book Chapter - Standard - Specification / PhD Thesis	Research Questions Study Aims & Objectives	Research Methodology	Research Q1 - Practical implementations of Enterprise Engineering and Enterprise Architecture	Research Q2 - Quantitative and qualitative approaches for Enterprise Engineering and Enterprise Architecture
2014	Enterprise Architecture: Twenty Years of the GERAM Framework	Bernus, Peter Noran, Ovidiu Molina, Arturo	Proceedings of the 19th World Congress The International Federation of Automatic Control	Conference Proceeding	the use of systems thinking and systems theory in EA and about how it is possible to reconcile and understand, based on a single overarching framework, the interplay of two major enterprise change endeavours: on the one hand enterprise engineering (i.e. deliberate change) and on the other hand evolutionary, organic change attempts to show how such change processes can be illustrated by employing systems thinking to construct dynamic business models: the evolution of these concepts is exemplified with some past applications in networked enterprise building and more recent proposals in environmental, disaster and healthcare management. Finally, the paper attempts to plot the way GERAM will continue to con- tribute to society in the context of future challenges and emerging opportunities	NA	NA	Qualitative

continued on following page

Table 7. Continued

Publication Year	Publication Title	Authors	Published in	Type Journal Article / Conference Proceeding / White Paper - Report / Book Chapter - Standard - Specification / PhD Thesis	Research Questions Study Aims & Objectives	Research Methodology	Research Q1 - Practical implementations of Enterprise Engineering and Enterprise Architecture	Research Q2 - Quantitative and qualitative approaches for Enterprise Engineering and Enterprise Architecture
2015	DisasterWarning System in the Philippines Through Enterprise Engineering Perspective: AStudy on the 2013 Super Typhoon Haiyan	Leelawat, Natt Suppasri, Anawat Kure, Shuichi Yi, Carine J. Mateo, Cherry May R Imamura, Fumihiko	Journal of DisasterResearch	Journal Article	to determine the system's essential components by us- ing the Design and Engineering Methodology for Or- ganizations (DEMO) contribute a practical aspect in the formof suggestions to planners and decision makers that may assist them in preparing mitigation plans for projected natural disasters	DEMO	Yes	Qualitative
2015	The Enterprise Engineering Domain	De Vries, Marne Gerber, Aurona Van Der Merwe, Alta	Enterprise Engineering Working Conference	Conference Proceeding	(1) the validation results of the proposed boundaries of the EE domain, and (2) a prioritisation of the phenomena of interest and core problems or topics of interest within the EE domain	NA	Yes	Quantitative
2015	A Case Study of Business Process Simulation in the Context of Enterprise Engineering	Liu, Yang Iijima, Junichi	Enterprise Engineering Working Conference	Conference Proceeding	to apply the DEMO++ based simulation in a real-world case study with the following objectives: to evaluate the advantages, potentials and limitations of DEMO++ based simulation; to further investigate how it can assist in business process change; and to find problems to be improved in the selected process of "Company C"	Na	Yes	Qualitative

continued on following page

213

Table 7. Continued

Publication Year	Publication Title	Authors	Published in	Type Journal Article / Conference Proceeding / White Paper - Report / Book Chapter / Standard - Specification / PhD Thesis	Research Questions Study Aims & Objectives	Research Methodology	Research Q1 - Practical implementations of Enterprise Engineering and Enterprise Architecture	Research Q2 - Quantitative and qualitative approaches for Enterprise Engineering and Enterprise Architecture
2015	Analysis of Federated Enterprise Architecture Models	Antunes, Goncalo Barateiro, Jose Caetano, Artur Borbinha, Jose	Twenty-Third European Conference on Information Systems	Conference Proceeding	(1) the specification of multiple enterprise architecture models as ontological schemas, (2) the integration of ontological schemas, and (3) the analysis of the integrated models.	Design Science Research	NA	Qualitative
2015	Extending Enterprise Architectures to Capture Consumer Values: The Case of TOGAF	Svee, Eric-Oluf Zdravkovic, Jelena	Advanced Information Systems Engineering Workshops	Conference Proceeding	how to make Enterprise Architecture (EA) aware of consumer values	NA	Yes	Qualitative
2015	Contemporary Enterprise Architecture Frameworks: A Comparative study of TOGAF and Zachmans ' EA frameworks	Singh, Alok Mudholkar, Pankaj Balani, Lovely Lakhmani	Research Gate	Conference Proceeding	conduct comparative study of two popular EA frameworks viz. TOGAF and Zach man's broad introduction to the field of enterprise architecture	NA	NA	Qualitative
2016	A Conceptual Framework for Analysing Enterprise Engineering Methodologies	Albani, Antonia Rabera, David Wintera, Robert	Enterprise Modelling And Information Systems Architectures	Journal Article	a systematical understanding and comparison of methodologies and for a facilitation of their composition (if necessary), a general conceptual framework proposed	Design Science Research	Yes	Qualitative

continued on following page

Table 7. Continued

Publication Year	Publication Title	Authors	Published in	Type *Journal Article / Conference Proceeding / White Paper - Report / Book Chapter - Standard - Specification / PhD Thesis*	Research Questions Study Aims & Objectives	Research Methodology	Research Q1 - Practical implementations of Enterprise Engineering and Enterprise Architecture	Research Q2 - Quantitative and qualitative approaches for Enterprise Engineering and Enterprise Architecture
2016	A Multidimensional Classification of 55 Enterprise Architecture Frameworks	Sultanow, Eldar Brockmann, Carsten Schroeder, Kai Cox, Sean	Twenty-second Americas Conference on Information Systems, 2016	Conference Proceeding	definition of classification system which is used to analyze 55 different EA frameworks to enable researchers and practical enterprise architects to navigate their way around in the proverbial jungle of enterprise architecture frameworks	NA	NA	Qualitative
2016	Enterprise Architecture Frameworks: The Fad of the Century	Kotusev, Svyatoslav	bsc.org - British Computer Society	White Paper - Report	How can it be that the most widely acknowledged EA frameworks inseparably associated with the very notion of EA turned out to be essentially unrelated to real EA practices? What does it all mean?	NA	NA	Qualitative
2016	Enterprise information systems state of the art: Past, present and future trends	Romero, David Vernadat, François	Computers in Industry	Journal Article	intended to set the scene for a special issue of the Computers in Industry Journal on "Future Perspectives on Next Generation Enterprise Information Systems"	NA	NA	Qualitative
2016	Interface-based software integration	Rais, Aziz Ahmad	Journal Of Systems Integration	Journal Article	Interface-based integration practice in order to help simplify the process of building such a software integration system.	NA	NA	Qualitative

continued on following page

Table 7. Continued

Publication Year	Publication Title	Authors	Published in	Type Journal Article / Conference Proceeding / White Paper - Report / Book Chapter / Standard - Specification / PhD Thesis	Research Questions Study Aims & Objectives	Research Methodology	Research Q1 - Practical implementations of Enterprise Engineering and Enterprise Architecture	Research Q2 - Quantitative and qualitative approaches for Enterprise Engineering and Enterprise Architecture
2016	The History of Enterprise Architecture: An Evidence-Based Review	Kotusev, Svyatoslav	Journal of Enterprise Architecture	Journal Article	Is Zachman's "A Framework for Information Systems Architecture" really the seminal publication of the EA discipline? Is it really the first EA framework? Did it really profoundly influence modern EA methodologies? an evidence-based history of EA and tracing the origins of all essential ideas constituting the basis of the modern concept of EA	NA	NA	Qualitative

Chapter 7

Sustainable Competitive Advantage Through Business Model Innovation:
The Indian Perspective

Purna Prabhakar Nandamuri
IFHE University, India

K. S. Venu Gopala Rao
IFHE University, India

Mukesh Kumar Mishra
IFHE University, India

ABSTRACT

Conventionally, businesses focus on their offerings for growth. But the increasingly unpredictable business environment is making them irrelevant in the market. So, businesses should resort to a system of dynamic management by innovating on the business models rather than a single aspect of the business. Business model innovation demands neither new technologies nor creation of new markets, but cares about delivering the existing products produced by existing technologies to the existing markets, through a unique model. Hence, defining, innovating, and evolving new business models have become the new basis of competition. A differentiated, hard-to-imitate, effective, and efficient business model is more likely to ensure higher profits and long-term survival. In this context, the present chapter attempts to furnish multiple global evidences and discuss the Indian perspective of business model innovation.

DOI: 10.4018/978-1-5225-5360-1.ch007

INTRODUCTION

If a man makes a better mouse-trap than his neighbor, though he builds his house in the woods, the world will make a beaten path to his door, said Ralph Waldo Emerson[1]. Organizations can achieve superior performance when they turn unique by doing something no other business does and through the ways that are difficult to imitate. The logic is very simple that a business will neither be at advantage nor prosper when all competitors offer similar products and services to the same set of customers by performing the same kinds of activities. Competitive advantage allows a business to generate higher sales, better margins and able to retain more customers than competitors, making it difficult for competitors to neutralize that advantage. Hence, achieving sustainable competitive advantage is the Holy Grail [2] for every business. But the present business environment is characterized by risk and instability owing to globalization and disruptive technological innovations. For example, in perhaps the most extensive study of long-term growth rates, researchers at the Corporate Executive Board found that only 13 percent of Global 100 companies have been able to sustain as little as two percent real annual revenue growth from one decade to the next over the past 50 years (Sherman, 2017). An executive survey of 1,035 C-level executives and board members representing the full range of regions, industries, and functional specialties, reported that 87 percent of executives and directors feel most pressured to demonstrate strong financial performance within two years or less, 65 percent say short-term pressure has increased over the past five years, and 55 percent of executives and directors in companies lacking a long-term culture say they would delay a new project to hit quarterly targets, even if it sacrificed long-term value (Barton, Bailey, & Zoffer, 2015). This phenomenon is coined as corporate short termism. On the other hand, the average revenue and earnings growth between 2001 and 2014 were 47 percent and 36 percent higher, and market capitalization grew 58 percent faster as well, among the firms that focused on the long term (Sherman, 2017). In another research, Reeves and Deimler (2011) found that the business operating margins, which remained largely static since 1950s, have been more than doubled since 1980s, making way for undisputed market leaders in each industry, creating a wide gap between the winners and losers. Consequently, businesses shifting in and out of the top three rankings in their industries increased to 14 percent by 2008, from two percent during 1960s, proving, on one hand, that market leadership to be an increasingly dubious prize and disproving, on the other hand, the strong correlation between profitability and market share in many sectors. The probability that the market leader is also the profitability leader, declined from 34 percent in 1950s to just a seven percent in 2007 (Reeves & Deimler, 2011). Further, it has become virtually impossible for some businesses to identify the right competitor from the right industry. Thus, time has proved that sustainable competitive advantage no longer arises exclusively from either market position or scale of operations. Rather, it stems from the second-order organizational capabilities of rapid adaptability to the dynamic business environment and act fast on the signals of change. Companies should work out to experiment rapidly, frequently, and economically, not only with products and services but also with processes, strategies, and even business models. In this context, the present chapter attempts to highlight the concept, practices and scope of the business model innovation for sustained competitive advantage with specific reference to the Indian business.

In the contemporary creative economy, businesses are struggling to exploit the next opportunity by understanding what customers really need and ready to pay for, to design better experiences, and to gain new efficiencies from existing assets. Many organizations have traditionally been involved in either process or product innovation in order to achieve competitive advantage in the long run. But, the cross industry research findings across different industries have proved that *invention breeds invention,*[3] as it is found that around 90 percent of all learning ultimately disperses to relevant competitors, making it harder to protect the process innovations (Reeves & Deimler, 2011). Product innovations also prove to be difficult to safeguard since comprehensive information on around 70 percent of new product innovations reaches competitors within a year of development, since imitation costs a third less than innovation and is a third quicker also (Ghemawat, 1986). Therefore, it is obvious that product and process innovations which are expensive, time-consuming, and require considerable investments, could not sustain the competitive advantage for a business for a relatively longer period. However, the role of process and product innovations, in achieving sustainability, can't be ignored. But, businesses should not stay too long with one model of competitive advantage and should keep looking for the next one always before the existing model becomes either exhausted or turns obsolete or copied by competitors. The product and process innovation efforts integrated with the other aspects of business such as marketing and organizational innovation proves to be better than the simple product or process innovation. For example, among the European Union Member States, out of 49.1 percent of the total organizations that reported some form of innovation activity during 2012–14, organizational innovation was recorded at 27.3 percent while product innovation accounted for 23.9 percent, marketing innovation at 22.8 percent, and process innovation at 21.6 percent. Further, a majority of the organizations have introduced more than one type of these innovations (Eurostat, 2017).

Thus, businesses are forced to cope with such competitive pressure where competitive advantage is transient and not sustainable, proving the search for the *holy grail* of 'sustainable competitive advantage' is futile making the future returns on the upfront investments uncertain. Customers have started looking for reliable and customized solutions, rather than simple products or services, while insisting on better, cheaper, quicker, and convenient delivery of the same. Consequently, the bargaining power has shifted from seller to buyer in the marketplace. This unprecedented market environment has augmented the necessity to address the soaring customer needs more astutely and capture value by providing required solutions through innovative and integrated business models. Hence, continuous and transformational innovation has become the new playbook for business survival, if not growth. Ever ongoing re-evaluation of the value propositions that business offers to customers, has become imperative to sustain the competitive advantage. Hence, businesses would not be able to capture value from their product and process innovations without a well-developed business model. The UK based grocery retailer-Tesco[4], serves an apt example for this phenomenon as it believes that its business is organized around the three pillars of customers, product and channels. Tesco prioritizes customer involvement along with the product and process innovations (Tesco, 2016). Tesco attempts to comprehend the early warning of shifts in customer behavior by analyzing the purchase patterns of more than 13 million members of its loyalty program, to customize its offerings for each store and each customer segment. Further, the analysis empowered the company to become a store without walls, through online platform, and to offer a broader range of products and services, including media and financial services, by extending the business model.

To refer another example, Ford Motor Company[5] could slash the time required to build Model-T[6] from around 12 hours to just 93 minutes, by shifting the production facility to an innovative assembly line at the nearby Highland Park in Michigan, from its existing production facility in Detroit, in1910, which allowed the price of the car to be dropped from $850 in 1908 to less than $300 in 1925. At such prices, Model T at times comprised as much as 40 percent of all cars sold in the United States, realizing Ford's goal to 'democratize the automobile'. Another successful company, Google[7], monitors the changing ad conditions within a split-second time, without human intervention, by linking its advertising data directly to its operations through advanced algorithms. The real-time tracking is done on the basis of an ad's relevance to an individual's search or website as well as the advertiser's bids on key words. Subsequently, the company could generate higher pay-per-click revenue by achieving higher click-through rate through enhancing the relevance of an ad. Another case in point is Procter & Gamble (P&G)[8], which uses a virtual 3-D walk-in store to run quicker, cheaper and efficient experiments through its *Connect + Develop*[9] model, leveraging *InnoCentive*[10] and other open-innovation networks to solve technical design problems, and *Vocalpoint*[11] and other online user communities to test-market new products with friendly audiences before a full launch. Among P&G's new-business initiatives, more than 80 percent utilize its virtual toolbox model. Similarly, when Ikea[12] entered the Russian market, they observed that the value of the real estate, surrounding their new stores, increased dramatically. By, exploiting the trend, Ikea made more profits by exploring two complimentary business models simultaneously - retailing through its stores as well as capturing the appreciation in real estate value through mall development.

On the other hand, Nokia[13] serves a unique example that missed the track due to the static and rigid business model. Nokia would still be leading the smartphone market, if the experience curve, leading to a strong cost position, and the early mover advantage coupled with the scale curve, helping to achieve market leadership, were the key indicators of success. But Nokia failed to read the signals of an entirely different kind of competition, as Stephen Elop, Nokia's CEO from 2010 to 2014, wrote to his staff that *our competitors aren't taking our market share with devices; they are taking our market share with an entire ecosystem*. Thus, an increasing number of adaptive companies are exploring an array of innovative methods and technologies such as virtual environments, to breed, test, and replicate inventive ideas faster, at lower cost, and with less risk than their competitors. Conventionally, many businesses focus on their offerings – the products and services, for innovation and growth. But in an increasingly turbulent and unpredictable business environment, the routines, business models, and strategies, also become obsolete rapidly. Adaptive companies, like Tesco, Ikea, P&G, Ford, and Google, etc., innovate with business models as well as product range, to leverage existing resources and capabilities.

BUSINESS MODEL INNOVATION

An organization's business model is a system of interconnected and interdependent activities that determines the way the company do business with its customers, partners and vendors. In other words, it is an activity system, integrating a bundle of specific activities, undertaken to fulfill the perceived needs of the market, along with the description of which parties - either company or its partners, conduct which activities, and how these activities are linked to each other. Further, a business model is a set of key decisions that together determine how a business earns its revenue, incurs its costs, and manages its risks. The innovation to the model aims at making changes to those decisions such as *what* should be the offerings, and *why*, *when* and *who* to make decisions. Integrated changes along these dimensions enhance the company's revenues, costs, as well as risks also. Business model innovation is considered to be a brilliant idea, among the business circles, since it demands neither new technologies nor creation of new markets. It is concerned about delivering the existing products produced by existing technologies to the existing markets, through a unique model. Further, it creates advantages that are hard to copy since the augmented changes are invisible to the outside world. *In today's climate, it is best to assume that most business models, even successful ones, will have a short lifespan,* says Alexander Osterwalder[14]. Business models must transform over time as the dynamic markets, technologies and legal structures dictate.

Business model innovation is considered to be the fourth industrial revolution. Every industry is organized around a set of implicit and long-standing beliefs about how to make money. For instance, the retail industry believes that the store format and purchasing power determine the bottom line. The telecommunications industry is organized around the fundamentals beliefs about the average revenue per user and customer retention. The pharmaceutical sector's success is believed to depend on the time required to get approvals from the US Food and Drug Administration (USFDA). The returns in oil and gas sector are believed to be determined by company assets and regulatory framework. The business models of different businesses in any industry are usually built around such predominant beliefs. New ideas and technologies are also commercialized through the business models only. The same idea or technology brought to the market through two different business models will yield two different economic outcomes. Hence, companies strive to develop the capability to innovate on business models. The economic value of a new idea or technology remains hidden until it is commercialized through a business model. The Xerox Corporation[15] serves the best evidence for this point. Xerox, during 1980s, was making industry leading copiers and printers. The company understood that the real profit was accrued through the sale of consumables - the toner and paper, rather than the core products. Therefore, the higher the consumables for each machine sold, the greater the returns for Xerox. Accordingly, Xerox has developed a business model that would enable faster and more copies, through an effective technology enabling the machines to handle very high volumes and maximum machine uptime and availability. This obviously resulted in a strong cognitive bias discouraging the development of low-speed personal copiers. At that same time, Xerox funded significant research on man-machine interfaces and point-and-click user interface and many other technologies. But, all these technologies couldn't contribute to increase the volume of copies by the machines and the sales and marketing department couldn't leverage on it. Thus, Xerox failed to integrate a new business model with an innovative technology to achieve competitive advantage.

Building a business is a lot similar to building a house - with all preliminary sketches. The entire business system, to produce and deliver goods or services to its target customers, is part of the business model (Itami & Nishino, 2010). The business system should also function as a learning system. Successful organizations such as Walmart[16] and Dell[17] have developed competitive advantage by making changes in the logistics process to save costs and ensure service quality to customers and thus, increased revenues and profits as well (Alvis, 2017). Innovative companies like Google and Skype[18] created and delivered value through interacting with clients, partners and other stakeholders to facilitate learning and innovation and were able to innovate 'freemium' business models by offering a product and charge only a section of the users. At the same time, many dot.com companies such as Yahoo![19] failed to understand the interdependencies of the innovation ecosystem and convert value into profit (Shafer, Smith, & Linder, 2005). Another appropriate example is electric automotive vehicle industry, where the value creation is an ecosystem of interdependencies among the automotive product, the battery technology industries, electricity services and the ICT[20] network service industries, which necessitates collaborative partnerships between the companies and even inter-industry partnerships at the sector level. Thus, any technological innovation is of diminutive value and less sustainable if not exploited through a differentiated business model.

However, developing an innovative business model to capture the desired value is not a trivial task (Chesbrough, 2010). Around 40 percent of the 27 companies founded during the past 25 years in the USA, did so through business model innovation and made their way to the *Fortune 500[21]* list in the past 10 years (Johnson, Christensen, & Kagermann, 2008). Thus, as Chesbrough (2007) observes, today, innovation must include business models, rather than just technology and R&D, as business models have become less durable than they used to be earlier. In the past, companies used to execute the same business model, once fixed in place, for years and even decades, better than their competitors to capture the economic value. But the modern market economy has been subjecting the business models to rapid displacement, disruption, and even outright destruction, in extreme cases. An updated business model enables the organization to realize the economic value of its products, services, and technology as per the dynamic market conditions. Hence, a clear business model is crucial to the success of any business in today's competitive global marketplace. An efficient business model answers the age-old questions that Peter Drucker[22] raised - *Who is the customer and what does the customer value?,* while clarifying the business managers about how and where to make money in that specific business and how to deliver value to customers at an appropriate cost. However, companies like Kodak[23], which failed to embrace digital cameras and photography, and Encyclopedia Britannica[24], which failed to respond to the disruptive impact of the internet, provide standard examples that business models do fail due to either poor execution or false assumptions about the markets or rapid changes in the external environment.

Consequently, defining, innovating and evolving the business models have become the core of the company's strategy work. In the modern liberalized global market, business models have become the new basis of competition. Working on multiple business models simultaneously has become essential for large and complex transnational companies to successfully participate in multiple industries and serve multiple target markets. Hence, companies need to think hard about innovating and sustaining their business models through the trial and error and ex-post adaptation models. The promise of business-model innovation has long captivated the sustainability field, generating plenty of hype. Profit seeking firms in competitive environments will endeavor to meet heterogeneous consumer needs through constant invention and presentation of new value propositions to the consumer. A business model articulates the logic and provides evidence on how a business creates and delivers value to customers by defining the value and outlining the architecture of revenues, costs, and profits associated. Developing a promising business model itself is not sufficient to ascertain competitive advantage as imitation has become often easy. A differentiated, hard to imitate, effective and efficient business model is more likely to yield profits. Further, business models must transform over time as the dynamic markets, technologies and legal structures allow. A business model pioneered by one company in one context may be adopted by another company for another setting as successful business models are shared, very often, by multiple competitors. In fact, a business model is more generic than a business strategy. Hence, developing an effective, efficient, and differentiated architecture for a business model is significant to establish competitive advantage for a business. Unlike other types of innovation, changes to the business model require changes to the foundational decisions upon which the business operates. Therefore, business model innovation will likely be radical, and in many cases, transformational. Changing the business model design brings much higher risk due to the potential for disruption to the current business. For large businesses, recognizing and managing this kind of transition can be critical to long term survival.

The importance of business model innovation was confirmed by a survey of 700 CEOs worldwide carried out by IBM[25](2008), which showed that those firms with the fastest-growing operating margins were placing twice as much emphasis on business model innovation as those which were showing under performance. The survey conceptualizes business model innovation (referred to as BMI hereafter) as a distinct category of innovation, quite different from the usual product/service/market or process/operational innovations (Bock, Opsahl, George, & Gann, 2012). Further, the survey found that BMI have not yet been sufficiently operationalized neither as a separate type of innovation nor as a combination of other innovation types and the 2012 edition of the survey suggests a taxonomy to distinguish between an industry model; a revenue model; and an enterprise model to redefine innovation, value chain, and internal structures. The 2006 edition identified that the CEOs are giving business model innovation as prominent a place on their agendas as products/services/markets innovation and operational innovation, even though the three areas are essential, equally important and inseparable from each other (IBM, 2006). The business leaders are now focusing almost 30 percent of their innovation efforts on their business models since it was evident that the companies that have grown their operating margins faster than their competitors were putting twice as much emphasis on business model innovation as underperformers. Moreover, it was found that business model innovation had a much stronger correlation with operating margin growth than the other types of innovation (IBM, 2006). Further, it was observed that the business model innovators are underrepresented in Europe whereas they are overrepresented in the US and Japan (Bock, Opsahl, George, & Gann, 2012).

Thus, BMI refers to radical or disruptive innovation that affects the entire business and not just incremental changes. Further, BMI can be undertaken in the public sector to increase concern for public, across a wide set of activities, such as health care, public transportation, labor administration, and eGovernance etc. Bason (2012) proposes a shift from the classic 'bureaucratic' model in public management to a 'networked governance' model, through collaboration between the general public and public services, and public-sector organizations and the private-sector. In some cases citizens are encouraged to take on participatory roles as co-producers of some of the services they expect. Companies that change and adapt their business model are more likely to achieve a sustainable competitive advantage, since innovative business models are often much more difficult to imitate than products and services.

GLOBAL EVIDENCES

As it was cited in the preceding part of this chapter, one key finding of the IBM Global CEO Survey of around 750 corporate and public sector leaders from around the world in 2006, was that 'competitive pressures have pushed business model innovation much higher than expected' on CEOs' priority list (George & Marc, 2006). The survey, further, reveals that the companies who emphasized twice on business model innovation than product or process innovation, could increase their operating margins faster than their peers. A survey of 4,018 executives worldwide and in-depth interviews with leading decision-makers around the globe, found that *how* companies do business will often be more important than *what* they do and a majority of the managers surveyed favored new business models over new products and services as a source of future competitive advantage (The Economist, 2005). European Commission (2014) policy brief has mapped the business model innovation in European Union and found that approximately six percent of the small and medium enterprises (SMEs) across all European Union members and sectors were classified as business model innovators. Among the countries, Portugal have the highest share of business model innovators with around 10 percent and Cyprus, Italy and Luxembourg also have larger shares of BMI whereas Romania, Hungary, Latvia and Bulgaria have the lowest share with less than two percent. A study by the American Management Association[26] found that the share of investments on business model innovation was not more than 10 percent of the total innovation budgets at global companies. General Motors[27] is another well-known company that filed for bankruptcy during the recent downturn. Even though, the economic crisis contributed to the troubles of the company, claiming the downturn as an exclusive reason for failure would be a misjudgment. Rather, the critical factor is the inability of the company to adjust the business model to the altered market conditions and competitive environment. Therefore, companies must dissect their business models regularly and redefine if necessary to be successful in the increasingly-complex business environment.

However, it is always possible to do things differently. When the digital revolution hit the old economy company like Warner Music[28], revenue turnover shrunk dramatically due to the irresistible drop in CD[29] sales. The company, within no time, improved the existing business model, aligning to the digital era by updating the value proposition for artists, developing new digital distribution channels, and establishing new cooperation models. As a result, the company could secure 21 percent market share, the highest for ten years, in the US market in 2008. Yet, Warner Music believes that this model will need to be continuously evolved in-tune with the market changes. Many global corporations such as Apple, Google, Dell, Netflix[30], Adidas[31], IBM, Amazon[32], Gillette[33] etc., have turned successful through innovating on business models. Apple Inc. is an example of success for business model innovation. It reached rock bottom in its history in 1997 as revenues dropped by around 36 percent in two successive years. Management was changed almost every year and suffered a loss of about $ 1billion plus on a turnover of $ 7 billion in 1997. Market share in the personal computer (PC) sector fell to a meagre two percent and the share price fell to an all-time low of $13. Fast forward nearly two decades, and it is a completely different picture now. A turnover of $43 billion was recorded during 2009, about 35 percent increase on the previous year's figures and profit also rose to $8 billion and the share price rose to over $185 in the same year. The company focused heavily on closed platforms, from hardware components to their own operating system, to gain great control over the supply chain as well as usability and sales was run through distribution partners. As Steve Jobs[34] left, the company's ability to innovate declined significantly and the existing products were milked heavily to the end of their product life cycle, instead of reaching the demanding customers with creative and innovative products. With the return of Steve Jobs in mid-nineties, the innovation potential of the company was reactivated to move from being a hardware and software producer to a supplier of 'digital entertainment' which turned the company around to make revenues from lifestyle products such as the *iPod[35]* and *iPhone[36]* and content, rather than hardware. The required software for the new entertainment business model - *iLife[37], iTunes[38], QuickTime[39] or MobileMe[40]* (presently *iCloud)* - was developed or purchased while building up new capabilities in digital content such as music and films to complement the entertainment products and achieve better market control. Apple was the first electronics company in the world to link legal music *iTunes,* the first of its kind unified development platform in the mobile market, download as an activity by radically transforming its business model to include an ongoing relationship with its hardware customers rather than trying to grow by simply introducing new hardware products to the market. Further, Apple entered smartphone market with *iPhone* in 2007, creating a similar type of business value that other competitors have created for around 10 years. But, Apple took around 16.9 percent of market share and achieved 71 percent of total market revenue in 2012 whereas, Samsung[41], its nearest competitor, was able to take only 37 percent of total market revenue at a market share of 32.6 percent during the same year (Capgemini, 2010). This indicates that Apple has followed different business model even though the created values are similar with other competitors. Thus, the locus of innovation was extended from the product space to the business model. The same has been extended ultimately to cellular phones also to emerge as the market leader by delivering unique value to customers and charge premium.

Another most innovative company, Dell, has replaced the traditional *build-to-stock* model of selling computers through retail stores and implemented an innovative customer-driven *build-to-order* business model allowing online customization, capitalizing on improved internet technology. The successful business model transformation required significant innovations in supply chain practices, which in turn resulted in significant changes in channel structures, processes, and supplier performance expectations in the manufacture of computers. However, Dell gained these insights over time and through continuous refinements to the business model. Dell had revolutionized the computer industry in the nineties, became one among the global top five companies in 1997, and emerged as the market leader for the first time in 2001. But, the fact that Dell has since forfeited this position, demonstrations the limited lifespan of business models and the ever-present need to reinvent continuously. Similarly, GE Aviation[42] has successfully switched the value proposition from selling jet engines to selling flight hours to its clients, with the engines rented and serviced by the company, shifting the risk of downtime from the airline customer to GE (Chesbrough, 2007). Walmart's fundamental changes to a networked enterprise structure and value chain also serves as a fitting trace to the fast-shifting business priorities to be sustainable amidst of uncertainties. Another example is the *pay as you go* approach by the auto insurance Progressive with its Pay-As-You-Drive (PAYD)[43] offer (Desyllas & Sako, 2013).

One more fitting example comes from the fashion retailer Inditex[44], a fast-growing Spanish firm that manages prestigious global brand such as Zara[45], has wisely designed an activity system to bring new fashionable garments from the design stage to the shop floor within record time, days as opposed to months, which made a big difference in the fast-moving fashion business. Despite the competitors' strong track records and capabilities in product innovation and logistics, Inditex could beat them to the punch through its innovative business model which linked and governed the deployment of existing resources and capabilities in novel ways. The company radically simplified and expedited communication channels across the entire organization, which reflected in shop layouts, and the means of communication across the stores, headquarters and production facilities, enabling the current fashion trends move quickly from customer to production. Due to a comparatively high share of in-house production, and frequent supply of smaller items, the company can respond faster to information than its competitors.

It would be inappropriate to continue the story without mentioning Google an innovative company since the developers at Google are encouraged to invest 20 percent of their working time in ideas and projects of their choice. This project has nothing to do with the core business of Google. Employees give constructive feedback and suggest new features instead of waiting for big strategic plans from the company's leadership. AdSense[46], Google Mail and Google News originated from *20% project*[47] only. Another similar path-breaking innovation could be found with Taco Bell, the Mexican-style fast food restaurant chain, which turned the restaurant's kitchen into a heating and assembly unit through a program called *K-minus*[48] in the late 1980s. The food preparation was shifted to outside vendors and the pre-cooked food is sent in plastic bags to about 300 restaurants where it could be heated, assembled and served. This incremental business model innovation allowed Taco Bell to realize economies of scale and improvements in efficiency and quality control, as well as increase space for customers within the restaurants (Santos, Spector & Van der Heyden, 2009). Another glorifying evidence of business model innovation comes from IBM, which turned around into a service provider by launching a range of new activities in consulting, IT maintenance, and other services, from being a hardware supplier for decades. As a result, more than half of IBM's $96 billion revenues came from these activities, by 2009.

The success of Volkswagen (VW)[49] owes much to a strategy of achieving commonality across components, whereby different models of cars under its brands share similar internal components. The innovation of shared components enables VW to switch production, at its plants, between different models, according to the demand swings and reduces demand variability for individual components. Amazon, in the late 1990s, has expanded from books into music, video, and games since all of them require similar logistics capabilities, to cover the risk of failing in any one of these categories with a potentially superior share in another. And today, the huge growth of the company necessitated to institute special technological competencies, in the form of highly scalable server structures for running the electronic trade platform efficiently. Amazon revealed a new area of business from this emerging core competency, namely, the leasing of just these structures, popular now as cloud computing, resulting in flexible costs for delivery. Amazon developed a complete business model around this newly created platform *EC2 (Elastic Compute Cloud)*[50], which is established under the umbrella of Amazon Web Services. LAN Airlines[51] uses the overnight flights to transport both passengers and cargo by using the downtime to handle cargo, while flying in international routes, whereas the popular American passenger-only airlines keep their planes on the ground for long periods and derive less than five percent of revenue from cargo. Moreover, hedging passengers with cargo allows the airline afford to serve destinations that other airlines avoid, by flying profitably even with lesser occupancy. Similar innovations have taken hold among other sectors, globally, such as automotive industry by leasing cars instead of selling, and office equipment or construction tools industry by renting out equipment instead of selling. Thus, an innovative business model would enable the business either to create a new market or to exploit new opportunities in existing markets.

THE INDIAN PERSPECTIVE

Business innovation is relatively a late phenomenon in the Asian region and specifically in the Indian corporate context, as the Indian economy was liberalized only during the early 90s. The first wave of business innovation in the Asian region occurred during the post-World War II period, through China's 'open door' policy, in 1978, which changed the competitive landscape of global manufacturing, followed by the deregulation efforts in India, transforming the global services industry. But, the first wave innovation was fundamentally established on the competitive advantage derived from lower factor costs in China and India, giving rise to *the China price*[52] concept across the world. This trend has been prevailing for more than two decades and the modern market economy breeds a subtle need to innovate on business models to succeed, as competition is catching up in all sectors, in emerging markets. Indian businesses also have come to understand the imperative of innovation for sustained economic growth. India is considered as the sixth most innovative country among the world (GE, 2012). However, it is still far from reaching its potential as it was found that the Indian companies spend only about 0.3 percent of their revenue towards innovation as compared to a three percent contributed by their counterparts in developed economies. And although Indian firms have been actively creating new business models, a significant proportion of these innovations have been borrowed, while very few are truly 'new-to-world'.

Business model plays critical role in emerging markets since it is the only mechanism for integrating a firm's value chain (Porter, 1985) or value network (Shafer, Smith, & Linder, 2005) within the larger business ecosystem (Leibold, Probst, & Gibbert, 2002). As the business model is a strategic reaction to an identified market opportunity and delineated market boundaries through a systematic competitor analysis (Porter, 1980) and market research (Narver & Slater, 1990), the market structures need to be already existing with known customer preferences and established competitor network. But, absence of such market structure in emerging markets restricts the initiation towards experimentation with business models since markets that don't exist can't be analyzed (Christensen, 2003). As both the business environment and the potential outcomes are greatly uncertain in emerging markets, firms experiment with business models through a process of *effectuation*[53] (Sarasvathy, 2001) to influence the collective action needed to construct a new market. Moreover, implementing a new business model successfully in emerging markets requires the integration of resources, partners, suppliers, customers and other agents into collaborative networks that evolve with market conditions (Sarasvathy & Dew, 2005). Hence, firms need to develop multiple hypothesized business models and work cooperatively, involving all stakeholders, to develop the strategic actions to create value (Morris, Schindehutte, & Allen, 2005). Over the course of time, these iterations endorse stakeholder commitment and build market conditions around a productive business model (Sarasvathy & Dew, 2005). As the emerging markets are flooded by a multitude of opportunities, entrepreneurs initially set out to develop a business model in alignment with the predetermined hypothesis of the market. Thus, effectuation plays a critical role in developing business models that become the *de facto* industry standards (Sarasvathy & Kotha, 2001).

India, being the future growth destination, is the 'laboratory' for business model innovation that create social impact at the *bottom of the pyramid*[54]. Many Western multinationals struggle to exploit the emerging opportunities by relentlessly cutting costs and preparing to accept zero-profits. But, the problem is that simply replicating their native matured market business models in the new and emerging markets won't work. Many Indian firms and the MNC subsidiaries are rushing to adopt innovative business models in many sectors like housing, healthcare, education, and financial services by creating better affordability to those living in the middle and bottom of the pyramid. The telecom industry is an apt example of business model innovation that stimulated growth and development. Jain Irrigation Systems[55], an Indian MNC, has designed a micro irrigation system specifically for smallholder farming conditions to reduce water usage considerably and proved that creating social value and economic returns can go hand in hand. Amazon entered into India, in 2013, by redesign their existing business model to suit to the unique Indian market conditions. German corporate, Bosch[56], also, has been creating new opportunities by developing technological solutions to address challenges in sectors such as water, health, sanitation and energy, aiming at the upcoming middle income and underserved population segments. Thus, much of the business model innovations happening in the emerging markets are considered to be the second wave of innovation. The most noteworthy innovations in emerging markets are undertaken by companies that have grown primarily in that particular market developing a deep local understanding. For instance, Kotak Mahindra Bank[57], India's fourth-largest private-sector bank, has launched a fully-integrated social bank account *Jifi,* transcending digital banking by seamlessly incorporating social networking platforms such as Twitter and Facebook with mainstream banking. It would be appropriate to discuss some noteworthy efforts in details, from some of the most happening industries in India.

FMCG Industry

Most of the Fast Moving Consumer Goods (FMCG) sector business models were catered only to the Indian urban markets until 2003. Hindustan Unilever lead the bandwagon of shifting focus towards rural India in 2004 by launching new products targeted to those segments by redesigning the packaging, distribution and warehousing models. Of late, some indigenous incumbents like Patanjali Ayurveda[58]are emerging to dominate the industry through different models.

Domestic Low-Cost Carrier Industry

The IndiGo airlines[59] could establish itself as the leader in the Indian low-cost carrier fraternity by revolutionizing the low-cost carrier industry in 2000 through adopting an efficiency-centered business model enabling lower fares, faster check-in, and excellent customer service. Most of the low cost carrier companies are imitating the IndiGo model which makes it imperative for the market leader to further innovate on its model.

Hospitality Industry

The future of business model innovation in Asia belongs to such companies like OYO Rooms[60], an *asset-light[61]* digital aggregator of budget hotel rooms in India. Following the original model of the US based Airbnb[62], OYO rooms tries to offer better value for money to the Indian travelers, where many budget hotel rooms in India lack comfort, cleanliness, convenience, and even basic customer service. The revenue is generated by charging commission for each OYO-vetted room from the hoteliers. OYO supports hotels through training to manage daily operations, and helps to increase asset utilization, and to optimize costs. The dynamic algorithmically determined pricing model optimizes profitability by balancing inventory and cost and taking market demand into account. However, OYO's business model have inspired imitation, as a good number of new competitors such as *Zen Rooms[63]* and *Value+[64]* that have entered the fray. Finally, the capacity to innovate on the business model to deliver higher value propositions to the clients as well as customers will turn sustainable.

Telecom Industry

Indian telecom industry, the world's second-largest telecom market, with around 105 Crore subscriber base with wireless tele-density of above 87 per cent, is valued at $40 billion. The sector has registered a strong CAGR[65] of 19.96 percent in subscriber base during the past decade. The sector has reached an inflection point, after a prolonged exponential expansion on traditional business models. The operating environment for Indian telecom companies is turning increasingly complex, as the consumption patterns are rapidly changing and value is moving not only to other stages of the value chain but also into completely different markets. The popularity of 'mobile' Internet as well as the cumulative use of social media is driving significant changes to traditional consumption patterns, eating into the traditional revenue streams. At the same time, the pricing models to monetize such traffic have turned ineffective. Moreover, the highly popular Facebook has been erecting a massive wall through extensive communication features, reducing the telecom operator's ability to monetize. The industry ARPU[66] has been dwindling between ₹125 to ₹131 per month during 2014 – 2016. In another significant development, 2016 has witnessed the entry of a Greenfield 4G operator, with aggressive tariff plans offering free voice calls and low-cost data. High debt and falling ARPUs started ringing warning bells for the weak players. Thus, the traditional business models of the telecom operators, grown on the back of conventional voice and data services are eventually crumbling and forcing a rapid evolution to survive. An innovative business model of infrastructure sharing at different levels and another feasible model of consolidation as some smaller players are making distress calls to their larger rivals, seems to be the future. Thus, the industry is heading towards a rapid innovation of its business models, in order to survive.

E-Commerce Industry

The advent of e-commerce in India has revolutionized the approach towards running a business at scale by creating high customer satisfaction. Entrepreneurs are innovating on clutter-breaking ideas to create newer verticals, giving rise to new shopping experiences to reach the customers in newer ways. The industry is set to hit $76 billion by 2021 from $13.6 billion in 2014 (Deloitte, 2015). Entrepreneurial ecosystem is still evolving with rapid innovation in both the existing and startups in promotion, pricing, sale, and even distribution channels, aiming at capturing the emerging mass market. As a result, the players have to manage the challenges associated with the diverse supplier and customer base, technological constraints, dwindling customer satisfaction, authenticity of information and grievance redressal etc. The predominant revenue models are built upon either of sales, transaction fee, subscription, advertising revenues, and still progressing into creating new types of revenue models whenever required. The companies derive competitive advantage through cost leadership, product differentiation and customization and wide assortment of products which can be sorted based on different criteria. Further, the customer centric approaches such as offering complete anonymity, ease of making payment through multiple modes like different cards, net banking, electronic fund transfer (EFT) and even cash on delivery (COD), faster and time bound delivery, easy replacement policy, equated monthly instalments (EMI) options, and tie-ups with various complimentary service organizations etc. form the integral components of the prevailing business models. E-commerce is dynamic and is throwing up new business models at a fast pace. The strategies like discounting and heavy spending on advertisement and marketing have rendered most of the companies unprofitable. However, the e-commerce business models deployed by Indian companies do not rake in *moolah* for their investors but promise growth over time. With the increasing competition in the e-commerce market, players who are able to adapt and innovate in the face of rapid digital disruption embracing new technologies will be in better position for success. While a typical e-commerce business model revolves around developing a marketplace, the future will be all about business models that innovate and transform the very value chain. The blooming ecommerce companies in India need to focus more on a business model that will be profitable in the short to long term for better survival.

IT Industry

The Indian IT industry has sustained high levels of growth in revenues and employment since the late 1980s, with an unmatched value proposition. Out of the US$163 Billion revenue earned during FY16, exports accounted about 66 percent. The industry is expected to maintain a growth rate of 8 to10 percent in the near future and achieve a revenue target of US$ 225 Billion by 2020. However, the economics that made Indian IT such a compelling proposition are fading rather than disappearing altogether, due to the high rates of technological change, shift towards automation, artificial intelligence, cloud computing, and increased competition has been forcing the businesses to innovate on business models. Further, the changing perception of clients about technology has come to be a bigger worry as spending on new digital services such as the Internet Of Things (IOT) is forecasted to rise from a tenth of total spending in 2014 to over a third in 2020 (The Economist, 2017). As computers slowdown as they age and before long must be replaced by newer models, same is true of the business models of Indian IT firms.

CONCLUSION

According to the GE (2012) Global Innovation Barometer, India enjoys the reputation of the sixth best innovative country in the world. However, it is still far from reaching its potential, as the Indian companies spend only about 0.3 percent of their revenue towards innovation as compared to a full three percent spent by their counterparts in developed countries. Even though Indian firms have been increasingly active in creating new business models, a significant proportion of these business models have been borrowed from elsewhere with very few that are truly 'new-to-world'. However, it is these new-to-the-world innovations that India needs to achieve sustained economic growth. India has declared 2010-2020 as the *Decade of Innovation*. The triumph of modern India is driven by profound technological change driven by ideas that have broken traditional barriers.

Furthermore, global consumer demand keeps evolving forcing the businesses to do more to meet expectations and deliver more and more value at different layers of the societies. Thus, the value delivery has emerged as the 'basic rule of the society' in the present-day markets. Most companies have now realized that sustainability can result in streamlined processes and those who have looked to the future are changing their business models to ensure sustainability. Across the world, innovative business models are emerging to exploit the new market opportunities. Businesses will look radically different in the future. Consumers don't just buy from businesses anymore - they reuse, re-sell, and use peer to peer platforms for services such as lending. This means that companies that want a sustainable future must find new ways of operating to fit in with the changing business landscape. Those businesses that innovate to find solutions that resolve costs with social and environmental issues, or who change their business models to accommodate the rapidly shifting consumer landscape, will find a sustainable future. This is more pertinent for the enterprises in emerging and developing economies where the need to lower market barriers and engage in new forms of collaborations to address new consumers and integrate the poor in economic activities, is more. Thus, the company of the future will be far different from the company of today.

REFERENCES

Alvis. (2017). *How walmart makes money? Understanding walmart business model*. Retrieved from: https://revenuesandprofits.com/how-walmart-makes-money-understanding-walmart-business-model/

Barton, D., Bailey, J., & Zoffer, J. (2015). *Rising to the challenge of short-termism*. Retrieved from: http://www.fcltglobal.org/docs/default-source/default-document-library/fclt-global-rising-to-the-challenge.pdf

Bason, C. (2012). *Designing co-production: Discovering new business models for public services*. Leading Innovation Through Design. 2012 International Design Management research Conference, Boston, MA.

Bock, A. J., Opsahl, T., George, G., & Gann, D. M. (2012). The effects of culture and structure on strategic flexibility during business model innovation. *Journal of Management Studies*, *49*(2), 279–305. doi:10.1111/j.1467-6486.2011.01030.x

CapGemini. (2010). *Business model innovation*. Retrieved from: https://www.capgemini.com/consulting-fr/wp-content/uploads/sites/31/2017/08/business_model_innovation_ capgemini_consulting.pdf

Chesbrough, H. (2007). Business model innovation: It's not just about technology anymore. *Strategy and Leadership*, *35*(6), 12–17. doi:10.1108/10878570710833714

Chesbrough, H. (2010). Business Model Innovation: Opportunities and Barriers. *Long Range Planning*, *43*(2–3), 354–363. doi:10.1016/j.lrp.2009.07.010

Christensen, C. M. (2003). *The innovator's dilemma: The revolutionary book that will change the way you do business*. New York: HarperCollins Publishers, Inc.

Deloitte. (2015). *Technology, Media & Telecommunications India Predictions 2015*. Retrieved from:http://www2.deloitte.com/in/en/pages/technology-media-and-telecommunications/ articles/tmt-india-predictions-2015.html

Desyllas, P., & Sako, M. (2013). Profiting from business model innovation: Evidence from Pay-As-You-Drive auto insurance. *Research Policy*, *42*(1), 101–116. doi:10.1016/j.respol.2012.05.008

European Commission. (2014). *The Need for Innovations in Business Models, Final Policy Brief*. Retrieved from https://ec.europa.eu/research/innovation-union/pdf/expert-groups/ERIAB-BMI_PB_new_business_models.pdf

Eurostat. (2017). *Innovation statistics*. Retrieved from: http://ec.europa.eu/eurostat/statistics-explained/index.php/Innovation_statistics

GE. (2012). *GE Global Innovation Barometer, 2012*. Retrieved from http://files.gecompany.com/gecom/innovationbarometer/GE_Global_Innovation_Barometer_Report_January_2012.pdf

George, P., & Marc, C. (2006). IBM's global CEO report 2006: Business model innovation matters. *Strategy and Leadership*, *34*(5), 34–40. doi:10.1108/10878570610701531

Ghemawat, P. (1986, September). Sustainable advantage. *Harvard Business Review*. Retrieved from https://hbr.org/1986/09/sustainable-advantage

IBM. (2006). *Expanding the innovation horizon- The Global CEO Study 2006*. Retrieved from: https://www-935.ibm.com/services/us/gbs/bus/pdf/ceostudy.pdf

IBM. (2008). *The enterprise of the future*. Retrieved from https://www-935.ibm.com/services/uk/gbs/pdf/ibm_ceo_study_2008.pdf

Itami, H., & Nishino, K. (2010). Killing two birds with one stone: Profit for now and learning for the future. *Long Range Planning*, *43*(2–3), 364–369. doi:10.1016/j.lrp.2009.07.007

Johnson, W. M., Christensen, M. C., & Kagermann, H. (2008). Reinventing your business model. *Harvard Business Review*, *86*(12), 1–12.

Leibold, M., Probst, G., & Gibbert, M. (2002). *Strategic Management in the Knowledge Economy: New Approaches and Business Applications*. New York: Wiley.

Morris, M., Schindehutte, M., & Allen, J. (2005). The entrepreneur's business Model: Toward a unified perspective. *Journal of Business Research*, *58*(6), 726–735. doi:10.1016/j.jbusres.2003.11.001

Narver, J. C., & Slater, S. F. (1990). The effect of a market orientation on business profitability. *Journal of Marketing*, *54*(4), 20–35. doi:10.2307/1251757

Porter, M. E. (1980). *Competitive strategy*. New York: Free Press.

Porter, M. E. (1985). *Competitive advantage: Creating and sustaining superior performance*. New York: Free Press.

Reeves, M., & Deimler, M. (2011). Adaptability-The new competitive advantage. *Harvard Business review*. Retrieved from https://hbr.org/2011/07/adaptability-the-new-competitive-advantage

Santos, J., Spector, B., & Van der Heyden, L. (2009). *Toward a theory of business model innovation within incumbent firms*. INSEAD Working Paper No. 2009/16/EFE/ST/TOM. Retrieved from https://flora.insead.edu/fichiersti_wp/inseadwp2009/2009-16.pdf

Sarasvathy, S. D. (2001). Causation and effectuation: Toward a theoretical shift from economic inevitability to entrepreneurial contingency. *Academy of Management Review*, *26*(2), 243–263.

Sarasvathy, S. D., & Dew, N. (2005). New market creation through transformation. *Journal of Evolutionary Economics*, *15*(5), 533–565. doi:10.100700191-005-0264-x

Sarasvathy, S. D., & Kotha, S. (2001). *Effectuation in the management of Knightian uncertainty: Evidence from the real networks case*. Retrieved from http://www.effectuation.org/wp-content/uploads/2016/06/2001-realnet-1.pdf

Shafer, S. M., Smith, H. J., & Linder, J. C. (2005). The power of business models. *Business Horizons*, *48*(3), 199–207. doi:10.1016/j.bushor.2004.10.014

Sherman, L. (2017). *If You're in a Dogfight, Become a Cat! – Strategies for Long–Term Growth*. New York: Columbia University Press. doi:10.7312her17482

Tesco. (2016). *Business model - Keeping it simple*. Retrieved from: https://www.tescoplc. com/media/ 264185/tescoar16_businessmodel.pdf

The Economist. (2005). *Business 2010 - Embracing the challenge of change*. A report from the Economist Intelligence Unit sponsored by SAP. Retrieved from http://graphics.eiu.com/files/ad_pdfs/business%202010_global_final.pdf

The Economist. (2017). *Reboot - Indian outsourcing specialists must reboot their strategies*. Retrieved from https://www.economist.com/news/business/21714994-it-firms-need-upgrade-face-technological-and-political-shifts-indian-outsourcing

ADDITIONAL READING

Adams, A. C. (2014). Sustainability and the company of the future. Retrieved from: https://drcaroladams.net/sustainability-and-the-company-of-the-future/

Ahluwalia, T. (2016). The future of Indian e-commerce lies in innovation. Retrieved from: https://yourstory.com/2016/03/indian-e_commerce-future/

Anthony, S. (2011). *Three innovation trends in Asia*. Retrieved from: https://hbr.org/2011/12/three-innovation-trends-in-asi

Benwell, S. (2013). The future of corporate sustainability is all about innovation. Retrieved from: http://www.huffingtonpost.co.uk/sara-benwell/corporate-sustainability-innovation_ b_ 3378683.html

Bonini, S., & Gorner, S. (2011). The business of sustainability: Putting it into practice. McKinsey & Co. Retrieved from: https://www.mckinsey.com/~/media/.../sustainability/pdfs/putting_it_into_practice.ashx

Deloitte. (2014). Beacons for business model innovation. Retrieved from: https://www2.deloitte.com/us/en/pages/strategy/articles/beacons-for-business-model-innovation.html

Denning, S. (2013a). The management revolution that's already happening. Retrieved from: https://www.forbes.com/sites/stevedenning/2013/05/30/the-management-revolution-thats-already-happening/#fb18f7370911

Denning, S. (2013b). It's official! The end of competitive advantage. Retrieved from: https://www.forbes.com/sites/stevedenning/2013/06/02/its-official-the-end-of-competitive-advantage/#6c868dc31565

IBM. (2012). *Leading through connections*. Retrieved from http://www-935.ibm.com/services/multimedia/anz_ceo_study_2012.pdf

Schaltegger, S., Lüdeke-Freund, F., & Hansen, G. E. (2011). Business cases for sustainability and the role of business model innovation - Developing a conceptual framework. Retrieved from: https://www2.leuphana.de/umanagement/csm/content/nama/downloads/download_ publikationen/Schaltegger_Luedeke_Freund_Hansen_Business_Case_Sustainability.pdf

Velu, C., & Khanna, M. (2013). Business model innovation in India. *Journal of Indian Business Research*, 5(3), 156–170. doi:10.1108/JIBR-08-2012-0068

ENDNOTES

[1]   Ralph Waldo Emerson was an American Transcendentalist poet, philosopher and essayist during the 19th century, who disseminated his thoughts through dozens of published essays and more than 1,500 public lectures across the United States.

[2]   The *Holy Grail*, in Christian mythology, was the dish, plate, cup or vessel that caught Jesus' blood during his crucifixion. It was said to have the power to heal all wounds. It is used in the modern sense to mean an object or goal that is sought after for its great significance.

[3]   Ralph Waldo Emerson's popular quote.

[4]   Tesco PLC, the British multinational grocery and general merchandise retailer, founded in 1919 by Jack Cohen as a group of market stalls, is the third largest retailer in the world measured by profits, and ninth-largest retailer in the world measured by revenues. It has stores in 12 countries across Asia and Europe and is the grocery market leader in the UK, Ireland, Hungary and Thailand.

[5]   The Ford Motor Company (commonly referred to as 'Ford') is an American multinational automaker. It was founded by Henry Ford in 1903. The company sells automobiles and commercial vehicles under the 'Ford' brand and most luxury cars under the 'Lincoln' brand.

[6]   The 'Model T' was an automobile built by the Ford Motor Company from 1908 until 1927. Conceived by Henry Ford as practical, affordable transportation for the common man, it quickly became prized for its low cost, durability, versatility, and ease of maintenance. Assembly-line production allowed the price of the car to be lowered from $850 in 1908 to less than $300 in 1925. At such prices the Model T at times comprised as much as 40 percent of all cars sold in the United States. The Ford Model T was named the most influential car of the 20th Century in the 1999 Car of the Century competition.

[7]   Google is an American multinational technology company, founded in 1998 by Larry Page and Sergey Brin, specialized in Internet-related services and products. These include online advertising technologies, search, cloud computing, software, and hardware etc.

[8]   The Procter & Gamble Company, (known as P&G), an American multinational, incorporated in 1905, is focused on providing branded consumer packaged goods to the consumers across the world. The Company operates through five segments: Beauty; Grooming; Health Care; Fabric & Home Care, and Baby, Feminine & Family Care. The Company sells its products in approximately 180 countries and territories.

[9]   P&G partners with the world's most innovative minds– from individual inventors and small businesses, to Fortune 500 companies, to deliver on the company's most challenging opportunities, through the 'Connect + Develop' model, which helps P&G engage with innovators and patent-holders to meet needs across the P&G business: for products, technology, in-store, ecommerce and the supply chain and to drive discontinuous, sustainable innovation and productivity.

[10]   InnoCentive is an American crowdsourcing company that accepts by commission research and development problems in engineering, computer science, math, chemistry, life sciences, physical sciences and business. The company frames these as 'challenge problems' for anyone to solve. It gives cash awards for the best solutions to solvers who meet the challenge criteria.

[11]   Vocalpoint is a community where women get free samples so they can try out new products. Vocalpoint members are emailed short surveys to see if they're a good fit to try out a new product. If selected, they'll receive free samples, free products or free coupons. After members have tried out the products, they'll be asked to share their opinion and experience with that product.

[12]   IKEA, the Swedish multinational group, founded in 1943, designs and sells ready-to-assemble furniture, kitchen appliances and home accessories. It has been the world's largest furniture retailer since 2008. As of August 2017, IKEA owns and operates 400 stores in 49 countries. The IKEA website contains about 12,000 products and is the closest representation of the entire IKEA range. There were over 2.1 billion visitors to IKEA's websites in the year from September 2015 to August 2016. The company is responsible for approximately 1% of world commercial-product wood consumption, making it one of the largest users of wood in the retail sector.

[13]   Nokia Corporation, founded in 1865, is a Finnish multinational communications, information technology and consumer electronics company. In 2014, Nokia did business in more than 150 countries and reported annual revenues of around €12.73 billion. It was the world's 274th largest company measured by 2013 revenues according to the Fortune Global 500.

[14]   Alexander Osterwalder (born 1974) is a Swiss business theorist, author and consultant, known for his work on business modeling and the development of the Business Model Canvas.

[15]   Xerox Corporation (also known as Xerox, stylized as xerox since 2008, and previously as XEROX from 1960 to 2008) is an American global corporation that sells document solutions and services, and document technology products in more than 160 countries.

[16]   Wal-Mart Stores, Inc, doing business as Walmart, is an American multinational retailing corporation that operates as a chain of hypermarkets, discount department stores, and grocery stores. The company was founded by Sam Walton in 1962 and incorporated in 1969. As of January 31, 2017, Walmart has 11,695 stores and clubs in 28 countries, under a total of 63 banners. Walmart is the world's largest company by revenue – approximately $480 billion according to the Fortune Global 500 list in 2016, as well as the largest private employer in the world with 2.3 million employees. Walmart is also one of the world's most valuable companies by market value and is also the largest grocery retailer in the U.S. In 2016, 62.3 percent of Walmart's US$478.614 billion sales came from its U.S. operations.

[17]   Dell Inc. (stylized as DELL), a subsidiary of Dell Technologies, is an American multinational computer technology company, and one of the largest technology companies in the world with 138,000 employees. Dell manufactures, sells,

repairs, and supports personal computers, servers, data storage devices, network switches, computer software, computer peripherals, high-definition televisions, cameras, printers, and electronics built by other manufacturers. The company is well known for its innovations in supply chain management and e-commerce, particularly its direct-sales model and its "build-to-order" or "configure to order" approach to manufacturing—delivering individual PCs configured to customer specifications.

[18]   Skype is an instant messaging app that provides online text message and video chat services and also facilitates exchange of digital documents such as images, text, and video and allows video conference calls. Skype implements a 'freemium model'. Much of the service is free, but Skype Credit or a subscription is required to call a landline or a mobile phone number. Skype serves over 300 million estimated active members each month as of August 2015.

[19]   Yahoo! is a US based web services provider, presently owned by Verizon Communications, but originally founded by Jerry Yang and David Filo in 1994 and was incorporated in 1995. Yahoo was one of the pioneers of the early Internet era in the 1990s. At its height it was one of the most popular sites in the United States, and in 2016, rated as the sixth most visited website globally with over 7 billion views per month.

[20]   Information and Communication Technology

[21]   The Fortune 500 is an annual list compiled and published by Fortune magazine, since 1955, that ranks 500 of the largest United States Corporations by total revenue for their respective fiscal years.

[22]   Peter Ferdinand Drucker (1909 –2005) was an Austrian-born American management consultant, educator, and author, whose writings contributed to the philosophical and practical foundations of the modern business corporation. He has been described as 'the founder of modern management'.

[23]   The Eastman Kodak Company (referred to simply as Kodak) is an American technology company, founded in 1888, that produces imaging products with its historic basis on photography

[24]   The Encyclopaedia Britannica is a general knowledge English-language encyclopaedia, written by about 100 full-time editors and more than 4,000 contributors, who include the Nobel Prize winners and five American presidents. The 2010 version of the 15th edition, which spans 32 volumes and 32,640 pages, was the last printed edition while digital content and distribution has continued since then.

[25]   IBM (International Business Machines Corporation) is an American multinational technology company with operations in over 170 countries. The company originated in 1911 as the Computing-Tabulating-Recording Company (CTR) and was renamed "International Business Machines" in 1924.

IBM manufactures and markets computer hardware, middleware and software, and offers hosting and consulting services in areas ranging from mainframe computers to nanotechnology. IBM is also a major research organization, holding the record for most patents generated by a business (as of 2017) for 24 consecutive years. Inventions by IBM include the automated teller machine (ATM), the PC, the floppy disk, the hard disk drive, the magnetic stripe card, and the relational database, the SQL programming language, the UPC barcode, and dynamic random - access memory (DRAM). IBM has continually shifted its business mix by commoditizing markets focusing on higher-value, more profitable markets. Nicknamed Big Blue, IBM is one of 30 companies included in the Dow Jones Industrial Average and one of the world's largest employers, with (as of 2016) nearly 380,000 employees. IBM employees have been awarded five Nobel Prizes, six Turing Awards, ten National Medals of Technology and five National Medals of Science.

[26] The American Management Association (AMA), is a non-profit membership organization that provides a variety of educational and management development services to businesses, government agencies and individuals. Founded in 1913, as the National Association of Corporation Schools, the AMA became the American Management Association in 1923.

[27] General Motors Company, known as GM, is an American multinational corporation that manufactures cars and trucks in 35 countries. The company was the largest automobile manufacturer from 1931 through 2007.

[28] Warner Music Group (referred to as Warner Music) is an American multinational entertainment and record label conglomerate. It is one of the "big three" recording companies and the third largest in the global music industry.

[29] Compact disc (CD) is a digital optical disc data storage format released in 1982 and co-developed by Philips and Sony.

[30] Netflix is an American entertainment company founded by Reed Hastings and Marc Randolph in 1997. It specializes in and provides streaming media and video-on-demand online and DVD by mail.

[31] Adidas AG is a German multinational corporation that designs and manufactures shoes, clothing and accessories. It is the largest sportswear manufacturer in Europe, and the second largest in the world.

[32] Amazon.com, Inc., known as simply Amazon, is an American electronic commerce and cloud computing company that was founded by Jeff Bezos in 1994. The tech giant is the largest Internet-based retailer in the world by total sales and market capitalization.

[33] Gillette is a brand of men's safety razors and other personal care products including shaving supplies, owned by the multi-national corporation Procter & Gamble (P&G).

[34]   Steve Jobs (1955–2011) was an American entrepreneur, businessman, inventor, and industrial designer. Jobs was the chairman, and the chief executive officer (CEO), and a co-founder of Apple Inc.

[35]   The iPod is a line of portable media players designed and marketed by Apple Inc.

[36]   iPhone is a line of smartphones designed and marketed by Apple Inc.

[37]   iLife is a software suite for macOS and iOS developed by Apple Inc. It consists of various programs for media creation, organization, editing and publishing. It was composed of: iTunes, iMovie, iPhoto, iDVD, iWeb and GarageBand.

[38]   iTunes is a media player, media library, online radio broadcaster, and mobile device management application developed by Apple Inc., used to play, download, and organize digital downloads of music, video and other types of media available on the iTunes Store, on personal computers running the mac OS and Microsoft Windows operating systems. The *iTunes Store* is a software-based online digital media store operated by Apple Inc., since 2003, and has been the largest music vendor in the United States since 2008, and the largest music vendor in the world since 2010.

[39]   QuickTime is an extensible multimedia framework developed by Apple Inc., capable of handling various formats of digital video, picture, sound, panoramic images, and interactivity.

[40]   MobileMe was a subscription-based collection of online services and software offered by Apple Inc. All services were being gradually transitioned and replaced by iCloud and the service ceased with transfers to *iCloud* available until July 31, 2012.

[41]   Samsung Group is a South Korean multinational conglomerate comprising numerous affiliated businesses under the Samsung brand, and is the largest South Korean *chaebol* (business conglomerate).

[42]   GE Aviation is among the top aircraft engine suppliers, and offers engines for the majority of commercial aircraft. GE Aviation is part of the General Electric conglomerate, which is one of the world's largest corporations.

[43]   Usage-based insurance also known as pay as you drive (PAYD) or mile-based auto insurance is a type of vehicle insurance whereby the costs are dependent upon type of vehicle used, measured against time, distance, behavior and place. This differs from traditional insurance, which attempts to differentiate and reward 'safe' drivers, giving those lower premiums or a no-claims bonus.

[44]   Industria de Diseño Textil, S.A. (Inditex) is a Spanish multinational clothing company. Inditex, the biggest fashion group in the world, operates over 7,200 stores in 93 markets worldwide. The company's flagship store is Zara.

[45]   Zara is the main clothing and accessories retailer brand of the Inditex group, the world's largest apparel retailer.

[46] Google AdSense is a program run by Google that allows publishers in the Google Network of content sites to serve automatic text, image, video, or interactive media advertisements, that are targeted to site content and audience. These advertisements are administered, sorted, and maintained by Google. They can generate revenue on either a per-click or per-impression basis.

[47] One of Google's most famous management philosophies is something called '20% time'. Founders Larry Page and Sergey Brin highlighted the idea in 2004, to encourage Google's employees, in addition to their regular projects, to spend 20% of their time working on what they think will most benefit Google. This empowers them to be more creative and innovative by creating a room to explore and power to be generated from those 'intrinsically interested'. Some of the 20% products include Google News, Gmail, and even AdSense.

[48] K-Minus, meaning Kitchen Minus, which means that much of Taco Bell's food preparation would be shifted to outside vendors.

[49] Volkswagen (VW), is a German automaker founded in 1937 by the German Labour Front. It is the flagship marque of the Volkswagen Group, the largest automaker by worldwide sales in 2016.

[50] Amazon Elastic Compute Cloud (Amazon EC2) provides scalable computing capacity in the Amazon Web Services (AWS) cloud. Using Amazon EC2 eliminates the need to invest in hardware up front, so user can develop and deploy applications faster. Amazon EC2 can be used to launch as many or as few virtual servers as needed, configure security and networking, and manage storage. Amazon EC2 enables to scale up or down to handle changes in requirements or spikes in popularity, reducing the need to forecast traffic.

[51] LATAM Airlines, formerly LAN Airlines S.A., is an airline based in Santiago, Chile. LAN is one of the largest airlines in Latin America, serving Latin America, North America, the Caribbean, Oceania, and Europe.

[52] 'The China Price' is a term business-people in the US began using around 2003 to describe ultra-low prices of goods made in china.

[53] Effectuation is a way of thinking that serves entrepreneurs in the processes of opportunity identification and new venture creation. Effectuation includes a set of decision-making principles expert entrepreneurs are observed to employ in situations of uncertainty. Situations of uncertainty are situations in which the future is unpredictable, goals are not clearly known and there is no independent environment that serves as the ultimate selection mechanism.

54   The bottom of the pyramid is the largest, but poorest socio-economic group. In global terms, this is the 2.7 billion people who live on less than $2.50 a day. Management scholar CK Prahalad popularised the idea of this demographic as a profitable consumer base in his Stuart Hart coauthored 2004 book *The Fortune at the Bottom of the Pyramid.*

55   Jain Irrigation Systems is an Indian multinational organization, with 32 manufacturing plants, manufactures a number of products, including drip and sprinkler irrigation systems and components, integrated irrigation automation systems, PVC and PE piping systems, plastic sheets, greenhouses, bio-fertilizers, solar water-heating systems, solar water pumps, turnkey biogas plants, and photovoltaic systems.

56   Robert Bosch GmbH or Bosch, a German multinational engineering and electronics company, is the world's largest supplier of automotive components measured by 2011 revenues.

57   Kotak Mahindra Bank is an Indian private sector bank with a network of 1,369 branches across 689 locations across the country, as of 31 March, 2017. It was the fourth largest private bank in India by market capitalization in 2016.

58   Patanjali Ayurved Limited is an Indian FMCG company. Patanjali is the fastest growing FMCG company valued at ₹30 billion (US$470 million).

59   IndiGo is an Indian low-cost airline operator. It is the largest airline in India by passengers carried and fleet size, with a 38.7% market share as of July 2017. It is also the largest individual Asian low-cost carrier in terms of jet fleet size and passengers carried, and the eighth largest carrier in Asia with over 41 million passengers carried in 2016.

60   OYO HOTELS, known as OYO, is an Indian hotel brand, founded in 2013, that owns and operates as well as aggregates standardized hotel rooms. It currently operates in more than 200 Indian towns, Malaysia and Nepal.

61   Asset-light business model is the capital-light business model, as it doesn't require a lot of money to put a venture into action and help companies move faster and, in the long term, may make them more sustainable.

62   Airbnb is an online marketplace and hospitality service, enabling people to lease or rent short-term lodging including vacation rentals, apartment rentals, homestays, hostel beds, or hotel rooms. The company does not own any lodging; it is merely a broker and receives commissions from both guests and hosts in conjunction with every booking. It has over 3,000,000 lodging listings in 65,000 cities and 191 countries.

[63] Zen Rooms, backed by Rocket Internet, is a budget hotel platform for Southeast Asia. In addition to Indian operations, it has already started operations in Indonesia, Thailand, and Singapore and plans to expand into Malaysia, Vietnam, Sri Lanka, and Pakistan, and eventually wants to become "the biggest budget hotel brand network in Southeast Asia."

[64] Nasdaq-listed online travel booking portal MakeMyTrip has launched Value+, its own new brand of budget rooms, days after blocking Oyo Rooms and Zo Rooms from its portal.

[65] Compound Annual Growth Rate

[66] Average Revenue Per User (ARPU) is a measure of how much income a business generates, given the size of its customer base. It is widely utilized in the technology and telecommunications sectors to determine the potential profitability of a firm.

Chapter 8

Thought Process of a New Graduate Which Leads to Behavioral Intention to Apply for a Job Vacancy:
A Conceptual Model

Shan Anjana Jayasinghe
University of Moratuwa, Sri Lanka

Galagedarage Dinesh Samarasinghe
University of Moratuwa, Sri Lanka

Theekshana Suraweea
Sri Lanka Institute of Information Technology, Sri Lanka

ABSTRACT

Due to inadequacy, there is a call for more research on the thought process of job seekers. This chapter argues that employers have to communicate their company's job-seeker value proposition to new graduates to create job-seeker perceived value in their minds. Job-seeker perceived value will lead to behavioral intention. Further, the chapter proposes that a company's job-seeker value proposition has a direct positive relationship with behavioral intention and the relationship is moderated positively by voluntariness and gender. The technology acceptance model and the unified theory of acceptance and use of technology (UTAUT) were used to develop arguments related to each relationship proposed in the conceptual framework. Marketing management literature was used to label both constructs: company's job-seeker value proposition and job-seeker perceived value; and the same is employed to complement the arguments borrowed from management information system. Theoretical contribution, practical contribution, limitations, and opportunities for future research are also discussed in the chapter.

DOI: 10.4018/978-1-5225-5360-1.ch008

INTRODUCTION

In strategic management, recruitment is one of the main functional areas of consideration in the process of developing the functional strategy of any organisation (Wheelen & Hunger, 2011). For any organisation which plans to adopt growth or stability strategies, recruitment is an area of strategic importance (Wheelen & Hunger, 2011). "Recruitment" will emerge as a topic of high importance in organizations involved in the industry of Information and Communication Technology (ICT) in Sri Lanka since the National ICT Workforce Survey 2013 (Information and Communication Technology Agency of Sri Lanka, 2013) highlights the short supply of ICT professionals in the country. The survey further reveals that even though there had been a demand of 6,246 ICT professionals in 2013, the supply had been restricted to 5,778 ICT professionals, hence, creating a shortage of 468 ICT professionals in the field. Additionally, according to the 'SLASSCOM Strategy Document 2016' published by the Sri Lanka Association of Software and Service Companies (SLASSCOM), Sri Lanka's ICT industry anticipates in creating 200,000 direct jobs by 2022 compared to 75,107 in 2013. Consequently, it is evident that the existing situation prevalent in the ICT job market (low unemployment rate) nurtures "recruitment" to be one of its most significant current and future Human Resource Management (HRM) challenges for HRM practitioners of the ICT industry in Sri Lanka: since in times of low unemployment, it is possible to expect intensifying competition for talent between competing organisations (Aguinis, Gottfredson & Joo, 2012; Guthridge, Komm & Lawson, 2008). Further, Taylor and Collins (2000) discuss the manner in which recruitment becomes a larger focus of academic interest in times of low unemployment. This study therefore has gathered its motivation from this challenging situation present in the job market of the ICT industry in Sri Lanka

Extant literature defines recruitment as a process of attracting and obtaining as many applications as possible from eligible job-seekers (Armstrong & Taylor, 2014; Aswathappa, 2005). Rynes (1989, p.1) mentions that "an organisation's success in recruiting defines the applicant population with which it will work; selection is more pleasant, if not easier, when restriction or skew of distribution is attributable to an overabundance of well-qualified applicants." Thus, for a recruitment campaign to be successful, the behavioural intention of eligible job-seekers to apply for job openings is an important requirement, since it is an important psychological phenomenon which determines the number of job applications received.

Gillhouse (2001) notes that during a period wherein the rate of unemployment remains high, the chances that a recruitment campaign would become successful in terms of the number of applications received, is high; he further goes on to saying that it would not however be the case during a period of low unemployment rates. Thus, existing and new knowledge on the behavioural intention of job-seekers when applying for available job vacancies is a vital topic of study that would enrich organisations involved not only in the ICT industry of Sri Lanka, but also those in any other industry experiencing low unemployment rates.

The decision regarding the choice of job and employer branding are two main research areas in HRM which discuss the psychology of job-seekers. Research regarding the choice of job has predominantly studied factors affecting job attractiveness, organisational attractiveness, job pursuit decision and the career choice decision. Employer branding is another area of research which focuses on the recruitment of potential job seekers for available positions. Research on employer branding argues over factors which create employer attraction in the minds of the job-seekers (Backhaus & Tikoo, 2004; Wallace, Lings, Cameron & Sheldon, 2014). Factors affecting employer attraction is not a novel research area, as mentioned above, researches carried out over the topic of the choice of the job has spoken heavily on this matter furthermore, the concepts of recruitment, retention, employee satisfaction and turnover have been discussed under a single topic thus contributing towards the popularity of employer branding (Wallace et al., 2014).

Despite being under the limelight as two research areas that have been captured by many scholars exposing the concepts into extensive study, the thought process of the job-seeker has been a perspective often overlooked by many. Breaugh (2008) emphasizes the importance of this notion as he discusses the targeted recruitment and job applicant thought process. This study aims at addressing this particular capacity of notable deficit in research related to recruitment by introducing a conceptual framework which would describe the means by which a behavioural intention to apply for a job opening is generated in the mind of a job-seeker.

In order to assist the development of the conceptual model, the Technology Acceptance Model (TAM) was employed. It presents the thought process of a user who would accept and use a particular technology (Lee, Kozar, & Larsen, 2003; Legris, Ingham, & Collerette, 2003; Pikkarainen, Pikkarainen, Karjaluoto, & Pahnila, 2004; Venkatesh & Bala, 2008; Venkatesh & Davis, 2000). This model had been used in the past to assess the thought process of ICT professionals (Hardgrave, Davis & Riemenschneider, 2003; Henderson, Sheetz & Trinkle, 2012; Riemenschneider & Hardgrave, 2001; Vijayasarathy & Turk, 2012; Wallace & Sheetz, 2014). Thus, the use of this very same model to assess the thought process of ICT professionals is defendable; however, it can also be argued that the usage of this model is not justifiable in terms of assessing the thought process related to a job seeker, since it was initially used to study the acceptance of technology. Extant literature has employed the TAM to understand the purchase intention of buyers (Lima, Osmanb, Salahuddinc, Romled & Abdullah, 2016). Purchase intention is not related to the acceptance of technology; however, since the TAM had been developed with the backing of the Theory of Reasoned Action (TRA), the previous studies have employed TAM to describe the thought process of buyers. Further, Pierce, Willy, Roncace and Bischoff (2014) have employed the thought process explained in the TAM to understand people's attitudes toward health care reform. Pierce et al. (2014) labelled the model they developed as the Policy Acceptance Model (PAM). PAM is yet another example which magnifies the usage of the TAM in recent times. It solidifies how contemporary researchers have used the TAM to explain thought processes of humans who are not related to the acceptance of technology. The concept of "technoculture" in Sociology also justifies the usage of the TAM in explaining the behavioural intention of humans in other scenarios away from those which involve technology. According to literature in "technoculture", humans are 'techno-bodies' inhabiting 'techno-spaces,' thus technology influences how humans understand the natural world and how the successive technological developments have influenced attitudes to work, art, space, language and the human body. This further justifies the usage of the TAM to explain the thought process of a job seeker. Value proposition, perceived value and behavioural intention are three concepts of marketing management that were utilized at the point of developing logic for the conceptual framework. M. Armstrong and Taylor (2014) justify the usage of these marketing management concepts as a result of their claim which refers to the current job market as one similar to a buyer-seller market.

When considering the nature of this study under the pretext of those mentioned above, it stands out as one which is quite progressive and timely in nature. The focus of the paper is to develop a conceptual framework to understand the behavioural intentions of a job seeker intrigued by a job market which at present experiences a short supply of talent; to apply for a job position. The following sections of the paper is organised under four sections, namely, the literature review, conceptual framework and hypotheses, discussion and conclusion.

LITERATURE REVIEW

The Literature review begins its discussion from the topic of the TAM. The three sub-sections which follow would then further clarify the use of the three concepts of marketing management which have been utilized for this study; namely – value proposition, perceived value and behavioural intention. Thereafter, the study will present a justification for the use of the TAM and the three concepts in marketing management in order to propose a conceptual model that would explain the behavioural intention that would prompt a job seeker to apply for a particular job opening. The later part of this section will then introduce and elaborate on the characterization of the constructs.

Technology Acceptance Model (TAM)

The Technology Acceptance Model (TAM) (refer Figure 1) presented in 1986 by F. D. Davis in his doctoral thesis explains how the perceived usefulness and perceived ease of use affect actual behaviour (as cited in Legris et al., 2003). Thus the three components critical for this section of the study are the external variables (such as image, job relevance, output quality, result demonstrability, etc), perceived usefulness together with the ease of use and the behavioural intention of the users towards using the system. According to the TAM there is an impact from external variables in creating perceived usefulness and perceived ease of use in the minds of system users (Legris et al., 2003). Once a sense of perception is developed, the attitude towards the information system is created (Legris et al., 2003); This results in the creation of a behavioural intention that is to be used and an information system which can be advocated in the minds of the users (Lee et al., 2003; Legris et al., 2003; T. Pikkarainen et al., 2004; Venkatesh & Bala, 2008; Venkatesh & Davis, 2000).

External variables, perceived value and behavioural intention are the three constructs that will be considered in this study.

Company's Consumer Value Proposition

A Company's Consumer Value Proposition is a set of benefits or values that a company has promised to deliver in order to consumer needs and wants (Armstrong, Agnihotri, Haque, & Kotler, 2014). This provides an answer to the question, "why should I buy your brand rather than a competitor's?" (Armstrong et al., 2014). A customer would find an answer to this question at the point of evaluating the difference between all benefits and costs of a market offering, relative to that of the competing offers (Armstrong et al., 2014). Resulting this evaluation process in terms of benefits and costs of competing offers, a particular sense of "consumer value" is created in the mind of the customer for every offer. The available literature on marketing management terms this sense of value created in the mind of the customer for a competing offer, the "customer-perceived value" (Armstrong et al., 2014). In other words, to generate a sense of "perceived-value" in the mind of a customer, organisations must communicate the value propositions - their products or services offer to the customer. Then the customer will evaluate the difference between all the benefits and costs of the offering and decide which offer to purchase (G. Armstrong et al., 2014).

Figure 1. Original Technology Acceptance Model (TAM)
© *[***Source:*** *Legris, Ingham, & Collerette, 2003]. Reproduced by permission of Paul Legris*

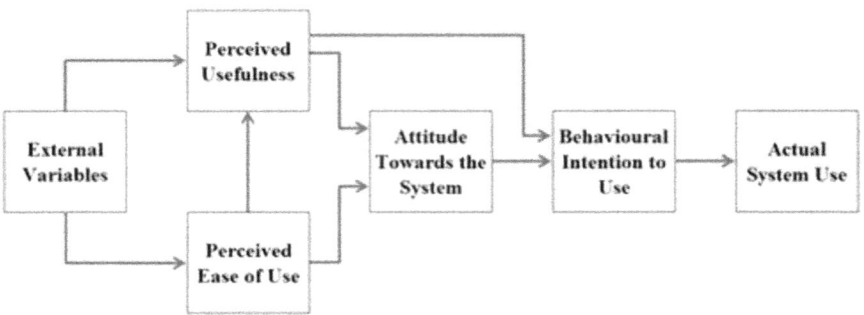

Perceived Value

Perceived value is defined as a trade-off between benefits and sacrifices perceived by customers in a supplier's offer (Eggert & Ulaga, 2002; Gallarza & Gil, 2008; McDougall & Levesque, 2000; Milfelner, Snoj, & Korda, 2011; Sánchez-Fernández & Iniesta-Bonillo, 2007; Yang & Peterson, 2004; Zeithml, 1988) relative to those of competing offers (Armstrong et al., 2014; Ulaga & Chacour, 2001).

Two main research approaches to perceived value can be found in extant literature, namely – uni – dimensional and multi - dimensional (Sánchez-Fernández & Iniesta-Bonillo, 2007). In a systematic review, Sánchez-Fernández and Iniesta-Bonillo (2007) concluded that perceived value is a complex and a multi-dimensional concept. Out of five multi-dimensional research streams Sánchez-Fernández and Iniesta-Bonillo (2007) have recommended to use Holbrook's Typology of Consumer Value (refer Figure 2) (Holbrook, 1999).

Sheth, Newman and Gross (1991) developed another multi - dimensional framework for perceived value. This framework consists of five values, namely - functional value, conditional value, social value, emotional value and epistemic value (Sheth et al., 1991). Roig, Garcia, Tena, and Monzonis (2006) analysed the dimensionality of the concept of perceived value in the banking sector. They summarised the most important studies of the multi-dimensionality of perceived value (refer Table 1). The summary shows that the model of Sheth et al. (1991) can be considered as the most robust model, because, it covers five dimensions of perceived value except logical value whereas other studies have considered maximum three values.

Figure 2. Holbrook's Typology of consumer value
©[**Source:** *Holbrook, 1999]. Reproduced by permission of Professor Morris B. Holbrook*

		Extrinsic	**Intrinsic**
Self-Oriented	**Active**	Efficinecy (O/I, Convenience)	Play (Fun)
	Reactive	Excellence (Quality)	Aesthetic (Beauty)
Other-Oriented	**Active**	Status (Success, Impression, Management)	Ethics (Justice, Virtue, Morality)
	Reactive	Esteem (Reputation, Materialism, Possession)	Spirituality (Faith, Ecstacy, Sacredness)

Table 1. Studies of multi-dimensionality of perceived value

Authors	**Cognitive**	**Emotional**	**Logical**	**Conditional**	**Social**	**Epistemic**
Mattson (1991)	×	×	×			
Sheth et al. (1991)	×	×		×	×	×
Gronroos (1997)	×	×				
De Ruyter et al. (1997)	×	×	×			
Sweeney & Soutar (2001)	×	×			×	
Sánchez et al. (2006)	×	×			×	
Roig et al. (2006)	×	×			×	

Source: Roig et al., 2006

Thus, it is clear that perceived value is a multi – dimensional construct and two main approaches have been introduced by Sheth et al. (1991) and Holbrook (1999) to explain the multi - dimensionality. This study considered the approach suggested by Sheth et al. (1991) when characterising one of the constructs in the conceptual framework and a detailed discussion on the choice is available in a following section of the literature review.

Behavioural Intention

According to the TAM shown in Figure 1, there is a direct relationship between the system user's perception about the usefulness of the system and the behavioural intention in using the system. Extant literature written on the Unified Theory of Acceptance and Use of Technology (UTAUT) model - a model that has used TAM and seven other models in information technology acceptance research indicates that external variables have a direct relationship on behavioural intention; voluntariness, experience, age and gender meanwhile moderate the relationship between external variables and the behavioural intention. (Venkatesh, Morris, Davis, & Davis, 2003; Wang & Wang, 2010) Wang and Wang (2010) have conducted a study to investigate the user acceptance of mobile internet based on the UTAUT model and they propose the fact that perceived value has a direct relationship with the behavioural intention and external variables also have a direct relationship with the behavioural intention. Further, Chen (2008) embarked on a study to investigate the structural relationships between service quality, perceived value, satisfaction, and behavioural intentions for air passengers; this study found that the perceived value leads to behavioural intention. Further, Hu (2011) also researched to understand the link between perceived value, customer satisfaction and purchase intention in e-commerce settings, he while endorsing the fact that perceived value and purchase intention has a direct relationship, stated that this relationship maximized on in the process of developing the conceptual framework of the study.

Based on the above discussion it can be concluded that, external variables have a direct relationship with behavioural intention while perceived value has a direct relationship with the behavioural intention. Further, the relationship between external variables and behavioural intention is positively moderated by four variables namely - voluntariness, experience, age and gender.

Deriving the Constructs of the Study

Perceived value is created as a result of getting to know about the value proposition, or in other words, it is a particular value attached to certain benefits or values of a particular product or service. In the TAM, perceived value is generated as a result of the external variables; relevant parties have to communicate benefits or values a particular information system has, in order to generate perceived ease of use and perceived usefulness in the minds of the potential system users. Thus, it is admissible to assume that the value proposition communicated to potential system users consists of external variables in the TAM as a result the value proposition communicated to the information system users creates a "perceived value" in the minds of those information system users. Further, the TAM proposes that perceived value has a direct relationship with behavioural intention and that it is consistent with the findings in marketing management. The UTAUT model proposes that the value proposition (external variables) has a direct relationship with behavioural intention and the relationship is positively moderated by four variables, namely – voluntariness, age, gender and experience.

The studies done by Vijayasarathy and Turk (2012), Wallace and Sheetz (2014), Hardgrave et al. (2003), Henderson et al. (2012) and Riemenschneider and Hardgrave (2001) have used the TAM to investigate the thought process of ICT professionals. Thus, the use of this very same model and the above mentioned relationships, to depict the thought process of an ICT professional related to the behavioural intention when applying for a job opening, is permissible since the TAM offers a noticeable contribution towards all relationships mentioned above.

According to the above discussion, three constructs will be employed in defining the thought process related to the behavioural intention of an ICT professional when apply for a job opening, namely – value proposition, perceived value and behavioural intention. Thereby to suit the domain of the study, i.e. recruitment, the three constructs can be named as company's job-seeker value proposition (identical to company's consumer value proposition in marketing management), job-seeker perceived value (identical to consumer perceived value in marketing management) and behavioural intention to apply for a job opening. Further, there are four other moderating variables in the thought process. The two subsequent sub-sections that are to follow will discuss regarding both the most recently introduced constructs of the domain of recruitment; namely – the company's job seeker value proposition and the job seeker perceived value.

Company's Job Seeker Value Proposition

A company's job-seeker value proposition can be defined as a set of benefits or values a company promises to deliver to job-seekers once they come on-board, in order to satisfy their intrinsic and extrinsic needs. Extant literature on job choice decision was referred to in the process of characterising the construct since it is an existing research area which discusses about the factors job-seekers are concerned of during their recruitment and selection process. Employer branding has also borrowed knowledge from research based on the decision of the choice of a job for studies related to attracting staff (Baum & Kabst, 2013; Uen, Ahlstrom, Chen & Liu, 2015). Past researchers who have studied the decision of the choice of job looked at factors affecting the four main dependent variables, namely - job attractiveness (Boswell, Roehling, LePine, & Moynihan, 2003; Grund, 2009), organisational attractiveness (Boswell et al., 2003; Dutta & Punnose, 2010; Terjesen, Vinnicombe & Freeman, 2007; Greening & Turban, 2000; Highhouse, Lievens, & Sinar, 2003; Highhouse,

Thornbury & Little, 2007; Lievens, Decaesteker, Coetsier, & Geirnaert, 2001; Roehling & Winters, 2000; Slaughter, Cable & Turban, 2014; Turban, 2001; Turban & Cable, 2003), job pursuit decision (Boswell et al., 2003; Cable & Turban, 2003) and career choice decision (Agarwala, 2008; Boswell et al., 2003). The independent variables of those studies are the factors that job-seekers are interested in. The present study assumes that those independent variables characterise a company's job-seeker value proposition.

Thus, job seeker value proposition can be characterised with seventeen unique factors, namely - autonomy at work, job security, pay, type of work, career development opportunities, benefits, learning and development (opportunities), responsibility at work, working conditions, work - life balance, company reputation, person – organisation fit, co – worker (sociable and competent), recruitment activities, geographical location, corporate social responsibility activities and company culture. According to M. Armstrong and Brown (2010), out of the seventeen factors, eleven factors, namely - autonomy at work, job security, pay, type of work, career development opportunities, benefits, learning and development (opportunities), responsibility at work, working conditions, work - life balance and company culture, can be categorised under the category of the 'total reward'. Fombrun (1999) and Chun (2005) on the other hand say that corporate social responsibility activities can be nested under company reputation. Thus, it is possible to conclude that, the job seeker value proposition can be characterised with six variables; namely – total reward, company reputation, person – organisation fit, co-workers (competent and sociable), geographical location and recruitment activities. The process of manoeuvring these six variables will in turn operationalize the construct.

The empirical focus of studies considered to characterise the construct have been focused on the new graduates. Thus, the model proposed is most suitable to determine the behavioural intention of freshly graduated candidates.

Job Seeker Perceived Value

The "job seeker perceived value" can be defined as the job-seeker's overall assessment of a particular job vacancy based on perceptions of what is received and what is given. As discussed above, in order to characterise the construct Holbrook's Typology and the framework for consumer choice behaviour can be used.

Holbrook's Typology, can be applied apart from its section concerning the 'Intrinsic Value'; since, available literature indicates only a consumption experience can grant Intrinsic Value (Holbrook, 1999). In this paper we argue that consumption experience is similar to getting the job and working in the organisation. According to Holbrook's Typology, extrinsic value consists of four experiences, namely – efficiency, excellence, status and esteem (Holbrook, 1999). He further notes that efficiency is a result of active use or consumption experience of a product in order to achieve a self-oriented purpose. Excellence thereby is a construct which arises as a result of the comparison done between actual the performance of a certain activity and its height of expectation (Holbrook, 1999). It is clear that both efficiency and excellence cannot be used for the present study as they are related to the post consumption stage of a product or service (Holbrook, 1999). Instead, status and esteem are identified as the two constructs that are suitable for the present study. It is said that people will consume a particular good or service if they feel that the product or service would contribute to the success and impression management (Holbrook, 1999). In terms of esteem, if a consumer feels that a particular good or service has potential to enhance his/her 'other-oriented' public image (Holbrook, 1999), there is a high chance that the consumer would consume the good or service, due to the perceived value generated in the mind of the consumer initially.

Sweeney and Soutar (2001) developed a multiple item scale to measure consumer perceived value and it is known as the PERVAL. This scale was derived from Sheth et al.'s (1991) study on consumer choice behaviour. Sweeney and Soutar (2001) have considered the emotional and social value as it is and have taken the two other constructs - quality and price as two subcomponents of functional value. Sweeney and Soutar (2001) have ignored epistemic value and conditional value when developing the scale with a justification.

When comparing the constructs of status and esteem in the PERVAL scale which were shortlisted from Holbrook's Typology, it is possible to assume that social value is similar to the constructs of status and esteem. One reason being, the fact that status and esteem are other-oriented constructs (Holbrook, 1999), whereas social value also transpires as an other-oriented construct since it consists of measures such as 'would help me to feel acceptable', 'would improve the way I'm perceived', etc (Sweeney & Soutar, 2001). According to Holbrook (1999), other(s) in 'other-oriented' value range from the micro level (family, friends, colleagues, etc) to an intermediate level (community, country, world) and even to the macro level (the Cosmos, Mother Nature and the Deity). It is possible to assume the same with social value as well. Emotional value is more of a self-oriented construct because it consists of measures such as 'is one that I would enjoy', 'would make me want to use it', etc. (Sweeney & Soutar, 2001). There is a construct named 'job quality' in available literature on Human Resource Management (OECD, 2013) and it can be considered as the identical counterpart to a product or service quality in Marketing Management. It is not feasible to look for a similar construct to price in Human Resource Management, since 'earnings' have also been captured as an indicator of job quality.

In summary, a job seeker perceived value is characterised with the use of three variables, namely – emotional value, social value and job quality.

CONCEPTUAL FRAMEWORK AND HYPOTHESES

As mentioned in the literature review, the hypotheses and conceptual framework proposed in this section are valid only for the behaviour of new graduates.

Extant literature on marketing management indicates the fact that there is a direct relationship between value proposition and perceived value (Armstrong et al., 2014). However, with evidence exclusively from marketing management it is not possible to hypothesise that such a relationship exists between the two constructs of a company's job-seeker value proposition and the job-seeker perceived value. According to the TAM, perceived value is generated in the minds of the potential system users as a result of getting to know about the value proposition or in other words its benefits or values attached with a new information system or technology (Lee et al., 2003; Legris et al., 2003; Pikkarainen et al., 2004; Venkatesh & Bala, 2008; Venkatesh & F.D. Davis, 2000). The TAM has been used to check the thought process of ICT professionals and thus, it is justifiable to hypothesise that a relationship exists between company's job-seeker value proposition and a job-seeker perceived value. To elaborate further, the TAM has been used to describe the thought processes of professionals who are in other professions as well (Legris et al., 2003). Thus, it is justifiable to form a general hypothesis to cover all types of job seekers in any industry which experience a short supply of talent.

- *H1: The company's job seeker value proposition will have a positive and significant influence on the job seeker-perceived value*

Studies in marketing management indicate that there is a direct relationship between perceived value and behavioural intention (Chen, 2008; Hu, 2011) and there is a direct relationship between the perceived value and behavioural intention according to the TAM as well. (Lee et al., 2003; Legris et al., 2003; Pikkarainen et al., 2004; Venkatesh & Bala, 2008; Venkatesh & Davis, 2000). Further, Wang and Wang (2010) who used the UTAUT model for their study proposed that the perceived value has a direct relationship with the behavioural intention; It was conducted to investigate the user acceptance of mobile internet. With these justifications from extant literature, the following hypothesis related to the direct relationship between the job-seeker perceived value and the behavioural intention of a job-seeker to apply for a job opening, can be proposed.

- *H2: The job seeker-perceived value will have a positive and significant influence on the behavioural intention of a job-seeker when applying for a job opening*

258

Studies on the TAM do not suggest any relationship between the value proposition and behavioural intention. Nevertheless, studies on the UTAUT model suggest that a value proposition has a direct relationship with behavioural intention (Venkatesh et al., 2003; Wang & Wang, 2010). Thus, it is justifiable to hypothesise that there is a direct relationship between company's job seeker value proposition and behavioural intention of a job-seeker when applying for a job opening.

- *H3: The company's job-seeker value proposition will have a positive and significant influence on the behavioural intention of a job-seeker when applying for a job opening*

Venkatesh et al. (2003) and Wang and Wang (2010) suggest that voluntariness, experience, age and gender positively moderate the relationship between value proposition and behavioural intention. As mentioned in the literature review, this study focuses its attention on fresh graduates. In terms of fresh graduates, it is reasonable to assume that they all are products of somewhat the similar age group and generation with no great degree in varying experience. This study assumed that those two variables are constants and it has not therefore considered including them in the conceptual framework. Thus, the study hypothesises that voluntariness and gender positively moderate the relationship between a company's job seeker value proposition and the behavioural intention of a job-seeker at the point of application for a job opening

- *H4: The influence of a company's job seeker value proposition on behavioural intention is positively moderated by gender and voluntariness new graduates*

The TAM proposes that the relationship between the value proposition and the behavioural intention is mediated by perceived usefulness (Legris et al., 2003). According to hypothesis 1, a job seeker's value proposition will have significant influences on the job seeker-perceived value. According to hypothesis 2, the job seeker-perceived value will have a significant influence on behavioural intentions of a job seeker when applying for a job opening. Thus, it is justifiable to hypothesise that the job seeker perceived value acts as a mediator in the relationship between the company's job seeker value proposition and the behavioural intention.

- *H5: The job seeker perceived value will mediate the direct relationship between a company's job seeker value proposition and the behavioural intention of a new graduate when applying for a job opening*

The conceptual framework proposed by this study is shown in Figure 3. The proposed hypotheses (except hypothesis 5) are labelled in Figure 3.

DISCUSSION

Theoretical Contribution

Based upon a literature review on extant literature in marketing management and management information systems (TAM), this conceptual paper makes three significant theoretical contributions. While there is a dearth of studies focusing on the thought process of job applicants (Breaugh, 2008), this study specifically focused on developing a conceptual framework which could explain the thought process related to the behavioural intention of new graduates when applying for job vacancies.

The problem related to this research prevailed in the ICT industry of Sri Lanka and the study occupied literature on the TAM in addition to marketing management in the process of developing the conceptual framework. Even though the TAM has been used by many past researchers to explain the thought process of ICT professionals, there have been numerous other instances where researchers have used the same model to explain the thought process of professionals employed in industries elsewhere. Thus, the conceptual model proposed by this study cannot be labelled as a framework that has the capability to explain the behavioural intention of a mere ICT professional. Therefore, the conceptual framework proposed by this study can be recognized as a general model that can be used to explain the thought process of any new graduate seeking occupation.

Figure 3. Conceptual framework
Source: *Authors developed through literature*

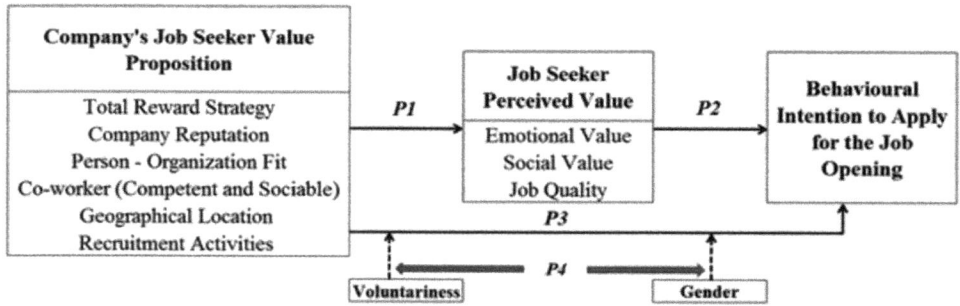

The second theoretical contribution of this study is the importation of knowledge from other disciplines to human resource management. McShane, Olekalns, Newman and Travaglione (2015) argue that organizational behaviour and human resource management are disciplines which should import knowledge from various other disciplines; since, during the past both the disciplines have benefited from knowledge of emerging fields such as communication, marketing and information systems. This study has imported knowledge from the disciplines of management information systems and marketing management. As a result of this knowledge importation, this study has introduced two novel terminologies to the discipline of human resource management, namely – a company's job-seeker value proposition and the job-seeker perceived value.

The third theoretical contribution of this research is the proposed chain relationship between the three main constructs, namely – the company's job seeker value proposition, a job seeker perceived value and the behavioural intention to apply for a job opening. The proposed relationship offered by this study has never been discussed by past researchers in human resource management. Baum and Kabst (2013) have proposed a conceptual framework which depicts a direct relationship between five factors (those factors were nested under "total reward" in the present study) and behavioural intention. Thus, the direct relationship between a company's job-seeker value proposition and a behavioural intention is by no means a novel phenomenon. The main novelty of the proposed conceptual framework however is the introduction of the mediating effect of the job seeker perceived value, as it is alien to the existing body of knowledge in human resource management.

Practical Contribution

An issue encountered by the present study is the short supply of talent in the ICT industry in Sri Lanka. In 2013, there had been a short supply of 468 employees and predictions on the behaviour of the ICT industry clearly shows that a short supply of talent is going to be one of the major challenges faced by human resource practitioners in the future. Thus, in addition to the theoretical contribution, this paper provides an advantageous edge for practitioners such as recruitment managers who are in industries which experience a short supply of employees and to those interested in recruiting new graduates. During such times wherein, an organization would embrace the loss of having a short supply of employees, the behavioural intention of job-seekers to apply for job openings become extremely critical, as, it determines the number of applications received for a recruitment campaign. Even though extant literature written on the decision of the choice of job and employer branding can be used when preparing a recruitment campaign, it is important to note that none of those studies have focused on the thought process of a new graduate (Breaugh, 2008).

This study aims at filling that gap and supporting recruitment managers to understand a portion of the thought process of a new graduate who is seeking a job through a recruitment and selection process. During the exercise, the study listed down six factors which characterise a company's job seeker value proposition. According to Armstrong et al. (2014) the value proposition consists of three components, which are to - chose the value, provide the value and communicate the value. The study thereby aids HRM practitioners to choose the correct value proposition that would generate a job-seeker perceived value and behavioural intention within the minds of the job-seekers when applying for job vacancies.

Further, the study also highlights three components which characterise a job seeker perceived value. These are some of the aspects that ought to be considered by recruitment practitioners when communicating the value proposition. They highlight the benefits a job-seeker would receive in relation to emotional value, social value and job quality.

Accordingly, there are two practical contributions of this study. Firstly, the study creates awareness about the thought process related to the behavioural intention of new graduates when applying for job openings by introducing the conceptual model and secondly, the study defines the scope that a recruitment manager should focus on when developing the company's job-seeker value proposition and the scope that a job-seeker would consider when deciding on the benefits or sacrifices (drawbacks).

Limitations

When developing the conceptual model for the study, its main contribution derived through the TAM; nevertheless the construct of "attitude towards the information system" (Lee et al., 2003; Legris et al., 2003; Pikkarainen et al., 2004; Venkatesh & Bala, 2008; Venkatesh & Davis, 2000), offered in the TAM was purposely avoided in this research. One could argue that the "attitude of the job seeker towards a job opening" should be presented in between the behavioural intention of the job seekers and the job seeker perceived value, for the conceptual model to be consistent with the famous TAM, however this was done to ensure that the model is consistent with the concepts presented in literature of marketing management. To further justify the non-usage of attitude, the UTAUT has also avoided considering this aspect of the "attitude".

The second limitation arose at the point of characterising the construct. The study on the company's job-seeker value proposition considered solely the factors which derived from extant literature regarding the choice of job related to fresh graduates. Thus, the conceptual framework proposed in the study is applicable only to the new graduate and it cannot be used to explain the thought process of graduates with experience as well as that of the non-graduate job-seeker.

The third limitation revolves around the validity of the conceptual framework. It is valid only when the job-seeker is more powerful than the employer. In other words, at times of short supply of talent, job-seekers possess the power to bargain. Thus, employers have to keep them informed regularly about what they offer. This is where company's job-seeker value proposition becomes important to employers. During times of abundant supply of talent, employers possess the power to bargain and therefore it is not a necessary to keep the job seekers informed about what they have to offer. Due to this reason, the proposed conceptual framework is valid only during periods of low unemployment rates.

FUTURE RESEARCH DIRECTIONS

The present research focused on five core constructs, i.e. a company's job-seeker value proposition, job-seeker perceived value, behavioural intention as well as voluntariness and gender. Those constructs were taken from extant literature on management information systems which focuses on studying the behavioural intention and actual behaviour of information system users. This study has not considered other closely related constructs such as attitude of the job-seeker, etc. Therefore, future research could reflect on such closely related constructs and strengthen the proposed conceptual framework further by including them in a logical manner.

The present research addressed the call for a focused study on the thought process of job-seekers by Breaugh (2008). Nonetheless, when thinking rationally, the thought process of a job-seeker contains several other steps, i.e. actual behaviour of applying for a job vacancy, behavioural intention to attend an interview, actual behaviour of attending an interview, behavioural intention to accept or reject a job offer and the actual behaviour of accepting or rejecting a job offer. The thought process of a job seeker from the very beginning instant wherein the job seeker is informed of the job opening until the point of accepting or rejecting the job, is a potential scope for future research.

As per Armstrong et al. (2014), communicating value is one of the main things associated with developing a correct value proposition. In conclusion, this study did not focus on the methods of communicating value proposition, since it did not belong to the scope of the study. Therefore, methods of communicating a company's job seeker value proposition are also an extremely vital topic which needs to be captured by researchers in the future.

CONCLUSION

Even though a rich body of extant literature on the psychology of job seekers is prevalent today, there remains a dearth of research discussing the thought process of job-seekers. The main objective of this study was to address this gap; as a result, the paper initiates its discussion on the present status of the job market in the ICT industry in Sri Lanka. Currently the industry is experiencing a low unemployment rate and the situation is expected to continue to remain the same until 2022. During times of low unemployment rates, the behavioural intention of the job-seekers to apply for job vacancies is crucial for any organisation, for it determines the success or failure of recruitment campaigns in terms of the number of applications received. Even though there are studies which have tried to understand the psychology of job-seekers, there is hardly any study which has focused on understanding the thought process of a job-seeker (Breaugh, 2008). Hence, based upon a literature review on the TAM as well as marketing management, this paper presents a conceptual framework backed by a steady logical thought, capable of explaining the thought process related to the behavioural intention of a new graduate when applying for a job vacancy. The proposed conceptual framework is applicable for any new graduate who is seeking employment in an industry which is experiencing a low unemployment rate.

The proposed conceptual framework presents the relationship between the company's job-seeker value proposition, job-seeker perceived value, behavioural intention, voluntariness and gender, which are the five main variables of the study. It attempts to explain the effect of a company's job-seeker value proposition and the job-seeker perceived value on the behavioural intention of the job-seeker when applying for a job vacancy. The job-seeker perceived value partially mediates the relationship between the company's job-seeker value proposition and behavioural intention while voluntariness and gender moderates the direct relationship between the company's job-seeker value proposition and the behavioural intention.

Further, out of the terminology used to label the constructs, two terminologies, namely the company's job seeker value proposition and job-seeker perceived value are novel to the field of human resource management. Therefore, even though relevant theoretical support and empirical research evidence to develop the conceptual model have been drawn from extant literature on marketing management and management information systems, the empirical validation of this conceptual framework would contribute towards the progress of this field of research.

Future researchers need to work on the limiting factors influencing the behavioural intention of new graduates to apply for job openings. This would help researchers enhance their understanding of the psychology of new graduates when applying for job vacancy. Further, future researchers should focus on understanding the thought process a new graduate beginning from the moment he/she gets to know about the job vacancy until the acceptance or rejection of the offer. This would then significantly benefit practitioners such as recruitment managers and line managers of various industries in making the right decisions when designing recruitment campaigns to attract new graduates.

REFERENCES

Agarwala, T. (2008). Factors Influencing Career Choice of Management Students in India. *Career Development International*, *13*(4), 362–376. doi:10.1108/13620430810880844

Aguinis, H., Gottfredson, R. K., & Joo, H. (2012). Using performance management to win the talent war. *Business Horizons*, *55*(6), 609–616. doi:10.1016/j.bushor.2012.05.007

Armstrong, G., Agnihotri, P. Y., Haque, E. U., & Kotler, P. (2014). *Principles of Marketing. Doring Kindersley* .

Armstrong, M., & Brown, D. (2010). *Strategic Rewards: Implementing More Effective Reward Management* (Indian Edition). New Delhi: Kogan Page India Private Limited.

Armstrong, M., & Taylor, S. (2014). *Armstrong's Handbook of Human Resource Management Practice*. London: Kogan Page Limited.

Aswathappa, K. (2005). *Human Resource and Personnel Management*. New Delhi: Tata McGraw-Hill Education.

Backhaus, K., & Tikoo, S. (2004). Conceptualizing and researching employer branding. *Career Development International*, *9*(5), 501–517. doi:10.1108/13620430410550754

Bauer, T. N., & Aiman-Smith, L. (1996). Green Career Choices: The Influence of Ecological Stance on Recruiting. *Journal of Business and Psychology*, *10*(4), 445–458. doi:10.1007/BF02251780

Baum, M., & Kabst, R. (2013). How to attract applicants in the Atlantic versus the Asia-Pacific region? A cross-national analysis on China, India, Germany, and Hungary. *Journal of World Business*, *48*(2), 175–185. doi:10.1016/j.jwb.2012.07.002

Boswell, W. R., Roehling, M. V., LePine, M. A., & Moynihan, L. M. (2003). Individual Job-Choice Decisions and the Impact of Job Attributes and Recruitment Practices: A Longitudinal Field Study. *Human Resource Management*, *42*(1), 23–37. doi:10.1002/hrm.10062

Breaugh, J. A. (2008). Employee recruitment: Current knowledge and important areas for future research. *Human Resource Management Review*, *18*(3), 103–118. doi:10.1016/j.hrmr.2008.07.003

Cable, D. M., & Judge, T. A. (1994). Pay Preferences and Job Search Decisions: A Person-Organization Fit Perspective. *Personnel Psychology*, *47*(2), 317–348. doi:10.1111/j.1744-6570.1994.tb01727.x

Cable, D. M., & Judge, T. A. (1996). Person–Organization Fit, Job Choice Decisions, and Organizational Entry. *Organizational Behavior and Human Decision Processes*, *67*(3), 294–311. doi:10.1006/obhd.1996.0081

Cable, D. M., & Turban, D. B. (2003). The Value of Organizational Reputation in the Recruitment Context: A Brand-Equity Perspective. *Journal of Applied Social Psychology*, *33*(11), 2244–2266. doi:10.1111/j.1559-1816.2003.tb01883.x

Chen, C.-F. (2008). Investigating Structural Relationships Between Service Quality, Perceived Value, Satisfaction and Behavioral Intentions for Air Passengers: Evidence from Taiwan. *Transportation Research Part A, Policy and Practice*, *42*(4), 709–717. doi:10.1016/j.tra.2008.01.007

Davis, F. D. Jr. (1986). *A technology acceptance model for empirically testing new end-user information systems: Theory and results*. Massachusetts Institute of Technology.

Davis, K. (1973). The Case for and against Business Assumption of Social Responsibilities. *Academy of Management Journal*, *16*(2), 312–322. doi:10.2307/255331

Dutta, A., & Punnose, E. M. (2010). Factors Affecting Choice of First Employer A Study of Indian Management Graduates. *Global Business Review*, *11*(3), 435–448. doi:10.1177/097215091001100308

Eggert, A., & Ulaga, W. (2002). Customer Perceived Value: A Substitute for Satisfaction in Business Markets? *Journal of Business and Industrial Marketing*, *17*(2/3), 107–118. doi:10.1108/08858620210419754

Feldman, D. C., & Arnold, H. J. (1978). Position choice: Comparing the importance of organizational and job factors. *The Journal of Applied Psychology*, *63*(6), 706–710. doi:10.1037/0021-9010.63.6.706

Fisher, C. D., & Yuan, X. Y. (1998). What motivates employees? A comparison of US and Chinese responses. *International Journal of Human Resource Management*, *9*(3), 516–528. doi:10.1080/095851998341053

Gallarza, M. G., & Gil, I. (2008). The Concept of Value and Its Dimensions: A Tool For Analysing Tourism Experiences. *Tourism Review*, *63*(3), 4–20. doi:10.1108/16605370810901553

Gatewood, R. D., Gowan, M. A., & Lautenschlager, G. J. (1993). Corporate image, recruitment image and initial job choice decisions. *Academy of Management Journal*, *36*(2), 414–427. doi:10.2307/256530

Gillhouse, J. R. (2001). *Recruitment and retention strategies to combat nationwide nursing shortages*. Academic Press.

Glueck, W. F. (1974). Decision Making: Organization Choice. *Personnel Psychology*, *27*(1), 77–93. doi:10.1111/j.1744-6570.1974.tb02064.x

Greening, D. W., & Turban, D. B. (2000). Corporate Social Performance As a Competitive Advantage in Attracting a Quality Workforce. *Business & Society*, *39*(3), 254–280. doi:10.1177/000765030003900302

Grund, C. (2013). Job preferences as revealed by employee-initiated job changes. *International Journal of Human Resource Management*, *24*(15), 2825–2850. doi: 10.1080/09585192.2013.804689

Guthridge, M., Komm, A. B., & Lawson, E. (2008). Making talent a strategic priority. *The McKinsey Quarterly*, *1*, 48.

Hardgrave, B. C., Davis, F. D., & Riemenschneider, C. K. (2003). Investigating Determinants of Software Developers' Intentions to Follow Methodologies. *Journal of Management Information Systems*, *20*(1), 123–151. doi:10.1080/07421222.200 3.11045751

Harris, M. M., & Fink, L. S. (1987). A Field Study of Applicant Reactions to Employment Opportunities: Does the Recruiter Make a Difference? *Personnel Psychology*, *40*(4), 765–784. doi:10.1111/j.1744-6570.1987.tb00623.x

Henderson, D., Sheetz, S. D., & Trinkle, B. S. (2012). The determinants of inter-organizational and internal in-house adoption of XBRL: A structural equation model. *International Journal of Accounting Information Systems*, *13*(2), 109–140. doi:10.1016/j.accinf.2012.02.001

Highhouse, S., Lievens, F., & Sinar, E. F. (2003). Measuring Attraction to Organizations. *Educational and Psychological Measurement*, *63*(6), 986–1001. doi:10.1177/0013164403258403

Highhouse, S., Thornbury, E. E., & Little, I. S. (2007). Social-identity functions of attraction to organizations. *Organizational Behavior and Human Decision Processes*, *103*(1), 134–146. doi:10.1016/j.obhdp.2006.01.001

Holbrook, M. B. (1999). Introduction to consumer value. *Consumer value: A framework for analysis and research*, 1-28.

Hu, Y. (2011). Linking Perceived Value, Customer Satisfaction, and Purchase Intention in E-Commerce Settings. In D. Jin & S. Lin (Eds.), *Advances in Computer Science, Intelligent System and Environment* (pp. 623–628). Berlin: Springer Berlin Heidelberg. doi:10.1007/978-3-642-23753-9_100

Information and Communication Technology Agency of Sri Lanka. (2013). National ICT Workforce Survey.

Judge, T. A., & Bretz, R. D. (1992). Effects of Work Values on Job Choice Decisions. *The Journal of Applied Psychology*, *77*(3), 261–271. doi:10.1037/0021-9010.77.3.261

Lee, Y., Kozar, K. A., & Larsen, K. R. (2003). The Technology Acceptance Model: Past, Present and Future. *Communications of the Association for Information Systems*, *12*(1), 50.

Legris, P., Ingham, J., & Collerette, P. (2003). Why do People Use Information Technology? A Critical Review of the Technology Acceptance Model. *Information & Management*, *40*(3), 191–204. doi:10.1016/S0378-7206(01)00143-4

Lievens, F., Decaesteker, C., Coetsier, P., & Geirnaert, J. (2001). Organizational Attractiveness for Prospective Applicants: A Person–Organisation Fit Perspective. *Applied Psychology*, *50*(1), 30–51. doi:10.1111/1464-0597.00047

Lim, Y. J., Osman, A., Salahuddin, S. N., Romle, A. R., & Abdullah, S. (2016). Factors Influencing Online Shopping Behavior: The Mediating Role of Purchase Intention. *Procedia Economics and Finance*, *35*, 401–410. doi:10.1016/S2212-5671(16)00050-2

McDougall, G. H. G., & Levesque, T. (2000). Customer Satisfaction with Services: Putting Perceived Value into he Equation. *Journal of Services Marketing*, *14*(5), 392–410. doi:10.1108/08876040010340937

McShane, S., Olekalns, M., Newman, A., & Travaglione, T. (2015). *Organisational Behaviour 5e; Emerging Knowledge. Global Insights*. McGraw-Hill Education Australia.

Milfelner, B., Snoj, B., & Korda, A. P. (2011). Measurement of Perceived Quality, Perceived Value, Image and Satisfaction Interrelations of Hotel Services: Comparison of Tourists from Slovenia and Italy. *Journal for General Social Issues*, *20*(3), 605–624. doi:10.5559/di.20.3.01

OECD. (2013). *How's Life? 2013: Measuring Well-Being*. OECD Publishing. doi:10.1787/9789264201392-

Phillips, C. R., Phillips, A. S., & Cappel, S. D. (1994). Research Note: How Management Students Select Prospective Employers. *International Journal of Manpower*, *15*(1), 55–59. doi:10.1108/01437729410053581

Pierce, T. P., Willy, C., Roncace, R., & Bischoff, J. (2014). Extending The Technology Acceptance Model [PAM]. *Policy Acceptance Model*, *5*(2), 16. doi:10.19030/ajhs.v5i2.8963

Pikkarainen, T., Pikkarainen, K., Karjaluoto, H., & Pahnila, S. (2004). Consumer Acceptance of Online Banking: An Extension of the Technology Acceptance Model. *Internet Research*, *14*(3), 224–235. doi:10.1108/10662240410542652

Posner, B. Z. (1981). Comparing Recruiter, Student and Faculty Perceptions of Important Applicant and Job Characteristics. *Personnel Psychology*, *34*(2), 329–339. doi:10.1111/j.1744-6570.1981.tb00946.x

Riemenschneider, C. K., & Hardgrave, B. C. (2001). Explaining Software Development tool Use with the Technology Acceptance Model. *Journal of Computer Information Systems*, *41*(4), 1–8. doi:10.1080/08874417.2001.11647015

Roehling, M. V., & Winters, D. (2000). Job Security Rights: The Effects of Specific Policies and Practices on the Evaluation of Employers. *Employee Responsibilities and Rights Journal*, *12*(1), 25–38. doi:10.1023/A:1007768817334

Roig, J. C. F., Garcia, J. S., Tena, M. A. M., & Monzonis, J. L. (2006). Customer Perceived Value in Banking Services. *International Journal of Bank Marketing*, *24*(5), 266–283. doi:10.1108/02652320610681729

Rynes, S. L. (1989). *Recruitment, job choice, and post-hire consequences: A call for new research directions*. CAHRS Working Paper Series, 398.

Rynes, S. L., & Barber, A. E. (1990). Applicant Attraction Strategies: An Organizational Perspective. *Academy of Management Review*, *15*(2), 286–310. doi:10.2307/258158

Rynes, S. L., Bretz, R. D. Jr, & Gerhart, B. (1991). The Importance of Recruitment in Job Choice: A Different Way of Looking. *Personnel Psychology*, *44*(3), 487–521. doi:10.1111/j.1744-6570.1991.tb02402.x

Rynes, S. L., & Lawler, J. (1983). A Policy-Capturing Investigation of the Role of Expectancies in Decisions to Pursue Job Alternatives. *The Journal of Applied Psychology*, *68*(4), 620–631. doi:10.1037/0021-9010.68.4.620

Sánchez-Fernández, R., & Iniesta-Bonillo, M. Á. (2007). The Concept of Perceived Value: A Systematic Review of the Research. *Marketing Theory*, *7*(4), 427–451. doi:10.1177/1470593107083165

Shaw, D. B. (2008). *Technoculture: The key concepts*. Berg.

Sheth, J. N., Newman, B. I., & Gross, B. L. (1991). Why We Buy What We Buy: A Theory of Consumption Values. *Journal of Business Research*, *22*(2), 159–170. doi:10.1016/0148-2963(91)90050-8

Slaughter, J. E., Cable, D. M., & Turban, D. B. (2014). Changing Job Seekers' Image Perceptions during Recruitment Visits: The Moderating Role of Belief Confidence. *The Journal of Applied Psychology*, *99*(6), 1146–1158. doi:10.1037/a0037482 PMID:25089859

Sri Lanka Association of Software and Service Companies & PricewaterhouseCoopers. (2016). *SLASSCOM Strategy Document 2016*. Author.

Sweeney, J. C., & Soutar, G. N. (2001). Consumer Perceived Value: The Development of a Multiple Item Scale. *Journal of Retailing*, *77*(2), 203–220. doi:10.1016/S0022-4359(01)00041-0

Taylor, M. S., & Collins, C. J. (2000). *Organizational recruitment: Enhancing the intersection of research and practice*. Academic Press.

Terjesen, S., Vinnicombe, S., & Freeman, C. (2007). Attracting Generation Y Graduates: Organisational Attributes, Likelihood to Apply and Sex Differences. *Career Development International*, *12*(6), 504–522. doi:10.1108/13620430710821994

Turban, D. B. (2001). Organizational Attractiveness as an Employer on College Campuses: An Examination of the Applicant Population. *Journal of Vocational Behavior*, *58*(2), 293–312. doi:10.1006/jvbe.2000.1765

Turban, D. B., & Cable, D. M. (2003). Firm Reputation and Applicant Pool Characteristics. *Journal of Organizational Behavior*, *24*(6), 733–751. doi:10.1002/job.215

Turban, D. B., Campion, J. E., & Eyring, A. R. (1995). Factors Related to Job Acceptance Decisions of College Recruits. *Journal of Vocational Behavior*, *47*(2), 193–213. doi:10.1006/jvbe.1995.1035

Turban, D. B., & Dougherty, T. W. (1992). Influences of Campus Recruiting on Applicant Attraction to Firms. *Academy of Management Journal*, *35*(4), 739–765. doi:10.2307/256314

Turban, D. B., Eyring, A. R., & Campion, J. E. (1993). Job Attributes: Preferences Compared with Reasons Given for Accepting and Rejecting Job Offers. *Journal of Occupational and Organizational Psychology*, *66*(1), 71–81. doi:10.1111/j.2044-8325.1993.tb00517.x

Turban, D. B., Forret, M. L., & Hendrickson, C. L. (1998). Applicant Attraction to Firms: Influences of Organization Reputation, Job and Organizational Attributes, and Recruiter Behaviors. *Journal of Vocational Behavior*, *52*(1), 24–44. doi:10.1006/jvbe.1996.1555

Turban, D. B., & Greening, D. W. (1997). Corporate Social Performance And Organizational Attractiveness To Prospective Employees. *Academy of Management Journal*, *40*(3), 658–672. doi:10.2307/257057

Uen, J. F., Ahlstrom, D., Chen, S., & Liu, J. (2015). Employer brand management, organizational prestige and employees' word-of-mouth referrals in Taiwan. *Asia Pacific Journal of Human Resources*, *53*(1), 104–123. doi:10.1111/1744-7941.12024

Ulaga, W., & Chacour, S. (2001). Measuring Customer-Perceived Value in Business Markets: A Prerequisite for Marketing Strategy Development and Implementation. *Industrial Marketing Management*, *30*(6), 525–540. doi:10.1016/S0019-8501(99)00122-4

Venkatesh, V., & Bala, H. (2008). Technology Acceptance Model 3 and a Research Agenda on Interventions. *Decision Sciences*, *39*(2), 273–315. doi:10.1111/j.1540-5915.2008.00192.x

Venkatesh, V., & Davis, F. D. (2000). A Theoretical Extension of the Technology Acceptance Model: Four Longitudinal Field Studies. *Management Science*, *46*(2), 186–204. doi:10.1287/mnsc.46.2.186.11926

Venkatesh, V., Morris, M. G., Davis, G. B., & Davis, F. D. (2003). User Acceptance of Information Technology: Toward a Unified View. *Management Information Systems Quarterly*, *27*(3), 425–478. doi:10.2307/30036540

Vijayasarathy, L., & Turk, D. (2012). Drivers of agile software development use: Dialectic interplay between benefits and hindrances. *Information and Software Technology*, *54*(2), 137–148. doi:10.1016/j.infsof.2011.08.003

Wallace, L. G., & Sheetz, S. D. (2014). The adoption of software measures: A technology acceptance model (TAM) perspective. *Information & Management*, *51*(2), 249–259. doi:10.1016/j.im.2013.12.003

Wallace, M., Lings, I., Cameron, R., & Sheldon, N. (2014). Attracting and Retaining Staff: The Role of Branding and Industry Image. In R. Harris & T. Short (Eds.), *Workforce Development: Perspectives and Issues* (pp. 19–36). Singapore: Springer Singapore. doi:10.1007/978-981-4560-58-0_2

Wang, H.-Y., & Wang, S.-H. (2010). User acceptance of mobile internet based on the Unified Theory of Acceptance and Use of Technology: Investigating the determinants and gender differences. *Social Behavior and Personality*, *38*(3), 415–426. doi:10.2224bp.2010.38.3.415

Wheelen, T. L., & Hunger, J. D. (2013). *Concepts in Strategic Management and Business Policy: Towards Global Sustainability*. Noida: Pearson Education India.

Williams, M. L., & Bauer, T. N. (1994). The Effect of a Managing Diversity Policy on Organizational Attractiveness. *Group & Organization Management*, *19*(3), 295–308. doi:10.1177/1059601194193005

Yang, Z., & Peterson, R. T. (2004). Customer Perceived Value, Satisfaction and Loyalty: The Role of Switching Costs. *Psychology and Marketing*, *21*(10), 799–822. doi:10.1002/mar.20030

Zeithaml, V. A. (1988). Consumer Perceptions of Price, Quality, and Value: A Means-End Model and Synthesis of Evidence. *Journal of Marketing*, *52*(3), 2–22. doi:10.2307/1251446

Compilation of References

Ableson, R. (2000, September 10). Can Respect Be Mandated? May be Not Here. *The New York Times*.

Adamson, J. (2000, Winter). How Denny's Went from Icon of Racism to Diversity Award Winner. *Journal of Organizational Excellence*, 55-68.

Agarwala, T. (2008). Factors Influencing Career Choice of Management Students in India. *Career Development International*, *13*(4), 362–376. doi:10.1108/13620430810880844

Aguinis, H., Gottfredson, R. K., & Joo, H. (2012). Using performance management to win the talent war. *Business Horizons*, *55*(6), 609–616. doi:10.1016/j.bushor.2012.05.007

AICEP. (2014). *Guia Pratico de Acesso ao Mercado*. Retrieved May 16, 2017, from http://www.portugalglobal.pt/PT/Internacionalizar/Paginas/MercadosExternos.aspx?marketId=71

AICEP. (2016a). *Alemanha- Sintese Pais*. Retrieved May 16, 2017, from http://www.portugalglobal.pt/PT/Biblioteca/Paginas/Detalhe.aspx?documentId=1719618b-fdd4-48f7-b4e1-1d6c16ba4665

AICEP. (2016b). *França- Condições Legais de Acesso ao Mercado*. Retrieved May 16, 2017, from http://www.portugalglobal.pt/PT/Biblioteca/Paginas/Detalhe.aspx?documentId=1f14b44c-db40-4119-a532-8d70137aaa03

AICEP. (2017a). *Alemanha- Vinhos- Breve Apontamento*. Retrieved May 16, 2017, from http://www.portugalglobal.pt/PT/Biblioteca/Paginas/Detalhe.aspx?documentId=320cdc40-6702-4b85-b2b9-a486d0653590

AICEP. (2017b). *Sintese Pais- Espanha*. Retrieved May 16, 2017, from http://www.portugalglobal.pt/PT/Biblioteca/Paginas/Detalhe.aspx?documentId=a8457fad-912d-4e56-914f-c1b6164df82c

AICEP. (2017c). *Espanha- Condições Legais de Acesso ao Mercado*. Retrieved May 16, 2017, from http://www.portugalglobal.pt/PT/Biblioteca/Paginas/Detalhe.aspx?documentId=d13154c8-9337-419a-8c14-d8cec898353a

AICEP. (2017d). *Sintese Pais- França*. Retrieved May 16, 2017, from http://www.portugalglobal.pt/PT/Internacionalizar/Paginas/MercadosExternos.aspx?marketId=03

Aier, S., Gleichauf, B. (2010). Applying design research artifacts for building design research artifacts: A process model for enterprise architecture planning. *Global Perspectives on Design Science Research*, 333-348.

Aier, S., & Gleichauf, B. (2010). Application of Enterprise Models for Engineering Enterprise Transformation. *Enterprise Modelling and Information Systems Architectures*, *1*(5), 58–75.

Aier, S., & Gleichauf, B. (2015). Application of enterprise models for engineering enterprise transformation. *Enterprise Modelling and Information Systems Architectures*, *5*(1), 58–75.

Aier, S., Riege, C., & Winter, R. (2008). Classification of Enterprise Architecture Scenarios – An Exploratory Analysis. *Enterprise Modelling and Information Systems Architectures*, *3*(1), 14–23.

Albani, A., & Dietz, J. (2010). Advances in Enterprise Engineering IV. In *6th International Workshop, CIAO 2010*. Springer.

Albani, A., Raber, D., & Winter, R. (2016). A Conceptual Framework for Understanding the Essence of Enterprise Engineering Methodologies. *Enterprise Modelling and Information Systems Architectures*, *11*(1), 1–26.

Alter, S. (2014, July). Potentially valuable overlaps between work system theory, DEMO, and enterprise engineering. In *Business Informatics (CBI), 2014 IEEE 16th Conference on* (Vol. 2, pp. 25-32). IEEE.

Alvis. (2017). *How walmart makes money? Understanding walmart business model*. Retrieved from: https://revenuesandprofits.com/how-walmart-makes-money-understanding-walmart-business-model/

Andersen, O. (1993). On the internationalization process of firms: A critical analysis. *Journal of International Business Studies*, *24*(2), 209–231. doi:10.1057/palgrave.jibs.8490230

ANSI/IEEE Std 1471-2000, IEEE Recommended Practice for Architectural Description of Software- Intensive Systems

Anttila, J., & Jussila, K. (2013). An advanced insight into managing business processes in practice. *Total Quality Management & Business Excellence*, *24*(7-8), 918–932. doi:10.1080/14 783363.2013.791105

Antunes, G., Barateiro, J., Caetano, A., & Borbinha, J. L. (2015, May). Analysis of Federated Enterprise Architecture Models. ECIS.

Arbab, F., Boer, F., Bonsangue, M., Lankhorst, M., Proper, E., & Torre, L. (2007). Integrating Architectural Models. *Enterprise Modelling and Information Systems Architectures*, *2*(May), 40–57.

Armistead, C., Pritchard, J. P., & Machin, S. (1999). Strategic business process management for organisational effectiveness. *Long Range Planning*, *32*(1), 96–106. doi:10.1016/S0024-6301(98)00130-7

Armour, F. J., Kaisler, S., & Liu, S. (1999). Building an Enterprise Architecture Step by Step‖. *IT Professional*, *4*(1), 31–39. doi:10.1109/6294.781623

Armstrong, G., Agnihotri, P. Y., Haque, E. U., & Kotler, P. (2014). *Principles of Marketing. Doring Kindersley* .

Armstrong, M., & Brown, D. (2010). *Strategic Rewards: Implementing More Effective Reward Management* (Indian Edition). New Delhi: Kogan Page India Private Limited.

Armstrong, M., & Taylor, S. (2014). *Armstrong's Handbook of Human Resource Management Practice*. London: Kogan Page Limited.

Aswathappa, K. (2005). *Human Resource and Personnel Management*. New Delhi: Tata McGraw-Hill Education.

Atwater, L. E., Brett, J. F., Waldman, D., DiMare, L., & Hayden, M. V. (2004). Men's and Women's Perceptions of the Gender Typing of Management Sub-roles. *Sex Roles*, *50*(3/4), 191–200. doi:10.1023/B:SERS.0000015551.78544.35

Austin, J., Stevenson, H., & Wei-Skillern, J. (2006). Social and Commercial Entrepreneurship: Same, Different, or Both? *Entrepreneurship Theory and Practice*, *30*(1), 1–22. doi:10.1111/j.1540-6520.2006.00107.x

Axelsson, B., & Johanson, J. (1992). Foreign market entry: The textbook vs the network view. In B. Axelsson & G. Easton (Eds.), *Industrial networks: A new view of reality* (pp. 218–234). London: Routledge.

Axelsson, B., & Johanson, J. (1992). Foreign market entry: The textbook vs. the network view. In B. Axelsson & G. Easton (Eds.), *Industrial networks: A new view of reality* (pp. 218–234). London: Routledge.

Backhaus, K., & Tikoo, S. (2004). Conceptualizing and researching employer branding. *Career Development International*, *9*(5), 501–517. doi:10.1108/13620430410550754

Barroero, T., Motta, G., & Pignatelli, G. (2010). Business Capabilities Centric Enterprise Architecture. *Enterprise Architecture, Integration and Interoperability IFIP TC 5 International Conference, EAI2N 2010*, 32–43. 10.1007/978-3-642-15509-3_4

Barton, D., Bailey, J., & Zoffer, J. (2015). *Rising to the challenge of short-termism*. Retrieved from: http://www.fcltglobal.org/docs/default-source/default-document-library/fclt-global-rising-to-the-challenge.pdf

Bason, C. (2012). *Designing co-production: Discovering new business models for public services*. Leading Innovation Through Design. 2012 International Design Management research Conference, Boston, MA.

Battilana, J., & Lee, M. (2014). Advancing Research on Hybrid Organizing – Insights from the Study of Social Enterprises. *The Academy of Management Annals*, *8*(1), 397–441. doi:10.1080/19416520.2014.893615

Battilana, J., Lee, M., Walker, J., & Dorsey, C. (2012). In Search of the Hybrid Ideal. *Stanford Social Innovation Review*, *10*, 51–55.

Battilana, J., Sengul, M., Pache, A. C., & Model, J. (2015). Harnessing productive tensions in hybrid organizations: The case of work integration social enterprises. *Academy of Management Journal*, *58*(6), 1658–1685. doi:10.5465/amj.2013.0903

Bauer, T. N., & Aiman-Smith, L. (1996). Green Career Choices: The Influence of Ecological Stance on Recruiting. *Journal of Business and Psychology*, *10*(4), 445–458. doi:10.1007/BF02251780

Baum, M., & Kabst, R. (2013). How to attract applicants in the Atlantic versus the Asia-Pacific region? A cross-national analysis on China, India, Germany, and Hungary. *Journal of World Business*, *48*(2), 175–185. doi:10.1016/j.jwb.2012.07.002

Becker, J., Pfeiffer, D., & Räckers, M. (2007). Domain Specific Process Modelling in Public Administrations – The PICTURE-Approach. In *Electronic Goverment: 6th International Conference, EGOV 2007, Proceedings*. Springer.

Beer, S. (1966). Decision and control: The meaning of operational research and management cybernetics. *Knowledge and Process Management*, *4*, 31–36.

Belkin, L. (2003, October 26). The Opt-Out Revolution. *New York Times Magazine*, 43-47, 58+.

Bell, J., McNaughton, R., & Young, S. (2001). 'Born-again global' firms. An extension to the 'born global' phenomenon. *Journal of International Management*, *7*(3), 173–189. doi:10.1016/S1075-4253(01)00043-6

Bell, S. T., Villado, A. J., Lukasik, M. A., Belau, L., & Briggs, A. L. (2011). Getting Specific about Demographic Variable and Team Performance Relationships: A Meta-Analysis. *Journal of Management*, *37*(3), 709–743. doi:10.1177/0149206310365001

Benner, M. J., & Tushman, M. (2002). Process Management and Technological Innovation: A Longitudinal Study of the Photography and Paint Industries. *Administrative Science Quarterly*, *47*(4), 676–706. doi:10.2307/3094913

Bergman, K. (2010). *Quality from Customer Needs to Customer Satisfaction*. Lund: Studentlitteratur AB.

Bernus, P., Noran, O., & Riedlinger, J. (2003). Using the Globemen Reference Model for Virtual Enterprise Design in after Sales Service. *VTT Symposium (Valtion Teknillinen Tutkimuskeskus)*, 71–90.

Bernus, P., Nemes, L., & Schmidt, G. (2003). *Handbook on Enterprise Architecture*. Springer. doi:10.1007/978-3-540-24744-9

Bernus, P., Noran, O., & Molina, A. (2015). Enterprise architecture: Twenty years of the GERAM framework. *Annual Reviews in Control*, *39*, 83–93. doi:10.1016/j.arcontrol.2015.03.008

BKCASE Editorial Board. (2017). *Guide to the Systems Engineering Body of Knowledge*. Author.

Black, J., & Mendenhall, M. (1990). Cross-Cultural Training Effectiveness: A Review and a Theoretical Framework for Future Research. *Academy of Management Review*, *15*, 113–136.

Bock, A. J., Opsahl, T., George, G., & Gann, D. M. (2012). The effects of culture and structure on strategic flexibility during business model innovation. *Journal of Management Studies*, *49*(2), 279–305. doi:10.1111/j.1467-6486.2011.01030.x

Boswell, W. R., Roehling, M. V., LePine, M. A., & Moynihan, L. M. (2003). Individual Job-Choice Decisions and the Impact of Job Attributes and Recruitment Practices: A Longitudinal Field Study. *Human Resource Management*, *42*(1), 23–37. doi:10.1002/hrm.10062

Boyer, K. K., & Pagell, M. (2000). Measurement issues in empirical research: Improving measures of operations strategy and advanced manufacturing technology. *Journal of Operations Management*, *18*(1), 361–374. doi:10.1016/S0272-6963(99)00029-7

Bradley, F. (2004). *International marketing strategy*. London: Prentice Hall.

Brandsen, T., & Karré, P. M. (2011). Hybrid Organizations: No Cause for Concern? *International Journal of Public Administration*, *34*(13), 827–836. doi:10.1080/01900692.2011.605090

Braun, C., & Winter, R. (2007). Integration of IT Service Management into Enterprise Architecture. *Applied Computing 2007, 1-2*, 1215–19.

Breaugh, J. A. (2008). Employee recruitment: Current knowledge and important areas for future research. *Human Resource Management Review*, *18*(3), 103–118. doi:10.1016/j.hrmr.2008.07.003

Broadbridge, A., & Simpson, R. (2011). 25 Years On: Reflecting on the Past and Looking to the Future in Gender and Management Research. *British Journal of Management*, *22*(3), 470–483. doi:10.1111/j.1467-8551.2011.00758.x

Browne, J., Harhen, J., & Shivnan, J. (1996). *Production Management Systems – An Integrated Perspective* (2nd ed.). Boston: Addison-Wesley.

Buckl, S., Ernst, A. M., Lankes, J., Matthes, F., Schweda, C. M., & Wittenburg, A. (2007). Generating visualizations of enterprise architectures using model transformations. Enterprise Modelling and Information Systems Architectures-An International Journal, 2(2).

Cable, D. M., & Judge, T. A. (1994). Pay Preferences and Job Search Decisions: A Person-Organization Fit Perspective. *Personnel Psychology*, *47*(2), 317–348. doi:10.1111/j.1744-6570.1994. tb01727.x

Cable, D. M., & Judge, T. A. (1996). Person–Organization Fit, Job Choice Decisions, and Organizational Entry. *Organizational Behavior and Human Decision Processes*, *67*(3), 294–311. doi:10.1006/obhd.1996.0081

Cable, D. M., & Turban, D. B. (2003). The Value of Organizational Reputation in the Recruitment Context: A Brand-Equity Perspective. *Journal of Applied Social Psychology*, *33*(11), 2244–2266. doi:10.1111/j.1559-1816.2003.tb01883.x

Campbell, K., & Vera, A. M. (2007). Gender Diversity in the Boardroom and Firm Financial Performance. *Journal of Business Ethics*. doi:10.100710551-007-9630-y

CapGemini. (2010). *Business model innovation*. Retrieved from: https://www.capgemini.com/consulting-fr/wp-content/uploads/sites/31/2017/08/business_model_innovation_ capgemini_ consulting.pdf

Carvalheira, A., & Moreira, A. C. (2016). Searching for opportunities and trust in internationalization markets. Entrepreneurial perspective of a traditional industry SME. In L. C. Carvalho (Ed.), *Handbook of research on entrepreneurial success and its impact on regional development* (pp. 675–701). Hershey, PA: IGI Global. doi:10.4018/978-1-4666-9567-2.ch028

Cesinger, B., Danko, A., & Bouncken, R. (2012). Born globals: (almost) 20 years of research and still not 'grown up'? *International Journal of Entrepreneurship and Small Business*, *15*(2), 171–190. doi:10.1504/IJESB.2012.045203

Checkland, P. (1999). *Systems thinking, systems practice*. New York: Wiley.

Checkland, P. B. (1981). *Systems Thinking Systems Practice*. Chichester, UK: Wiley.

Chen, C.-F. (2008). Investigating Structural Relationships Between Service Quality, Perceived Value, Satisfaction and Behavioral Intentions for Air Passengers: Evidence from Taiwan. *Transportation Research Part A, Policy and Practice*, *42*(4), 709–717. doi:10.1016/j.tra.2008.01.007

Chen, D., & Vernadat, F. (2004). Standards on Enterprise Integration and Engineering–State of the Art. *International Journal of Computer Integrated Manufacturing*, *17*(3), 235–253. doi:10.1080/09511920310001607087

Chen, H., Tian, Y., & Daugherty, P. J. (2009). Measuring process orientation. *International Journal of Logistics Management*, *20*(2), 213–227. doi:10.1108/09574090910981305

Chen, Q., & Hsu, M. (2001). Interenterprise collaborative business process management. *Proceedings of the 17th IEEE International Conference on Data Engineering*, 253–260. 10.1109/ICDE.2001.914836

Chesbrough, H. (2007). Business model innovation: It's not just about technology anymore. *Strategy and Leadership*, *35*(6), 12–17. doi:10.1108/10878570710833714

Chesbrough, H. (2010). Business Model Innovation: Opportunities and Barriers. *Long Range Planning*, *43*(2–3), 354–363. doi:10.1016/j.lrp.2009.07.010

Childs, J. T. (2005). *Workplace Diversity: A global HR topic that has arrived in 'The Future of Human Resource Management* (M. Losey, S. Meisinger, & D. Ulrich, Eds.). Society for Human Resource Management.

Choong, K. K. (2013). Are PMS Meeting the Measurement Needs of BPM? A Literature Review. *Business Process Management Journal*, *19*(3), 535–574. doi:10.1108/14637151311319941

Christensen, C. M. (2003). *The innovator's dilemma: The revolutionary book that will change the way you do business*. New York: HarperCollins Publishers, Inc.

Ciocoiu, M., Gruninger, M., & Nau, D. (2001). Ontologies for integrating en-gineering applications. *Journal of Computing and Information Science in Engineering, 1*(1), 45–60. doi:10.1115/1.1344878

Cochran, D. S., Sereno, R., & Aldrich, W. (2014). *Enterprise Engineering of Lean Accounting and Value Stream Structure through Collective System Design*. Academic Press.

Cornforth, C. (2014). Understanding and combating mission drift in social enterprises. *Social Enterprise Journal, 10*(1), 3–20. doi:10.1108/SEJ-09-2013-0036

Costanzo, F., Kanda, Y., Kimura, T., Kühnle, H., Lisanti, B., Singh Srai, J., . . . Williams, P. M. (2009) Enterprise Organization and Operation. Applications in Mechanical Engineering. doi:10.1007/978-3-540-30738-9_15

Coviello, N. (2015). Re-thinking research on born globals. *Journal of International Business Studies, 46*(1), 17–26. doi:10.1057/jibs.2014.59

Cox, T. H. Jr, & Blake, S. (1991). Managing Cultural Diversity: Implications for Organizational Competitiveness. *The Academy of Management Executive, 5*(3), 45–56. doi:10.5465/AME.1991.4274465

Cumming, D., Leung, T. Y., & Rui, O. (2015). Gender Diversity and Securities Fraud. *Academy of Management Journal, 58*(5), 1572–1593. doi:10.5465/amj.2013.0750

Cunningham, G. B. (2009). The Moderating Effect of Diversity Strategy on the Relationship between Racial Diversity and Organizational Performance. *Journal of Applied Social Psychology, 39*(6), 1445–1460. doi:10.1111/j.1559-1816.2009.00490.x

Curtis, E. F., & Dreachslin, J. L. (2008). Diversity Management Interventions and Organizational Performance: A Synthesis of Current Literature. *Human Resource Development Review, 7*(1), 107–136. doi:10.1177/1534484307311700

Dana, L. P. (2001). Networks, internationalization & policy. *Small Business Economics, 16*(2), 57–62. doi:10.1023/A:1011199116576

Dantas, J. G., Moreira, A. C., & Valente, F. M. (2015). Entrepreneurship and national culture: How cultural differences among countries explain entrepreneurial activity. In L. C. Carvalho (Ed.), *Handbook of research on internationalization of entrepreneurial innovation in the global economy* (pp. 1–28). Hershey, PA: IGI Global. doi:10.4018/978-1-4666-8216-0.ch001

Dantas, J. G., Moreira, A. C., & Valente, F. M. (2017). National culture, societal values and type of economy. Are they relevant to explain entrepreneurial activity? In L. C. Carvalho (Ed.), *Handbook of research on entrepreneurial ecosystems and social dynamics in a globalized world*. Hershey, PA: IGI Global.

Davenport, T. H. (1993). *Process Innovation: Reengineering Work through Information Technology*. Boston, MA: Harvard Business School.

Davenport, T. H., & Short, J. E. (1990). The New Industrial Engineering – Information Technology and Business Process Redesign. *Sloan Management Review*, *31*(4), 11–27.

Davenport, T. H., & Short, J. E. (1990). The New Industrial Engineering: Information Technology and Business Process Redesign. *Sloan Management Review*, *31*(4), 11–27.

Davis, F. D. Jr. (1986). *A technology acceptance model for empirically testing new end-user information systems: Theory and results*. Massachusetts Institute of Technology.

Davis, K. (1973). The Case for and against Business Assumption of Social Responsibilities. *Academy of Management Journal*, *16*(2), 312–322. doi:10.2307/255331

De Bruin, T., & Rosemann, M. (2005). Towards a Business Process Management Maturity Model. *ECIS 2005 Proceedings of the Thirteenth European Conference on Information Systems*.

de Vries, M., Gerber, A., & van der Merwe, A. (2014, April). The Nature of the Enterprise Engineering Discipline. In EEWC (pp. 1-15). doi:10.1007/978-3-319-06505-2_1

de Vries, M., Gerber, A., & van der Merwe, A. (2015, June). The enterprise engineering domain. In *Enterprise Engineering Working Conference* (pp. 47-63). Springer.

Debbabi, M., Hassaïne, F., Jarraya, Y., Soeanu, A., & Alawneh, L. (2010). Architecture Frameworks, Model-Driven Architecture, and Simulation. In Verification and Validation in Systems Engineering (pp. 15-35). Springer Berlin Heidelberg.

Deloitte. (2015). *Technology, Media & Telecommunications India Predictions 2015*. Retrieved from:http://www2.deloitte.com/in/en/pages/technology-media-and-telecommunications/ articles/ tmt-india-predictions-2015.html

Deschamps, F., de Lima, E. P., Santos, E. A. P., & Van Aken, E. (2013, January). Development of Enterprise Engineering Guidelines for Enterprise Diagnosis and Design. In *IIE Annual Conference. Proceedings* (p. 807). Institute of Industrial and Systems Engineers (IISE).

Desyllas, P., & Sako, M. (2013). Profiting from business model innovation: Evidence from Pay-As-You-Drive auto insurance. *Research Policy*, *42*(1), 101–116. doi:10.1016/j.respol.2012.05.008

DeToro, I., & McCabe, T. (1997). How to Stay Flexible and Elude Fads. *Quality Progress*, *30*, 55–60.

Díaz Garrido, E., Martín-Peña, M. L., & García-Muiña, F. (2007). Structural and infrastructural practices as elements of content operations strategy. The effect on a firm's competitiveness. *International Journal of Production Research*, *45*(9), 2119–2140. doi:10.1080/00207540600735480

Dicken, P. (2015). *Global shift. Mapping the changing contours of the world economy*. New York, NY: Guilford Press.

Dietz, J. L. G. (2011). *Enterprise Engineering Manifesto*. Retrieved from www.ciaonetwork. org. www.ciaonetwork.org

Dietz, J. L. G., & Hoogervorst, J. A. P. (2011). A Critical Investigation of TOGAF - Based on the Enterprise Engineering Theory and Practice. *Enterprise Engineering Working Conference 2011*, 76–90.

Dietz, J. L. G. (2006). *Enterprise Ontology – theory and methodology*. Heidelberg, Germany: Springer. doi:10.1007/3-540-33149-2

Dietz, J. L. G., & Hoogervorst, J. A. P. (2012). The principles of enterprise engineering. *Second Enterprise Engineering Working Conference, EEWC 2012*, 15–30.

Dietz, J. L., Hoogervorst, J. A., Albani, A., Aveiro, D., Babkin, E., Barjis, J., & Mulder, H. (2013). The discipline of enterprise engineering. *International Journal of Organisational Design and Engineering*, *3*(1), 86–114. doi:10.1504/IJODE.2013.053669

Doherty, B., Haugh, H., & Lyon, F. (2014). Social Enterprises as Hybrid Organizations: A Review and Research Agenda. *International Journal of Management Reviews*, *16*(4), 417–436. doi:10.1111/ijmr.12028

Dominguez, N. (2016). Risk-seeking behaviours in SMEs' internationalization. In H. Etemad, S. Denicolai, B. Hagen, & A. Zucchella (Eds.), *The changing global economy and its impact on international entrepreneurship* (pp. 66–95). Cheltenham, UK: Edward Elgar.

Dülger, M. (2011). *Significance of Team-Based Organizations in Business Process Orientation and Effectiveness: An Application to Service Firms in Turkey*. İstanbul, Turkey: Boğaziçi University.

Dunning, J. (1993). *Multinational enterprises and the global economy*. Reading, MA: Addison-Wesley.

Dutta, A., & Punnose, E. M. (2010). Factors Affecting Choice of First Employer A Study of Indian Management Graduates. *Global Business Review*, *11*(3), 435–448. doi:10.1177/097215091001100308

Dwyer, S., Richard, O. C., & Chadwick, K. (2003). Gender diversity in management and firm's performance: The influence of growth orientation and organizational culture. *Journal of Business Research*, *56*(12), 1009–1019. doi:10.1016/S0148-2963(01)00329-0

Earl, M. J. (1996). Business process reengineering: A phenomenon of organisation. In M. J. Earl (Ed.), *Information management. The organisational dimension* (pp. 53–76). New York: Oxford University Press.

Ebrahim, A., Battilana, J., & Mair, J. (2014). The governance of social enterprises: Mission drift and accountability challenges in hybrid organizations. *Research in Organizational Behavior*, *34*, 81–100. doi:10.1016/j.riob.2014.09.001

Eggert, A., & Ulaga, W. (2002). Customer Perceived Value: A Substitute for Satisfaction in Business Markets? *Journal of Business and Industrial Marketing*, *17*(2/3), 107–118. doi:10.1108/08858620210419754

Embry, A., Padgett, M. Y., & Caldwell, C. B. (2008). Can Leaders Step Outside of the Gender Box? An Examination of Leadership and Gender Role Stereotypes. *Journal of Leadership & Organizational Studies*, *15*(1), 30–45. doi:10.1177/1548051808318412

Espino-Rodriguez, T. F., & Gil-Padilla, M. (2014). The structural and infrastructural decisions of operations management in the hotel sector and their impact on organizational performance. *Tourism and Hospitality Research*, *15*(1), 3–18. doi:10.1177/1467358414553866

European Commission. (2014). *The Need for Innovations in Business Models, Final Policy Brief*. Retrieved from https://ec.europa.eu/research/innovation-union/pdf/expert-groups/ERIAB-BMI_PB_new_business_models.pdf

Eurostat. (2017). *Innovation statistics*. Retrieved from: http://ec.europa.eu/eurostat/statistics-explained/index.php/Innovation_statistics

Executive Office of the President of the United States. (2007). *Federal Enterprise Architecture (FEA) Consolidated Reference Model: Version 2.3*. Author.

Farmer, S. M., & Fedor, D. B. (2001). Changing the focus on volunteering: An investigation of volunteers' multiple contributions to a charitable organization. *Journal of Management*, *27*(2), 191–211. doi:10.1177/014920630102700204

Fattah, A. (2009). *IBM Enterprise Reference Architecture*. Academic Press.

Feldman, D. C., & Arnold, H. J. (1978). Position choice: Comparing the importance of organizational and job factors. *The Journal of Applied Psychology*, *63*(6), 706–710. doi:10.1037/0021-9010.63.6.706

Feltus, C., Petit, M., & Vernadat, F. (2009). Refining the Notion of Responsibility in Enterprise Engineering to Support Corporate Governance of IT. *IFAC Proceedings Volumes, 13*(1), 924–29. 10.3182/20090603-3-RU-2001.0126

Fields, J. (2007). *Conducting a Business Process Analysis*. The Dream Institute.

Fischer, R., Aier, S., & Winter, R. (2007). A Federated Approach to Enterprise Architecture Model Maintenance. *Enterprise Modelling and Information Systems Architectures*, *2*, 14. doi:10.1145/253260.253294

Fisher, C. D., & Yuan, X. Y. (1998). What motivates employees? A comparison of US and Chinese responses. *International Journal of Human Resource Management*, *9*(3), 516–528. doi:10.1080/095851998341053

Foorthuis, R., & Brinkkemper, S. (2008). Best Practices for Business and Systems Analysis in Projects Conforming to Enterprise Architecture. *International Journal of Enterprise Modelling and Information Systems Architectures*, *3*(August), 36–47.

Forsgren, M. (2002). The concept of learning in the Uppsala internationalization process model: A critical review. *International Business Review*, *11*(3), 257–277. doi:10.1016/S0969-5931(01)00060-9

Forsythe, J. (March 28, 2004). Winning with Diversity. *New York Times Magazine*, 65-72.

Francoeur, C., Labelle, R., & Desgagne, B. S. (2007). Gender Diversity in Corporate Governance and Top Management. *Journal of Business Ethics*, *81*(1), 83–95. doi:10.100710551-007-9482-5

Franco, M., Mainardes, E., & Martins, O. (2011). A review of inter-organizational networks: Evidence from studies published in 2005-2008. *Cuadernos Americanos*, *24*(43), 133–155.

Franke, U., Ekstedt, M., Lagerström, R., Saat, J., & Winter, R. (2010). Trends in Enterprise Architecture practice–A survey. *Trends in Enterprise Architecture Research*, 16-29.

Franke, U., Ekstedt, M., Lagerström, R., Saat, J., Winter, R. (2010). Trends in Enterprise Architecture practice–A survey. *Trends in Enterprise Architecture Research*, 16-29.

Frank, U., & Strecker, S. (2007). Open Reference Models: Community-Driven Collaboration to Promote Development and Dissemination of Reference Models. *Enterprise Modelling and Information Systems Architectures*, *2*(2), 32–41.

Gaaloul, K., & Molnar, W. (2014, November). Research Methodologies in Enterprise Engineering: Insights from a Workshop. In *Advanced Information Systems for Enterprises (IWAISE), 2014 International Workshop on* (pp. 58-64). IEEE.

Galbraith, J. R. (1994). *Competing with Flexible Lateral Organizations*. Wesley Publication Company.

Galbraith, J. R. (1995). *Designing Organizations: An Executive Briefing on Strategy, Structure And Process*. Jossey-Bass Publishers.

Gallarza, M. G., & Gil, I. (2008). The Concept of Value and Its Dimensions: A Tool For Analysing Tourism Experiences. *Tourism Review*, *63*(3), 4–20. doi:10.1108/16605370810901553

Gammelgård, M. (2007). Business Value Assessment of It Investments. KTH, Royal Institute of Technology.

Gatewood, R. D., Gowan, M. A., & Lautenschlager, G. J. (1993). Corporate image, recruitment image and initial job choice decisions. *Academy of Management Journal*, *36*(2), 414–427. doi:10.2307/256530

GE. (2012). *GE Global Innovation Barometer, 2012*. Retrieved from http://files.gecompany. com/gecom/innovationbarometer/GE_Global_Innovation_Barometer_Report_January_2012.pdf

Geiger, I., Dost, F., Schönhoff, A., & Kleinaltenkamp, M. (2015). Which types of multi-stage marketing increase direct customers' willingness-to-pay? Evidence from a scenario-based experiment in a B2B setting. *Industrial Marketing Management*, *47*, 175–189. doi:10.1016/j. indmarman.2015.02.042

Geldres-Weiss, V., Uribe-Bórquez, C., Coudounaris, D., & Monreal-Pérez, J. (2016). Innovation and experiential knowledge in firm exports: Applying the initial U-model. *Journal of Business Research*, *69*(11), 5076–5081. doi:10.1016/j.jbusres.2016.04.083

George, P., & Marc, C. (2006). IBM's global CEO report 2006: Business model innovation matters. *Strategy and Leadership*, *34*(5), 34–40. doi:10.1108/10878570610701531

Ghemawat, P. (1986, September). Sustainable advantage. *Harvard Business Review*. Retrieved from https://hbr.org/1986/09/sustainable-advantage

Giachetti, R. E. (2010). *Design of Enterprise Systems*. Boca Raton, FL: CRC Press.

Gillhouse, J. R. (2001). *Recruitment and retention strategies to combat nationwide nursing shortages*. Academic Press.

Glavan, L. M., Vukšić, V. B., & Vlahović, N. (2015). Decision tree learning for detecting turning points in business process orientation: A case of Croatian companies. *Croatian Operational Research Review*, *6*(1), 207–224. doi:10.17535/crorr.2015.0017

Glazner, C. G. (2009). *Understanding Enterprise Behavior Using Hybrid Simulation of Enterprise Architecture*. Massachusetts Institute of Technology.

Globemen21. (1999). *Global Engineering and Manufacturing in Enterprise Networks*. Globemen.

Glueck, W. F. (1974). Decision Making: Organization Choice. *Personnel Psychology*, *27*(1), 77–93. doi:10.1111/j.1744-6570.1974.tb02064.x

Goranson, H. T. (1999). *The Agile Virtual Enterprise—Cases, Metrics, Tools*. Quorum Books.

Gordijn, J., & Akkermans, J. M. (2003). Does e-Business Modeling Really Help? In *36th Hawaii International Conference On System Sciences*. Hawaii, HI: IEEE.

Gorman, M. (2004). Enterprise's Architecture. Enterprise Architectures, 1–10.

Graves, T. (2008). *Tetradian enterprise-architecture series Real Enterprise-Architecture: Beyond IT to the Whole Enterprise*. Academic Press.

Greefhorst, D., & Proper, E. (2011). The Role of Enterprise Architecture. *Architecture Principles*.

Greefhorst, D., & Proper, E. (2011). The Role of Enterprise Architecture. Architecture Principles. doi:10.1007/978-3-642-20279-7_2

Greening, D. W., & Turban, D. B. (2000). Corporate Social Performance As a Competitive Advantage in Attracting a Quality Workforce. *Business & Society*, *39*(3), 254–280. doi:10.1177/000765030003900302

Gregor, S. (2006). The nature of theory in information systems. *Management Information Systems Quarterly*, *30*(3), 611–642. doi:10.2307/25148742

Grudin, J. (1994). Computer-supported cooperative work: History and focus. *Computer*, *27*(5), 19–26. doi:10.1109/2.291294

Grund, C. (2013). Job preferences as revealed by employee-initiated job changes. *International Journal of Human Resource Management*, *24*(15), 2825–2850. doi:10.1080/09585192.2013.804689

Grünig, R., & Morschett, D. (2017). *Developing international strategies*. Berlin: Springer-Verlag. doi:10.1007/978-3-662-53123-5

Gulick, L. (1937). Notes on the theory of organization. In L. Gulick & L. Urwick (Eds.), *Papers on the science of administration* (pp. 1–45). New York: Institute of Public Administration, Columbia University.

Guthridge, M., Komm, A. B., & Lawson, E. (2008). Making talent a strategic priority. *The McKinsey Quarterly, 1,* 48.

Hadjikhani, A. (2015). A note on the criticisms against the internationalization process model. In M. Forsgren, U. Holm, & J. Johanson (Eds.), *Knowledge, Networks and Power* (pp. 64–87). London: Palgrave Macmillan. doi:10.1057/9781137508829_3

Håkansson, H., & Snehota, I. (2006). "No business is an island" 17 years later. *Strategic Management Journal, 22*(3), 271–274.

Hall, C., & Harmon, P. (2005). *BPTrends.com The Enterprise Architecture, Process Modeling, and Simulation Tools Report.* Academic Press.

Hammer, M. (1990). Reengineering Work: Don't Automate, Obliterate. *Harvard Business Review, 68*(4), 104–113.

Hammer, M. (1996). *Beyond Reengineering: How the Process-Centered Organization is Changing Our Work and Our Lives.* HarperCollins Publishers.

Hammer, M., & Champy, J. (1993). *Reengineering the Corporation – A Manifesto for Business Revolution.* New York: HarperCollins Publishers.

Hammer, M., & Champy, J. (1993). *Reengineering the Corporation: A Manifesto for Business Revolution.* New York: Harper Business.

Hardgrave, B. C., Davis, F. D., & Riemenschneider, C. K. (2003). Investigating Determinants of Software Developers' Intentions to Follow Methodologies. *Journal of Management Information Systems, 20*(1), 123–151. doi:10.1080/07421222.2003.11045751

Harmon, P. (2003). *Business Process Change: A Manager's Guide to Improving, Redesigning, and Automating Processes.* San Francisco: Morgan Kaufmann Publishers.

Harmon, P. (2004). Evaluating an Organization's Business Process Maturity. *Business Process Trends, 2*(3), 1–11.

Harmon, P. (2015). The scope and evolution of business process management. In *Handbook on business process management 1* (pp. 37–80). Springer Berlin Heidelberg. doi:10.1007/978-3-642-45100-3_3

Harrington, J. (2006). *Process Management Excellence – The Art of Excelling in Process Management.* Paton Press LLC.

Harris, R. (2001, May). The Illusion of Inclusion. *CFO,* 42-50.

Harris, M. M., & Fink, L. S. (1987). A Field Study of Applicant Reactions to Employment Opportunities: Does the Recruiter Make a Difference? *Personnel Psychology*, *40*(4), 765–784. doi:10.1111/j.1744-6570.1987.tb00623.x

Heineke, J. (1995). Strategic operations management decisions and professional performance in U.S. HMOs. *Journal of Operations Management*, *13*(4), 255–272. doi:10.1016/0272-6963(95)00035-6

Henderson, D., Sheetz, S. D., & Trinkle, B. S. (2012). The determinants of inter-organizational and internal in-house adoption of XBRL: A structural equation model. *International Journal of Accounting Information Systems*, *13*(2), 109–140. doi:10.1016/j.accinf.2012.02.001

Henriques, M., Tribolet, J., & Hoogervorst, J. (2010). *Enterprise Governance and DEMO* (Doctoral dissertation). Department of Computer Science and Engineering, Technical University of Lisboa, Instituto Superior Técnico, Lisboa.

Highhouse, S., Lievens, F., & Sinar, E. F. (2003). Measuring Attraction to Organizations. *Educational and Psychological Measurement*, *63*(6), 986–1001. doi:10.1177/0013164403258403

Highhouse, S., Thornbury, E. E., & Little, I. S. (2007). Social-identity functions of attraction to organizations. *Organizational Behavior and Human Decision Processes*, *103*(1), 134–146. doi:10.1016/j.obhdp.2006.01.001

Hofstede, G. (1991). *Cultures and organizations: Software of the mind*. London: McGraw-Hill.

Hofstede, G. (2001). *Culture consequences. Comparing values, behaviors, institutions, and organizations across nations*. Thousand Oaks, CA: Sage Publications.

Holbrook, M. B. (1999). Introduction to consumer value. *Consumer value: A framework for analysis and research*, 1-28.

Holm, D. B., Eriksson, K., & Johanson, J. (1996). Creating value through mutual commitment to business network relationships. *Strategic Management Journal*, *20*(5), 467–486. doi:

Hoogervorst, J. A. (2009). *Enterprise governance and enterprise engineering*. Springer Science & Business Media. doi:10.1007/978-3-540-92671-9

Hung, R. Y. (2006). Business Process Management as Competitive Advantage: A Review and Empirical Study. *Total Quality Management*, *17*(1), 21–40. doi:10.1080/14783360500249836

Hurbean, L., & Doina, F. (2014). *ERP III the promise of a new generation*. 13th International Conference on Informatics in Economy, Education, Research & Business Technologies, ASE, Bucharest, Romania.

Hu, Y. (2011). Linking Perceived Value, Customer Satisfaction, and Purchase Intention in E-Commerce Settings. In D. Jin & S. Lin (Eds.), *Advances in Computer Science, Intelligent System and Environment* (pp. 623–628). Berlin: Springer Berlin Heidelberg. doi:10.1007/978-3-642-23753-9_100

IBM. (2006). *Expanding the innovation horizon- The Global CEO Study 2006*. Retrieved from: https://www-935.ibm.com/services/us/gbs/bus/pdf/ceostudy.pdf

IBM. (2006). *IBM Industry Models for Financial Services The Information FrameWork (IFW)*. Overview.

IBM. (2008). *The enterprise of the future*. Retrieved from https://www-935.ibm.com/services/uk/gbs/pdf/ibm_ceo_study_2008.pdf

Ibrahim, S. E. (2010). An alternative methodology for formulating an operations strategy: The case of BTC-Egypt. *Management Decision*, *48*(6), 868–893. doi:10.1108/00251741011053442

IDEF. (1993). *Federal Information Processing Standards Publication 183: Integration Definition For Function Modeling (IDEF0)*. IDEF.

IEEE. (1999). *Draft for Standard, IEEE P1471/D5.1 Draft Recommended Practice for Architectural Description, October 1999*. IEEE.

Impact of Diversity Initiatives on the Bottom Line. A SHRM Survey of the Fortune 1000. (June 3, 2001). *Fortune*. Retrieved from http://www.fortune.com/sections

INCOSE. (2012). Systems Engineering Handbook: A Guide for System Life Cycle Processes and Activities, version 3.2.2. San Diego, CA: International Council on Systems Engineering (INCOSE), INCOSE-TP-2003-002-03.2.2.

Information and Communication Technology Agency of Sri Lanka. (2013). National ICT Workforce Survey.

ISO 15704:2000 Industrial automation systems — Requirements for enterprise-reference architectures and methodologies

ISO. (2008/2009). *ISO 9000 Quality Management Systems*. Geneva: Author.

ISO/IEC, ISO/IEC/IEEE 42010 Systems and Software Engineering—Architecture Description, 2011

Itami, H., & Nishino, K. (2010). Killing two birds with one stone: Profit for now and learning for the future. *Long Range Planning*, *43*(2–3), 364–369. doi:10.1016/j.lrp.2009.07.007

Iyamu, T., Mphahlele, L., & Hamunyela, S. (2014). The Connective Scheme between the Enterprise Architecture and Organisational Structure. In *New Perspectives in Information Systems and Technologies* (Vol. 2, pp. 9–21). Cham: Springer. doi:10.1007/978-3-319-05948-8_2

Jäger, U. P., & Schröer, A. (2013). Integrated Organizational Identity: A Definition of Hybrid Organizations and a Research Agenda. *Voluntas*, *25*(5), 1281–1306. doi:10.100711266-013-9386-1

Jaklic, J., Groznik, A., Huber, T., Svetina, M., Trkman, P., & Indihar Stemberger, M. (2012). A Link-up between Business Process Orientation and Efficiency Improvements in a Supply Chain: The Case Study from the Wholesale Business. *Transformations in Business & Economics*, *11*(2/26), 117-133.

Johanson, J., & Mattsson, L. G. (1987). Interorganizational relations in industrial systems: A network approach compared with the transaction-cost approach. *International Studies of Management & Organization*, *17*(1), 34–48. doi:10.1080/00208825.1987.11656444

Johanson, J., & Mattsson, L. G. (2015). Internationalisation in industrial systems — A network approach. In M. Forsgren, U. Holm, & J. Johanson (Eds.), *Knowledge, Networks and Power* (pp. 111–132). London: Palgrave Macmillan. doi:10.1057/9781137508829_5

Johanson, J., & Mattsson, L.-G. (1988). Internationalisation in industrial system: A network approach. In N. Hood & J.-E. Vahlne (Eds.), *Strategies in global competition*. London: Croom Helm.

Johanson, J., & Vahlne, J. E. (1977). The internationalization process of the firm – A model of knowledge development and increasing foreign market commitments. *Journal of International Business Studies*, *8*(1), 23–32. doi:10.1057/palgrave.jibs.8490676

Johanson, J., & Vahlne, J. E. (2009). The Uppsala internationalization process model revisited: From liability of foreignness to liability of outsidership. *Journal of International Business Studies*, *40*(9), 1411–1431. doi:10.1057/jibs.2009.24

Johanson, J., & Vahlne, J.-E. (1990). The mechanism of internationalization. *International Marketing Review*, *7*(4), 11–24. doi:10.1108/02651339010137414

Johanson, J., & Vahlne, J.-E. (1992). Management of foreign market entry. *Scandinavian International Business Review*, *1*(3), 9–27. doi:10.1016/0962-9262(92)90008-T

Johanson, J., & Wiedersheim-Paul, F. (1975). The internationalization of the firm: Four Swedish cases. *Journal of Management Studies*, *12*(3), 305–322. doi:10.1111/j.1467-6486.1975.tb00514.x

Johnson, W. M., Christensen, M. C., & Kagermann, H. (2008). Reinventing your business model. *Harvard Business Review*, *86*(12), 1–12.

Jonkers, H., Groenewegen, L., Bonsangue, M., van Buuren, R., Quartel, D. A., Lankhorst, M. M., & Aldea, A. (2017). A language for enterprise modelling. In *Enterprise Architecture at Work* (pp. 73–121). Springer Berlin Heidelberg. doi:10.1007/978-3-662-53933-0_5

Jorgensen, H. D., Lillehagen, F., & Karlsen, D. (2005). Collaborative Modelling and Metamodelling with the Enterprise Knowledge Architecture. *Enterprise Modelling and Information Systems Architectures*, *1*, 36–45.

Judge, T. A., & Bretz, R. D. (1992). Effects of Work Values on Job Choice Decisions. *The Journal of Applied Psychology*, *77*(3), 261–271. doi:10.1037/0021-9010.77.3.261

Karlsen, A. (2011). Enterprise Modeling Practice in ICT-Enabled Process Change. *IFIP Working Conference on The Practice of Enterprise Modeling 2011*, 208–22. 10.1007/978-3-642-24849-8_16

Kathuria, R., & Davis, E. B. (2001). Quality and work force management practices: The managerial performance implication. *Production and Operations Management*, *10*(4), 460–477. doi:10.1111/j.1937-5956.2001.tb00087.x

Kathuria, R., & Partovi, F. Y. (1999). Work force management practices for manufacturing flexibility. *Journal of Operations Management*, *18*(1), 21–39. doi:10.1016/S0272-6963(99)00011-X

Katsikeas, C., Leonidou, L., & Samiee, S. (2009). Research into exporting: Theoretical, methodological, and empirical insights. In M. Kotabe & K. Helsen (Eds.), *The Sage handbook of international marketing* (pp. 165–182). Los Angeles, CA: Sage. doi:10.4135/9780857021007.n8

Keen, P. G. W. (1997). *The Process Edge-Creating Value Where It Counts*. Boston, MA: Harvard Business School Press.

Kelly, K. (1995). *Out of Control: The New Biology of Machines, Social Systems and the Economic World*. Perseus Books.

Khalili Shavarini, S., Salimian, H., Nazemi, J., & Alborzi, M. (2013). Operations strategy and business strategy alignment model (case of Iranian industries). *International Journal of Operations & Production Management*, *33*(9), 1108–1130. doi:10.1108/IJOPM-12-2011-0467

Khosravi, A. (2016). Business process rearrangement and renaming: A new approach to process orientation and improvement. *Business Process Management Journal*, *22*(1), 116–139. doi:10.1108/BPMJ-02-2015-0012

Kleinaltenkamp, M., Rudolph, M., & Claßen, M. (2012). Multi-stage marketing. In M. Glynn & A. Woodside (Eds.), *Business-to-business marketing management: Strategies, cases, and solutions, advances in business marketing and purchasing* (Vol. 18, pp. 141–174). Bingley, UK: Emerald Group Publishing Ltd.

Knight, G. A., & Cavusgil, S. T. (1996). The born global firm: A challenge to traditional internationalization theory. *Advances in International Marketing*, *8*, 11–26.

Knight, G. A., & Cavusgil, S. T. (2004). Innovation, organizational capabilities, and the born-global firm. *Journal of International Business Studies*, *35*(2), 124–141. doi:10.1057/palgrave.jibs.8400071

Kohlbacher, M. (2009). The perceived effects of business process management. *Proceedings of Science and Technology for Humanity (TIC-STH), 2009 IEEE Toronto International Conference*, 399-402. 10.1109/TIC-STH.2009.5444467

Kohlbacher, M. (2010). The Effects of Process Orientation: A Literature Review. *Business Process Management Journal*, *16*(1), 135–152. doi:10.1108/14637151011017985

Kosanke, K., Vernadat, F., & Zelm, M. (1999). CIMOSA: Enterprise Engineering and Integration. *Computers in Industry*, *40*(2), 83–87. doi:10.1016/S0166-3615(99)00016-0

Kotusev, S. (2016a). *British Computer Society Enterprise Architecture Frameworks: The Fad of the Century*. Academic Press.

Kotusev, S. (2016b). The History of Enterprise Architecture: An Evidence-Based Review. *Journal of Enterprise Architecture*, *12*(1), 29–37.

Kuras, M.l., & White, B.E. (2005). *Engineering Enterprises Using Complex-System Engineering*. INCOSE Foundation.

Lee, J., Lee, D., & Sungwon, K. (2007). *An overview of the business process maturity model (BPMM). International workshop on process aware information systems (PAIS 2007)*. Springer.

Leelawat, N., Suppasri, A., Kure, S., Carine, J. Y., Mateo, C. M. R., & Imamura, F. (2015). Disaster Warning System in the Philippines Through Enterprise Engineering Perspective: A Study on the 2013 Super Typhoon Haiyan. *Journal of Disaster Research*, *10*(6), 1041–1050. doi:10.20965/jdr.2015.p1041

Lee, Y., Kozar, K. A., & Larsen, K. R. (2003). The Technology Acceptance Model: Past, Present and Future. *Communications of the Association for Information Systems*, *12*(1), 50.

Legris, P., Ingham, J., & Collerette, P. (2003). Why do People Use Information Technology? A Critical Review of the Technology Acceptance Model. *Information & Management*, *40*(3), 191–204. doi:10.1016/S0378-7206(01)00143-4

Leibold, M., Probst, G., & Gibbert, M. (2002). *Strategic Management in the Knowledge Economy: New Approaches and Business Applications*. New York: Wiley.

Lennie Copeland, L. (1988, June). Valuing Diversity, Part I: Making the Most of Cultural Differences at the Workplace. *Personnel*, 52–60.

Leonidou, L., & Katsikeas, C. (1996). The export development process: An integrative review of empirical models. *Journal of International Business Studies*, *27*(3), 517–551. doi:10.1057/palgrave.jibs.8490846

Lievens, F., Decaesteker, C., Coetsier, P., & Geirnaert, J. (2001). Organizational Attractiveness for Prospective Applicants: A Person–Organisation Fit Perspective. *Applied Psychology*, *50*(1), 30–51. doi:10.1111/1464-0597.00047

Li, L. X., Benton, W. C., & Leong, G. K. (2002). The impact of strategic operations management decisions on community hospital performance. *Journal of Operations Management*, *20*(1), 389–408. doi:10.1016/S0272-6963(02)00002-5

Liles, D. H., & Presley, A. R. (1996). Enterprise Modeling Within An Enterprise Engineering Framework. *The 1996 Winter Simulation Conference*.

Liles, D.H., Huff, B.L., & Rogers, K.J. (2001). A Manufacturing Reference Model For The Enterprise Engineer. *The Journal of Engineering Valuation and Cost Analysis*.

Liles, D. H., Johnson, M. E., & Meade, L. (1996). The enterprise engineering discipline. *Proceedings of the Fifth Industrial Engineering Research Conference*, 479–484.

Lillis, B., & Sweeney, M. (2013). Managing the fit between the views of competitive strategy and the strategic role of service operations. *European Management Journal*, *31*(6), 564–590. doi:10.1016/j.emj.2012.10.001

Lim, Y. J., Osman, A., Salahuddin, S. N., Romle, A. R., & Abdullah, S. (2016). Factors Influencing Online Shopping Behavior: The Mediating Role of Purchase Intention. *Procedia Economics and Finance*, *35*, 401–410. doi:10.1016/S2212-5671(16)00050-2

Lindström, Å., Johnson, P., Johansson, E., Ekstedt, M., & Simonsson, M. (2006). A survey on CIO concerns-do enterprise architecture frameworks support them? *Information Systems Frontiers*, *8*(2), 81–90.

Liu, Y., & Iijima, J. (2015, June). A Case Study of Business Process Simulation in the Context of Enterprise Engineering. In *Enterprise Engineering Working Conference* (pp. 96-110). Springer.

Lowson, R. H. (2001). Retail Operational Strategies in Complex Supply Chains. *International Journal of Logistics Management*, *12*(1), 97–111. doi:10.1108/09574090110806253

Lowson, R. H. (2002). Operations strategy: Genealogy, classification and anatomy. *International Journal of Operations & Production Management*, *22*(10), 1112–1129. doi:10.1108/01443570210446333

Lowson, R. H. (2003). The nature of an operations strategy: Combining strategic decisions from the resource-based and market-driven viewpoints. *Management Decision*, *41*(6), 538–549. doi:10.1108/00251740310485181

Madarasz, L., Timko, M., & Racek, M. (2005). Enterprise Modeling and Its Applications in Company Management Systems. *Proceedings of 5th International Symposium of Hungarian Researchers on Computational Intelligence*, 1–82.

Malhotra, N. K. (2017). *Marketing research: An applied approach*. Harlow: Pearson Education.

Marashi, E., & Davis, J.P. (2005). A Systems Approach to Resolving Complex Issues in a Design Process. *Complexity in Design and Engineering*, 160–69.

Marques, A. F., Borges, J. G., Sousa, P., & Pinho, A. M. (2011). An Enterprise Architecture Approach to Forest Management Support Systems Design: An Application to Pulpwood Supply Management in Portugal. *European Journal of Forest Research*, *130*(6), 935–948. doi:10.100710342-011-0482-8

Martinez, C., Cane, S., Abdul-Rauf, S., Smith, K., & Lee, K. (2008). *Application of network visualization to identify gaps in complex information system architectures*. The Mitre Corporation.

Martin, J. (1995). *The Great Transition. Using the Seven Principles of Enterprise Engineering to Align People, Technology and Strategy*. American Management Association.

Martín-Peña, M. L., & Díaz-Garrido, E. (2008a). Typologies and taxonomies of operations strategy: A literature review. *Management Research News*, *31*(3), 200–218. doi:10.1108/01409170810851294

Ma, S., & Wang, R. (2013). A Study on Meta-synthesis Mode of the Systems Engineering of Governance of Large Enterprise Group. In *Proceedings of the Sixth International Conference on Management Science and Engineering Management* (pp. 761–771). Springer London; doi:10.1007/978-3-319-19297-0_7.

McAdam, R. (1996). An integrated business improvement methodology to refocus business improvement efforts. *Business Process Re-engineering & Management Journal*, 2(1), 63–71. doi:10.1108/14637159610111482

McCormack, K. (2001, January). Business Process Orientation: Do You Have It? *Quality Progress*, 51–58.

McCormack, K. (2007). Introduction to the theory of business process orientation. In K. McCormack (Ed.), *Business Process Maturity. Theory and Application* (pp. 1–18). Booksurge Publishing.

McCormack, K. P., & Johnson, W. C. (2001). *Business Process Orientation – Gaining the E-Business Competitive Advantage*. St. Lucie Press. doi:10.1201/9781420025569

McCormack, K., Willems, J., van den Bergh, J., Deschoolmeester, D., Willaert, P., Indihar Štemberger, M., ... Vlahovic, N. (2009). A Global Investigation of Key Turning Points in Business Process Maturity. *Business Process Management Journal*, 15(5), 792–815. doi:10.1108/14637150910987946

McDermott, C. M., Markman, G. D., & Balkin, D. B. (2003). Operations strategy and new venture formation. *Management Research*, 1(2), 195–205.

McDougall, G. H. G., & Levesque, T. (2000). Customer Satisfaction with Services: Putting Perceived Value into he Equation. *Journal of Services Marketing*, 14(5), 392–410. doi:10.1108/08876040010340937

McDougall, P. P., & Oviatt, B. M. (2000). International entrepreneurship: The intersection of two research paths. *Academy of Management Journal*, 43(5), 902–906. doi:10.2307/1556418

McShane, S., Olekalns, M., Newman, A., & Travaglione, T. (2015). *Organisational Behaviour 5e; Emerging Knowledge. Global Insights*. McGraw-Hill Education Australia.

Milfelner, B., Snoj, B., & Korda, A. P. (2011). Measurement of Perceived Quality, Perceived Value, Image and Satisfaction Interrelations of Hotel Services: Comparison of Tourists from Slovenia and Italy. *Journal for General Social Issues*, 20(3), 605–624. doi:10.5559/di.20.3.01

Millette, V., & Gagné, M. (2008). Designing volunteers' tasks to maximize motivation, satisfaction and performance: The impact of job characteristics on volunteer engagement. *Motivation and Emotion*, 32(1), 11–22. doi:10.100711031-007-9079-4

Milliken, F. J., & Martins, L. I. (1996). Searching for Common Threads: Understanding the Multiple Effects of Diversity in Organizational Groups. *Academy of Management Review*, 21(2), 402–433.

Mintzberg, H. (1991). The Effective Organization: Forces and Forms. *Sloan Management Review*, 54(Winter), 54–69.

Mitre Corporation. (2014). Retrieved from http://www2.mitre.org/public/eabok/pdf/Using-EAs-14-1210.pdf

Moller, C. (2004). ERP II: next-generation extended enterprise resource planning. In J. Damsgaard, J. Hørlück, P. Kræmmergaard, & J. Rose (Eds.), Organizing for Networked Information Technologies: Readings in Process Integration and Transformation, Aalborg Universitet sforlag (pp. 108–118). Aalborg: Academic Press.

Molnar, W. A., & Korhonen, J. J. (2014). Research paradigms and topics in Enterprise Engineering analysis of recent conferences and workshops. *Proc - Int Conf Res Challenges Inf Sci*. 10.1109/RCIS.2014.6861071

Molnar, W. A., & Proper, H. A. (2013, June). Engineering an enterprise: Practical issues of two case studies from the luxembourgish beverage and tobacco industry. In *Working Conference on Practice-Driven Research on Enterprise Transformation* (pp. 76-91). Springer. 10.1007/978-3-642-38774-6_6

Monge, P. R. (1990). Theoretical and Analytical Issues in Studying Organizational Processes. *Organization Science*, *1*(4), 23–34. doi:10.1287/orsc.1.4.406

Moreira, A. C., & Alves, C. (2016). Commitment-trust dynamics in the internationalization process: A case study of market entry in the Brazilian market. In Information Resources Management Association (Ed.), International business: Concepts, methodologies, tools, and applications, (vol. 3, pp. 1206-1229). Hershey, PA: IGI Global. Doi:10.4018/978-1-4666-9814-7.ch057

Moreira, A. (2004). Breve ensaio sobre a internacionalização. *Politécnica*, *15*, 23–33.

Moreira, A. C. (2007). La internacionalización de Pymes industriales a través de multinacionales. Presentación de algunos casos de los sectores automotor y electrónico. *Cuadernos de Administración*, *20*(34), 89–114.

Moreira, A. C. (2009). The evolution of internationalisation: Towards a new theory? *Global Economics and Management Review*, *14*(1), 41–59.

Moreira, A. C., & Silva, P. M. (2015). New product development and the challenges of internationalization. In L. C. Carvalho (Ed.), *Handbook of research on internationalization of entrepreneurial innovation in the global economy* (pp. 65–87). Hershey, PA: IGI Global; doi:10.4018/978-1-4666-8216-0.ch004

Morgan, J., & Katsikeas, C. (1997). Theories of international trade, foreign direct investment and firm internationalization: A critique. *Management Decision*, *35*(1), 68–77. doi:10.1108/00251749710160214

Morris, M., Schindehutte, M., & Allen, J. (2005). The entrepreneur's business Model: Toward a unified perspective. *Journal of Business Research*, *58*(6), 726–735. doi:10.1016/j.jbusres.2003.11.001

Moustaghfir, K. (2008). The dynamics of knowledge assets and their link with firm performance. *Measuring Business Excellence*, *12*(2), 10–24. doi:10.1108/13683040810881162

Mulder, P. (2017). *Bureaucratic Theory by Max Weber*. Retrieved November 9, 2017 from: https://www.toolshero.com/management/bureaucratic-theory-weber/

Nadarajah, D., & Latifah Syed Abdul Kadir, S. (2014). A Review of the Importance of Business Process Management in Achieving Sustainable Competitive Advantage. *The TQM Journal*, *26*(5), 522–531. doi:10.1108/TQM-01-2013-0008

Nakakawa, A., van Bommel, P., & Proper, E. (2010, June). Towards a Theory on Collaborative Decision Making in Enterprise Architecture. In DESRIST (pp. 538-541). doi:10.1007/978-3-642-13335-0_40

Nakakawa, A., van Bommel, P., & Erik Proper, H. A. (2010). On Supporting Collaborative Problem Solving in Enterprise Architecture Creation. *Working Conference on Practice-Driven Research on Enterprise Transformation PRET 2010*, 156–81. 10.1007/978-3-642-16770-6_7

Narver, J. C., & Slater, S. F. (1990). The effect of a market orientation on business profitability. *Journal of Marketing*, *54*(4), 20–35. doi:10.2307/1251757

Nightingale, D. J., & Rhodes, D. H. (2004). Enterprise Systems Architecting : Emerging Art and Science within Engineering Systems. *Proceedings of the ESD External Symposium*, 1–13.

Nishii, L. H. (2013). The Benefits of Climate for Inclusion for Gender-Diverse Groups. *Academy of Management Journal*, *56*(6), 1754–1774. doi:10.5465/amj.2009.0823

Noran, O. (2007). Discovering and Modelling Enterprise Engineering Project Processes. Handbook of Enterprise Systems Architecture in Practice. doi:10.4018/978-1-59904-189-6.ch003

Noran, O. (2009). A Decision Support System for Enterprise Engineering. *Information Systems Development: Challenges in Practice, Theory, and Education,* 93–104.

Novotná, L., Martins, I., & Moreira, A. C. (2017). Trade between the Czech Republic and Portugal: Analysis of the 2000-2015 period. In T. Dorożyński & A. Kuna-Marszałek (Eds.), *Outward foreign direct investment (FDI) in emerging market economies* (pp. 200–225). Hershey, PA: IGI Global. doi:10.4018/978-1-5225-2345-1.ch010

OECD. (2013). *How's Life? 2013: Measuring Well-Being*. OECD Publishing. doi:10.1787/9789264201392-

Ogush, M., Coleman, D., & Beringer, D. (2000). *Hewlett Packard A Template for Documenting Software and Firmware Architectures*. Academic Press.

Ollapally, A., & Bhatnagar, J. (2009). The Holistic Approach to Diversity Management: HR Implications. *Indian Journal of Industrial Relations*, *44*(3), 454–472.

Olsen, J. E., & Martins, L. L. (2012). Understanding organizational diversity management programs: A theoretical framework and directions for future research. *Journal of Organizational Behavior*, *33*(8), 1168–1187. doi:10.1002/job.1792

Op'tLand, M., Proper, H. A., Waage, M., Cloo, J., & Steghuis, C. (2008). *Enterprise architecture—creating value by informed governance*. Berlin: Springer.

Ortner, E. (2008). From Software Engineering to Enterprise Engineering–Introduction to a Language-Critical. *Innovative Techniques in Instruction Technology*, 135–143.

Österle, H., & Winter, R. (2003). Business Engineering. In Business Engineering – Auf demWeg zum Unternehmen des Informationszeitalters (Vol. 2). Springer.

Osterwalder, A. (2004). The Business Model Ontology A Proposition. In *A Design Science Approach*. UNIVERSITE DE LAUSANNE.

Oviatt, B. M., & McDougall, P. P. (1994). Toward a theory of international new ventures. *International Business Studies*, *25*(1), 45–64. doi:10.1057/palgrave.jibs.8490193

Pache, A.-C., & Santos, F. (2012). Inside the Hybrid Organization: Selective Coupling as a Response to Competing Institutional Logics. *Academy of Management Journal*, *56*(4), 972–1001. doi:10.5465/amj.2011.0405

Pall, G. A. (1987). *Quality Process Management*. Englewood Cliffs, NJ: Prentice-Hall.

Palmberg, K. (2009). Exploring Process Management: Are There Any Widespread Models and Definitions? *The TQM Journal*, *21*(2), 203–215. doi:10.1108/17542730910938182

Paulk, M. C., Curtis, B., Chrissis, M. B., & Weber, C. V. (1993). *The Capability Maturity Model for Software, Version 1.1 (No. CMU/SEI-93-TR-24)*. Software Engineering Institute. doi:10.21236/ADA263403

Phillips, C. R., Phillips, A. S., & Cappel, S. D. (1994). Research Note: How Management Students Select Prospective Employers. *International Journal of Manpower*, *15*(1), 55–59. doi:10.1108/01437729410053581

Phusavat, K., & Kanchana, R. (2008). Competitive priorities for service providers: Perspectives from Thailand. *Industrial Management & Data Systems*, *108*(1), 5–21. doi:10.1108/02635570810844052

Pierce, T. P., Willy, C., Roncace, R., & Bischoff, J. (2014). Extending The Technology Acceptance Model [PAM]. *Policy Acceptance Model*, *5*(2), 16. doi:10.19030/ajhs.v5i2.8963

Pikkarainen, T., Pikkarainen, K., Karjaluoto, H., & Pahnila, S. (2004). Consumer Acceptance of Online Banking: An Extension of the Technology Acceptance Model. *Internet Research*, *14*(3), 224–235. doi:10.1108/10662240410542652

Podsiadlowski, A., Groschke, D., Kogler, M., Springer, C., & Zee, K. (2013). Managing a culturally diverse workforce: Diversity perspectives in organizations. *International Journal of Intercultural Relations*, *37*(2), 159–175. doi:10.1016/j.ijintrel.2012.09.001

Popp, J., Milward, H., MacKean, G., Casebeer, A., & Lindstrom, R. (2014). *Inter-organizational networks. A Review of the literature to inform practice*. Washington, DC: IBM Center for The Business of Government.

PorData. (2017). *Fluxos migratorios internacionais*. Retrieved April 28, 2017, from http://www.pordata.pt/Europa/Fluxos+migrat%C3%B3rios+internacionais-1622

Porter, M. (1985). *Competitive Advantage: Creating and Sustaining Superior Performance*. New York: Free Press.

Porter, M. E. (1980). *Competitive strategy*. New York: Free Press.

Porter, M. E. (1985). *Competitive advantage: Creating and sustaining superior performance*. New York: Free Press.

Posner, B. Z. (1981). Comparing Recruiter, Student and Faculty Perceptions of Important Applicant and Job Characteristics. *Personnel Psychology*, *34*(2), 329–339. doi:10.1111/j.1744-6570.1981. tb00946.x

Powell, G. N., Butterfield, D. A., & Parent, J. D. (2002). Gender and Managerial Stereotypes: Have the Times Changed? *Journal of Management*, *28*(2), 177–193. doi:10.1177/014920630202800203

Presley, A. R., Huff, B. L., & Liles, D. H. (1993). A Comprehensive Enterprise Model for Small Manufacturers. In *Proceedings of the 2nd Industrial Engineering Research Conference* (pp. 430-434). Institute of Industrial Engineers, Atlanta, Georgia

Rabelo, L., Helal, M., Jones, A., & Min, H. S. (2007). *Enterprise simulation: a hybrid system approach. Int J Comput Integr Manuf*. doi:10.1080/09511920400030138

Ragins, B. (1989). Barriers to Mentoring: The Female Manager's Dilemma. *Human Relations*, *42*(1), 1–22. doi:10.1177/001872678904200101Ragins, B. R., Townsend, B., & Mattis, M. (1998). Gender Gap in the Executive Suite. *The Academy of Management Executive*, *12*(1), 28–42.

Rais, A. A. (2016). Interface-Based Software Integration. *Journal of Systems Integration*, (3).

Raymond, L., & Croteau, A.-M. (2009). Manufacturing Strategy and Business Strategy in Medium-Sized Enterprises: Performance Effects of Strategic Alignment. *IEEE Transactions on Engineering Management*, *56*(2), 192–202. doi:10.1109/TEM.2008.922646

Reeves, M., & Deimler, M. (2011). Adaptability-The new competitive advantage. *Harvard Business review*. Retrieved from https://hbr.org/2011/07/adaptability-the-new-competitive-advantage

Reijers, H. A. (2006). Implementing BPM systems: The role of process orientation. *Business Process Management Journal*, *12*(4), 389–409. doi:10.1108/14637150610678041

Ribau, C. P., Moreira, A. C., & Raposo, M. (2015). Internationalisation of the firm theories: A schematic synthesis. *International Journal of Business and Globalisation*, *15*(4), 528–554. doi:10.1504/IJBG.2015.072535

Ribau, C. P., Moreira, A. C., & Raposo, M. (2017). SME internationalization research: Mapping the state of the art. *Canadian Journal of Administrative Sciences*. doi:10.1002/CJAS.1419

Rice, F. (1994, August 8). How to Make Diversity Pay. *Fortune*, 78-86.

Riemenschneider, C. K., & Hardgrave, B. C. (2001). Explaining Software Development tool Use with the Technology Acceptance Model. *Journal of Computer Information Systems*, *41*(4), 1–8. doi:10.1080/08874417.2001.11647015

Roberson, Q. M. (2006). Disentangling the Meanings of Diversity and Inclusion in Organizations. *Group & Organization Management*, *31*(2), 212–236. doi:10.1177/1059601104273064

Rocha, Á., Correia, A. M., Tan, F. B., & Stroetmann Editors, K. A. (2014). *Advances in Intelligent Systems and Computing 276 New Perspectives in Information Systems and Technologies* (Vol. 2). Springer.

Roehling, M. V., & Winters, D. (2000). Job Security Rights: The Effects of Specific Policies and Practices on the Evaluation of Employers. *Employee Responsibilities and Rights Journal*, *12*(1), 25–38. doi:10.1023/A:1007768817334

Rohloff, M. (2011). Advances in business process management implementation based on a maturity assessment and best practice exchange. *Information Systems and e-Business Management*, *9*(3), 383–403. doi:10.100710257-010-0137-1

Roig, J. C. F., Garcia, J. S., Tena, M. A. M., & Monzonis, J. L. (2006). Customer Perceived Value in Banking Services. *International Journal of Bank Marketing*, *24*(5), 266–283. doi:10.1108/02652320610681729

Romero, D., & Vernadat, F. (2016). Enterprise information systems state of the art: Past, present and future trends. *Computers in Industry*, *79*, 3–13. doi:10.1016/j.compind.2016.03.001

Rosemann, M., de Bruin, T., & Power, B. (2006). A Model to Measure Business Process Management Maturity and Improve Performance. In J. Jeston & J. Nelis (Eds.), *Business process management*. Oxford, UK: Butterworth-Heinemann.

Rosemann, M., & vom Brocke, J. (2015). The six core elements of business process management. In *Handbook on business process management 1* (pp. 105–122). Springer Berlin Heidelberg. doi:10.1007/978-3-642-45100-3_5

Ross, J.W., Weill, P., & Robertson, D.C. (2006). Enterprise Architecture as Strategy. *Enterprise Architecture as Strategy*, 1–10.

Ross, J. E. (1995). *Total Quality Management: Text, Cases and Readings*. St. Lucie Press.

Roth, A. V., & Menor, L. J. (2003). Insights into service operations management: A research agenda. *Production and Operations Management*, *12*(2), 145–164. doi:10.1111/j.1937-5956.2003.tb00498.x

Roy, K., & Karna, A. (2015). Doing social good on a sustainable basis: Competitive advantage of social businesses. *Management Decision*, *53*(6), 1355–1374. doi:10.1108/MD-09-2014-0561

Rummler, G., & Brache, A. (1990). *Improving Performance*. San Francisco, CA: Jossey-Bass.

Rungtusanatham, M. J., Choi, T. Y., Hollingworth, D. G., Wu, Z., & Forza, C. (2003). Survey research in operations management: Historical analyses. *Journal of Operations Management*, *21*(4), 475–488. doi:10.1016/S0272-6963(03)00020-2

Ruzzier, M., Hisrich, R., & Antoncic, B. (2006). SME internationalization research: Past, present, and future. *Journal of Small Business and Enterprise Development*, *13*(4), 476–497. doi:10.1108/14626000610705705

Rynes, S. L. (1989). *Recruitment, job choice, and post-hire consequences: A call for new research directions.* CAHRS Working Paper Series, 398.

Rynes, S. L., & Barber, A. E. (1990). Applicant Attraction Strategies: An Organizational Perspective. *Academy of Management Review*, *15*(2), 286–310. doi:10.2307/258158

Rynes, S. L., Bretz, R. D. Jr, & Gerhart, B. (1991). The Importance of Recruitment in Job Choice: A Different Way of Looking. *Personnel Psychology*, *44*(3), 487–521. doi:10.1111/j.1744-6570.1991. tb02402.x

Rynes, S. L., & Lawler, J. (1983). A Policy-Capturing Investigation of the Role of Expectancies in Decisions to Pursue Job Alternatives. *The Journal of Applied Psychology*, *68*(4), 620–631. doi:10.1037/0021-9010.68.4.620

Rytter, N. G., Boer, H., & Koch, C. (2007). Conceptualizing operations strategy processes. *International Journal of Operations & Production Management*, *27*(10), 1093–1114. doi:10.1108/01443570710820648

Sakas, D., & Kutsikos, K. (2014). An adaptable decision making model for sustainable enterprise interoperability. *Procedia: Social and Behavioral Sciences*, *148*, 611–618. doi:10.1016/j. sbspro.2014.07.087

Salomon, R., & Shaver, J. (2005). Export and domestic sales: Their interrelationship and determinants. *Strategic Management Journal*, *26*(9), 855–871. doi:10.1002mj.481

Sánchez-Fernández, R., & Iniesta-Bonillo, M. Á. (2007). The Concept of Perceived Value: A Systematic Review of the Research. *Marketing Theory*, *7*(4), 427–451. doi:10.1177/1470593107083165

Santos, J., Spector, B., & Van der Heyden, L. (2009). *Toward a theory of business model innovation within incumbent firms.* INSEAD Working Paper No. 2009/16/EFE/ST/TOM. Retrieved from https://flora.insead.edu/fichiersti_wp/inseadwp2009/2009-16.pdf

Santos, F. M., Pache, A.-C., & Birkholz, C. (2015). Making Hybrids Work: Aligning business models and organizational design for social enterprises. *California Management Review*, *57*(3), 36–58. doi:10.1525/cmr.2015.57.3.36

SAP. (2007). *Sap Eaf Overview Guide*. SAP.

Sarasvathy, S. D., & Kotha, S. (2001). *Effectuation in the management of Knightian uncertainty: Evidence from the real networks case.* Retrieved from http://www.effectuation.org/wp-content/uploads/2016/06/2001-realnet-1.pdf

Sarasvathy, S. D. (2001). Causation and effectuation: Toward a theoretical shift from economic inevitability to entrepreneurial contingency. *Academy of Management Review*, *26*(2), 243–263.

Sarasvathy, S. D., & Dew, N. (2005). New market creation through transformation. *Journal of Evolutionary Economics*, *15*(5), 533–565. doi:10.100700191-005-0264-x

Scandura, T. A., & Williams, E. A. (2000). Research methodology in management: Current practices, trends, and implications for future research. *Academy of Management Journal*, *43*(6), 1248–1264. doi:10.2307/1556348

Scheer, A. W., & Schneider, K. (2005). ARIS – Architecture of Integrated Information Systems. In P. Bernus, K. Mertins, & G. Schmidt (Eds.), *Hand- book on Architectures of Information Systems* (Vol. 2, pp. 605–623). Berlin: Springer.

Schekkerman, J. (2003). *Extended Enterprise Architecture Maturity Model*. Institute for Enterprise Architecture Developments.

Schekkerman, J. (2006). Creating or Choosing an Enterprise Architecture Framework. In *How to Survive in the Jungle of Enterprise Architecture Frameworks: Creating or Choosing an Enterprise Architecture Framework*. Academic Press.

Schueffel, P., Baldegger, R., & Amann, W. (2014). Behavioral patterns in born-again global firms: Towards a conceptual framework of the internationalization activities of mature SMEs. *Multinational Business Review*, *22*(4), 418–441. doi:10.1108/MBR-06-2014-0029

Schutta, J. T. (2006). *Business Performance through Lean Six Sigma: Linking the Knowledge Worker, the Twelve Pillars, and Baldrige*. Milwaukee, WI: ASQ Quality Press.

SEE. (1995). *Society For Enterprise Engineering Conference Announcement, 1995*. SEE.

SEFORÏS. (2016). *SEFORÏS Cross-Country Report*. Retrieved from http://www.seforis.eu/cross-country-report

Sembiring, J., & Siregar, M. I. H. (2013). A Decision Model for IT Risk Management on Disaster Recovery Center in an Enterprise Architecture Model. *Procedia Technology*, *11*, 1142–1146. doi:10.1016/j.protcy.2013.12.306

Senge, P. (1990). *The fifth discipline: The Art and Practice of the Learning Organization*. New York: Doubleday Currency.

Sethi, V., & King, W. (2003). *Organizational Transformation through Business Process Reengineering*. Pearson Education.

Shafer, S. M., Smith, H. J., & Linder, J. C. (2005). The power of business models. *Business Horizons*, *48*(3), 199–207. doi:10.1016/j.bushor.2004.10.014

Shane, S. (1993). Cultural influences on national rates of innovation. *Journal of Business Venturing*, *8*(1), 59–73. doi:10.1016/0883-9026(93)90011-S

Shaw, D. B. (2008). *Technoculture: The key concepts*. Berg.

Sherman, L. (2017). *If You're in a Dogfight, Become a Cat! – Strategies for Long–Term Growth*. New York: Columbia University Press. doi:10.7312her17482

Sheth, J. N., Newman, B. I., & Gross, B. L. (1991). Why We Buy What We Buy: A Theory of Consumption Values. *Journal of Business Research*, *22*(2), 159–170. doi:10.1016/0148-2963(91)90050-8

Shore, L. M., Randel, A. E., Chung, B. G., Dean, M. A., Ehrhart, K. H., & Singh, G. (2011). Inclusion and Diversity in Work Groups: A Review and Model for Future Research. *Journal of Management*, *37*(4), 1262–1289. doi:10.1177/0149206310385943

Sikdar, A., & Payyazhi, J. (2014). A Process Model of Managing Organizational Change During Business Process Redesign. *Business Process Management Journal*, *20*(6), 971–998. doi:10.1108/BPMJ-02-2013-0020

Simon, H. A. (1962). The architecture of complexity. *Proceedings of the American Philosophical Society*, *106*(6), 467–482.

Singh, A., Mudholkar, P., & Balani, L.L. (2015). *Contemporary Enterprise Architecture Frameworks (A Comparative Study of TOGAF and Zachmans â€™ EA Frameworks)*. Academic Press.

Škrinjar, R., Bosilj-Vukšić, V., & Indihar-Štemberger, M. (2008). The Impact of Business Process Orientation on Financial and Non-Financial Performance. *Business Process Management Journal*, *14*(5), 738–754. doi:10.1108/14637150810903084

Slack, N., Chambers, S., & Johnston, R. (2001). *Operations managment* (3rd ed.). Harlow: Financial Times Prentice Hall.

Slaughter, J. E., Cable, D. M., & Turban, D. B. (2014). Changing Job Seekers' Image Perceptions during Recruitment Visits: The Moderating Role of Belief Confidence. *The Journal of Applied Psychology*, *99*(6), 1146–1158. doi:10.1037/a0037482 PMID:25089859

Smart, P. A., Maddern, H., & Maull, R. S. (2009). Understanding Business Process Management: Implications for Theory and Practice. *British Journal of Management*, *20*(4), 491–507. doi:10.1111/j.1467-8551.2008.00594.x

Smith, A., & Fingar, P. (2003). *Business Process Management: The Third Wave*. Meghan – Kiffer Press.

Smith, N., Smith, V., & Verner, M. (2006). Do women in top management affect firm performance? A panel study of 2500 Danish firms. *International Journal of Productivity and Performance Management*, *55*(7), 569–593. doi:10.1108/17410400610702160

Smith, W. K., Gonin, M., & Besharov, M. L. (2013). Managing Social-Business Tensions. *Business Ethics Quarterly*, *23*(3), 407–442. doi:10.5840/beq201323327

Snow, C. C., & Miles, R. E. (1983). The Role of Strategy in the Development of a General Theory of Organizations. *Advances in Strategic Management*, *2*, 231–259.

Sousa, P., Lima, J., Sampaio, A., & Pereira, C. (2009). An Approach for Creating and Managing Enterprise Blueprints: A Case for IT Blueprints. *Advances in Enterprise Engineering III, 5th International Workshop, CIAO! 2009, and 5th International Workshop, EOMAS 2009*, 70–84. 10.1007/978-3-642-01915-9_6

Spanyi, A. (2006). *More for Less: The Power Of Process Management*. Meghan – Kiffer Press.

Sri Lanka Association of Software and Service Companies & PricewaterhouseCoopers. (2016). *SLASSCOM Strategy Document 2016*. Author.

Stanisauskaite, V., & Kock, S. (2016). The dynamic development of international entrepreneurial networks. In H. Etemad, S. Denicolai, B. Hagen, & A. Zucchella (Eds.), *The changing global economy and its impact on international entrepreneurship* (pp. 119–135). Cheltenham, UK: Edward Elgar. doi:10.4337/9781783479849.00012

Strnadl, C. F. (2006). Aligning Business and IT: The Process-Driven Architecture Model. *Information Systems Management*, *23*(4), 67–77. doi:10.1201/1078.10580530/46352.23.4.20 060901/95115.9

Sujansky, J. (2004, February). Lead a Multi-Generational Workforce. *The Business Journal of Tri-Cities*, 21-23.

Sultanow, E., Brockmann, C., Schroeder, K., & Cox, S. (2016). *A multidimensional Classification of 55 Enterprise Architecture Frameworks*. Academic Press.

Sumukadas, N., & Sawhney, R. (2004). Workforce agility through employee involvement. *IIE Transactions*, *36*(10), 1011–1021. doi:10.1080/07408170490500997

Survey results reported in "Diversity Initiatives Shown to Be Critical to Job Seekers". (2003, September 14). *The New York Times Magazine,* 100.

Svee, E. O., & Zdravkovic, J. (2015, June). Extending enterprise architectures to capture consumer values: the case of TOGAF. In *International Conference on Advanced Information Systems Engineering* (pp. 221-232). Springer. 10.1007/978-3-319-19243-7_22

Sweeney, J. C., & Soutar, G. N. (2001). Consumer Perceived Value: The Development of a Multiple Item Scale. *Journal of Retailing*, *77*(2), 203–220. doi:10.1016/S0022-4359(01)00041-0

Talwar, R. (1993). Business Re-Engineering - A Strategy-Driven Approach. *Long Range Planning*, *26*(6), 22–40. doi:10.1016/0024-6301(93)90204-S

Tamm, T., Seddon, P. B., Shanks, G., & Reynolds, P. (2011). How Does Enterprises Architecture Add Value to Organisations? *Communications of the Association for Information Systems*, *28*(1), 141–168.

Tang, A., Han, J., & Chen, P. (2004). A Comparative Analysis of Architecture Frameworks Technical Report: CeCSES Centre Report. Software Engineering Conference, 2004. 11th Asia-Pacific, 640–647.

Tang, J., Pee, L. G., & Iijima, J. (2013). Investigating the Effects of Business Process Orientation on Organizational Innovation Performance. *Information & Management*, *50*(8), 650–660. doi:10.1016/j.im.2013.07.002

Tatli, A. (2011). A Multi-layered Exploration of the Diversity Management Field: Diversity Discourses, Practices and Practitioners in the UK. *British Journal of Management*, *22*(2), 238–253. doi:10.1111/j.1467-8551.2010.00730.x

Tatli, A., & Ozbilgin, M. F. (2012). An Emic Approach to Intersectional Study of Diversity at Work: A Bourdieuan Framing. *International Journal of Management Reviews*, *14*(2), 180–200. doi:10.1111/j.1468-2370.2011.00326.x

Taylor, M. S., & Collins, C. J. (2000). *Organizational recruitment: Enhancing the intersection of research and practice*. Academic Press.

Tenner, A. R., & DeToro, I. J. (1997). *Process Redesign: The Implementation Guide for Managers*. Reading, MA: Addison-Wesley.

Terjesen, S., Vinnicombe, S., & Freeman, C. (2007). Attracting Generation Y Graduates: Organisational Attributes, Likelihood to Apply and Sex Differences. *Career Development International*, *12*(6), 504–522. doi:10.1108/13620430710821994

Tesco. (2016). *Business model - Keeping it simple*. Retrieved from: https://www.tescoplc.com/media/264185/tescoar16_businessmodel.pdf

The Economist. (2005). *Business 2010 - Embracing the challenge of change*. A report from the Economist Intelligence Unit sponsored by SAP. Retrieved from http://graphics.eiu.com/files/ad_pdfs/business%202010_global_final.pdf

The Economist. (2017). *Reboot - Indian outsourcing specialists must reboot their strategies*. Retrieved from https://www.economist.com/news/business/21714994-it-firms-need-upgrade-face-technological-and-political-shifts-indian-outsourcing

The IT Governance Institute. (2007). *0 The IT Governance Institute TOGAF TM and COBIT Mapping of TOGAF 8.1 with COBIT 4.0*. Author.

Thun, J. H. (2008). Empirical analysis of manufacturing strategy implementation. *International Journal of Production Economics*, *113*(1), 370–382. doi:10.1016/j.ijpe.2007.09.005

Timmers, P. (1998). *Business Models for Electronic Markets. Journal on Electronic Markets*, *8*(2), 3–8.

Törnroos, J. Å. (2002). Internationalisation of the firm–a theoretical review with implications for business network research. In *18th IMP Conference*, Dijon, France.

Towers Perrin and Hudson Institute. (1990). *Workforce 2000: Competing in a Seller' Market*. Valhalla, NY: Towers Perrin.

Treasury Board of Canada. (2004). *Business Transformation Enablement Program Strategic Design & Planning Methodology*. Author.

Triandis, H. (2004). The many dimensions of culture. *The Academy of Management Executive*, *18*(1), 88–93. doi:10.5465/AME.2004.12689599

Tribolet, J., Sousa, P., & Caetano, A. (2014). The role of enterprise governance and cartography in enterprise engineering. Enterprise Modelling and Information Systems Architectures-An International Journal, 9(1).

Trkman, P. (2013). Increasing Process Orientation with Business Process Management: Critical Practices. *International Journal of Information Management*, *33*(1), 48–60. doi:10.1016/j.ijinfomgt.2012.05.011

Trompenaars, F. (1993). *Riding the waves of culture – Understanding cultural diversity in business*. London: Nicholas Brealey Publishing.

Trudgen, R., & Freeman, S. (2014). Measuring the Performance of Born-Global Firms Throughout Their Development Process: The Roles of Initial Market Selection and Internationalisation Speed. *Management International Review*, *54*(4), 551–579. doi:10.100711575-014-0210-y

Turban, D. B. (2001). Organizational Attractiveness as an Employer on College Campuses: An Examination of the Applicant Population. *Journal of Vocational Behavior*, *58*(2), 293–312. doi:10.1006/jvbe.2000.1765

Turban, D. B., & Cable, D. M. (2003). Firm Reputation and Applicant Pool Characteristics. *Journal of Organizational Behavior*, *24*(6), 733–751. doi:10.1002/job.215

Turban, D. B., Campion, J. E., & Eyring, A. R. (1995). Factors Related to Job Acceptance Decisions of College Recruits. *Journal of Vocational Behavior*, *47*(2), 193–213. doi:10.1006/jvbe.1995.1035

Turban, D. B., & Dougherty, T. W. (1992). Influences of Campus Recruiting on Applicant Attraction to Firms. *Academy of Management Journal*, *35*(4), 739–765. doi:10.2307/256314

Turban, D. B., Eyring, A. R., & Campion, J. E. (1993). Job Attributes: Preferences Compared with Reasons Given for Accepting and Rejecting Job Offers. *Journal of Occupational and Organizational Psychology*, *66*(1), 71–81. doi:10.1111/j.2044-8325.1993.tb00517.x

Turban, D. B., Forret, M. L., & Hendrickson, C. L. (1998). Applicant Attraction to Firms: Influences of Organization Reputation, Job and Organizational Attributes, and Recruiter Behaviors. *Journal of Vocational Behavior*, *52*(1), 24–44. doi:10.1006/jvbe.1996.1555

Turban, D. B., & Greening, D. W. (1997). Corporate Social Performance And Organizational Attractiveness To Prospective Employees. *Academy of Management Journal*, *40*(3), 658–672. doi:10.2307/257057

U.S. Government. (2009). *Improving Agency Performance Using Information and Information Technology*. Author.

Uen, J. F., Ahlstrom, D., Chen, S., & Liu, J. (2015). Employer brand management, organizational prestige and employees' word-of-mouth referrals in Taiwan. *Asia Pacific Journal of Human Resources*, *53*(1), 104–123. doi:10.1111/1744-7941.12024

Ulaga, W., & Chacour, S. (2001). Measuring Customer-Perceived Value in Business Markets: A Prerequisite for Marketing Strategy Development and Implementation. *Industrial Marketing Management*, *30*(6), 525–540. doi:10.1016/S0019-8501(99)00122-4

UML ISO IEC - UML Specification, Version 1.4.2, formal/05-04-01 (2005)

Urbaczewski, L., & Mrdalj, S. (2006). A comparison of enterprise architecture frameworks. *Issues in Information Systems*, *7*(2).

Vahlne, J. E., Ivarsson, I., & Johanson, J. (2011). The tortuous road to globalization for Volvo's heavy truck business: Extending the scope of the Uppsala model. *International Business Review*, *20*(1), 1–14. doi:10.1016/j.ibusrev.2010.05.003

Van Der Aalst, W. M. (2013). Business Process Management: A Comprehensive Survey. *Software Engineering*, *2013*, 1–37. doi:10.1155/2013/507984

Van der Aalst, W. M. P., ter Hofstede, H. N., & Weske, M. (2003). Business Process Management: A Survey. *Proceedings of the International Conference of Business Process Management*. 10.1007/3-540-44895-0_1

Van Der Beek, W.T.H., Trienekens, J., & Grefen, P. (2012). The Application of Enterprise Reference Architecture in the Financial Industry. *Lecture Notes in Business Information Processing, 131*, 93–110.

Van Looy, A., De Backer, M., & Poels, G. (2011). Defining Business Process Maturity. A Journey towards Excellence. *Total Quality Management & Business Excellence*, *22*(11), 1119–1137. doi:10.1080/14783363.2011.624779

Velitchkov, I. (2008). Integration of IT Strategy and Enterprise Architecture Models. *International Conference on Computer Systems and Technologies*, 1–6. 10.1145/1500879.1500955

Venkatesh, V., & Bala, H. (2008). Technology Acceptance Model 3 and a Research Agenda on Interventions. *Decision Sciences*, *39*(2), 273–315. doi:10.1111/j.1540-5915.2008.00192.x

Venkatesh, V., & Davis, F. D. (2000). A Theoretical Extension of the Technology Acceptance Model: Four Longitudinal Field Studies. *Management Science*, *46*(2), 186–204. doi:10.1287/mnsc.46.2.186.11926

Venkatesh, V., Morris, M. G., Davis, G. B., & Davis, F. D. (2003). User Acceptance of Information Technology: Toward a Unified View. *Management Information Systems Quarterly*, *27*(3), 425–478. doi:10.2307/30036540

Vernadat, F. (2014). Enterprise Modeling in the context of Enterprise Engineering: State of the art and outlook. *International Journal of Production Management and Engineering*, *2*(2), 57–73. doi:10.4995/ijpme.2014.2326

Vernadat, F. B. (1996). *Enterprise Modeling and Integration: Principles and Applications.* London: Chapman & Hall.

Vesterager, J., Tølle, M., & Bernus, P. (2003). VERA: Virtual Enterprise Reference Architecture. *VTT Symposium (Valtion Teknillinen Tutkimuskeskus),* 39–51.

Vijayasarathy, L., & Turk, D. (2012). Drivers of agile software development use: Dialectic interplay between benefits and hindrances. *Information and Software Technology, 54*(2), 137–148. doi:10.1016/j.infsof.2011.08.003

von Bertalanffy, L. (1968). *General System Theory: Foundations, Development, Applications* (rev. ed.). New York: Braziller.

Walker, J. (2015). Hybrid Organizations: Origins, Strategies, Impacts and Implications. *California Management Review, 57*(3), 5–13. doi:10.1525/cmr.2015.57.3.5

Wallace, L. G., & Sheetz, S. D. (2014). The adoption of software measures: A technology acceptance model (TAM) perspective. *Information & Management, 51*(2), 249–259. doi:10.1016/j.im.2013.12.003

Wallace, M., Lings, I., Cameron, R., & Sheldon, N. (2014). Attracting and Retaining Staff: The Role of Branding and Industry Image. In R. Harris & T. Short (Eds.), *Workforce Development: Perspectives and Issues* (pp. 19–36). Singapore: Springer Singapore. doi:10.1007/978-981-4560-58-0_2

Wan, H., Luo, A., & Luo, X. (2014, May). How Enterprise Architecture Formative Critical Success Facets Might Affect Enterprise Architecture Success: A Literature Analysis. In ICISO (pp. 197-209). doi:10.1007/978-3-642-55355-4_20

Wang, H.-Y., & Wang, S.-H. (2010). User acceptance of mobile internet based on the Unified Theory of Acceptance and Use of Technology: Investigating the determinants and gender differences. *Social Behavior and Personality, 38*(3), 415–426. doi:10.2224bp.2010.38.3.415

Weerawardena, J., Mort, G. S., Liesch, P. W., & Knight, G. (2007). Conceptualizing accelerated internationalization in the born global firm: A dynamic capabilities perspective. *Journal of World Business, 42*(3), 294–306. doi:10.1016/j.jwb.2007.04.004

Welch, L. S., & Luostarinen, R. (1988). Internationalization: Evolution of a concept. *Journal of General Management, 14*(2), 83–98. doi:10.1177/030630708801400203

Wellington, S., Brumit Kropf, M., & Gerkovich, P. R. (2003, June). What's Holding Women Back? *Harvard Business Review,* 18–19.

Wheelen, T. L., & Hunger, J. D. (2013). *Concepts in Strategic Management and Business Policy: Towards Global Sustainability.* Noida: Pearson Education India.

Wheelwright, S. C., & Hayes, R. H. (1985). Competing through manufacturing. *Harvard Business Review, 63*(1), 99–109.

Whitman, L., & Huff, B. (2001). On the Use of Enterprise Models. *International Journal of Flexible Manufacturing Systems*, *13*(2), 195–208. doi:10.1023/A:1011187602935

Williams, M. L., & Bauer, T. N. (1994). The Effect of a Managing Diversity Policy on Organizational Attractiveness. *Group & Organization Management*, *19*(3), 295–308. doi:10.1177/1059601194193005

Wilson, F., & Post, J. E. (2011). Business models for people, planet (& profits): Exploring the phenomena of social business, a market-based approach to social value creation. *Small Business Economics*, *40*(3), 715–737. doi:10.100711187-011-9401-0

Winter, R., Zhao, J. L., & Aier, S. (2010). Global Perspectives on Design Science Research. *5th International Conference, Desrist 2010.* 10.1007/978-3-642-13335-0

Wolff, F. (2008). An Evaluation Framework for Enterprise Architecture Modelling. *Enterprise Modelling and Information Systems Architectures*, *3*(1), 48–60.

Wong, W. P., Ahmad, N. H., Nasurdin, A. M., & Mohamad, M. N. (2014). The Impact of External Environmental On Business Process Management and Organizational Performance. *Service Business*, *8*(4), 559–586. doi:10.100711628-013-0207-9

Wood, J. T. (1994). *Organismic Modeling of Organizations: A Dynamic Enterprise Model.* Arlington, VA: The University of Texas at Arlington.

Yang, Z., & Peterson, R. T. (2004). Customer Perceived Value, Satisfaction and Loyalty: The Role of Switching Costs. *Psychology and Marketing*, *21*(10), 799–822. doi:10.1002/mar.20030

Yin, R. K. (2004). *Case study methods. Complementary methods for research in education.* Washington, DC: American Educational Research Association.

Zaheer, A., Rehman, K. U., & Khan, M. A. (2010). Development and Testing of a Business Process Orientation Model to Improve Employee and Organizational Performance. *African Journal of Business Management*, *4*(2), 149–161.

Zairi, M. (1997). Business Process Management: A Bounderyless Approach to Modern Competitiveness. *Business Process Management Journal*, *3*(1), 64–80. doi:10.1108/14637159710161585

Zander, I., McDougall-Covin, P., & Rose, E. (2015). Born globals and international business: Evolution of a field of research. *Journal of International Business Studies*, *46*(1), 27–35. doi:10.1057/jibs.2014.60

Zeithaml, V. A. (1988). Consumer Perceptions of Price, Quality, and Value: A Means-End Model and Synthesis of Evidence. *Journal of Marketing*, *52*(3), 2–22. doi:10.2307/1251446

Zia, M. J., Azam, F., & Allauddin, M. (2011). A survey of enterprise architecture analysis using multi criteria decision making models (MCDM). *Intelligent Computing and Information Science*, 631-637.

About the Contributors

Carolina Machado received her PhD degree in Management Sciences (Organizational and Politics Management area / Human Resources Management) from the University of Minho in 1999, and Master degree in Management (Strategic Human Resource Management) from Technical University of Lisbon in 1994. Teaching in the Human Resources Management subjects since 1989 at University of Minho, she is since 2004 Associated Professor, with experience and research interest areas in the field of Human Resource Management, International Human Resource Management, Human Resource Management in SMEs, Training and Development, Management Change and Knowledge Management. She is Head of Human Resources Management Work Group at University of Minho, as well as Chief Editor of the International Journal of Applied Management Sciences and Engineering (IJAMSE), Guest Editor of journals, books Editor and books Series Editor, as well as reviewer in different international prestigious journals. In addition, she has also published both as editor/co-editor and as author/co-author several books, book chapters and articles in journals and conferences.

J. Paulo Davim received the Ph.D. degree in Mechanical Engineering in 1997, the M.Sc. degree in Mechanical Engineering (materials and manufacturing processes) in 1991, the Mechanical Engineer degree (MEng-5 years) in 1986, from the University of Porto (FEUP), the Aggregate title (Full Habilitation) from the University of Coimbra in 2005 and the D.Sc. from London Metropolitan University in 2013. He is Eur Ing by FEANI-Brussels and Senior Chartered Engineer by the Portuguese Institution of Engineers with a MBA and Specialist title in Engineering and Industrial Management. Currently, he is Professor at the Department of Mechanical Engineering of the University of Aveiro, Portugal. He has more than 30 years of teaching and research experience in Manufacturing, Materials and Mechanical Engineering with special emphasis in Machining & Tribology. He has also interest in Management & Industrial Engineering and Higher Education for Sustainability & Engineering Education. He has guided large numbers of postdoc, Ph.D. and masters students. He has received several scientific awards. He has worked as evaluator of projects for international research agencies as well as examiner of Ph.D. thesis for many universities. He is the Editor in Chief of several international journals, Guest Editor of journals, books Editor, book Series Editor and Scientific Advisory for many international journals and conferences. Presently, he is an Editorial Board member of 25 international journals and acts as reviewer for more than 80 prestigious Web of Science journals. In addition, he has also published as editor (and co-editor) more than 100 books and as author (and co-author) more than 10 books, 70 book chapters and 400 articles in journals and conferences (more than 200 articles in journals indexed in Web of Science core collection/h-index 43+/5500+ citations and SCOPUS/h-index 52+/7500+ citations).

* * *

Victor Alves has a Bachelor's degree in Tourism from the University of Aveiro. He has been actively involved Tourism students community, holding Public Relations responsibilities with the business fabric. He is finishing his Master's degree in Management, also at the University of Aveiro, where he is specializing in Marketing and International Business.

Marlene Amorim is an assistant professor at the Department of Economics Management Industrial Engineering and Tourism at the University of Aveiro and researcher at GOVCOPP, Research Unit in Governance Competitiveness and Public Policies. Currently she serves as Pro-rector for Internationalization at the University of Aveiro. She received her PhD degree in Management from IESE Business School of University of Navarra in Spain, and had completed a Master degree in Management of Science Technology and Innovation from the University of Aveiro and a degree in Economics from the University of Porto. Marlene conducts research in the area of service operations and service quality, notably in topics related to service process design and customer participation in service delivery. She currently integrates the editorial team of the International Journal of Supply Chain and Operations Resilience.

Liliana Ávila is a PhD candidate at the Department of Economics, Management, Industrial Engineering and Tourism at the University of Aveiro. She has a Bachelor and a Master degree in Management and Industrial Engineering from the University of Aveiro. Since 2012, Liliana has been involved in several projects at the regional level for the promotion of social innovation and entrepreneurship in a straight collaboration with local municipalities, as well as projects at the international level including SEFORIS – Social Entrepreneurship as Force for More Inclusive and Innovative Societies, a multi-disciplinary, multi-method international research project on social enterprise funded by the European Commission. Liliana currently conducts research on social enterprises, namely in topics related to the operations management in such organizations and has presented some communications in academic and project meetings.

Sónia Cristina Marques Conceição obtained her Bachelor's degree in Marketing and Advertising from the Instituto Superior de Gestão e Tecnologia de Santarém, Portugal. Currently she is finishing the Master in Management from the University of Aveiro, Portugal. She has experience working and participating in Advertising and Promotion campaigns in the Retailing Industry. She has worked as a marketing assistant for a fuel distribution company. She was executive assistant at ACAPO - Association of the Blind and Amblíopes of Portugal. She has extensive experience in catering and customer service.

Meral Dülger was awarded her Ph.D. degree in the Management and Organizations Program from Boğaziçi University, Department of Management. She is an assistant professor in the Department of Business Administration (lectured in English) of Marmara University. Along with her administrative duties, Dülger teaches in several undergraduate programs as well as executive education programs. She currently gives lectures on Strategic Management, Small Business Management, Innovation Management, Entrepreneurship, Global Business and Contemporary Management. Her research interests center on team-based structures, organizational design, strategic management, process design and re-engineering along with organizational learning and entrepreneurship.

Luís Miguel D. F. Ferreira is an Assistant Professor at the Department of Mechanical Engineering of the University of Coimbra. He received his PhD from the Universidade Técnica de Lisboa. His main research interest is in Supply Chain Management. He has significant consultancy experience, both in the private and public sectors and has published in several journals, including: Production Planning and Control and Supply Chain Management: An International Journal.

Shan Anjana Jayasinghe holds a Bachelor's Degree in Engineering (Electronic and Telecommunication Engineering) from University of Moratuwa. He obtained his postgraduate degree (Master of Business Administration in Management of Technology) from the same university. Currently he is working at Dialog Axiata PLC, a premiere mobile telecommunication company is Sri Lanka, as a Senior Project Manager. He has 6 years' experience in telecommunication industry, initially as an engineer and later as a project manager.

Huseyin Selcuk Kilic is currently an instructor in the Department of Industrial Engineering in Marmara University. He received the BSc, MSc and PhD degrees in Industrial Engineering from Istanbul Technical University. He studied in-plant logistics design for his PhD dissertation. His main research areas are plant logistics, reverse logistics, lean production, decision making and ergonomics. He has research papers in journals that include Applied Mathematical Modelling, Decision Support Systems, Computers and Industrial Engineering, International Journal of Advanced Manufacturing Technology, and Assembly Automation.

Tatiana Martins has a Bachelor's degree Marketing from ISCA-University of Aveiro, Portugal. He was awarded a merit diploma for her outstanding performance. Currenntly, Tatiana is finishing her Master's degree in Management, at the Department of Economics, Management, Industrial Engineering and Tourism, University of Aveiro. She has experience working in Sales for a Italian Multinational company. She is involved in Veg volunteering activities and as an animal rights activist. Tatiana was the first person of her family to attend university.

Mukesh Kumar Mishra is a dynamic research oriented faculty in Area of Marketing, Currently working as Associate Professor in IBS Hyderabad He did his MBA from Sahara Arts & Management Academy, Lucknow affiliated to UPTU, Lucknow(India) (2004) and Ph.D from North Orissa University, Baripada(India) (2011). He is having 5 years of rich Corporate experience in Direct sales and Channel Sales of companies like ICICI HOME FINANCE, NESTLE, HUL, PEPSICO and DABUR, and 9 Years of academic experience. Prior to joining IBS he was working with Regional College of Management Autonomous, Bhubaneswar, India as Asst. Professor in marketing area. He is very passionate about training and consultancy. He has trained people from reputed organizations in private sectors as well as public sectors.

António C. Moreira obtained a Bachelor's degree in Electrical Engineering and a Master's degree in Management, both from the University of Porto, Portugal. He received his PhD in Management from UMIST-University of Manchester Institute of Science and Technology, England. He has a solid international background in industry leveraged working for a multinational company in Germany as well as in Portugal. He has also been involved in consultancy projects and in research activities. He is Assistant Professor at the Department of Economics, Management, Industrial Engineering, and Tourism, University of Aveiro, Portugal, where he headed the Bachelor and Master Degrees in Management for five years. He is member of GOVCOPP research unit.

Purna Prabhakar Nandamuri has an overall experience of around 32 years, of which 20 years executive experience with Indian Railways - Government Of India, and 12 years in academics. In addition to Doctorate in Strategic Management, his education spreads across Masters in Management, Psychology, and English Language and Literature. He has been handling Business Strategy and Business Ethics & Corporate Governance subjects at post graduate level of the Management course. He has published one book and more than 50 research papers in national and international journals, and many chapters in edited book volumes internationally. He serves as an active resource person for several Management Development and Faculty Development Programs at his university.

Alamuri Narayana is the former Dean, Faculty of Management, Osmania University.

João Manuel Branco Marques Pereira obtained his Bachelor's degree in Marketing Manegement at IPAM - Instituto Português de Administração e Marketing, Portugal. He is finihsing his Master's degree in Management at the University of Aveiro, Portugal. He works for Worten Portugal, the largest appliance retailer in Portugal, which is part of the SONAE Group.

Liliana Sofia Pais Pinto obtained a Bachelor's degree in Public Administration and is currently attending the Master in Management, both from the University of Aveiro, Portugal. As the Best Student in Public Administration, she was awarded the "Municipio de Aveiro" Prize. She currently works as a junior consultant.

Maria Manuel Leite Brito Bento Ribeiro obtained her Bachelor's degree in Public Administration in 2016 at the University of Aveiro, Portugal. She is currently finishing her Master's in Management, also from the University of Aveiro. She is currently a trainee at Altice Labs, a company based in Aveiro, in the area of Investment Distribution.

Dinesh Samarasinghe is the current head of Department of Management of Technology, Faculty of Business, University of Moratuwa Sri Lanka. He graduated from University of Sri Jayewardenepura with a first class honours degree. Later he went on to complete his Master of Business Administration and Doctor of Philosophy postgraduate degrees from University of Colombo. He focuses more on to research in Marketing Management.

Bahar Sennaroglu is an Associate Professor in the Industrial Engineering Department of Faculty of Engineering of Marmara University. Dr. Sennaroglu received her MSc and PhD degrees in Industrial Engineering from Marmara University. Her research interests include design and analysis of experiments, decision techniques, forecasting techniques, project management, production and quality systems. She was an academic visitor for the academic year 2016-2017 in the Department of Engineering and the Built Environment of Faculty of Science and Technology of Anglia Ruskin University. Her ORCID ID is orcid.org/0000-0002-6809-634X.

Theekshana Suraweera is the founder Dean of the Faculty of Business, SLIIT. Prior to joining SLIIT, Theekshana was a Senior Academic at the University of Canterbury, New Zealand, served in the United Nations Development Programme (UNDP) as a MIS Specialist and has been a Sri Lanka Administrative Service (SLAS) served in senior Positions in Govt. Departments and Ministries. He holds PhD (Canterbury- New Zealand), MBA (Sri J- Sri Lanka), MSc (Reading-UK), MSc (Sri.j) and the Postgraduate Diploma in International Affairs from Bandaranayke Centre for International Studies, Sri Lanka. His current teaching at SLIIT focuses on Business Research Methodology, Change Management, Knowledge Management, Emotional Intelligence, Professional & Skill Development.. Theekshana's main research interests are in the field of IT application in Business and Education, and has presented research papers in the refereed international journals and conferences. He has published the Sinhala adaptations of 'our Iceberg is Melting' by John Kotter and 'Who Moved My Cheese' by Spenser Johnson'. "Edutainment Unlimited", an innovative fun filled workshop series created and presented by Dr Theekshana, aimed at developing learning and study skills among secondary school children has become very popular .in Sri Lankan Schools. He is an excellent communicator and was the Charter President of SLIIT Toastmasters Club.

Pinar Yildiran is a PhD Student in Industrial Engineering in Faculty of Engineering of Marmara University. She received her MSc degree in Engineering Management from Marmara University. She has bachelor degree in Physics Engineering in Istanbul Technical University. Actively she is PMO Manager in Zorlu Holding IT department. Her research interests include decision techniques, project management, IT Enterprise Architecture Systems and Enterprise Engineering.

Index

Stay Current on the Latest Emerging Research Developments

Become an IGI Global Reviewer for Authored Book Projects

Premier Reference Source

Emerging GIS Applications for Emergency and Disaster Management

Premier Reference Source

Managerial Strategies and Green Solutions for Project Sustainability

Premier Reference Source

Comparative Approaches to Using R and Python for Statistical Data Analysis

Premier Reference Source

Solutions for High-Touch Communications in a High-Tech World

The overall success of an authored book project is dependent on quality and timely reviews.

In this competitive age of scholarly publishing, constructive and timely feedback significantly decreases the turnaround time of manuscripts from submission to acceptance, allowing the publication and discovery of progressive research at a much more expeditious rate. Several IGI Global authored book projects are currently seeking highly qualified experts in the field to fill vacancies on their respective editorial review boards:

Applications may be sent to:
development@igi-global.com

Applicants must have a doctorate (or an equivalent degree) as well as publishing and reviewing experience. Reviewers are asked to write reviews in a timely, collegial, and constructive manner. All reviewers will begin their role on an ad-hoc basis for a period of one year, and upon successful completion of this term can be considered for full editorial review board status, with the potential for a subsequent promotion to Associate Editor.

If you have a colleague that may be interested in this opportunity, we encourage you to share this information with them.

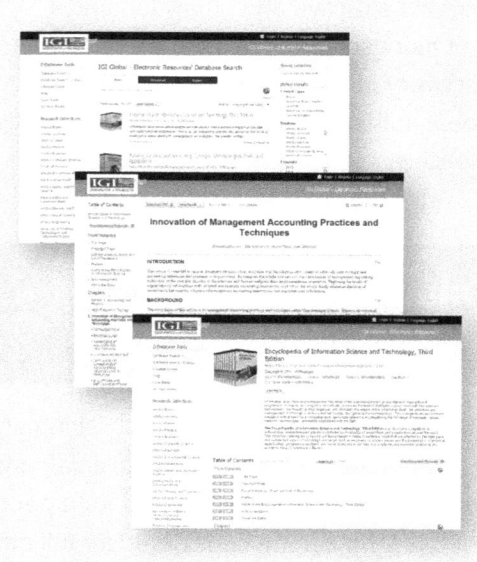

Lightning Source UK Ltd.
Milton Keynes UK
UKHW05n0403050618
323729UK00007B/147/P

9 781522 553601